An Introduction to Anthropological Theories and Theorists

An Introduction to Anthropological Theories and Theorists

Third Edition

Jerry D. Moore

RAWAT PUBLICATIONS
Jaipur • New Delhi • Bangalore • Hyderabad • Guwahati

ISBN 978-81-316-0425-0

First Indian Reprint, 2011

First published in 2009 under the title *Vision of Culture: An Introduction to Anthropological Theories and Theorists*.

This edition published by arrangement with Rowman & Littlefield Publishers, Inc. A wholly owned subsidiary of The Rowman & Littlefield Publishing Group, Inc. 4501, Forbes Boulevard, Suite 200, Lanham, MD 20706 USA.
www.altamirapress.com

For sale in India, Pakistan, Bangladesh, Nepal, Sri Lanka, Bhutan and the Maldives.

Published by
Prem Rawat for **Rawat Publications**
Satyam Apts., Sector 3, Jawahar Nagar, Jaipur - 302 004 (India)
Phone: 0141 265 1748 / 7006 Fax: 0141 265 1748
E-mail : info@rawatbooks.com
Website: rawatbooks.com

New Delhi Office
4858/24, Ansari Road, Daryaganj, New Delhi 110 002
Phone: 011-23263290

Also at *Bangalore, Hyderabad* and *Guwahati*

Printed at Chaman Enterprises, New Delhi

Contents

Acknowledgments

This book was written for students, and since 1993 various versions of the chapters have been tested on my students at California State University, Dominguez Hills. I want to thank them for their patience, questions, and puzzling looks—and for forcing me to be clear in exposition and intent. When I was writing the chapter on Edward Sapir, I felt an immediate empathy for the Ottawa period in his life when he lacked students; to lack the exchange of ideas with students would be a great loss, and I thank my students for their contributions to this book.

I would also like to acknowledge four of my teachers who taught me anthropological theory as an undergraduate and graduate student: Michael Seelye, Joel Canby, Charles Erasmus, and Albert Spaulding. I thank Dr. James W. Fernandez for answering my request for information on his anthropological career. I also want to thank Dr. Marshall Sahlins for providing me with a copy of his curriculum vitae, an important source for writing about his career and publications.

I cannot sufficiently express my gratitude to my wife and colleague, Janine Gasco, who read draft chapters, listened to theoretical and editorial problems, and whose advice was unfailingly sound. In addition, I have discussed aspects of this book with my friends and colleagues Andrew Stewart, Brenda Bowser, and Susan Needham; I appreciate their comments, tolerance, and encouragements.

At AltaMira Press, I was fortunate to work on the first and second editions with Mitch Allen, whose confidence in this book—even in the face of scathing reviews—is the principal reason this project was completed. More recently, I have had the pleasure of working with Alan McClare, whose enthusiasm and support for the third edition of *Visions of Culture* are very much appreciated. I would also like to acknowledge the contributions made by the ten anonymous reviewers who have read different versions of this manuscript in its three editions. Dr. Aletta Biersack caught an error in the second edition in the chapter on Claude Lévi-Strauss and was kind enough to notify me. I also appreciate comments I have received from other readers.

Finally, I would like to thank the student, whose name I never knew, who asked one of the best questions anyone can pose: "What's the goddamn point of it all?" This book is dedicated to him.

Introduction

What's the Point?

Years ago I attended a weekend conference organized by a group of undergraduate anthropology students from a major Midwestern public university. The annual conference was held in a group of cabins on the edge of a beautiful lake. The setting was conducive to serious presentations and also provided an opportunity for professors and students to discuss ideas in an informal environment, an informality enhanced by several kegs of beer.

Toward the end of an exhausting day of dialogue, the discussion turned to theoretical matters. Many of the students were enrolled in Professor X's course on anthropological theory and theorists, and they began to complain about the course, emboldened by beer and the absence of Professor X, who was simply too busy to attend the conference.

A young man stood up and said, "We start off with Edward Tylor, but Professor X tells us that Tylor was just an armchair anthropologist. So we read Malinowski who everyone says was a good fieldworker, but then Professor X says Malinowski was a racist. And then we read Margaret Mead, and Professor X says Mead was a liar."

The young man swayed slightly and demanded, "What's the goddamn point of it all?"

It was a very good question.

It is commonplace to assert that anthropology is in a crisis, but if that is true, it is a crisis of our own making. James Peacock, a former president of the American Anthropological Association, summarized anthropology's potential contributions and reflected on its shortcomings: "Poised for victory, we retreat, turn within, luxuriate in ourselves, squander our resources in silly arguments, shrink our vision to the smallest world, fiddle while Rome burns and barbarians are at the gate" (1994:1).

In a field as diverse as anthropology, it is inevitable that conflicting opinions exist. But in the midst of conflict, we lose sight of the intellectual achievements of anthropology and the personal contributions of anthropologists. And worse, we fail as teachers to communicate to our students the legacies of anthropologists who are worthy of attention, scrutiny, and respect.

This book is written for anthropology students. It is an introduction to the principal theorists and theories that shaped and continue to influence modern anthropology. Organized in a series of profiles, I summarize the major theoretical concepts of twenty-five scholars and relate those concepts to each scholar's formative influences, anthropological research, and intellectual framework.

The chapters are organized into six thematic sections beginning with a brief introductory essay outlining the problems and issues common to the anthropologists discussed in the section. Each chapter introduces a scholar's contribution to anthropology, profiles her/his professional life with an emphasis on fieldwork and publications, and discusses major aspects of the anthropologist's work: Morgan's comparative approach to kin systems, Durkheim's conscience collective, Malinowski's theory of needs, Lévi-Strauss's structural approach to myth, Victor Turner's concept of social drama, Ortner's analysis of key symbols, and so on. The chapter conclusion is followed by a list of references students can pursue in more depth; I have tried to cite readily available sources. While the reference list is not exhaustive, it is a representative cross section listing principal bibliographical sources and recent critical assessments.

Visions of Culture is organized differently from other texts on anthropological theory. First, I have attempted to represent a broader range of anthropological viewpoints than, for example, Adam Kuper describes in his excellent study of British social anthropologists (Kuper 1983). Second, I have attempted to sample more current trends in anthropology than are discussed in Elvin Hatch's (1973) *Theories of Man and Culture*. Third, I try to provide a balanced, though not uncritical, reading of each anthropologist's contribution to anthropological theory. I do not personally advocate a specific theory as Marvin Harris (1968) does in *The Rise of Anthropological Theory*. The scholars discussed in *Visions of Culture* are not straw men or whipping boys. Each anthropologist discussed in this book has intellectual merit; they were included because their ideas are important and deserve to be understood.

Finally, I have presented each anthropologist in the context of her/his intellectual milieu; I have not measured each scholar against current theoretical trends in anthropology. Today, for example, cultural ecology and cultural evolution have fallen into disfavor, but they were important theoretical lines of inquiry from roughly 1945 to 1975. The several variations on functionalism were important to anthropology from the mid-1920s to the mid-1960s, although they are less so now. Because of their impact in the development of anthropological theory, I discuss these works even if some current theorists might consider such positions hopelessly outdated.

Visions of Culture is organized around the women and men who shaped modern anthropology. Other texts on anthropological theory emphasize ideas over individuals, but I believe there are good reasons for a biographical structure. Ideas do not exist in the ether; they take shape in the experiences of individuals. Obviously, certain ideas become generally held, common properties. The organic analogy, the idea of progress, the function of society, the postmodernist critique, and so on, have broad existences; they are not the single-handed creations of "Great Men." In my reading of anthropologists' theories, such broad concepts seem to be generic foundations on which specific scholars build their theoretical structures. Other factors and more immediate issues configure individual anthropologists' ideas.

Preeminent among these is the experience of anthropological fieldwork. Repeatedly, one discovers that anthropologists arrive at their theoretical positions in the process of trying to understand another human culture. Benedict and the Zuni, Mead and the Samoans, Radcliffe-Brown and the Andamanese, Malinowski and the Trobriand Islanders, Evans-Pritchard and the Azande, Steward and the Shoshone, Harris and rural Brazilians,

Turner and the Ndembu, Geertz and the Javanese, Fernandez and the Fang, Ortner and the Sherpas, Bourdieu in Algeria, Sahlins and historic Oceana—there is a recurrent dialectic that occurs in the context of research. In general discussions of theory, the empirical contexts of fieldwork are too often ignored. This is a shame since ethnographic research is anthropology's most important addition to the social sciences, and our translations of other cultures' experiences are anthropology's most lasting contribution to intellectual life.

Obviously, I could not write about every major anthropological figure, so my selections require justification. First, I have considered anthropologists who dealt with central issues, such as: "What is the nature of culture?" "What is the relationship between the individual and society?" and "How can another culture be understood by an anthropological outsider?" These are fundamental issues with which anthropologists have struggled since the late nineteenth century, but not all anthropologists have focused on these theoretical issues. I realize that I have ignored major figures who made significant theoretical and substantive contributions to anthropology, and I apologize to them, their students, and their posthumous advocates. Second, I have not considered scholars whose works were important during their lifetimes but have since become marginal to major currents in the field (see, for example, Ackerman [1987:1–4] on Sir James Frazer). Third, I have selected anthropologists who reflect basic trends within anthropology—unilineal evolution, Boasian historicism, functionalism, cultural materialism, structuralism, semiotics, feminism, practice theory, and postmodernism. Fourth, I have limited myself to anthropologists from the United States, Great Britain, and France and emphasize Anglo-American anthropology, which I assume is of most interest to my audience. Finally, I have not discussed social thinkers in related fields who have made huge impacts on anthropology: Marx, Freud, Weber, Giddens, and so on. That would involve writing a biographical encyclopedia of the social sciences, which is not my goal, intention, or desire.

The final selection of twenty-five anthropologists—Edward Tylor, Lewis Henry Morgan, Franz Boas, Émile Durkheim, Alfred Kroeber, Ruth Benedict, Edward Sapir, Margaret Mead,

Marcel Mauss, Bronislaw Malinowski, A. R. Radcliffe-Brown, Edward Evans-Pritchard, Leslie White, Julian Steward, Marvin Harris, Eleanor Burke Leacock, Claude Lévi-Strauss, Victor Turner, Clifford Geertz, Mary Douglas, James Fernandez, Sherry Ortner, Pierre Bourdieu, Eric Wolf, and Marshall Sahlins—is not an exhaustive list, but a starting point for further research, classroom discussion, and student inquiry into the ideas and individuals who have shaped anthropology by contributing their particular and creative visions of culture.

References

Ackerman, Robert
1987 *James Frazer: A Life.* Cambridge: Cambridge University Press.

Harris, Marvin
1968 *The Rise of Anthropological Theory: A History of Theories of Culture.* New York: Thomas Y. Crowell.

Hatch, Elvin
1973 *Theories of Man and Culture.* New York: Columbia University Press.

Kuper, Adam
1983 *Anthropology and Anthropologists: The Modern British School.* London: Routledge & Kegan Paul.

Peacock, James
1994 The AAA President's Report: Challenges Facing the Discipline. *Anthropology Newsletter* 35(9):1, 5.

I

FOUNDERS

Anthropology addresses a series of questions that humans have considered for millennia: What is the nature of society? Why do cultures change? What is the relationship between the person as an individual and the person as a member of a distinctive social group? What are the distinguishing characteristics of humanness? Why are cultures different?

The written record of such inquiries covers at least twenty-five hundred years. In fourth-century BC Athens, Aristotle pondered the organization of the state and used the organic analogy—the comparison of society to a living organism—which became a recurrent theme in nineteenth- and twentieth-century anthropology. The fourteenth-century Arab geographer Ibn Khaldun explained the differences between cultures in terms of climate—passionate, expressive societies exist in warmer climates while restrained, impassive cultures exist in northern climates. In 1725 Giovanni Battista Vico, a poor scholar in Italy, wrote *Principii d' una scienza nuova* and outlined a historical model of the evolution of human society. By the 1700s a wide range of moral philosophers were considering the nature of human cultures, drawing on ethnographic sources from Herodotus, Garcilaso de la Vega, Joseph-François Lafitau, and others.

So how can we call four men—Edward Tylor, Lewis Henry Morgan, Émile Durkheim, and Franz Boas—the "founders" of anthropology? First, because there are direct connections between modern anthropological issues and the ideas of these late nineteenth-century and early twentieth-century scholars. A significant change occurred in the social sciences with the publication of Charles Darwin's *On the Origin of Species*. The directness of Darwin's impact has been discussed by Stocking (1968, 1987), but it seems clear that the Darwinian theory of biological variation served as a model for inquiry into the nature of human cultural differences. The mid-nineteenth century is a threshold: earlier writers may have thought about cultural differences and the nature of humanity, but their approaches to understanding are distinct from post-Darwinian science. It is not that earlier scholars were unaware of cultural differences, but rather that they lacked "the slightest clue as to how cultural differences might be scientifically explained" (Harris 1968:18). Morgan, Tylor, Durkheim, and Boas stand on this side of that intellectual divide, and thus their ideas remain more immediate and direct.

Before 1860, according to the *Oxford English Dictionary*, "anthropology" meant the study of human nature encompassing physiology and psychology; after 1860, the word denotes a science of humankind "in its widest sense." This shift in usage marks a change in an intellectual field that the works of Morgan, Tylor, Boas, and Durkheim partly created.

Second, all these men were founders in a practical sense: they were instrumental in establishing anthropology as an academic discipline. Between 1860 and 1900, anthropology changed from a loose collection of shared interests into a formally defined science of humankind. Tylor, Morgan, Durkheim, and Boas were directly involved in the creations of new anthropological institutions. Tylor held the first professorship of anthropology at Oxford, and he wrote the first anthropology textbook. Morgan obtained support for anthropological research from the Smithsonian Institution and the U.S. government. Durkheim outlined a new curriculum of social inquiry, founded influential journals, and established a cadre of students and colleagues who in turn would shape French social science through the 1970s. Boas would supervise the first American Ph.D. in anthropology, establish new journals and associations, and literally set the broad investigative boundaries of American anthropology.

Finally, Tylor, Morgan, Durkheim, and Boas—though drawing on existing conceptual frameworks and ideas—articulated new sets of anthropological problems and proposed methods for their scientific study. In so doing, they developed ways of thinking about human culture that continue to inform our inquiries, and that shaped the course of current anthropology. Tylor's definition of culture, Morgan's examination of social evolution, Durkheim's creation of a science of society, and Boas's insistence on viewing cultures in specific historical contexts—these positions form the landscape of the emergent field of anthropology as it developed from the late nineteenth century to the present. These men were founders.

References

Darwin, Charles

1859 *On the Origin of Species by Means of Natural Selection, or, The Preservation of Favoured Races in the Struggle for Life.* London: J. Murray.

Harris, Marvin

1968 *The Rise of Anthropological Theory: A History of Theories of Culture.* New York: Thomas Y. Crowell.

Stocking, George W., Jr.

1968 *Race, Culture, and Evolution: Essays in the History of Anthropology.* New York: Free Press.

1987 *Victorian Anthropology.* New York: Free Press.

1

Edward Tylor

The Evolution of Culture

Edward Burnett Tylor (1832–1917) is considered the founding father of British anthropology. Tylor was the first professor of anthropology at Oxford; he was active in establishing anthropological associations and institutions; and his ideas contributed to the intellectual debates of the late nineteenth century sparked by Darwin's *On the Origin of Species*. His friend A. C. Haddon wrote that Tylor's books, "while replete with vast erudition, are so suggestive and graced by such quiet humour that they have become 'classics,' and have profoundly influenced modern thought. From their first appearance it was recognized that a mastermind was guiding the destinies of the nascent science" (1910:159). When a contemporary, the religious scholar Max Müller, dubbed anthropology "Mr. Tylor's science," it was a recognition of Tylor's impact on the definition of a scholarly field.

Central to Tylor's contribution was his definition of culture: "Culture or Civilization, taken in its wide ethnographic sense, is that complex whole which includes knowledge, belief, art, morals, law, custom, and any other capabilities and habits acquired by man as a member of society" (1958:1). In these opening lines of his major work, *Primitive Culture*, Tylor first defined culture in "its modern technical or anthropological meaning" (Kroeber and Kluckhohn 1952:9; compare Stocking 1963). It is a definition of culture that Bohannan and Glazer note "is the only one most anthropologists can quote correctly, and the one they fall back on when others prove too cumbersome" (1988:62).

Yet one of his most careful modern readers, George W. Stocking Jr., writes, "To judge by current textbooks, Tylor has little to say to anthropology today" (1968:176). Contending that many of his later readers simply misunderstood his concept of culture (Stocking 1963), Stocking concludes that Tylor was not "one of the major investors in the general intellectual capital of the modern human sciences," dwarfed by figures like Marx, Freud, Weber, or Durkheim (1987:301–302).

Ironically, Tylor's lasting influence was greater on American anthropology than on subsequent British social anthropology (see, for example, Evans-Pritchard's [1981:91–94] curiously curt discussion of his eminent predecessor at Oxford). In contrast, an American anthropologist like Robert Lowie (1937) lauded Tylor as a careful scholar with a "serene willingness to weigh evidence." Varying assessments of Tylor and his American contemporary, Lewis Henry Morgan, led Meyer Fortes (1969) to suggest that Morgan gave birth to British social anthropology, while the very British Tylor fathered American cultural anthropology.

How do we make sense of such contradictory assessments? Why was Tylor so influential in his time? What is the lasting value of his ideas?

Background

Tylor's family were Quakers, then a religious minority, though one firmly part of the British middle class. Tylor's religion precluded education at Oxford or Cambridge, which only granted degrees to members of the Church of England. Tylor was educated in Quaker schools before joining the family foundry business at the age of sixteen. Tylor's Quaker upbringing also led to an agnosticism that tempered his studies of the origins of religion. Ackerman observes that Tylor's agnosticism led him to approach religions as intellectual systems rather than expressions of belief, noting that Tylor "cared more about creed than consolation" (1987:77).

In his early twenties, Tylor exhibited preliminary symptoms of tuberculosis, and "secure of a modest competency" in Marett's (1936:13) discreet phrase, Tylor left the family business and traveled to warmer latitudes to regain his health. In Cuba he met Henry Christy, a British businessman and avid archaeologist, and the two set off for a four-month journey through Mexico described in Tylor's first book, *Anahuac: Or, Mexico and the Mexicans, Ancient and Modern* (1861). *Anahuac* is a travelogue informed by wide reading and crafted with an eye for telling detail and an ear for dialogue.

From the port of Veracruz, Tylor and Christy traveled inland by stagecoach to Mexico City with frequent stops as the archaeologist Christy searched roadside gullies for obsidian arrowheads (Tylor 1861:35). The travelers visited archaeological sites like Teotihuacán and Cholula, searched for potsherds in newly plowed fields, and compared the artifacts of Mexico with recent finds from Europe.

But most of *Anahuac* describes modern, not ancient, Mexico. Tylor and Christy toured sugar plantations, textile factories, pulque shops, and haciendas. He describes Mexico's political instability and poverty. Tylor's anticlerical upbringing erupts in a rash of diatribes against the Catholic Church. His criticisms are so stinging that Tylor himself admits, "It seems hard to be always attacking the Roman Catholic clergy," but then proceeds to blame priests for the "doleful ignorance" and poverty of the population (1861:126). In *Anahuac* Tylor shows himself as an informed and observant, though not unprejudiced, writer.

Over the next four years, Tylor matured into a more serious student of human culture. In 1865 he published *Researches into the Early History of Mankind and the Development of Civilization,* which outlined the analytical themes that he developed the rest of his life. "The early Culture History of Mankind," Tylor wrote, "is capable of being treated as an Inductive Science, by collecting and grouping facts" (1964:137).

Tylor sifted through missionaries' accounts, explorers' journals, ancient texts, and ethnological reports to search for similarities in human cultures. "When similar arts, customs, beliefs or legends are found in several distant regions, among peoples not known to be of the same stock," Tylor asked, "how is this similarity to be accounted for?" (1964:3). Essentially there are two possible explanations: the similarity is either the result of parallel invention—"the like working of men's minds under like conditions" (1964:3)—or it is evidence of contacts—direct or indirect, contemporary or historical—between the societies and the consequent diffusion of cultural knowledge.

Tylor's consideration of diffusion marks his early work, yet Stocking notes that Tylor increasingly emphasized the importance of evolution over diffusion or parallel invention (1963:788). Sixteen years later, the scholar would conceive of his textbook *Anthropology* as "a series of chapters demonstrating the *fact* and *course* of progression in various areas of life," almost exclusively emphasizing evolution (Stocking 1982:79).

Evolution and progress were important themes even in Tylor's first serious ethnological book. Nearly half of *Researches into the Early History of Mankind* considers the evolution of language and symbols. Although admitting that there is "no evidence of man ever having lived in society without use of spoken language," Tylor describes certain societies with "a speech so imperfect that even if talking of ordinary matters they have to eke it out by gestures." Weighing alternate hypotheses, he suggests that such societies either are "the strongest case of degeneration known in the history of the human race or supply a telling argument that the gesture-language is part of the original utterance of mankind" (Tylor 1964:62–64). In his first serious anthropological book, Tylor sketches a handful of themes he will develop in later work: the interpretation of myth, native rationales of dreams, and the logic of sympathetic magic, among others. *Researches* also contains his initial methodological musings about how to document the evolution of human society (see, for example, Tylor 1964:236–241).

Researches into the Early History of Mankind and the Development of Civilization was published by John Murray and Sons, publishers of the most important scientific writings of the nineteenth century, including Lyell's *Principles of Geology* and Darwin's *On the Origin of Species*. It was a measure of Tylor's growing status in the scientific community. By the late 1860s, Tylor "had climbed into the scientific establishment," Joan Leopold writes (1980), becoming the friend of Alfred Russel Wallace, Thomas Henry Huxley, and other eminent Victorians; publishing articles and reviews in major periodicals; and giving public lectures. Tylor's achievement was marked by his election as a fellow of the Royal Society in 1871 and the publication of *Primitive Culture*.

Primitive Culture

In *Primitive Culture* Tylor sets out to reconstruct the history of human culture and immediately faces a major problem: How can humanity's prehistoric, unwritten history be known? Tylor closely followed contemporary archaeological discoveries of stone tools and extinct mammals in Great Britain and France, but fragments of bone and stone were not enough to reconstruct the "complex whole" of culture or civilization. And so Tylor crafted his reconstruction on two principles: uniformitarianism and the concept of survivals.

> The condition of culture among the various societies of mankind, insofar as it is capable of being investigated on general principles, is a subject apt for the study of laws of human thought and action. On the one hand, the uniformity which so largely pervades civilization may be ascribed, in great measure, to the uniform action of uniform causes: while on the other hand its various grades may be regarded as stages of development or evolution, each the outcome of previous history, and about to do its proper part in shaping the history of the future. (Tylor 1958:1)

Uniformitarianism was derived from Charles Lyell's multivolume *Principles of Geology* (1830–1833). Lyell argued that the geological processes observable today—erosion, sedimentation, and so on—were the same processes that shaped the earth in the past rather than spectacular, unique catastrophes like Noah's Flood. Observations of modern processes allowed for reconstructing the history of the earth because the same geological processes were at work then as now.

This was also true for culture, Tylor argued, because culture was created by universally similar human minds and governed by the same basic laws of cognition. "Surveyed in a broad view," Tylor writes,

> the character and habit of mankind at once display that similarity and consistency which led the Italian proverb-maker to declare "all the world is one country." . . . To general likeness in human nature on the one hand, and to general likeness in

> the circumstances of life on the other, this similarity and consistency may no doubt be traced, and they may be studied with especial fitness comparing races near the same grade of civilization. (1958:6)

Setting aside for the moment the issue of "grade of civilization," Tylor's key point is that the processes of culture are similar for all people, regardless of where or when they lived, because human minds are similar (Tylor 1958:159). This is the central logic of Tylor's uniformitarianism: culture or civilization consists of knowledge, beliefs, art, morals, customs, and other mental constructs; since human mental processes are universal, human societies have developed culture along similar trajectories, characterized by progress and expressed in the evolution of culture.

This has three implications. First, race does not explain cultural differences. Believing that it was "possible and desirable to eliminate considerations of hereditary varieties or races of man," Tylor contended his study demonstrated "that stages of culture may be compared without taking into account how far tribes who use the same implement, follow the same custom, or believe the same myth, may differ in their bodily configuration and the colour of their skin and hair" (1958:7). Rather, if two societies have analogous cultural traits (pottery or monotheism or stock markets), it is because either (1) the trait has diffused from one society to another, or (2) because independent inventions have developed due to the similarly constructed human minds encountering similar situations.

Second, it means that societies with similar cultural traits may represent analogous stages in the development of human culture. Citing Samuel Johnson's fairly predictable insult "one set of savages is like another," Tylor surprisingly exclaims, "How true a generalization this really is, any Ethnological Museum may show" (1958:6). Tylor quickly explains that these similarities are most pronounced in the realm of technology—the tools for hunting, fishing, fire making, cooking, and so on—although cross-cultural similarities also exist in mythology, kinship, and other aspects of social life. Such parallels reflect similar stages of cultural development among existing societies and also allow us to reconstruct prehistoric societies. Since the laws of mind are uniform, the patterns of contemporary "primitive" societies must be similar to those of extinct prehistoric peoples, a "hypothetical primitive condition [that] corresponds in a considerable degree to that of modern savage tribes, who in spite of their difference and distance, have in common certain elements of civilization, which seem remains of an early state of the human race at large" (Tylor 1958:21). Tylor essentially asserted, as Robert Ackerman states, that "human nature and development being relatively homogeneous, one might legitimately discover, in the behaviour of contemporary primitive peoples, living links in the evolutionary chain" (1987:78).

Third, Tylor's uniformitarianism allowed him to reconstruct the specific processes leading to a particular belief, moral, or set of cultural knowledge. Since culture was a cognitive construction created by similar human minds solving the problems of existence in a rational though often erroneous way, it was possible for Tylor to retrace the logical steps that led to a superstition, folk belief, or "irrational" practice.

Tylor's reconstruction of the evolution of human culture relied on the comparative method and the doctrine of survivals. The comparative method is based on a straightforward logic: similar objects are historically related. Apes, monkeys, and humans have five digits because those animals are historically related. The words "no," *non*, and *nein* are similar because English, French, and German share historical roots. By Tylor's time the comparative method had produced major advances in different fields. The method was evident in Georges Cuvier's (1769–1832) comparative zoology and in the major advances in comparative linguistics, particularly the discovery of a proto-Indo-European language reconstructed from linguistic fragments found in Sanskrit (Hoeningswald 1963).

The comparative method forms the basis of a history of origins. Tylor presents his version of the comparative method as a natural history of human culture: "A first step in the study of civilization is to dissect it into details, and to classify these in their proper groups" (1958:7). For example, "myths" may be classified into myths about the sun, myths about eclipses or earthquakes, myths about the names of places, myths about the establishment of a tribe, and so on. Each of these, he argues, is a species of the genus "myth," and ethnography becomes natural history. Tylor states, "The ethnographer's business is to classify such details with a view of making out their distribution in geography and history, and the relations which exist among them" (1958:8).

Temporal and spatial distributions of cultural traits may reflect different processes. Some patterns could result from contacts between different cultures and the diffusion of cultural traits. Other patterns could represent parallel resolution of similar problems of existence: fishnets are similar worldwide because there are only certain ways you can catch fish, but patterns could also be reflections of earlier stages of human culture, traits that Tylor named "survivals."

For example, throughout the United States you see signs like "Ye Olde Steak House" or "Ye Olde Coffee Shoppe" or (my personal favorite) "Ye Olde Pizza Parlor." Most Americans will pronounce the word as "yee" and recognize it as an archaic English word but not know that "Y" was a symbol for the "th" sound and thus that "Ye" is simply "The." The symbol has survived, although its meaning is not really understood. "Ye" is a survival.

Tylor defines survivals as "processes, customs, opinions, and so forth, which have been carried by force of habit into a new state of society different from that in which they had their original home and they remain as proofs and examples of an older condition of culture out of which a newer has been evolved" (1958:16). We say "God bless you" or "Gesundheit" when someone sneezes because it is a survival, not because we still believe the soul is leaving the body. We celebrate Halloween because it is a survival, not because we are placating the wild spirits on the night before All Souls' Day. We shake hands as a form of greeting because it is a custom, not to show that we are unarmed. We frequently use words, gestures, sayings, and practices whose original meanings have been lost but in our daily encounters nonetheless survive.

Survivals, Tylor argues, are not merely quaint customs, but are the vestiges of previous culture. "Children's sports, popular sayings, absurd customs, may be practically unimportant, but are not philosophically insignificant bearing as they do on one of the most instructive phases of early culture" (1958:111). Such "relics of primitive barbarism" allow the ethnographer to reconstruct earlier cultural patterns and ultimately define the evolution of culture.

Human history, Tylor believed, was characterized by progress. In technology, the development of firearms showed a clear progression from matchlock to wheel lock to flintlock to percussion cap to automatic weapon. The order of technological change is obvious: one innovation leads to another. The crossbow is clearly derived from the longbow, and no one would doubt the relationship even without a written record (Tylor 1958:15). Similarly, other dimensions of culture can be seen as having a progressive relationship, demonstrating "that the main tendency from primaeval up to modern times has been from savagery towards civilization" (Tylor 1958:21).

At this point Tylor pursues a tenuous line of logic: just as specific cultural traits may be vestigial survivals of an earlier culture, entire societies may reflect earlier stages of human evolution. A society that in the late nineteenth century used stone tools was not simply a society without metal tools, but literally a vestige of prehistory, a "Stone Age" culture. The study of extant "primitive" societies is the investigation of "primaeval monuments of barbaric thought and life" leading to a reconstruction of the stages of evolution through which humans—at least some—have progressed (Tylor 1958).

At this point Tylor's cautious argument swerves into essentially unreflective assumption and prejudice. Civilization, Tylor writes,

> may be looked upon as the general improvement of mankind by higher organization of the individual and society, to the end of promoting at once man's goodness, power and happiness. This theoretical civilization does in no small measure correspond with actual civilization, as traced by comparing savagery with barbarism, and barbarism with modern educated life. So far as we take into account only material and intellectual culture, this is especially true. Acquaintance with the physical laws of the world, and the accompanying power of adapting nature to man's own ends, are, on the whole, lowest among savages, mean among barbarians, and highest among modern educated nations. (1958:27)

Not surprisingly, Tylor's "physical laws" are the principles of Western science; alternative epistemologies are merely error-filled remnants of prescientific barbarism. Based on a society's mastery of "material and intellectual culture," one can assign a relative rank on an evolutionary scale: "Thus, on the definite basis of compared facts, ethnographers are able to set up at least a rough scale of civilization. Few would dispute that the following races are arranged rightly in order of culture:—Australian, Tahitian, Aztec, Chinese, Italian" (Tylor 1958:27). Obviously many people would dispute this order, particularly Australians, Tahitians, Aztecs, and Chinese. How can any ranking of societies be untainted by prejudice? The violent convulsions of the past century make it difficult to assume that "modern educated nations" successfully promote humanity's goodness, power, and happiness. Most modern readers will stumble on the very ideas that Tylor took for granted.

Perhaps less obvious is the problem in considering entire societies as evolutionary survivals of earlier stages of human progress. The concept of a survival suggests that a cultural practice—"Ye" or "Gesundheit"—has been carried unchanged from the past into the present, and we can cite examples of such survivals. But it is another matter to assume that an entire human group has been static, a fossilized representative of an earlier cultural stage. Tylor had no reason to think that the histories of the Australians or Tahitians were either brief or static and no basis to believe that such societies reflected earlier forms of human culture rather than just different, contemporary patterns. Simply, this was justified by Tylor's assumption of human progress.

Progress and *Anthropology*

Progress is the backbone of Tylor's *Anthropology*, the first textbook on the subject. Written for a popular audience, Tylor deletes most of the references to nonevolutionary processes, focusing instead on the developmental issues of "how mankind came to be as they are, and to live as they do" (1960:1). He emphasizes the progress of cultural development: "History . . . shows arts, sciences, and political institutions beginning in ruder states, and becoming in the course of ages more intelligent, more systematic, more perfectly arranged or organized to answer their purposes" (1960:11). In the balance of *Anthropology*, Tylor summarizes his discussions of language, technology, and religion with a clarity and purpose rarely present in *Researches into the Early History of Mankind* or *Primitive Culture*.

Tylor's evolution exhibits an uneven determinism. On the one hand, human history is framed by progress rather than degeneration, by transformation from the simple to complex, and by the trajectory from savagery to civilization. Progress, Tylor believed, did not end in the nineteenth century but was transformed from an unconscious tendency to a conscious tenet: "Acquainted with events and their consequences far and wide over the world, we are able to direct our own course with more confidence toward improvement" (1960:275). Anthropology contributes to human progress, Tylor argued; knowing the course of human history "from the remote past to the present, will not only help us to forecast the future, but may guide us in our duty of leaving the world better than we found it" (1960:275). Tylor writes that "the science of culture is essentially a reformer's science" (1964:539). Perhaps Tylor's Quaker liberalism led him to embrace progress and reform (Stocking 1968).

Most of Tylor's adult life was spent in Oxford where he became keeper of the University Museum in 1883. In 1884 Tylor was given a readership in anthropology and held that position until 1896, when he was named the first professor of anthropology. He lectured on the origins of human culture, myth and magic, and the distribution of cultural traits. After the publication of *Anthropology*, Tylor spent his time teaching and developing academic institutions and anthropological associations rather than writing new works. But Tylor remained extremely influential on the development of British anthropology. He developed potential questions for researchers to ask in the field; influenced scholars like James Frazer, A. C. Haddon, and W. R. Rivers; and gave numerous public lectures. *Primitive Culture* was reprinted ten times and was translated into Russian, German, French, and Polish during Tylor's lifetime.

Tylor retired from Oxford in 1909 as professor emeritus, and his achievements were recognized by a knighthood in 1912. His final years were marked by decreasing mental clarity, and his friends lamented that Tylor never produced another work as great as *Primitive Culture* (Lang 1907; Stocking 1968).

Conclusion

Edward Burnett Tylor shaped the development of anthropology as a field of inquiry. Tylor's comparative method was emulated by many scholars and later fiercely attacked by Franz Boas and other American cultural anthropologists. Tylor's ideas about the origins of religion would lead others, like James Frazer, to investigate religions as systems of knowledge, and Tylor's concept of animism would remain a key contribution in comparative studies of religion (Sharpe 1986:56–58).

But of his contributions, it was Tylor's definition of the concept of culture that is most enduring. By arguing for the nonbiological basis of social difference, Tylor stepped away from the racial explanations that characterized Western thought since the ancient Greeks (compare Harris 1968:140–141). By outlining general principles of social life, Tylor gave new directions to comparative inquiry into human life. Finally, in defining the cultural dimension of human existence, Edward Tylor created anthropology, the study of humankind.

References

Ackerman, Robert
1987 *J. G. Frazer: His Life and Work*. Cambridge: Cambridge University Press.

Bohannan, Paul, and Mark Glazer
1988 *High Points in Anthropology*. New York: Knopf.

Evans-Prichard, Edward
1981 *A History of Ethnological Thought*. New York: Basic Books.

Fortes, Meyer
1969 *Kinship and the Social Order: The Legacy of Lewis Henry Morgan*. Chicago: Aldine.

Freire-Marreco, Barbara
1907 A Bibliography of Edward Burnett Tylor. In *Anthropological Essays Presented to Edward Tylor in Honour of His 75th Birthday, October 2, 1907*. W. Rivers, R. Marett, and N. Thomas, eds. Pp. 375–409. Oxford: Clarendon Press.

Haddon, A. C.
1910 *A History of Anthropology*. New York: G. P. Putnam's Sons.

Harris, Marvin
1968 *The Rise of Anthropological Theory: A History of Theories of Culture.* New York: Thomas Y. Crowell.

Hoenigswald, Henry
1963 On the History of the Comparative Method. *Anthropological Linguistics* 5:1–11.

Kroeber, A. L., and Clyde Kluckhohn
1952 *Culture; A Critical Review of Concepts and Definitions.* Cambridge, Mass.: The Museum.

Lang, Andrew
1907 Edward Burnett Tylor. In *Anthropological Essays Presented to Edward Tylor in Honour of His 75th Birthday, October 2, 1907.* W. Rivers, R. Marett, and N. Thomas, eds. Pp. 1–15. Oxford: Clarendon Press.

Leopold, Joan
1980 *Culture in Comparative and Evolutionary Perspective: E. B. Tylor and the Making of Primitive Culture.* Berlin: Reimer.

Lowie, Robert
1937 *The History of Ethnological Theory.* New York: Holt, Farrar & Rinehart.

Marett, R.
1936 *Tylor.* New York: Wiley and Sons.

Sharpe, Eric
1986 *Comparative Religions: A History.* La Salle, Ill.: Open Court Press.

Stocking, George W., Jr.
1963 Matthew Arnold, E. B. Tylor and the Uses of Invention. *American Anthropologist* 65:783–799.
1968 Edward Tylor. In *International Encyclopedia of the Social Sciences,* vol. 16. D. L. Sills, ed. Pp. 170–177. New York: Macmillan.
1982 *Race, Culture, and Evolution: Essays in the History of Anthropology.* Chicago: University of Chicago Press.
1987 *Victorian Anthropology.* New York: Free Press.

Tylor, Edward
1861 *Anahuac: Or, Mexico and the Mexicans, Ancient and Modern.* London: Longman, Green, Longman and Roberts.
1958 *Primitive Culture.* New York: Harper & Row. [Originally published 1871.]
1960 *Anthropology.* Ann Arbor: University of Michigan Press. [Originally published 1881.]
1964 *Researches into the Early History of Mankind and the Development of Civilization.* Chicago: University of Chicago Press. [Originally published 1865.]

2

Lewis Henry Morgan

The Evolution of Society

It is commonly alleged that the Victorian evolutionists based their conclusions solely on library research, sheltered from the vagaries of anthropological fieldwork or the complexities of interacting with real people. Bronislaw Malinowski, who revolutionized anthropological fieldwork in the twentieth century (see chapter 10), characterized the nineteenth-century evolutionists as "satisfied in reaching a rigid, self-contained entity" uncomplicated by the messy facts of cultural life (1944:31). Lewis Henry Morgan was the great exception.

Drawn to ethnography by his personal and professional ties to the Seneca Nation, a tribe of the Iroquois League, Morgan made extensive visits among various Iroquois groups. His notebooks and journals indicate "an acute and resourceful observer" (White 1959:4). Morgan also studied Native American groups in Kansas and Nebraska (1859–1860), the upper Missouri (1862), and the American Southwest (1878)—trips that involved intensive, if not prolonged, fieldwork. Robert Lowie, an anthropologist and expert on the Crow, remarked that Morgan's description of the Crow kinship system, though based on a brief trip, "was vastly superior to my own original attempt in this direction" (1936:169–170). Lowie admitted that "my error seems the less pardonable because the essential facts had already been grasped by Morgan." Combining field observations with extensive cross-cultural data, Morgan produced masterful compilations of anthropological information.

So is there any truth to Malinowski's criticism? Perhaps—but in Morgan's case it is misplaced. It is not that Morgan was unconcerned with ethnographic data, but that Morgan analyzed those data within a single evolutionary framework. Morgan's evolutionary approach was attacked by Boas, Kroeber, and others, but it also influenced the materialist approaches of Karl Marx, Friedrich Engels, and Leslie White. For example, Engels's 1884 *Origin of the Family, Private Property and the State* is subtitled "which is based on the Findings of L. H. Morgan in his *Ancient Society*." Charles Darwin considered Morgan America's most eminent social scientist, and even a strict antievolutionist such as Lowie could admire Morgan as "not a flashy intellect, but one of unusual honesty, depth, and tenacity" (1936:181). His career, one biographer suggested, "is one of the strangest in American intellectual history" (Resek 1960:vii).

Background

Born in 1818, Lewis Henry Morgan was raised on the frontier of western New York and lived his life against the backdrop of manifest destiny, economic expansion and collapse, and the American Civil War. Trained as a lawyer, a Whig in personality and politics, an ardent supporter of the market and the Republic, it is hard to imagine a less likely contributor to Marxist theory than Morgan.

Educated at Union College in Schenectady, New York, Morgan embodied progress as an inevitable social process and as a personal code. Admitted to the bar in 1842 but unable to find legal work because of a lingering economic depression, Morgan occupied himself by penning lectures and articles on temperance, parallels between ancient Greece and mid-nineteenth-century America, and other topics. In late 1844, Morgan opened a legal practice in Rochester, New York. Like many men of his time and class, Morgan joined a social club, the Order of the Gordian Knot, which originally drew on Greco-Roman themes. Yet gradually, the association changed to emphasize uniquely American qualities and was renamed the Grand Order of the Iroquois, a change proposed by Morgan.

Morgan became consumed with the study of Iroquois culture, incorporating ethnographic facts into the protocols of the club. More serious activities soon followed. In the late 1840s, Morgan immersed himself in Iroquois studies. As he devoted more time to ethnology, Morgan's legal practice suffered, and Morgan decided to summarize his Iroquois research and then turn back to law. In six months, Morgan completed *League of the Ho-dé-no-sau-nee or Iroquois*.

The *League* summarized Morgan's studies about Iroquois religion, domestic architecture, government and social organization, material culture, language, and place-names. Richly illustrated with figures and maps, the monograph presented detailed ethnographic data, such as word lists, place-names, and plans; it remains an invaluable source of information. Morgan's work received generally, but not universally, positive reviews. The American explorer and ethnologist John Wesley Powell described it as "the first scientific account of an Indian tribe given to the world" (1880:114). In contrast, the historian Francis Parkman argued that Morgan overemphasized the uniqueness of the Iroquois regarding "as the peculiar distinction of the Iroquois, that which is in fact common to many other tribes" (cited in Resek 1960:44). Parkman's criticism had merit: at this point in his studies, Morgan's anthropological knowledge was profound but provincial.

During the next decade, Morgan attended to law and business, developing a modest fortune based on mining, land, and railroad interests. But in the late 1850s, Morgan returned to ethnology, and specifically to studies of Iroquois kinship and social organizations.

Morgan discussed Iroquois kinship in the *League*, but in 1857 he read an expanded paper, "Laws of Descent of the Iroquois," to the American Association for the Advancement of Science. The Iroquois kinship system surprised Morgan. For example, collateral kin were classified as lineal kin—the same terms are used for "father" and "father's brother," for "mother" and "mother's sister," and for siblings and parallel cousins. Descent among the Seneca was reckoned through the mother's line, and thus a child is a member of his or her mother's lineage, not his or her father's. Morgan further observed that Iroquois political organization was an extension of kinship. "In fact," Morgan wrote, "their celebrated League was but an elaboration of these relationships into a complex, and even stupendous system of civil polity" (1858:132).

In 1859 Morgan discovered that similar kinship systems were used by the Ojibwa of upper Michigan and possibly among the Dakota and Creek (White 1959:6–7). This led Morgan to a new approach to ethnographic data. Rather than solely document the folklore of the Iroquois, Morgan began to explore the relationships between different societies as reflected in shared systems of kinship. Morgan's greatest discovery, as anthropologist Leslie White put it, was "the fact that customs of designating relatives have scientific significance" (1957:257).That discovery was documented in Morgan's (1871) magnum opus, *Systems of Consanguinity and Affinity of the Human Family.*

Kinship and Evolution

Morgan began a global inquiry about kinship systems. Supported by the Smithsonian Institution and the U.S. State Department, Morgan sent a printed questionnaire requesting information about kinship terms to consular officials, missionaries, and scientists around the world. This cross-cultural survey, combined with Morgan's own field research, resulted in kinship data from 139 different groups in North America, Asia, Oceania, and ancient and modern Europe. (Africa, South America, and Australia remained essentially unknown.)

Morgan's goal was to trace the connections between systems of kinship and to explore their "progressive changes" as man developed through "the ages of barbarism" (Morgan 1871:vi). At this point, Morgan had not outlined the evolutionary scheme that forms the explanatory structure of his *Ancient Society.* Rather, Morgan approached kinship systems as if they were languages and modeled his analysis on the comparative method (see pp. 11–12). Just as scholars had demonstrated the development and historical relationships between different language families based on linguistic similarities, Morgan argued that "in the systems of relationship of the great families of mankind some of the oldest memorials of human thought and experience are deposited and preserved" (1871:vi).

Morgan argued that all kinship systems could be divided into two large groups—descriptive systems and classificatory systems. Descriptive systems, such as that used in English, distinguish between lineal relatives and collateral kin; "father" and "father's brother" are not given the same term. In descriptive systems, there are fewer special kin terms, and these terms are applied to kin who are relatively close to the speaker, referred to as "Ego" (Morgan 1871:468–469).

In contrast, classificatory systems treat lineal and collateral kin as if they were the same, distinguishing generation (Ego's father versus Ego's father's father) and gender (Ego's male cousins versus Ego's female cousins), but using the same term for "father" and "father's brother," for "mother" and "mother's sister," and so on, similar to the pattern Morgan first identified among the Iroquois.

In his survey, Morgan identified six families of kinship systems—three descriptive ones (Semitic, Aryan, and Uralian) and three classificatory ones (Malayan, Turanian, and Ganowanian). Semitic kin systems were found among Arabs, Hebrews, and Armenians; Aryan systems were used by speakers of Persian, Sanskrit, and all the European language groups, modern and ancient; and Uralian kin systems were found among Turk, Magyar, Finn, and Estonian populations. Of the classificatory systems, "Ganowanian" was a term Morgan invented (after the Seneca words for "bow and arrow") to cover all native North Americans; Turanian included Chinese, Japanese, Hindu, and other groups of the Indian subcontinent; while Malayan subsumed Hawaiians, Maoris, and all the other Oceanic groups in the sample.

These six families of kinship systems may be divided, Morgan wrote, "into two great divisions. Upon one side are the Aryan, Semitic, and Uralian, and upon the other the Ganowanian, the Turanian, and Malayan, *which gives nearly the line of demarcation between civilized and uncivilized nations*" (1871:469; emphasis added). This is a startling conclusion: the difference between classificatory and descriptive kinship systems marks the distinction between uncivilized and civilized. How could Morgan conclude this? How could he link differences in kinship systems to the levels of cultural advancement?

Morgan's logic was subtle but flawed. First, Morgan argued that kinship systems were based on "natural suggestions," primitive ruminations "which arise spontaneously in the mind with the exercise of normal intelligence" (1871:472), a point similar to Tylor's emphasis on the mental construction of culture (see pp. 9–11). Descriptive systems were natural inferences about descent when marriage was based on monogamy. Kinfolk, Morgan argued, would attempt to explain their relationships by referring to a series of married ancestors (1871:472). Like Tylor, Morgan viewed culture as rationalizations about reality made by "savage philosophers," rationales that could be reconstructed by the ethnographer.

But then how do classificatory systems develop? Classificatory systems, Morgan argued, are also inferences from social relationships, but those where marriage is either polygamous, communal, or promiscuous. For example, Morgan discussed the Hawaiian kin classification in which Ego uses the same kin term for "father," "father's brother," and "mother's brother" and another term for "mother," "mother's sister," and "father's sister." Morgan interpreted Hawaiian kinship as reflecting

> promiscuous intercourse within prescribed limits. The existence of this custom necessarily implies an antecedent condition of promiscuous intercourse, involving the cohabitation of brothers and sisters, and perhaps of parents and child; thus finding mankind in a condition akin to that of the inferior animals, and more intensely barbarous than we have been accustomed to regard as a possible state of man. (1871:481)

The classification systems are reasonable inferences based on promiscuous sex and indeterminate parentage (Morgan 1871:482–483). (I refer to my brothers' children as my children because I have intercourse with my brothers' wives, and how can I tell whose kid is whose? We're just one big happy family.)

Morgan inferred different social relations from distinct kinship systems and then arranged them on a continuum from "most primitive" to "most civilized," from promiscuous intercourse to monogamy. But given the "natural stability of domestic institutions" (Morgan 1871:15), why would one system give rise to another? Why would classificatory systems evolve into descriptive ones? Why would kinship ever change?

Morgan offers a mix of explanations, each envisioning the "reform" of a previous state of society. When communal husbands defend their communal wives from other men, promiscuous society is partially "reformed." This begins a process that ultimately leads to "the family as it now exists" (Morgan 1871:481), that is, the independent nuclear family based on monogamous marriage.

But the real change follows the invention of private property; at this point, Morgan dramatically expands the implications of his study:

> There is one powerful motive which might under certain circumstances tend to the overthrow of the classificatory form and the substitution of the descriptive, but it would arise after the attainment of civilization. This is the inheritance of estates. Hence the growth of property and the settlement of its distribution might be expected to lead to a more precise discrimination of consanguinity. (1871:14)

With the "rise of property, . . . the settlement of its rights, and above all, with the established certainty of its transmission to lineal descendants," descriptive kin systems evolve, and the nuclear family eventually develops. The family "became organized and individualized by property rights and privileges" (Morgan 1871:492). Social structure and economy are thus linked.

The British social anthropologist Meyer Fortes has written of Morgan's "combination of insight and confusion," arguing that Morgan's appeal to the role of private property was "pure guesswork—a projection of his private values as an American of his day in a society undergoing rapid economic expansion" (1969:32). Rife with assumption and reliant on conjectural history, Morgan had no evidence that Hawaiian kin terms were remnants of a promiscuous horde or that "barbarous nations" were ignorant of inherited property (Morgan 1871:492).

Yet, Morgan was among the first to explore the importance of kin systems and their relationship to other aspects of human life, such as economy and politics. What began as a method for understanding the historical connections between societies was transformed into a scheme for understanding the development of all human society, the framework he elaborated in *Ancient Society.*

Ancient Society

The central tenets of Morgan's classic are stated in the opening paragraph:

> The latest investigations respecting the early condition of the human race are tending to the conclusion that mankind commenced their career at the bottom of the scale and worked their way up from savagery to civilization through the slow accumulation of experimental knowledge. As it is undeniable that portions of the human family have existed in a state of savagery, other portions in a state of barbarism, and still other portions in a state of civilization, it seems equally so that these three distinct conditions are connected with each other in a natural as well as necessary sequence of progress. (1877:3)

Thus the different portions of humanity—whether in Asia, Europe, Africa, Australia, or the Americas—represented different points along a common line of progress. "The history of the human race," Morgan observed, "is one in source, one in experience, and one in progress" (1877:vi). Savagery in one culture, barbarism in another, and civilization in a third were not the result of different races being genetically condemned to backwardness or development; they were simply societies perched at different stages on a common progression of cultural evolution. Morgan writes,

> It may be remarked finally that the experience of mankind has run in nearly uniform channels; that human necessities in similar condition have been substantially the same; and that the operations of the mental principle have been uniform in virtue of the specific identity of the brain of all the races of mankind. (1877:8)

For Morgan the terms "savagery," "barbarism," and "civilization" represented well-defined stages of progress measured by four sets of cultural achievements: (1) inventions and discoveries, (2) the idea of government, (3) the organization of the family, and (4) the concept of property. The lines of progress were clearest in the field of inventions and discoveries because certain inventions necessarily preceded others (fire before pottery, hunting before pastoralism). Therefore, Morgan chose technological developments as the primary but not sole "test of progress" marking the different stages of cultural evolution.

Morgan divided the earliest stage, or "ethnical period," into "Lower Status of Savagery," which began with the earliest humans and ended with knowledge of fire and fishing; "Middle Status of Savagery," which began with fire and fishing and lasted until the invention of the bow and arrow; and "Upper Status of Savagery," which began with the bow and arrow but ended with the development of pottery.

The invention of pottery marked the divide between savagery and barbarism. Lower Status of Barbarism began with pottery and ended with the domestication of animals in the Old World and the irrigated agriculture and substantial architecture in the New World. Those developments marked the Middle Status of Barbarism, which lasted until the invention of smelting iron ore. The Upper Status of Barbarism began with iron smelting and continued until the development of a phonetic alphabet, which marks the development of "Civilization," a stage that continues, without additional subdivisions, to this day.

Morgan argued that the "successive arts of subsistence" were the foundation on which "human supremacy on the earth depended," suggesting that "the great epochs of human progress have been identified, more or less directly, with the enlargement of the sources of subsistence" (1877:19). This materialist basis of cultural evolution has been considered Morgan's principal legacy by subsequent evolutionists such as Marx, Engels, Leslie White (chapter 13), Marvin Harris (chapter 15), and Eleanor Leacock (chapter 16). And yet, *Ancient Society* is not a coherently materialist theory since it incorporates mentalistic explanations for changes in other arenas, such as government, family, and property (see Service 1985:48–53).

Morgan's discussion of "Growth of the Idea of Government" comprises 60 percent of *Ancient Society*. By "government," Morgan referred to what modern anthropologists call social organization and political organization. Morgan explicitly distinguished social order based on kin ties (societas) from social order based on political ties (civitas):

> The experience of mankind . . . has developed but two plans of government, using plan in its scientific sense. Both were definite and systematic organizations of society. The first and most ancient was social organization, founded upon gentes, phratries and tribes. The second and latest in time was a political organization founded upon territory and upon property. Under the first a gentile society was created, in which the government dealt with persons through their relation to a gens and tribe. These relations were purely personal. Under the second a political society was created, in which the government dealt with persons through their relations to territory, e.g. the township, the county, and the state. These relations were purely territorial. The two plans were fundamentally different. One belongs to ancient society, the other to modern. (1877:62)

Morgan briefly described the organization of society based on sex, reprising his reconstruction of the communal and brother-sister families, and then proceeded to his principal concern: the nature of the gens or, in modern anthropological terms, the lineage. In Morgan's terms, the gens is a named social group of consanguineal kin (that is, kin related by "blood," not marriage) descended from a common ancestor (1877:63).

Whether matrilineal or patrilineal, the gens (plural: gentes) was the "fundamental basis of ancient society" found in cultures around the world and spanning the ethnical periods from savagery to civilization (Morgan 1877:64). When bound together into groups of two or more gentes—which Morgan called "phratries," but today are known as "clans"—such kin-based social institutions provided the structure for the distribution of rights, property, and political offices. When a group of gentes or phratries also had a single name for the entire group, spoke a single dialect, and had a supreme government and an identified territory, then social order had reached the level of the tribe (Morgan 1877:102–103). In turn, when tribes coalesced into a single entity, a nation existed. Thus, Morgan argued that government evolved from promiscuous horde to brother-sister group families, from group families to gens, and then progressively through stages of phratry, tribe, and nation.

Morgan's scheme for the evolution of the family largely restates his discussions in *Systems of Consanguinity and Affinity of the Human Family*, but his treatment of property is more developed in *Ancient Society*. Arguing that the growth of property would "keep pace with the progress of inventions and discoveries" and that the possession and inheritance of property was regulated by progressive forms of social organization, Morgan directly linked concepts of property with technological and social evolution (1877:525–526). During the stage of savagery, property was minimal and not inherited since it was buried as grave goods when the owner died. In the Lower Status of Barbarism, property increased in quantity but was distributed among the gens on a member's death without specific inheritance by spouses (Morgan 1877:530–531). By the Middle Status of Barbarism and with the development of agriculture, property increased in quantity and variety. New relationships developed between people and land, such as forms of communal land ownership in which individuals had the right to use, but not sell, it (Morgan 1877:535–536). By the end of the Upper Status of Barbarism, two forms of land tenure evolved—state ownership and individual ownership—which became well established by the ethnical period of Civilization (Morgan 1877:552).

But how did Morgan determine the relationship between ethnical periods, essentially defined by technological inventions, and forms of government and property? Basically in two ways. First, he proposed a plausible but conjectural history, arguing that different forms of social organization or of property were necessarily based on earlier, simpler forms in the same way that metallurgy presumed the prior invention of fire.

Second, Morgan assumed that primitive societies were representative of earlier stages of social evolution, producing a relative ordering of social and property forms. With the exception of the Lower Status of Savagery, for which "no exemplification of tribes of mankind in this condition remained to the historical period," primitive, non-Western societies represented the stages in cultural evolution, a point Tylor also made (see pp. 9–11) and that was later echoed by the French social theorist Émile Durkheim (see chapter 4). Morgan held that

> the domestic institutions of the barbarous, and even of the savage ancestors of mankind, are still exemplified in portions of the human family with such completeness that, with the exception of the strictly primitive period [i.e., Lower Savagery], the several stages of this progress are tolerably well preserved. They are seen in the organization of society upon the basis of sex, then upon the basis of kin, and finally upon the basis of territory; through the successive forms of marriage and of the family with the systems of consanguinity thereby created; and through house life and architecture; and through progress in usages with respect to the ownership and inheritance of property. (1877:7)

Thus, an ethnographic study of the Australian aborigines or the Iroquois or ancient Romans was not a study of different cultures, but of representatives of specific stages of cultural evolution. Civilized nations had progressed through similar stages and profited by the "heroic exertions and the patient toil" of barbarian and savage ancestors, which was "part of the plan of the Supreme Intelligence to develop a barbarian out of a savage, and a civilized man out of this barbarian" (Morgan 1877:554).

Conclusion

In many ways *Ancient Society* was Morgan's most important work and least convincing; it was influential and enraging. As noted above, Morgan's statements about the relationships between property relationships and social order were developed by Engels, and through Engels's work Morgan's ideas were spread worldwide. In response, Franz Boas would mount a severe critique of Morgan's and Tylor's "comparative method," attacking the idea that humanity had passed through unilineal, progressive stages (see pp. 40–42).

In the 1940s, Morgan's emphasis on the technological realm was recast by Leslie White (see chapter 13) into a theory of cultural evolution; in fact, Morgan never seemed certain that "the arts of subsistence" were the causal determinants that White proposed, nor does White's work contain the mentalist elements found throughout *Ancient Society* suggesting that cultural developments were produced by individual will and rational choice (Colson 1974:10–11).

Though not without flaws, Morgan's contributions to anthropology remain essential and permanent. First, Morgan outlined the importance of the study of kinship systems, recognizing the significance of classificatory systems, the role of lineal descent groups in social organization, and the complementary patterns of kin-based political orders and those based on non-kin relationships. Second, Morgan conducted research that attempted to be systematic and global, anticipating by a century large-scale cross-cultural studies such as the Human Relations Area Files. Finally, Morgan attempted to organize anthropological data in terms of an explicit framework of cultural evolution rather than simply treat cultural differences as ethnographic curios.

Morgan died on December 17, 1881; he was sixty-three years old. His longtime friend, the Reverend Joshua McIlvaine (to whom *Systems of Consanguinity and Affinity of the Human Family* is dedicated), delivered the benediction, but only after first presenting an analysis of the classificatory kinship system. It was a fitting tribute to Morgan's lifework, a body of work in which his confidence in reason's ability to discover the laws of nature is present on every page.

References

Colson, Elizabeth

1974 *Tradition and Contract: The Problem of Order*. Chicago: Aldine.

Fortes, Meyer

1969 *Kinship and the Social Order: The Legacy of Lewis Henry Morgan*. Chicago: Aldine.

Lowie, Robert

1936 Lewis H. Morgan in Historical Perspective. In *Essays in Anthropology: Presented to A. L. Kroeber in Celebration of His Sixtieth Birthday, June 11, 1936*. R. Lowie, ed. Pp. 169–181. Berkeley: University of California Press.

Malinowski, Bronislaw
1944 *A Scientific Theory of Culture and Other Essays*. Chapel Hill: University of North Carolina Press.

Morgan, Lewis H.
1858 Laws of Descent among the Iroquois. *Proceedings of the American Association for the Advancement of Science for August 1857* 11:132–148. Cambridge, Mass.
1871 *Systems of Consanguinity and Affinity of the Human Family*. Smithsonian Contributions to Knowledge, 17. Washington, D.C.: Smithsonian Institution. [Facsimile reprint 1970. The Netherlands: Anthropological Publications.]
1877 *Ancient Society; Or, Researches in the Lines of Human Progress from Savagery through Barbarism to Civilization*. New York: Henry Holt. [Facsimile reprint 1978. Palo Alto: New York Labor News.]
1901 *League of the Ho-dé-no-sau-nee or Iroquois*. Edited and annotated by H. Lloyd. New York: Dodd, Mead. [Originally published 1851; facsimile reprint 1966. New York: Burt Franklin.]
1959 *The Indian Journals, 1859–1862*. Edited and with an introduction by Leslie White. Ann Arbor: University of Michigan Press.
1965 *Houses and House-Life of the American Aborigines*. Chicago: University of Chicago Press. [Originally published in 1881 in *Contributions to North American Ethnology*. Vol. 4. Washington, D.C.]

Powell, John Wesley
1880 Sketch of Lewis Henry Morgan. *Popular Science Monthly* 18:114–121.

Resek, Carl
1960 *Lewis Henry Morgan: American Scholar*. Chicago: University of Chicago Press.

Service, Elman
1985 A *Century of Controversy: Ethnological Issues from 1860 to 1960*. New York: Academic Press.

White, Leslie
1937 Extracts from the European Travel Journal of Lewis H. Morgan. *Rochester Historical Society Publications* 16:221–390.
1942 Lewis H. Morgan's Journal of a Trip to Southwestern Colorado and New Mexico, 1878. *American Antiquity* 8:1–26.
1944 Morgan's Attitude toward Religion and Science. *American Anthropologist* 46:218–230.
1951 Lewis H. Morgan's Western Field Trips. *American Anthropologist* 53:11–18.

1957 How Morgan Came to Write *Systems of Consanguinity and Affinity*. *Papers of the Michigan Academy of Science, Arts, and Letters* 42:257–268.
1959 Lewis Henry Morgan: His Life and Researches. In *The Indian Journals, 1859–1862*. L. White, ed. Pp. 3–12. Ann Arbor: University of Michigan Press.

3

Franz Boas

Culture in Context

Franz Boas (1858–1942) shaped the direction of twentieth-century American anthropology. His former student, Alfred Kroeber, wrote shortly after Boas's death that "the world lost its greatest anthropologist and America one of its most colorful intellectual figures" (1943:5). Echoing this assessment thirty years later, George Stocking Jr. wrote, "There is no real question that [Boas] was the most important single force in shaping American anthropology in the first half of the 20th century" (1974:1). Boas's influence was institutional, intellectual, and personal. Like Tylor and Durkheim, Boas played a pivotal role in moving anthropology into academia, in establishing associations and journals, and by creating essential networks of institutional support from the public, policy makers, and other scientists.

Boas defined the principal fields of inquiry that American anthropologists would pursue. His wide interests—spanning from biological anthropology to linguistics—gave American anthropology a topical breadth that is not really present in Great Britain or France, where anthropology is preeminently social anthropology, and archaeology and biological anthropology are separate fields. The fact that American anthropology has included sociocultural anthropology, linguistics, physical anthropology, and archaeology—the so-called four fields approach—is partly a reflection of Boas's broad interests.

Boas created an anthropology very different from those of Morgan, Tylor, or Durkheim. Rather than assuming that cultural practices were explicable only in reference to broad evolutionary stages, Boas argued that they were understandable only in specific cultural contexts.

For example, Boas and the anthropologist O. T. Mason engaged in a spirited debate about the organization of ethnographic materials in museum displays; it is an unlikely subject for a fierce debate, but it produced an illuminating exchange. Mason, an evolutionist, proposed organizing ethnographic displays in the Smithsonian Institution by artifact classes—pottery, stone tools, musical instruments—regardless of their place of origin, displaying what Mason called "similarities in the products of industry." Mason wanted to illustrate the evolutionary parallels in human nature, arguing that cultural products stemmed from similar, universal causes.

Boas's response was quick and telling. Boas contended that cultural traits first must be explained in terms of specific cultural contexts rather than by broad reference to general evolutionary trends. "In the collections of the national museum," Boas wrote, "the marked character of the North-West American tribes is almost lost, because the objects are scattered in different parts of the building and are exhibited among those from other tribes" (1887:486). Instead of being presented in technological "stages," ethnographic collections should be "arranged according to tribes, in order to teach the peculiar style of each group. The art and characteristic style of a people can be understood only by studying its productions as a whole."

Over the next decade, Boas expanded this critique into a larger-scale attack on the theories of Morgan, Tylor, and other evolutionists. Boas's basic approach (culture was to be understood from detailed studies of specific cultures) was passed on to the first cohort of professional American anthropologists, individuals who would literally shape the field of anthropological inquiry: Alfred Kroeber (chapter 5), Ruth Benedict (chapter 6), Edward Sapir (chapter 7), Margaret Mead (chapter 8), and many others. In turn, Boas's students, as anthropologist Marvin Harris wrote, "set forth the main lines of development of anthropological research and instruction at crucial institutions around the country" (1968:251). Thus Boas's personal contacts with his students extended his intellectual influence and shaped the institutions of American anthropology.

And yet, as Kroeber noted, "It has long been notoriously difficult to convey the essence of Boas' contribution in anthropology to non-anthropologists" (1943:24; a task at which Kroeber also failed). This difficulty, and the fact that Boas played a pivotal role in the establishment of American anthropology, requires an examination of Boas's essential contribution.

Background

The founder of American anthropology was born in northwestern Germany into a prosperous Jewish family that was committed to progressive education and politics. He wrote that he was raised "in a German home in which the ideals of the Revolution of 1848 were a living force," referring to the European revolutions that fought for universal suffrage, freedoms of press and assembly, and other liberal democratic reforms—revolts ultimately repressed by the military and monarchy. Of his parents' Judaism, Boas wrote, "My father had retained an emotional affection for the ceremonial of his parental home, without allowing it to influence his intellectual freedom," and concluded, "My parents had broken through the shackles of dogma" (1939:19). By his own account, these influences shaped Boas's anthropology and his social activism.

Boas was educated in his hometown and then went off to study physics, mathematics, and geography in a string of universities. "My university studies were a compromise," Boas recalled, between an "emotional interest in the phenomena of the world," which led to geography, and an "intellectual interest" in the formal analyses of mathematics and physics (1939:20). His doctoral dissertation was on the color of water, a topic emphasizing physics over geography; he received his doctorate in 1881 at the age of twenty-three. Kroeber contended that Boas's education "as a physicist heavily determined his whole intellectual career," creating his "gifts for dealing with abstract form or structure and of intellectual precision and rigor" (1943:7).

After a year of military service, Boas was at loose ends; he wanted to study human societies but lacked financial support. After a string of setbacks, in June 1883 Boas joined a German expedition to the Arctic to pursue research on the Inuit in order "to discover how far one can get, by studying a very special and not simple case, in determining the relationship between the life of a people and environment" (Boas 1974:44). Supported by writing freelance articles for a Berlin newspaper, Boas spent a year on Baffin Island in the Canadian Arctic. Traveling by dogsled during the Arctic winter in −50-degree temperatures, Boas charted the Baffin coastline, collected Inuit legends, and observed rites and ceremonies. Ultimately, Boas was unsatisfied with his ethnographic research, calling it "shallow" and a "disappointment"; nevertheless, he recognized that the year in the Arctic "had a profound influence upon the development of my views . . . because it led me away from my former interests and toward the desire to understand what determines the behavior of human beings" (1939:20–21).

Boas returned from the Arctic to uncertain prospects, unsuccessfully applying for jobs and fellowships in the United States, then working in Germany for eighteen months before returning to America. In the fall of 1886 he worked for the Canadian Geological Survey in southern British Columbia conducting a brief ethnographic survey in the vicinity of Vancouver Island (Rohner and Rohner 1969). Returning to New York in 1887, Boas accepted a job as assistant editor of *Science*, and with some financial security, married and became an American citizen.

From his position at *Science*, Boas extended his influence almost immediately. In 1888 the British Association for the Advancement of Science (BAAS) asked Boas to collect ethnographic data on the Northwest Coast. After a successful trip, the BAAS supported a second field trip to the Northwest Coast in 1889 in which Boas studied native languages, made anthropometric measurements, and investigated social organizations of the Kwakiutl and Tsimshian (Boas 1974). In 1889 Boas obtained a teaching position at the newly founded Clark University in Worcester, Massachusetts, where the first American Ph.D. in anthropology was granted under his leadership in 1892 (Kroeber 1943:12). In 1892 financial turmoil at Clark University led to a massive faculty resignation. Boas also left to join the anthropological staff at the Chicago World's Columbian Exposition who were working on displaying Native American materials. A short-term position at the newly established Field Museum of Natural History in Chicago was followed by part-time work for the Smithsonian, another field trip to the Northwest Coast sponsored by the BAAS, and unfulfilled hopes of a position at the American Museum of Natural History in New York. This professional turmoil was deepened by the death of his child (Hyatt 1990:33).

It was a dark and difficult time. Boas's letters from the field oscillate from quick descriptions of research accomplished to depressed accounts of financial insecurities, underscored by a deep longing for his wife and surviving children.

But in 1895 things began to change. John Wesley Powell offered Boas an editorial position at the Smithsonian's Bureau of American Ethnology, which galvanized the American Museum of Natural History (AMNH) into making a counterproposal that Boas accepted. Appointed to the AMNH in December 1895, Boas finally obtained a permanent position. "No longer concerned with economic survival," Hyatt writes, "he began to concentrate on the science of anthropology and its many applications" (1990:35).

From his base in New York, Boas began to influence American anthropology. In May 1896 he was hired as lecturer in physical anthropology at Columbia College and was appointed professor in 1899. He maintained his position at the AMNH throughout this period and became curator of anthropology in 1901, weaving close ties between the AMNH and Columbia. Boas seized his opportunity with extraordinary energy and expertise. Harris, a prolific scholar in his own right (see chapter 15), wrote,

> Boas' accomplishments as a teacher, administrator, researcher, founder and president of societies, editor, lecturer, and traveler are exhausting to behold. To anyone who has ever worried about publishing or perishing, the fact that all this activity was accompanied by the publication of a torrent of books and articles is well nigh terrifying. (1968:252)

From 1895 till his death in 1942, Boas's résumé becomes a blur of publications and accomplishments, almost as if he wanted to compensate for the frustrations of his early career.

Boas became full professor at Columbia University in 1899 and was elected to the National Academy of Sciences in 1900. He helped establish the American Anthropological Association and revived the journal *American Anthropologist*. Boas founded the *International Journal of American Linguistics* in 1917, which continues to be published; helped establish an archaeological field school in Mexico; and presided over a series of field research projects, particularly in the Northwest Coast, while continuing to publish constantly.

Boas authored six books and more than seven hundred articles; his bibliography records his diverse research (Andrews 1943). Most numerous are his articles and reports on his investigations in the Arctic and Northwest Coast; Boas's publications on the Kwakiutl, Tsimshian, and other Northwest Coast societies total over ten thousand printed pages (Codere 1959). Boas made major contributions in the study of language. For four decades Boas taught two seminars at Columbia University: one on statistical methods, the other on North American Indian languages. Boas published extensively on Northwest Coast Indian languages and established a research agenda for recording Native American languages (Boas 1966d).

Third, Boas's work in anthropometry was a major field of endeavor with significant implications for public policy. In Boas's time, race was considered a fixed biological category; individual races were thought to have specific properties—physical, mental, and cultural. Many formal studies defined racial variation based on cranial measurements rather than "obvious" characteristics like skin color. Skull form, it was thought, was a more stable property and thus a better basis for defining racial categories, yet the stability of cranial form had been assumed, never demonstrated. In 1911 Boas published the results of a massive study of the head form of 17,821 immigrants and conducted sophisticated statistical analyses of the data (remember, this was done without computers). Boas showed that cranial form was anything but stable, with significant differences between immigrant parents and their American-born children (Boas 1966b; Gravlee, Bernard, and Leonard 2003). Boas demonstrated that traits thought to be fixed (genetically inherited) traits were actually modified by environment. And if such a stable racial trait as cranial form was influenced by environment, then all other racial classifications and characterizations became suspect.

In 1931 Boas gave his presidential address, entitled "Race and Progress," to the American Association for the Advancement of Science (AAAS). Boas summarized four decades of research, applying it to America's most cancerous social problem, racism. Throughout his career, Boas attacked racist pseudoscientific studies linking race and intelligence (Baker 1998:120–126). Arguing that variations among individuals were greater than those between races, Boas concluded that "biological differences between races are small. There is no reason to believe that one race is by nature so much more intelligent, endowed with great will power, or emotionally more stable than another" (1931:6). Not only was Boas offended by bad science, but he drew on his personal experience of anti-Semitism; these factors produced an informed and fervent rejection of racism. Boas was involved in the establishment of the National Association for the Advancement of Colored People and wrote about race in popular magazines as well as in scientific journals (Hyatt 1990:83–99).

His 1931 speech was a central statement about a long battle against racism. Boas argued that because of intermarriage and mating, there were no biologically "pure" races and that, contrary to a then common view, the "mixture" of races had no harmful consequences. Further, variations between individuals within races were greater than differences between races. Boas questioned the significance of IQ tests and discounted studies showing racial variations in intelligence. In addition to attacking the biological concept of race, he attacked the social concept. "Among us race antagonism is a fact," Boas stated (1931:6). He then argued that America's great problem is a social stratification based on racial characteristics that leads to divisive conflicts. Boas concluded his AAAS address with this essential challenge:

> As long as we insist on [socioeconomic] stratification in racial layers, we shall pay the penalty in the form of interracial struggle. Will it be better for us to continue as we have been doing, or shall we try to recognize the conditions that lead to the fundamental antagonisms that trouble us? (1931:8)

Boas continued to speak out against racism and by 1933 he was an early critic of Nazism. Boas attacked their racist policies, argued that Hitler and his leading supporters should be confined to an insane asylum, and wrote anti-Nazi polemics that the Allied underground smuggled into Germany (Herskovits 1943:45–46). Boas was a committed, public intellectual. (For more detailed discussions of Boas's diverse accomplishments in academic and public life, see Cole 1999; Herskovits 1953; Hyatt 1990; Spier 1959; and Stocking 1974.)

The Integration of Cultures

Like any developing scholar, Boas's opinions evolved over the course of his career, but his most consistently held position was that cultures were integrated wholes produced by specific historical processes rather than reflections of universal evolutionary stages. In his earliest works Boas wrote passages that could have been penned by Edward Tylor: "The frequent occurrence of similar phenomena in cultural areas that have no historical contact . . . shows that the human mind develops everywhere according to the same laws" (1966a:637). By the late 1890s, however, Boas had developed his critique of evolutionary frameworks and the comparative method. Boas argued that the comparative approaches of Morgan and Tylor were undercut by three flaws: (1) the assumption of unilineal evolution, (2) the notion of modern societies as evolutionary survivals, and (3) the classification of societies based on weak data and inappropriate criteria. These flaws were the targets of the Boasian attack.

Boas dismissed the evolutionary frameworks of Morgan, Tylor, and others as untested and untestable. In his "The Methods of Ethnology," Boas summarizes the evolutionary position, which

> presupposes that the course of historical changes in the cultural life of mankind follows definite laws which are applicable everywhere, and which bring it about that cultural development, in its main lines, is the same among all races and all peoples. *As soon as we admit that the hypothesis of a uniform evolution has to be proved before it can be accepted the whole structure loses its foundation.* (1920:311–312, emphasis added)

Boas undercut the entire basis of nineteenth-century cultural evolution. We might agree with Tylor and Morgan that certain technological processes have an inherent evolutionary order—fire must precede pottery making, flintlocks were invented before automatic rifles—but there is no ethnographic evidence indicating that matrilineal kin systems preceded patrilineal kin systems or that religions based on animism developed before polytheistic religions. Boas argued that this unilineal ordering is a simple assumption; there is no proven historical relationship nor any way to prove such a relationship. Therefore, evolutionary frameworks were unproven assumptions imposed on the data, not theories derived from ethnographic data.

Further, Boas argued, the unilineal classification of different societies assumed that different societies with similar cultural patterns (e.g., they used Hawaiian kinship classifications [see p. 23] or the bow and arrow) were at similar evolutionary levels. On the contrary, he believed that very similar cultural practices may arise from different causes. Anthropology's primary task, according to Boas, was to provide "a penetrating analysis of a unique culture describing its form, the dynamic reactions of the individual to the culture and of the culture to the individual" (1966c:310–311). Boas did not assume (as some of his students did) that general laws of human behavior did not exist, but rather that those laws could be derived only from an understanding of specific historical processes.

> We agree that certain laws exist which govern the growth of human culture, and it is our endeavor to discover these laws. The object of our investigation is to find the processes by which certain stages of culture have developed. The customs and beliefs themselves are not the ultimate objects of research. We desire to learn the reasons why such customs and beliefs exist—in other words, we wish to discover the history of their development.
>
> . . . A detailed study of customs in their bearings to the total culture of the tribe practicing them, and in connection with an investigation of their geographical distribution among neighboring tribes, affords us almost always a means of determining with considerable accuracy the historical causes that led to the formation of the customs in question and to the psychological processes that were at work in their development. The results of inquiries may be three-fold. They may reveal the environ-

> mental conditions which have created or modified elements; they may clear up psychological factors which are at work in shaping culture; or they may bring before our eyes the effects that historical connections have had upon the growth of the culture. (Boas 1896:905)

Thus Boas suggests that lawlike generalizations can be based on adaptational, psychological, or historical factors, but only if documented by well-established ethnographic cases:

> The comparative method and the historical method, if I may use these terms, have been struggling for supremacy for a long time, but we may hope that each will soon find its appropriate place and function. The historical method has reached a sounder basis by abandoning the misleading principle of assuming connection wherever similarities of culture are found. The comparative method, notwithstanding all that has been said and written in its praise, has been remarkably barren of definite results, and I believe it will not become fruitful until we renounce the vain endeavor to construct a uniform systematic history of the evolution of culture, and until we begin to make our comparisons on the broader and sounder basis which I venture to outline. Up to this time we have too much reveled in more or less ingenious vagaries. The solid work is still all before us. (1896:908)

Conclusion

Franz Boas argued that detailed studies of particular societies had to consider the entire range of cultural behavior, and thus the concepts of anthropological holism and cultural particularism became twin tenets of American anthropology. In later years Boas grew even more skeptical about the possibility of deriving cultural laws. Writing in 1932, Boas concludes,

> Cultural phenomena are of such complexity that it seems to me doubtful whether valid cultural laws can be found. The causal conditions of cultural happenings lie always in the interaction between individual and society, and no classificatory study of societies will solve this problem. The morphological classifica-

> tion of societies may call to our attention some problems. It will not solve them. In every case it is reducible to the same source, the interaction between the individual and society. (1932:612)

Unfortunately, Boas did not articulate the relationship between cultural elements and cultural wholes. Stocking poses the unresolved paradox: "On the one hand, culture was simply an accidental accretion of individual elements. On the other, culture—despite Boas' renunciation of organic growth—was at the same time an integrated spiritual totality that somehow conditioned the form of its elements" (1974:5–6).

Boas demolished the evolutionary framework, provided methodologies for the investigation of specific cultures, and hinted at the relationship between individuals and society, cultural elements, and cultural wholes—but never really answered how cultures become integrated wholes.

Due to Boas's enormous influence on the practice of anthropology in America, anthropological research took a decidedly antitheoretical turn in the early twentieth century, when research began to focus on the differences rather than the similarities between societies. When cultural elements were held in common, they were interpreted as evidence of historical contact and diffusion and not unilineal evolution. The antievolutionary position would dominate American anthropology until the 1940s, when an evolutionary approach would be reformulated in the work of Leslie White (chapter 13) and Julian Steward (chapter 14).

Until his death in 1942, Boas continued his remarkably detailed, stunningly diverse studies of humanity, and his influence was felt for decades later as many of his students turned their attention to what Boas saw as the key nexus, the relationship between the individual and society.

References

Andrews, H.
1943 Bibliography of Fanz Boas. In *Franz Boas*, 1858–1942. R. Linton, ed. Pp. 67–109. American Anthropological Association, Memoir 61. [Reprinted 1969. New York: Krauss Reprint.]

Baker, Lee

1998 *From Savage to Negro: Anthropology and the Construction of Race, 1896–1954*. Berkeley: University of California Press.

Boas, Franz

1896 The Limitations of the Comparative Method of Anthropology. *Science* 4:901–908.

1887 The Occurrence of Similar Inventions in Areas Widely Apart. *Science* 9:485–86.

1920 The Methods of Ethnology. *American Anthropologist* 22(4):311–321.

1931 Race and Progress. *Science* 74:1–8.

1932 The Aims of Anthropological Research. *Science* 76:605–613.

1939 An Anthropologist's Credo. In *I Believe*. C. Fadiman, ed. Pp. 19–29. New York: Simon & Schuster.

1966a The Aims of Ethnology. In *Race, Language and Culture*. Pp. 626–638. New York: Free Press. [Originally published 1888.]

1966b Changes in Bodily Form of Descendants of Immigrants. In *Race, Language and Culture*. Pp. 60–75. New York: Free Press.

1966c History and Science in Anthropology: A Reply. In *Race, Language and Culture*. Pp. 305–311. [Originally published 1936.]

1966d Introduction: International Journal of American Linguistics. In *Race, Language and Culture*. Pp. 199–210. New York: Free Press. [Originally published 1917.]

1974 Fieldwork for the British Association, 1888–1897. In *The Shaping of American Anthropology, 1883–1911; A Franz Boas Reader*. G. Stocking Jr., ed. Pp. 88–197. New York: Basic Books. [Originally published 1898.]

Codere, Helen

1959 *The Understanding of the Kwakiutl in the Anthropology of Franz Boas*. W. Goldschmidt, ed. Pp. 61–75. American Anthropological Association, Memoir 89.

Cole, Douglas

1999 *Franz Boas: The Early Years, 1858–1906*. Seattle: University of Washington Press.

Gravlee, Clarence, H. Russel Bernard, and William Leonard

2003 Heredity, Environment, and Cranial Form: A Reanalysis of Boas's Immigrant Data. *American Anthropologist* 105(1):125–138.

Harris, Marvin

1968 *The Rise of Anthropological Theory: A History of Theories of Culture*. New York: Thomas Y. Crowell.

Herskovits, Melville
1943 Franz Boas as Physical Anthropologist. In *Franz Boas*, 1858–1942. R. Linton, ed. Pp. 39–51. American Anthropological Association, Memoir 61. [Reprinted 1969. New York: Krauss Reprint.]
1953 *Franz Boas*. New York: Scribner.

Hyatt, Marshall
1990 *Franz Boas, Social Activist: The Dynamics of Ethnicity*. New York: Greenwood Press.

Kroeber, Alfred
1943 Franz Boas: The Man. In *Franz Boas, 1858–1942*. American Anthropological Association, Memoir 61. [Reprinted 1969. New York: Krauss Reprint.]

Rohner, Ronald, and Evelyn C. Rohner
1969 Introduction. In *The Ethnography of Franz Boas: Letters and Diaries of Franz Boas Written on the Northwest Coast from 1886 to 1931*. Compiled and edited by R. Rohner. Pp. xiii–xxx. Chicago: University of Chicago Press.

Spier, Leslie
1959 Some Central Elements in the Legacy. In *The Anthropology of Franz Boas: Essays on the Centennial of His Birth*. W. Goldschmidt, ed. Pp. 146–155. American Anthropological Association, Memoir 89. Menasha, Wis.: American Anthropological Association.

Stocking, George, Jr.
1974 Introduction: The Basic Assumptions of Boasian Anthropology. In *The Shaping of American Anthropology, 1883–1911; A Franz Boas Reader*. G. Stocking Jr., ed. Pp. 1–20. New York: Basic Books.

4

Émile Durkheim

The Organic Society

The tradition of anthropological inquiry concerned with the character of social integration descends from the works of the French sociologist and educator Émile Durkheim (1858–1917). This line passes from Durkheim to his students, particularly Marcel Mauss (chapter 9), and through them to the British school of social anthropology exemplified by A. R. Radcliffe-Brown (see chapter 11), Evans-Pritchard (chapter 12), Mary Douglas (chapter 20), and many others. These scholars share a concern with the arrangement and articulation of basic social segments: how are different kin groups, classes, and political and religious units structured such that a given, coherent society exists? With his analytical focus on social integration, Durkheim's influence permeates a wide range of anthropological endeavors, including British social anthropology, anthropological approaches to religion, and questions about the origins of the state and the evolution of social complexity.

Given the influence of Durkheim's ideas, it is hard to understand how little impact Durkheim had on early American anthropology. As one historian has noted, "The American school of anthropologists (Ruth Benedict, Clyde Kluckhohn, Margaret Mead) owed a good deal to him, even, or chiefly, when they contradicted several of his conclusions" (Peyre 1960:23). The anthropologist Paul Bohannan wrote, "A few cultural anthropologists have roundly rejected Durkheim; others have rephrased him to their own ends; most have simply ignored him" (1960:77).

Why this lack of appreciation and indifference? Partly it was due to the barriers of language; only one of Durkheim's books,

The Elementary Forms of the Religious Life, was translated into English during his lifetime (in 1915), and his other classic, *The Division of Labor in Society*, originally written in 1893, was not translated into English until 1933. Some American anthropologists dismissed Durkheim for his lack of fieldwork, his assumption that certain societies (like the Arunta of Australia) were archetypically primitive, and for his apparent lack of concern with the details of ethnographic data. Yet, the more fundamental barrier that existed between American anthropologists and Durkheim and the scholars he influenced was a basic distinction between culture and society.

As discussed in chapter 1, Tylor's definition of culture emphasized the intellectual, ideational aspects of culture—culture was shared, learned, patterned "knowledge." For much of the twentieth century, American anthropology has approached "culture" in this manner, distinguishing "culture" from "society." For example, Alfred Kroeber (1952b:118–119) cited the "existence of cultureless or essentially cultureless subhuman societies" like those of ants or bees as evidence for the difference between society and culture (see pp. 69–70). Durkheim, intent on creating "a science of society," was viewed as somewhat irrelevant by American cultural anthropologists. In an address to the 1950 American Anthropological Association, Kroeber dealt with Durkheim in a surprisingly casual manner:

> Durkheim, to sum him up, may be rated a positivist; an empiricist in principle, but with only mild urge toward the use of wide context; like most of his countrymen [Kroeber engages in anti-French slurs] more interested in sharp principles than in variety of comparative data; not ethnocentric but yet little given to relativistic and pluralistic recognitions; and continuing to the end to believe that cultural phenomena can be adequately subsumed under purely social concepts. Durkheim left a school, but his actual constructive influence outside France has been slight, except on and through Radcliffe-Brown. (1952a:146)

From a current perspective, Kroeber's assessment of Durkheim is not only insulting but incorrect. Clearly this misappreciation involved more than language barriers; Kroeber, Lowie, and many other American anthropologists were cosmopolitan scholars comfortable in French. So either Durkheim's current status is misplaced or Kroeber and his colleagues were unable to understand the lasting value of Durkheim's ideas.

Background

Émile Durkheim was born in 1858 to a Jewish family in the Alsace region of eastern France. Much of Durkheim's life was framed by conflicts between Germany and France, first in the Franco-Prussian War (1870–1871), in which France was crushed, Napoleon III captured, and Alsace ceded to the Germans, second in World War I. The destruction experienced by France and the Allies was severe, and like so many others, Durkheim lost many loved ones, including his son, André, and every one of his students except for Marcel Mauss. By all accounts, the war aged him before his time; he died at the age of fifty-nine. But this was all in the future.

As a youth, Durkheim was recognized for his brilliance and began to advance through the centralized hierarchy of the French educational system. Durkheim spent his adult life within this system, as an instructor at several lycées teaching philosophy to teenage boys, and after a year's sabbatical in Germany, as a professor of social science at the University of Bordeaux. He was "called" to the University of Paris in 1902 and became a full professor there in 1906, teaching courses in education, philosophy, and sociology.

For Durkheim, sociology was "the science of societies" (1960:325); his sociology lacked the emphasis on Western, industrialized society typical of American sociology. In the French university, sociology was taught as a dimension of philosophy, but the implications of Durkheim's teaching were felt in a number of other disciplines. Peyre writes that "sociology became a catalyst that transformed a number of other disciplines" (1960:15), such as law, economics, geography, and anthropology and ethnology, exemplified by the works of Mauss (see chapter 9) and Claude Lévi-Strauss (chapter 17) and several generations of French social scientists.

And so the paradox reemerges: how could such an influential scholar have so little impact on the early years of American anthropology? The answer relates, in part, to the interpretation of two of Durkheim's central themes: the ideas of mechanic solidarity versus organic solidarity, and the *conscience collective*.

Mechanic and Organic Solidarity

In the preface to his first classic, *The Division of Labor in Society*, Durkheim begins with an acute phrase, "We do not wish to extract ethics from science, but to establish the science of ethics, which is quite different. Moral facts are phenomena like others; they consist of rules of action recognizable by certain distinctive characteristics" (1964:33). When we understand that for Durkheim, "moral" implies not only value (as in the *moral* of a story) but also outlook (as in *morale*), then it becomes clear that he is describing the study of values, worldview, and beliefs and proposing that they are amenable to scientific inquiry (see Bohannan and Glazer 1988:232). The specific focus of Durkheim's work was, in his words,

> the question of the relations of the individual to social solidarity. Why does the individual, while becoming more autonomous, depend more upon society? How can he be at once more individual and more solidary. Certainly these two movements, contradictory as they appear, develop in parallel fashion. This is the problem we are raising. (1964:37)

A moment's reflection shows that Durkheim is on to something. A hunter and gatherer, living as an integral part of a band, can also survive on his own; his social identity is as a member of a group even though he has all the skills necessary for individual survival. We, members of industrialized societies, living independently and often in isolation, rely on others to raise our food, fix our cars, determine the value of our labors, and so on; we are socially independent, but we cannot survive without others. *The Division of Labor in Society* is not about the sexual division of labor, but rather about how society can be alternately segmented or unitary and characterized by homogeneity or heterogeneity and yet, somehow, stay together.

In Durkheim's era, the division of labor was not an esoteric subject; it characterized the transformation of European life during the Industrial Revolution. It was at the heart of Adam Smith's analysis of *The Wealth of Nations*; it was central to Marx's critique of capitalism; and it was relevant to issues that touched off massive social upheavals, such as the revolt of the Paris Commune in 1871, which was bloodily suppressed. The division of labor and the emergence of new social classes were themes for social analysis with real impacts, much like academic discussions of race and ethnic relations are immediately relevant to people in the United States today. And so Durkheim was attempting to understand, at least partially, how his own society had come into being.

To explore this question, Durkheim chose a comparative method, but it is a comparative method different in logic and intent than the comparative method employed by Tylor and Morgan (see pp. 11–14, 21–29), which involved identifying similarities in cultural traits to reconstruct historical connections. For Durkheim, the comparative method consisted of contrasting entire societies in order to identify dimensions of social integration.

Durkheim proposed that societies have different configurations of social integration or "solidarity." He argued that different societies could have distinct types of solidarity as the basis of social existence, and he called these "mechanical solidarity" and "organic solidarity." Mechanical solidarity "comes from a certain number of states of conscience which are common to all the members of the same society" (Durkheim 1964:109). Mechanical solidarity applies to societies in which all members have a common, shared social experience, but who do not necessarily depend on each other to survive. This form of solidarity is called mechanical, Durkheim wrote, not because "it is produced by mechanical or artificial means. We call it that only by analogy to the cohesion which unites the elements of an inanimate body, as opposed to that which makes a unity out of the elements of a living body" (1964:130). In mechanical solidarity societies, Durkheim believed, the individual was directly and equally attached to society, normative values were shared and more important than individual ones, and special subdivisions within a society were either absent or weak.

This contrasts with societies in which diverse, interdependent subdivisions are linked by formal institutions into a single society. This form of solidarity Durkheim called "organic," in the sense of a complex biological organism:

> This solidarity resembles that which we observe among the higher animals. Each organ, in effect, has its special physiognomy, its autonomy. And moreover, the unity of the organism is as great as the individuation of the parts is more marked. Because of this analogy we propose to call the solidarity which is due to the division of labor, *organic*. (1964:131; emphasis added)

Thus Durkheim outlined two models of social integration that characterized two contrasting societal structures. A mechanical solidarity society was "an absolutely homogeneous mass whose parts were not distinguished from one another, and which consequently had no structure" (Durkheim 1972:141). Organic solidarity societies, on the other hand,

> are formed not by the repetition of similar, homogeneous segments, but by a system of different organs each of which has a special role, and which are themselves formed of differentiated parts. Not only are social elements not of the same nature, but they are not distributed in the same way. They are . . . coordinated and subordinated one to another around the same central organ which exercises a moderating action over the rest of the organism. (Durkheim 1972:143)

For example, many institutions in American society are in some sense dependent on the legal system: corporations, marriages and families, nonprofit organizations, political offices, and so on. Each of these institutions is separate and different but subordinate to the rule of law, which thus exercises its "moderating influence" over the different organs of American society.

The differences between mechanical solidarity and organic solidarity were so marked that the development of one form could only be at the expense of the other, and historically that meant the evolution of organic solidarity as mechanical solidarity declined.

Durkheim culled his examples of traditional, non-Western societies from the Bible, classical texts, and primitive ethnographies to show that such different groups as the Australian aborigines, the unspecified tribes of native America and Africa, and the tribes of Israel all exhibit mechanical solidarity (Durkheim 1964:176–178). In contrast, such different societies as the Franks and the early Roman republic exhibit organic solidarity (Durkheim 1964:183–185). On such slender empirical grounds, Durkheim deduced a set of historical expectations, a set of developmental hypotheses.

First, Durkheim proposed that "whereas lower societies are spread over immense areas relative to the size of their populations, among more advanced peoples population tends to become more and more concentrated" (1972:152). This process begins with the development of agriculture, "since it necessitates a life in a fixed territory," and intensifies with industrialization. Second, the development of towns marks a threshold between mechanical and organic solidarity. Towns, Durkheim writes, "always result from the need of individuals to put themselves constantly in the closest possible contact with each other," presumably because their diverse tasks, parceled out by the division of labor, must be exchanged to be of value. In contrast, "As long as society is essentially segmental [and solidarity is mechanical], towns do not exist" (Durkheim 1972:152). Concurrently, the shift from mechanical to organic solidarity is marked by the "number and rapidity of the means of communication and transportation" (Durkheim 1972:153), the network that binds together the disparate organs of society.

Thus Durkheim outlined a model that not only categorized existing and historically known societies, but also provided a theory about the evolution of different social forms. The shift from mechanical to organic solidarity resulted from the greater division of labor; with greater numbers of separate tasks, the need for integrating structures increased. In turn, the division of labor became more marked as greater concentrations of people lived in one place; that is because, as Durkheim hypothesizes, "If work becomes progressively divided as societies become more voluminous and dense, it is not because external circumstances are more varied, but because struggle for existence is more acute" (1972:153). Borrowing directly from Darwin, Durkheim argued that as more people live together, competition over resources intensifies and, in response, people pursue different economic niches, evolving into different social groups. Once the trend to greater concentration of population begins, a series of social consequences follows expressed by differences in the fundamental organization of society.

But apart from the laws and contracts and markets that bind a society together, what is it that gives a society a distinctive, common identity? Durkheim analyzed that question with a concept that is one of the more misunderstood ideas in the social sciences, the conscience collective.

The Conscience Collective

As anthropologist Paul Bohannan noted, "Durkheim, like all original thinkers, had to stretch the language he used for the exposition of his ideas to the limits, and perhaps beyond" (1960:77–78). The difficulty in understanding the notion of the conscience collective stems from the inherent ambiguity of the term, compounded by the definitional nuances lost in the translation of the phrase from French to English. The French *conscience* combines both the sense of awareness associated in English with "consciousness" and the sense of a regulating function associated with "conscience." But in addition, "conscience" implies "that of which someone is (or many persons are) aware." Paul Bohannan wrote, "The only suitable English word for this notion is the anthropologist's term 'culture.' Thus the French term *conscience* means three things: internalized sanctions, awareness, and perceived culture" (1960:78–79).

This combination of two concepts—being aware of something and the object of awareness—makes the term "conscience" so slippery for English speakers, and yet so important to Durkheim's work. "This ambiguous assimilation of the knowing instrument and the known thing—of consciousness and culture—into a single concept was vital to Durkheim's thought," Bohannan observed (1960:79). "Encompassing what are for English-speaking thinkers, at least those in social science, two substantives, the knower and the known, Durkheim focused his attention on the verbal connection between them: the 'knowing,' or, as he called, it the process of representation" (Bohannan 1960:79).

The subtleties of conscience collective may have contributed to Durkheim's neglect in early American anthropology. For Boas (pp. 41–43) and Kroeber (pp. 69–70), culture consisted of learned and shared knowledge and behavior, expressed in such different ways as technology, social organization, or language. Further, cultural knowledge was both separate from the process by which it was obtained and distinct from the society that held that knowledge. Finally, few American anthropologists were interested in the process of cultural acquisition (enculturation) until the 1930s. And so not only did Durkheim's conscience collective combine two terms that English speakers would distinguish, but it also drew attention to the process of cultural knowing that early American anthropologists did not often consider. No wonder the idea seemed confusing or useless.

Yet conscience collective was pivotal in Durkheim's work because it connected the different patterns of social solidarity to the processes of enculturation within a particular society. Conscience collective has different properties in societies based on mechanical solidarity versus those based on organic solidarity. First, in mechanical solidarity the individual tends to have values or views that are shared with all other members of society; in that sense, as Giddens writes, "individual 'consciousness' is simply a microcosm of conscience collective" (1972:5), which is not the case under organic solidarity. Second, in societies characterized by mechanical solidarity, the conscience collective has a greater intellectual and emotional hold over the individual. Third, in societies characterized by mechanical solidarity, the conscience collective has greater rigidity; certain behaviors are required or prohibited and everyone knows what they are, whereas in organic societies—such as our own—there may be constant debates about acceptable behaviors or appropriate values. Finally, there is a difference in content. In societies associated with mechanical solidarity, the conscience collective is broadly associated with religion; the sanctions for social norms come from the supernatural. In societies characterized by organic solidarity, the role of religion is diminished. Durkheim writes,

> But, if there is one truth that history teaches us beyond doubt, it is that religion tends to embrace a smaller and smaller portion of social life. Originally, it pervades everything; everything social is religious; the two words are synonymous. Then, little by little, political, economic, scientific functions free themselves from the religious function, constitute themselves apart and take on a more and more acknowledged temporal character. God, who was at first present in all human relations, progressively withdraws from them; he abandons the world to men and their disputes. (1964:169)

In this dramatic manner, Durkheim highlights the pervasive importance of religion in society, something that had not been studied systematically by social scientists to that point. Durkheim bemoaned the lack of "any scientific notion of what religion is" (1964:168) and set out to change that situation in his classic, *The Elementary Forms of the Religious Life*.

The Elementary Forms of the Religious Life

In this work, Durkheim set out to describe the basic elements of religious life by studying the most primitive society he knew of: the native peoples of central Australia. He outlined his method in the opening paragraph of the book:

> [We] propose to study the most primitive and simple religion which is actually known, to make an analysis of it, and to attempt an explanation of it. A religious system may be said to be the most primitive which one can observe when it fulfills the two following conditions: in the first place, when it is found in a society whose organization is surpassed by no others in simplicity; and secondly, when it is possible to explain it without making use of any element borrowed from a previous religion. (1968:13)

Durkheim thus attempted to identify not only the elemental constituents of religion, but the origins of religion. Previously, two basic ideas had been advanced about the origins of religion. First was animism, an idea developed by Tylor, which characterized religion as originating with an individual's explanation of misunderstood phenomena. Animism is the idea that spirits occupy all sorts of objects. Just as humans have different states of being—asleep and awake, living and dead—that imply the existence of an animating force, objects also have anima, and primitive religious activities revolve around avoiding, propitiating, or placating those spirits. An alternative concept, naturism, saw religion as an expression of natural forces and objects—weather, fire, the sea, lightning, and so on. Durkheim quotes a major proponent of naturism, Max Müller, as writing, "At first sight, nothing seemed less natural than nature. Nature was the greatest surprise, a terror, a marvel, a standing miracle" (1968:92). Religion, Müller held, arose from attempts to understand these phenomena. Thus animism and naturism similarly view religion as originating with individuals' explanations of natural phenomena.

Durkheim's approach was fundamentally different:

> Religion is something eminently social. Religious representations are collective representations which express collective realities; the rites are a manner of acting which take rise in the midst of assembled groups and which are destined to excite, maintain or recreate certain mental states in these groups. So if the categories are of religious origins they ought to participate in this nature common to all religious facts; they too should be social affairs and the product of collective thought. (1968:22)

For that reason, Durkheim was interested in the totem as expressed by native peoples of central Australia. "Totem" refers to a category of things—animals, plants, celestial bodies, ancestral mythic beings—associated with a social group. The name of the totem, for example, "red kangaroo," refers to the clan associated with that totem. The totem is the name and emblem of the clan and is incorporated into the liturgy of religious practices. The totem is, Durkheim writes, "the very type of sacred thing" (1968:140). Its sacredness is imparted to those things associated with it, its loss is the greatest imaginable disaster, and specific taboos transform the animal or object into embodiments of sacredness. Yet, a specific totem is only sacred to a particular clan and not to any other. Such a brief synopsis hardly does justice to Durkheim's analysis of totemism or the vast literature subsequent to his work, but it illustrates how Durkheim perceived the social nature of religion.

Durkheim emphasized the elemental properties of religion: "A religion is a unified system of beliefs and practices relative to sacred things, that is to say, things set apart and forbidden—beliefs and practices which unite into one single moral community, called a Church, all those who adhere to them" (1968:62).

What makes religion distinctive is its focus on the sacred, which is itself a social construction. There is nothing inherently sacred or profane in the world. A place, a symbol, or a personality becomes sacred because it is socially classified as sacred. It is impossible to separate the object of worship from the process of socially defining the sacred; in other words, the knower and the known (to use Bohannan's phrase) are indivisible, mutually created by the process of knowing.

What was true of sacredness was equally true of other shared cognitive categories, what Durkheim called "collective representations." Collective representations include such systems of knowledge as cardinal directions, temporal divisions, color categories, and social distinctions—classifications unique to different societies. The arbitrary yet very systematic nature of collective representations (e.g., all Americans agree that south is opposite of north and that there are sixty minutes in an hour) indicate they are not simply products of individual musings about the nature of existence. The collective representations of religion are not derived from individual psychology because, Durkheim writes,

> between these two sorts of representations there is all the difference which exists between the individual and the social, and one can no more derive the second from the first than he can deduce society from the individual, the whole from the part, the complex from the simple. Society is a reality *sui generis*; it has its own peculiar characteristics, which are not found elsewhere and which are not met with again in the same form in all the rest of the universe. (1968:29)

Collective representations exist because there are two different spheres of human knowledge, the individual and the social, and Émile Durkheim developed a theory of the social basis of cultural knowledge.

Conclusion

The early American anthropologists criticized Durkheim's lack of fieldwork experience, his overreliance on a few ethnographies, and his simplistic classification of very different societies into the category "primitive." But many American anthropologists also seem to have misunderstood what Durkheim was trying to do—attempting to build a theory of society.

Among Durkheim's many contributions to social science, this may be his most profound: the idea that there is a distinct realm of human existence, society, that is not derived from any other source. Society has characteristic structures that allow us to distinguish social forms, those based on mechanical solidarity versus those based on organic solidarity. We can perceive the origins of organic solidarity in those pure examples of mechanical solidarity that Durkheim called "the veritable social protoplasm, the germ out of which all social types would develop" (1964:174). Change occurred systematically, caused by innovations in the economy that affected human population densities, which then led to the increasing division of labor. Such developments are paralleled by changes in the conscience collective: in the degree to which an individual's belief represents everybody's belief, in the controlling power of belief, in the diminishing importance of religious institutions and the domination of secular ones. That issue Durkheim explores by showing that religion is eminently social and not the extrapolation of individual musings to a larger audience. Along with other categories, the boundaries between sacred and profane are collective social representations.

Therefore, understanding the different currents of human existence requires focusing on the social dimensions because it is there that the differences are created, defined, expressed, and transmitted. These are some of the key notions in the science of society created by Émile Durkheim.

References

Bohannan, Paul
1960 Conscience Collective and Culture. In *Emile Durkheim, 1858–1917.* K. Wolff, ed. Pp. 77–96. Columbus: Ohio State University Press.

Bohannan, Paul, and Mark Glazer

1988 *High Points in Anthropology*. New York: McGraw-Hill.

Durkheim, Émile

1960 The Dualism of Human Nature and Its Social Conditions. In *Emile Durkheim, 1858–1917*. K. Wolff, ed. Pp. 325–40. Columbus: Ohio State University Press.

1964 *The Division of Labor in Society*. G. Simpson, trans. New York: Free Press of Glencoe.

1968 *The Elementary Forms of the Religious Life*. J. Swain, trans. New York: Free Press.

1972 *Selected Writings*. Edited, translated, and introduced by A. Giddens. Cambridge: Cambridge University Press.

Giddens, Anthony

1972 Introduction: Durkheim's Writings on Sociology and Social Philosophy. In *Emile Durkheim: Selected Writings*. A. Giddens, ed., trans., and intro. Pp. 1–50. Cambridge: Cambridge University Press.

Kroeber, Alfred

1952a The Concept of Culture in Science. In *The Nature of Culture*. Pp. 118–135. Chicago: University of Chicago Press.

1952b Introduction. In *The Nature of Culture*. Pp. 3–11. Chicago: University of Chicago Press.

Peyre, Henri

1960 Durkheim: The Man, His Time, and His Intellectual Background. In *Emile Durkheim, 1858–1917*. K. Wolff, ed. Pp. 3–31. Columbus: Ohio State University Press.

Wolff, Kurt

1960 An Introductory Durkheim Bibliography. In *Emile Durkheim, 1858–1917*. K. Wolff, ed. Pp. 437–445. Columbus: Ohio State University Press.

II

THE NATURE OF CULTURE

The Boasian critique of the comparative method and evolutionary schemes created an analytical vacuum. If cultural patterns are not the reflections of earlier stages of human development that has run "in nearly uniform channels" in Tylor's phrase, then what do cultural patterns reflect? If cultures are essentially the accidental accumulations of diverse traits and values brought together by specific historical circumstances of innovation, diffusion, and migration, how is it that cultures are integrated wholes? If, as Boas had written, "the causal conditions of cultural happenings lie always in the interaction between individual and society" (1932:612), what is the nature of that interaction? What holds cultures together? What gives cultures their distinctive essences?

These questions plagued Boas's students like Alfred Kroeber, Ruth Benedict, Edward Sapir, and Margaret Mead. And although the answers they arrived at were different, their respective explorations were framed by three concepts: the causal priority of culture, the concept of the microcosm, and the recognition that cultural knowledge was rapidly vanishing.

Boas's specific critiques of unilineal evolution and racial explanations of behavior led to the general conclusion that culture could only be explained in reference to specific cultural patterns, that culture explains culture, a position known as cultural determinism (Hatch 1973:49). Thus, the idea of cultural relativism holds that one can only understand a specific society's practices within its specific cultural context (Hatch 1983).

Similarly, explanation requires understanding how historical processes of diffusion, migration, and invention produced a particular cultural pattern, the idea of historical particularism (Harris 1968:250–289). More broadly, the above implies that culture cannot be explained by reference to human biology, individual psychology, or any factors other than cultural ones.

But how can such factors be identified? Boas and his students believed that the laws governing culture, if they existed, could be discovered only through the study of small-scale societies in which culture could be examined in microcosm. During the early twentieth century, there was a general assumption that small-scale societies—the isolated camp, the primitive village—provided a discrete analytical unit where the patterns of culture could be observed in microcosm. In such "simple societies" it would be possible for the anthropologist to observe clearly dimensions of culture obscured in larger, more complex societies.

But those small, traditional cultures were disappearing rapidly. In American and British anthropology there was a broad recognition that traditional cultural knowledge was being lost in the face of Western colonization and globalization. Anthropologists responded by going into the field to "salvage" the last vestiges of traditional culture. Anthropologists George Marcus and Michael Fischer observe that "the main motif that ethnography as a science developed was that of salvaging cultural diversity. The ethnographer would capture in writing the authenticity of changing cultures, so they could be entered into the record for the great comparative project of anthropology" (1986:24).

From that comparative project would emerge the general laws of culture, laws inferred from specific studies of small-scale traditional societies. Working from this common set of assumptions, Kroeber, Benedict, Sapir, and Mead each attempted to understand the patterning of culture from different analytical angles.

For Kroeber, culture is a phenomenon distinct from that of society, the individual, or the organism. Culture exists on its own analytical level, irreducible to other levels of phenomena and explicable in terms of its own particular characteristics. Culture is learned and shared as Tylor had said, but it is also variable, plastic, value laden, superpersonal, and anonymous. Cultural innovations are not the products of lone genius, but expressions of "regularities of form and style and significance" (Kroeber 1952:104). Changes in some dimensions of culture, most notably in matters of style, may actually be governed by a superorganic oscillation that occurs unbeknownst to the individual members of a culture. And thus culture is distinct from and dominant over the individual.

For Benedict, cultures are more than the sum of their parts; they are configurations based on fundamental values of existence that differ between cultures. Cultures have a distinctive essence because key values are learned by individuals as members of particular cultures. American society has its outline—dynamic, constantly changing, fragmentary—because we value individualism, innovation, and success. The connection between the individual and society is based on values; individuals who through temperament and training share the values of their society are successful, those who don't are deviants. And yet those core values are not the same for all societies, and thus the successful person in one culture is the deviant in another.

Mead took a very similar approach. Like Benedict, Mead saw the relation between individual and society as based on values, but they are very specific values transmitted during child rearing. Rather than concerning herself with overall configurations, Mead was much concerned with rather specific sets of cultural values: is adolescent sex traumatic or easy; is a baby breast-fed on demand or rudely weaned; is food shared or hoarded? In these and other cases, the way children are raised determines the adults they become and that process gives societies their distinctiveness and shape.

Sapir's explanation was very different. Sapir contended that culture is a constantly edited document created by individuals engaged in public discourse. Far from being the passive creations of culture, individuals build cultures in their actions and words. Rather than collective expressions of fundamental, timeless values, Sapir argued that even the most basic contentions of culture are fodder for debate and disagreement. There are limits to points of disagreement, however, and the boundaries are set by language. The categories of different languages express basic ideas about how the universe is perceived, how causality is explained, how time, mass, space, number, and so on are conceptualized. Speakers of the same language will tend to use similar linguistic categories. For example, if we set a time for a meeting, we may argue about whether I am late, but not about the number of minutes in an hour. Such linguistic categories are instilled unthinkingly as a child learns a language, becoming so ingrained that we don't argue about them. And thus the use of language and symbols allows humans to actively create new cultural forms, but the linguistic categories inherent in language give an overall shape to cultural experience.

It is often said that Boas cast an enormous influence over American anthropology, but perhaps nowhere is that more evident than in his students' efforts to understand the nature of culture.

References

Boas, Franz
1932 The Aims of Anthropological Research. *Science* 76:605–613.

Harris, Marvin
1968 *The Rise of Anthropological Theory: A History of Theories of Culture.* New York: Thomas Y. Crowell.

Hatch, Elvin
1973 *Theories of Man and Culture.* New York: Columbia University Press.
1983 *Culture and Morality.* New York: Columbia University Press.

Kroeber, A. L.
1952 *The Nature of Culture.* Chicago: University of Chicago Press.

Marcus, George E., and Michael M. J. Fischer
1986 *Anthropology as Cultural Critique: An Experimental Moment in the Human Sciences.* Chicago: University of Chicago Press.

5

Alfred Kroeber

Configurations of Culture

It is tempting to call Alfred Kroeber (1876–1960) the last Renaissance man of anthropology. During his eighty-five-year lifetime, Kroeber lived through and shaped major changes in anthropology, which changed from merely documenting the exotic to concerning itself with the different arenas of human life and developed a holistic view of humans within our cultural and biological contexts. Alfred Kroeber ranged across all those fields; he was the last anthropological generalist.

Since Kroeber's time, the number of anthropologists and the quantity of anthropological research has grown so enormously that it is difficult to keep up with the literature in one field, let alone another. Between 1892 and 1901, a total of eight Ph.D.'s in anthropology were granted by American universities, Kroeber's among them (Bernstein 2002); in 1995, 484 Ph.D.'s in anthropology were awarded (Givens and Jablonski 1996). Although anthropology as a field retains the ideology of being a holistic and multidimensional endeavor (Borofsky 2002), few anthropologists pursue more than a single field; we are sociocultural anthropologists or archaeologists or physical anthropologists or linguists. Within such fields we are even further specialized as California archaeologists or Andean archaeologists or linguists specializing in Mayan, Romance, or Austronesian languages.

The lack of generalists since Kroeber's time both mirrors an information explosion and the growing emphasis on specialization of all academic disciplines. But Kroeber's breadth was exceptional even for his time and reflects a deeply original, creative mind at work at a time when almost everything in American anthropology was new.

Background

Alfred Kroeber was born in New Jersey in 1876, the year of Custer's defeat at Little Big Horn; much of his research on Native American life and language occurred during the twilight of American Indian independence. Kroeber's family were upper-middle-class German Americans who insisted on a challenging educational regime of tutors, private schools, and hard work. He entered Columbia College at the age of sixteen and majored in English, later receiving an M.A. with a thesis on British plays. Kroeber's early education directly led to his more "humanistic" approach to anthropology. Kroeber drifted into anthropology when he took a seminar in American Indian languages from Franz Boas, a seminar that met around Boas's dining room table (Steward 1973:6). Kroeber received the first Ph.D. in anthropology at Columbia University (Jackins 2002). Boas supervised Kroeber's doctoral dissertation on the art of the Arapaho; it was only twenty-eight pages long (Kroeber 1901).

Kroeber's dissertation may have been brief, but he was an extremely prolific writer. In 1936 when he was honored on his sixtieth birthday, a bibliography of his writings included 175 entries (this seems to have been an underestimate; a subsequent list shows 306 works). In the following twenty-five years of his life—at a time when most people slow down—Kroeber's writings grew to 532 publications: articles, monographs, reviews, book introductions, essays, and so on (Gibson and Rowe 1961).

A review of these titles indicates Alfred Kroeber's major research interests. First is his work on the native peoples of California (e.g., Kroeber 1904, 1906, 1907a, 1907b, 1909, 1910, 1911, 1925, 1929, 1932). Kroeber was one of the first members of the anthropology department at the University of California, Berkeley. He was hired to study the Indians of California, essentially doing "salvage ethnography" to recover the vestiges of precontact language and society before they were completely wiped out by

Euro-American society. Kroeber published some seventy writings on the ethnology of native California, but his magnum opus was the *Handbook of the Indians of California* (1925). This one-thousand-page tome summarized Kroeber's investigations of every native group in California. It is a remarkable compendium, including aboriginal population estimates, lists of native toponyms, and details of subsistence, cosmology, kinship, and social organization. Kroeber made numerous field trips, interviewed dozens of informants, summarized published sources, and scoured mission registers. It remains an important source of information, in many cases the only source.

Kroeber shared this desire to preserve rapidly disappearing cultural knowledge with other American anthropologists like Boas and Mead and also with British anthropologists (Kuper 1983:5–6). As anthropologists began to conduct fieldwork it quickly became apparent that traditional societies were being destroyed. The Cambridge anthropologist and psychologist W. H. R. Rivers wrote in 1913, "In many parts of the world the death of an old man brings with it the loss of knowledge never to be replaced" (quoted in Kuper 1983:5). In the United States and Great Britain there was a shared sense that major theoretical issues could be addressed only with information that was disappearing daily, and this sparked a concerted effort to gather the available empirical data.

Kroeber's salvage ethnography led to a basic approach of ethnographic analysis: the culture element distribution list (Aginsky 1943; Driver 1937, 1939; Drucker 1950; Stewart 1941; Klimek 1935; Kroeber 1935, 1939; Wheeler-Voeglin 1941; for discussion, see Heizer 1963). He faced a basic set of problems (Kroeber 1939:4–6): (1) How are cultures to be defined? (2) How are their precontact practices to be reconstructed from current knowledge? and (3) How are the interactions between cultures to be measured? In native North America there were some obvious differences in the geographical distribution of cultural practices: Indians in the American Southwest and east of the Mississippi grew maize; Indians of the Northwest Coast and Great Basin did not. But such rough classifications failed to capture more subtle variations within particular cultural areas, nor did they account for the blurred edges of all such areas, and they assumed that certain aspects of culture—for example, agriculture—were more important than others. As Kroeber worked within California, it became obvious that there were significant differences among California Indians; for example, native Californians had the highest linguistic diversity of any region in North America, leading one scholar to call it "the Babel of ancient America" (Moratto 1984:530). Such cultural diversity had to be measured and explained, and Kroeber designed the cultural element lists to deal with this problem. Kroeber often approached the analysis of cultures as a natural historian, specifically like a Linnaean taxonomist interested in classifying species rather than a modern evolutionary taxonomist concerned with variations in a population. The cultural element survey reflects this approach.

Kroeber divided culture into minimal units that could be characterized qualitatively. For example, did a specific group practice "polyandry" or "cremation," did they use a "sinew-backed bow" or "beaver-teeth dice," "eat acorn mush" or did their young men drink a dangerous hallucinogenic made from jimsonweed? These lists were prepared, and graduate students were sent out to interview native informants and check off the elements; the results were tabulated and published. Julian Steward, one of Kroeber's graduate students, wrote,

> Kroeber obtained funds for an ambitious four-year field project of element list surveys which was carried out by 13 field workers and included 254 tribes and tribal subdivisions west of the Rocky Mountains. The lists ranged from 3,000 to more than 6,000 elements, the presence and absence of which were recorded for each local group. (1961:1057)

The element surveys were plotted in space in an attempt to understand the boundaries of particular cultures, and that led to the issue of interaction between cultures. Steward continues,

> The territorial plotting of element distributions raised questions about the mechanism of diffusion of each element, which had usually been conceived of as a fairly simple process through which one society transmitted cultural features to another merely because of contiguity. Kroeber modified this concept . . . by showing that cultural products may be imitated by

> peoples who had no direct contact with their originators. (1961:1057)

In hindsight, the element survey approach has a number of flaws. First, it atomizes culture into bits and pieces and considers each element to be of equal significance (certainly the use of beaver teeth dice and the practice of polyandry have different levels of importance). Second, the approach assumes that the presence of that cultural element in one society is equivalent to the presence of that cultural element in another. For example, the swastika was used in native North America, India, Nazi Germany, and is used in the United States today. Even though the swastika is found in all these places, it clearly has several different meanings. Third, the cultural element survey created a static, synchronic view of a society, implying that the only mechanisms of cultural change were invention (an individual's creation of a new cultural trait), migration (the movement of a society with new cultural traits into a new area), and diffusion (the spread of cultural traits without migration). But for all its flaws, the cultural elements survey met one important goal: it produced systematic information on societies that were being destroyed.

Culture and Configurations

Kroeber was not interested in mere minutiae; he was also concerned with the broad patterns of culture that characterized entire societies, or what he referred to as major styles that marked particular cultural configurations. Analogous to Benedict's concept discussed in chapter 6, Kroeber states that "patterns are those arrangements or systems of internal relationship which give to any culture its coherence or plan, and keep it from being a mere accumulation of random bits" (1948:131). Such patterns "or configurations or Gestalts," Kroeber wrote, "are what seem to me to be most productive to distinguish or formulate in culture" (1952c:5).

Kroeber drew a sharp definitional boundary between culture and society. Society occurs whenever there is group life—including among social insects like bees and ants—but culture consists of learned and shared elements of custom and belief (Kroeber 1952a:118–119). Further, Kroeber believed that such customs and beliefs existed independently of the individuals who held such beliefs. In a brief after-dinner talk in 1946 to a group of anthropologists, Kroeber outlined his position. Culture is transmitted by human interactions, "not by the genetic mechanism of heredity but by the interconditioning of zygotes." Regardless of its origins, "culture quickly tends to become supra-personal and anonymous," falling "into patterns, or regularities of form and style and significance." And finally, Kroeber argued that culture "embodies values, which may be formulated (overtly as mores) or felt (implicitly, as in folkways) by the society carrying the culture, and which it is part of the business of the anthropologist to characterize and define" (1952b:104). Thus Kroeber's basic definition of culture is that it is learned, shared, patterned, and meaningful.

Kroeber tried to steer his analysis between two extremes that dominated early twentieth-century ways of thinking about humans: racial determinism and the Great Man theory. Very early in his career (1917)—and clearly showing Boas's influence (see pp. 38–40)—Kroeber attacked the notion that different races have different innate properties. He questioned a number of assumptions linking genetic background to behavior, such as that the Eskimo innately desires blubber or the French are inherently facile with language, and also the tendency to equate "race" and "civilization."

At the same time, Kroeber argued against the Great Man theory, contending that even geniuses did not so much shape their cultures as represent them. Kroeber found repeated examples of multiple geniuses—like the independent invention of calculus by Leibnitz in 1684 and Newton in 1687, the development of the theory of natural selection by Charles Darwin and Alfred Russel Wallace, and the invention of the steamboat by Robert Fulton and at least four other contemporary inventors. "The history of inventions," Kroeber wrote, "is a chain of parallel instances" (1952d:45). The co-occurrence of such inventions, he concluded, was evidence that something larger was at work, some force greater than either genetic inheritance or genius. That force was greater than the organism—it was superorganic:

> The reason why mental heredity has so little if anything to do with civilization, is that civilization is not mental action but a body or stream of products of mental exercise. The social or cultural . . . is in its essence non-individual. Civilization as such begins only where the individual ends; and whoever does not in some measure perceive this fact . . . can find no meaning in civilization, and history for him must be only a wearying jumble, or an opportunity for the exercise of art [that is, by making things up]. (Kroeber 1952d:40)

For Kroeber, that organizing force was culture—nongenetic, shared, anonymous, and patterned knowledge. The configurations of culture are produced by the history of a particular set of cultural values. Kroeber noted "that it is of the nature of culture to be heavily conditioned by its own cumulative past, so that the most fruitful approach to its understanding is a historical one" (1952c:4). The historical approach showed broader and broader connections between cultural elements as they were expressed in space and time (Kroeber 1952c:5). Placing these elements in this manner, one could identify configurations and their development, prominence, decline, and replacement. That, Kroeber felt, was the nature of explanation.

Kroeber turned his attention to scores of topics—Peruvian archaeology, American Indian linguistics, and so on—but arguably his most intriguing analysis was of a subject that might seem strange: changes in women's dress. It was a topic that Kroeber wrote about at least twice, first in 1919 and then again in 1940. Kroeber was drawn to study women's fashion because it reflected "pure" style and because changes in fashion could be dated by studying historic Parisian fashion magazines. By the time of the second study, Kroeber had data ranging from 1787 to 1936. Kroeber measured a range of variables, such as dress length and dress width, and then conducted a statistical and time series analysis. What he found was that certain major fluctuations had different periodicities; for example, dress length was greatest in the eighteenth century and the mid- and late nineteenth century, with shorter dresses most common at about 1815 and 1931. Further, Kroeber found some interesting patterns in the variation of style. Most years, variation from the central trend was minor, whether the tendency was for long dresses or short dresses, but in some periods there was a great degree of variation before the central tendency was reasserted. Kroeber considered a variety of historical causes—such as, did periods of political instability cause greater variation in hem length?—and failed to find any causes for such patterns other than the simple, superorganic fluctuation of style.

> The primary factor [for such fashion changes] would seem to be adherence to or departure from an ideal though unconscious pattern for formal clothing in women. The consistent conformity of variability to certain magnitudes of proportion—mostly a conformity of low variabilities to high magnitudes [that is, when skirts are shortest, everyone's skirts are short]—leaves little room for any other conclusion. (Richardson and Kroeber 1952:368)

In sum, Kroeber studied women's fashion because it exemplified his conception of what culture was. Clearly nongenetic, fashion was obviously free of the influences of heredity. Obviously shared, fashion was more than the idiosyncratic exercise of genius. Reducible to elements, fashion traits could be plotted in time; in this case space was held constant by considering only Parisian fashion. Clearly patterned, fashion underwent long-term systematic fluctuations. And finally, his explanation was historical because changes in fashion could not be understood by appeal to outside factors but only explained within their specific cultural configuration. And thus Kroeber's analysis of this unlikely topic captured the basic characteristics of his approach to culture.

Kroeber attempted to repeat his microcosmic analysis in the narrow field of Parisian fashion in a parallel, enormous study of world civilization, *Configurations of Culture Growth* (1944). During his earlier cultural element distribution studies, Kroeber had developed the notion of culture climax. A culture climax is when "historically known cultural growths . . . show a virtual coincidence of florescence in the several faces of culture" (Kroeber 1939:5). Since Kroeber had long argued that cultural innovations were not the products of "Great Men" but rather of "parallel instances," a study of superior inventions demonstrates "the frequent habit of societies to develop their cultures to their highest levels spasmodically: especially in their intellectual and aesthetic aspects, but also in more material and practical aspects" (1944:5). If genius were simply the result of genetics, then superior innovations should occur randomly; that they do not indicates "the causal participation of a cultural factor, the intervention of a superpersonal element in the personal activity of genius" (Kroeber 1944:13). Yet, Kroeber found "no evidence of any true law in the phenomena dealt with; nothing cyclical, regularly repetitive, or necessary" (1944:761). If anything, this simply strengthened Kroeber's idea of the irreducibility of culture.

For Kroeber, culture was a mental construct completely distinct from other phenomena. Culture, he wrote, "is superorganic and superindividual in that, although carried, participated in and produced by organic individuals, it is acquired; and it is acquired by learning" (1948:254). Culture cannot be explained by organic individual needs as Malinowski claimed (Kroeber 1948:309–310; on Malinowski, see pp. 139–43), and it cannot be treated as equivalent to "society" (Kroeber 1948:847–849). Cultural patterns can be understood only within a historical approach that emphasizes change through time, the cultural antecedents of new cultural patterns, and the importance of understanding cultural phenomena within particular configurations (Kroeber 1957, 1963a, 1963b; see Hatch 1973:94–95 for discussion).

Conclusion

Kroeber's broad contributions to anthropology make any brief summary of his career nearly impossible, but Steward's (1961) obituary captures many of Kroeber's basic ideas. Kroeber believed "that culture derived from culture" and that psychological, adaptational, or organic explanations were indefensible. His historical approach was "superorganic and supra-individual" and twofold, first characterizing cultures "by the minutiae of their content" while also seeking "major styles, philosophies, and values" (Steward 1961:1050).

Kroeber's contribution to American anthropology has a mixed legacy. There is little question of his substantive contributions to ethnology, ethnography, linguistics, and archaeology, but in contrast there is little current enthusiasm for Kroeber's concerns with the superorganic, the style and patterns of civilization, or the anonymity of culture. As a theoretician, Kroeber's position is more frequently argued against than embraced (Benedict 1959:231; Harris 1968:320–337). And yet, Kroeber's attempt to find the unifying basis of culture was a central problem faced by many of his contemporaries, including Benedict, Sapir, and Mead.

References

Aginsky, Bernard

1943 *Central Sierra*. Culture Element Distributions XXIV. Anthropological Records, vol. 8, no. 4. Berkeley: University of California Press.

Benedict, Ruth

1959 *Patterns of Culture*. 1934. Reprint, New York: Houghton Mifflin.

Bernstein, Jay

2002 First Recipients of Anthropological Doctorates in the United States, 1891–1930. *American Anthropologist* 104(2):551–564.

Borofsky, Robert

2002 The Four Subfields: Anthropologists as Mythmakers. *American Anthropologist* 104(2):463–480.

Driver, Harold

1937 *Southern Sierra Nevada*. Culture Element Distributions VI. Anthropological Records, vol. 1, no. 2. Pp. 53–154. Berkeley: University of California Press.

1939 *Northwest California*. Culture Element Distributions X. Anthropological Records, vol. 1, no. 6. Pp. 297–433. Berkeley: University of California Press.

Drucker, Philip

1950 *Northwest Coast*. Culture Element Distributions XXVI. Anthropological Records, vol. 9, no. 3. Berkeley: University of California Press.

Gibson, Anne, and John Rowe

1961 A Bibliography of the Publications of Alfred Louis Kroeber. *American Anthropologist* 63:1060–1087.

Givens, Douglas, and Timothy Jablonski

1996 Degrees, FYI. *Anthropology Newsletter* 37(5):7.

Hatch, Elvin
1973 *Theories of Man and Culture*. New York: Columbia University Press.

Heizer, Robert
1963 Foreword. In *Cultural and Natural Areas of Native North America*. 4th ed. By A. L. Kroeber. Berkeley: University of California Press. [Originally published 1939.]

Jackins, Ira
2002 The First Boasian: Alfred Kroeber and Franz Boas, 1896–1905. *American Anthropologist* 104(2):520–532.

Klimek, Stanislaw
1935 *The Structure of California Indian Culture*. Culture Element Distributions I. University of California Publications in American Archaeology and Ethnology, vol. 37, no. 1. Pp. 12–70. Berkeley: University of California Press.

Kroeber, Alfred
1901 Decorative Symbolism of the Arapaho. *American Anthropologist* 3:308–336.
1904 *The Languages of the Coast of California South of San Francisco*. University of California Publications in American Archaeology and Ethnology, vol. 2, no. 2. Pp. 29–80. Berkeley: University of California Press.
1906 The Dialect Divisions of the Moquelumnan Family in Relation to the Internal Differentiation of Other Linguistic Families of California. *American Anthropologist* 8:652–663.
1907a *The Washo Language of East Central California and Nevada*. University of California Publications in American Archaeology and Ethnology, vol. 4, no. 5. Pp. 251–317. Berkeley: University of California Press.
1907b *The Yokuts Language of South Central California*. University of California Publications in American Archaeology and Ethnology, vol. 2, no. 5. Pp. 163–377. Berkeley: University of California Press.
1909 *Some Notes on the Shoshonean Dialects of Southern California*. University of California Publications in American Archaeology and Ethnology, vol. 8, no. 5. Pp. 235–269. Berkeley: University of California Press.
1910 *The Chumash and Costanoan Languages*. University of California Publications in American Archaeology and Ethnology, vol. 9, no. 2. Pp. 237–271. Berkeley: University of California Press.
1911 *The Languages of the Coast of California North of San Francisco*. University of California Publications in American Archaeology and

Ethnology, vol. 9, no. 3. Pp. 37–271. Berkeley: University of California Press.

1920 *California Culture Provinces*. University of California Publications in American Archaeology and Ethnology, vol. 17, no. 2. Pp. 151–170. Berkeley: University of California Press.

1925 *Handbook of the Indians of California*. Bureau of American Ethnology, Bulletin 78. Washington, D.C.: Smithsonian Institution.

1929 *The Valley Nisenan*. University of California Publications in American Archaeology and Ethnology, vol. 24, no. 4. Pp. 253–290. Berkeley: University of California Press.

1932 *The Patwin and Their Neighbors*. University of California Publications in American Archaeology and Ethnology, vol. 29, no. 4. Pp. 253–423. Berkeley: University of California Press.

1935 Preface. In *The Structure of California Indian Culture*. Culture Element Distributions I. By S. Klimek. University of California Publications in American Archaeology and Ethnology, vol. 37, no. 1. Pp. 1–11. Berkeley: University of California Press.

1939 *Cultural and Natural Areas of Native North America*. University of California Publications in American Archaeology and Ethnology, vol. 38. Pp. 1–240. Berkeley: University of California Press.

1944 *Configurations of Culture Growth*. Berkeley: University of California Press.

1948 *Anthropology: Race, Language, Culture, Psychology, Pre-History*. New York: Harcourt, Brace.

1952a The Concept of Culture in Science. In *The Nature of Culture*. Pp. 118–135. Chicago: University of Chicago Press.

1952b Culture, Events, and Individuals. In *The Nature of Culture*. Pp. 104–106. Chicago: University of Chicago Press.

1952c Introduction. In *The Nature of Culture*. Pp. 3–11. Chicago: University of Chicago Press.

1952d The Superorganic. In *The Nature of Culture*. Pp. 22–51. Chicago: University of Chicago Press. [Originally published 1917.]

1957 *Style and Civilizations*. Ithaca: Cornell University.

1963a An Anthropologist Looks at History. In *An Anthropologist Looks at History*. Theodora Kroeber, ed. Pp. 152–159. Berkeley: University of California Press.

1963b History and Anthropology in the Study of Civilizations. In *An Anthropologist Looks at History*. Theodora Kroeber, ed. Pp. 160–171. Berkeley: University of California Press.

Kuper, Adam

1983 *Anthropology and Anthropologists: The Modern British School*. London: Routledge & Kegan Paul.

Moratto, Michael
1984 *California Archaeology*. New York: Academic Press.

Richardson, Jane, and Alfred Kroeber
1952 Three Centuries of Women's Dress Fashions: A Quantitative Analysis. In *The Nature of Culture*. Pp. 358–72. 1940 Reprint. Chicago: University of Chicago Press.

Steward, Julian
1961 Alfred Louis Kroeber, 1876–1960. *American Anthropologist* 63:1038–1087.
1973 *Alfred Kroeber*. New York: Columbia University Press.

Stewart, Omer
1941 Culture Element Distributions XIV: Northern Paiute. *Anthropological Records* 4 (3):361–446. Berkeley: University of California Press.

Wheeler-Voeglin, Erminie
1942 Culture Element Distributions XX: Northeast California. *Anthropological Records* 7(2): 47–251.

6

Ruth Benedict
Patterns of Culture

Ironically, interest in Ruth Benedict's life story overshadows her ideas as an anthropologist, which focused on the relationship between the individual and society. Benedict is the subject of three biographies (Caffrey 1989; Mead 1974; Modell 1983) and another study examining her relationship with Margaret Mead (Lapsley 1999). Benedict is a captivating subject for biographers because she was not only a brilliant anthropologist, but also a brilliant woman who was an anthropologist. Benedict was one of the first women to attain prominence as a social scientist, and her life exemplifies the difficult, often conflicting choices that women face in American society. The trajectories of her life and career in anthropology were shaped by that fact.

Background

Ruth Benedict (née Fulton) was educated at Vassar College, which was established in the 1860s with the goal of educating women on an equal plane with men. Although women's university education had existed for twenty years when Ruth Benedict enrolled in 1905, it was still sufficiently new that *Ladies' Home Journal* in October 1905 published an article titled "Madcap Frolics of College Girls," followed in the November issue by the riveting article "What College Girls Eat" (Caffrey 1989:43). Ruth Benedict studied literature and poetry, and later in her life she published poems in poetry magazines and journals. But her exposure to critical analysis, even more than to poetry, was to impact on her anthropology. At Vassar she was exposed to a wide range of progressive political issues and modernist artistic trends and to a challenging body of English and German literature, particularly the works of Friedrich Nietzsche.

Nietzsche's works are not read by most Americans today, but many of us know the opening notes of *2001: A Space Odyssey*, actually a tone poem composed by Richard Strauss based on Nietzsche's *Thus Spake Zarathustra*. Nietzsche chose to write a collection of philosophical statements as if they were spoken by the Persian philosopher Zarathustra (Zoroaster); in fact, they were Nietzsche's own recipes calling for creativity, revolt against conformity, and vigorous engagement with life. Caffrey writes,

> Nietzsche advocated creative iconoclasm. The Self desires to create beyond itself, he wrote: "Creating—that is the great salvation from suffering, and life's alleviation." The creativity he advocated was the creativity of new values. . . . [Nietzsche] advocated the destruction of conventional morality and conformity because they suffocated creativity. He affirmed physical joy. He called for a renunciation of materialism and for his readers to develop God within themselves. All of these were qualities Ruth believed most important. . . . *Thus Spake Zarathustra* gave her a sense of freedom from that restrictive past and a purpose for living out her future. (1989:54–55)

In 1914 Ruth Fulton married Stanley Benedict, but over the years their marriage unraveled. After stints of unsatisfying participation in social work and repressing her own interests for the sake of her marriage, she went back to school at the age of thirty-one at the New School for Social Research. After a year she was encouraged to take graduate courses at Columbia University where she began an association with Franz Boas that lasted from 1921 until Boas's death in 1942.

Boas supervised Benedict's dissertation—"The Concept of the Guardian Spirit in North America"—which was later published by the American Anthropological Association (Benedict 1923). The dissertation was based on library research rather than fieldwork, but the fact that she obtained her Ph.D. in three semesters is still remarkable. Except for a brief 1922 study of the

Serrano in Southern California (Benedict 1924), all of Benedict's early writings were based on library research (for example, Benedict 1922). Beginning in the mid-1920s, however, Benedict went to the American Southwest for summer field research projects among the Zuni (1924), Zuni and Cochiti (1925), O'otam (1927), and Mescalero Apache (1931). Benedict's Zuni research would become central to her 1934 book *Patterns of Culture.*

During this period Benedict was developing her interests in personality and culture, editing the *Journal of American Folklore,* and teaching at Columbia, where the relationship between Boas and Benedict continued to evolve. After serving as her mentor, Boas became her professional colleague when he got her a position in the Department of Anthropology, which he chaired. Gradually, Benedict was made a full-fledged faculty member, and at her death in 1948, she was one of Columbia University's most eminent professors.

Patterns of Culture

Patterns of Culture was an extremely popular book from the time it was published in 1934. Translated into a dozen languages, issued in 1946 as a paperback that sold for twenty-five cents, as of 1974 *Patterns of Culture* had sold 1.6 million copies (Mead 1974:1). It is still in print. The ideas of the book spread outside of academia into the American society in general. Because the ideas have permeated modern American culture, we now take them as commonplace. *Patterns of Culture* was written for the nonanthropologist, and as Caffrey observes, "it acted as a signal of and a catalyst for the final acceptance of a profound paradigm change in the social sciences and in American society" (1989:209). Benedict found alleviation from suffering, in Nietzsche's phrase, in the creativity of intellect; *Patterns of Culture* is clear evidence of that intellect at work.

First, it emphasized the importance of culture versus biology; by contrasting the starkly different patterns of life among the Zuni, Dobu, and Kwakiutl, Benedict demonstrated the causal primacy of culture in understanding differences between modern humans. By extension, the profiles of these three societies so different from American society further weakened the grip of Victorian mores on American life.

Second, Benedict's emphasis on patterns of culture was a new twist on a fairly twisted idea. The concept of patterns was similar in some ways to the culture-element complexes that Kroeber and others had discussed (see pp. 67–69): patterned co-occurrences of cultural traits that marked different cultural groups. For example, anthropologist Clark Wissler described the horse complex among Plains Indians, a constellation of cultural practices including the tepee, travois, buffalo hunting, raiding, and the Sun Dance—all of which revolved around the horse. Similarly, we could define an American car culture in which a wide range of cultural elements—billboards, cellular phones, commuter schools, and so on—are all linked by the presence of automobiles.

But Benedict and other anthropologists were searching for something more subtle and profound, the relationship not only between a set of things and behaviors, but between the underlying ideas, values, and mores that characterize a particular society. The notion of the "Gestalt" configuration was influential at this time. Coming from the German word for the outline of a physical shape, psychologists had applied the notion to experiments in learning behavior that suggested people learn in response to underlying patterns called forth by a specific event rather than by direct stimulus response. Thus we learn that boisterous behavior is inappropriate in a church, but then extend that knowledge to cathedrals and synagogues, certain public monuments (the Lincoln Memorial), backyard weddings, and so on. Even in new situations we follow previously learned instructions because the new situation calls forth a basic learned pattern. "The Gestalt idea of configuration," Margaret Caffrey writes, "fell on open minds in America. A configuration was a form of pattern that linked facts and events with the attitudes and beliefs underlying them" (1989:154). Ruth Benedict made this notion of the Gestalt/configuration/pattern central to her work:

> Gestalt (configuration) psychology has done some of the most striking work in justifying the importance of this point of departure from the whole rather than from the parts.

> Gestalt psychologists have shown that in the simplest sense-perception no analysis of the separate precepts can account for the total experience. It is not enough to divide perceptions up into objective fragments. The subjective framework, the forms provided by past experience, are crucial and cannot be omitted. (1959:51)

When Benedict contrasts "objective" and "subjective," she is not using "subjective" as a synonym for "mere opinion" or an ethnocentric projection; she is attempting to characterize the subjective values that explain why members of a particular society behave in certain ways. Benedict used the concept of pattern to refer to a society's underlying "values of existence." She wrote, "Cultures . . . are more than the sum of their traits. We may know all about the distribution of a tribe's form of marriage, ritual dances, and puberty initiations and yet understand nothing of the culture as a whole which has used these elements to its own purpose" (1959:47).

Benedict exposed the differences in cultural patterns by contrasting three relatively well-studied and markedly different societies: the Pueblo Indians (Zuni and Hopi); the Dobu, who live on an island east of New Guinea; and the Northwest Coast Indians (Tsimshian, Kwakiutl, Coast Salish) who live between Puget Sound and southwestern Alaska. The three ethnographic cases were based on research by anthropologists whose work Benedict trusted: Reo Fortune had studied the Dobu (he was married to Margaret Mead at the time, see p. 106–7), Boas had worked on the Northwest Coast, and Benedict herself had conducted research at Zuni Pueblo. They were also completely different societies with fundamentally different cultural configurations. Marshaling extensive ethnographic detail, Benedict sifted out the fundamental elements of the cultural pattern. For example, she wrote of the Dobu:

> The Dobuan . . . is dour, prudish, and passionate, consumed with jealousy and suspicion and resentment. Every moment of prosperity he conceives himself to have wrung from a malicious world by a conflict in which he has worsted his opponent. The good man is the one who has many such conflicts to his credit, as anyone can see from the fact that he has survived

> with a measure of prosperity. It is taken for granted that he has thieved, killed children and his close associates by sorcery, cheated whenever he dared. (1959:168–169)

Contrast this with the Zuni ideal of the good man:

> The ideal man in Zuni is a person of dignity and affability who has never tried to lead, and who has never called forth comment from his neighbours. Any conflict, even though right is on his side, is held against him. . . . He should "talk lots," as they say—that is, he should always set people at their ease—and he should without fail co-operate easily with others either in the field or in ritual, never betraying a suspicion of arrogance or a strong emotion. (1959:99)

Benedict was not just reciting her own prejudices about people; she was proposing ethnographically informed generalizations about the distinct values of different societies. Such societies were so fundamentally different that Benedict turned to Nietzsche's work to borrow two concepts: the Apollonian and Dionysian approaches to existence. Benedict contrasted the configuration of the Zuni and other Puebloan Indians with that of the Kwakiutl and many other North American groups in their pursuit of

> the values of existence. The Dionysian pursues them through [as Nietzsche observed] "the annihilation of the ordinary bounds and limits of existence"; he seeks to attain in his most valued moments escape from the boundaries imposed upon him by his five senses, to break through into another order of existence. The desire of the Dionysian, in personal experience or in ritual, is to press through it toward a certain psychological state, to achieve excess. [The Dionysian] values the illuminations of frenzy. The Apollonian distrusts all this. . . . He knows but one law, measure in the Hellenic sense. He keeps within the middle of the road, stays within the known map, does not meddle with disruptive psychological states. In Nietzsche's fine phrase, even in the exaltation of the dance he "remains what he is, and retains his civic name." (1959:78–79)

"The Southwest Pueblos are Apollonian," Benedict wrote, and in contrast to many North American groups, "Zuni ideals and institutions . . . are rigorous on this point. The known map, the middle of the road to any Apollonian, is embodied in the common tradition of his people" (1959:80). Outside of the Pueblos, and despite the many differences in Native American language and culture, Benedict saw a common emphasis on Dionysian behavior: "They valued all violent experience, all means by which human beings may break through the usual sensory routine, and to all such experiences they attributed the highest value" (1959:80). The most conspicuous evidence was the vision quest, in which an individual—through fasting, drugs (tobacco), and self-mutilation—attempts to break through commonplace existence and obtain a personal vision through direct contact with the supernatural. Such a set of core values shaped larger cultural practices, resulting in distinctive patterns of culture.

Yet, not all individuals comfortably fit into the accepted patterns of cultural life, and Ruth Benedict knew this from her own experience. She had, as a person, reached a point when she could no longer conform to the normal values for American women in the 1920s; she had not accepted all the core values of her own culture. Benedict saw the potential for conflict between the individual and culture in her own life and assumed that this would occur in other societies. One of her students would state, "Ruth pursued anthropology to answer her own private questions about the individual's fate" (Cole 2002:533).

Thus, the final part of *Patterns of Culture* addresses this problem. "We have seen that any society selects some segment of the arc of possible human behavior," Benedict wrote, "and in so far as it achieves integration its institutions tend to further the expression of its selected segment and inhibit opposite expressions" (1959:254). Human nature is so malleable, the lessons of one's culture are so explicit, and the sanctions for disobedience so severe that the vast majority of people not only accept the core values but assume that "their particular institutions reflect an ultimate and universal sanity" (Benedict 1959:254). And yet not everyone finds the institutions of a given culture "equally congenial . . . favored are those . . . whose potentialities most nearly coincide with the type of behavior selected by their society" (Benedict 1959:255). Benedict argues that "deviation" is essentially a conflict between individual personality and a given culture's values and not a singular dimension true for all humans. The deviant in Dobu society is "the man who was naturally friendly" (Benedict 1959:258); the honored man in a Dionysian society is the despised pariah in an Apollonian culture.

So *Patterns of Culture* poses an interesting conflict between the individual and culture: on the one hand, culture is an expression of core values that most people learn and absorb; on the other hand, there are individual personalities that lie outside the particular segment of the arc of possibilities that defines that culture. Therefore, not only are cultural values relative, but the very definition of deviance as well. Benedict's book is one of the founding anthropological texts on the relationship between culture and personality.

Conclusion

Benedict wrote more than just *Patterns of Culture*, of course. During World War II, Benedict worked for the Office of War Information, sifting through published materials about other cultures in support of the American war effort and conducting studies of "cultures at a distance." The best-known study, *The Chrysanthemum and the Sword* (1946), was an examination of the core values of Japanese society and how such values influenced Japanese behavior during the war and the postwar American occupation. Less well known is Benedict's earlier study of the people and culture of Thailand (1952; written in 1943), which anticipates the methods of *The Chrysanthemum and the Sword*.

Benedict contributed to the war effort in another, very different way. In 1943 she and Gene Weltfish wrote a ten-cent antiracist pamphlet entitled *The Races of Mankind*. In the face of Nazi racial policies and racial conflicts within the United States, and as American troops fought around the globe, issues of race were paramount. Benedict and Weltfish summarized the current scientific views on race and argued that racial differences were minimal when compared to cultural differences. This argument was also advanced in *Patterns of Culture* and echoed Boas's discussion of race (see pp. 38–40). When the U.S. Army decided to distribute the pamphlet, conservative congressmen attacked it as "Communist propaganda." This patently absurd charge attracted publicity and helped sell over 750,000 copies of the pamphlet, which was translated into seven languages (Edwards 1968).

Other successes notwithstanding, none of Benedict's works surpassed *Patterns of Culture,* in terms of theoretical impact. Its clear argument exposed the basic patterns of a society, the set of basic values that form a cultural chord. As the shift from major to minor keys in the opening notes of *Thus Spake Zarathustra* conveys a sense of the universe's majesty and mystery, the Apollonian and Dionysian archetypes evoke certain fundamentals of a society. Note that Benedict was not trying to create a classification system for cultures. "Categories become a liability," she wrote, "when they are taken as inevitable and applicable alike to all civilizations and events" (1959:238). Cultures were not ragtag assortments of elements tossed together by historical accident; rather, Benedict showed that cultural differences were multifaceted expressions of a society's most basic core values. The goal of anthropology was to document these different patterns. Benedict wrote about the social outcome of that process in the last lines of her *Patterns of Culture*: "We shall arrive then at a more realistic social faith, accepting as grounds of hope and as new bases for tolerance the coexisting and equally valid patterns of life which mankind has created for itself from the raw materials of existence" (1959:278).

References

Benedict, Ruth

1922 The Vision in Plains Culture. *American Anthropologist* 24:1–23. [Reprinted 1959 in *An Anthropologist at Work: Writings of Ruth Benedict.* By Margaret Mead. New York: Houghton Mifflin.]

1923 *The Concept of the Guardian Spirit in North America.* American Anthropological Association, Memoir 29. [Reprinted 1974. Millwood, N.J.: Kraus Reprint.]

1924 A Brief Sketch of Serrano Culture. *American Anthropologist* 26:366–392. [Reprinted 1959 in *An Anthropologist at Work: Writings of Ruth Benedict.* By Margaret Mead. New York: Houghton Mifflin.]

1931 *Tales of the Cochiti Indians*. Bureau of American Ethnology, Bulletin 98. Washington, D.C.: Smithsonian Institution.
1932 Configurations of Culture in North America. *American Anthropologist* 34:1–27. [Reprinted 1974 in *Ruth Benedict*. By Margaret Mead. New York: Columbia University Press.]
1946 *The Chrysanthemum and the Sword: Patterns of Japanese Culture*. New York: Houghton Mifflin.
1952 *Thai Culture and Behavior: An Unpublished War Time Study Dated September, 1943*. Data Paper no. 4. Ithaca, N.Y.: Southeast Asia Program, Department of Far Eastern Studies, Cornell University.
1959 *Patterns of Culture*. New York: Houghton Mifflin. [Originally published 1934.]
1968 *Race: Science and Politics*. Including *The Races of Mankind* by Ruth Benedict and Gene Weltfish. New York: Viking Press. [Originally published 1940.]

Caffrey, Margaret
1989 *Ruth Benedict: Stranger in the Land*. Austin: University of Texas Press.

Cole, Sally
2002 "Mrs. Landes Meet Mrs. Benedict": Culture Pattern and Individual Agency in the 1930s. *American Anthropologist* 104(2):533–543.

Edwards, Violet
1968 Note on *The Races of Mankind*. In *Race: Science and Politics*. By Ruth Benedict. Pp. 167–168. New York: Viking Press.

Lapsley, Hilary
1999 *Margaret Mead and Ruth Benedict: The Kinship of Women*. Amherst: University of Massachusetts Press.

Mead, Margaret
1966 *An Anthropologist at Work: Writings of Ruth Benedict*. New York: Atherton Press.
1974 *Ruth Benedict*. New York: Columbia University Press.

Modell, Julia
1983 *Ruth Benedict: Patterns of a Life*. Philadelphia: University of Pennsylvania Press.

7

Edward Sapir

Culture, Language, and the Individual

Edward Sapir (1884–1939), a former student wrote, "was one of those rare men among scientists and scholars who are spoken of by their colleagues in terms of genius" (Mandelbaum 1968:v). In her obituary of Sapir in *American Anthropologist*, Ruth Benedict wrote, "Few men in academic life have been so brilliantly endowed as Professor Sapir, and the loss which linguistics and anthropology have sustained cannot be measured. To those of us who have been his friends, his death leaves a vacancy which can never be filled" (1939:468).

Sapir was recognized as the most brilliant linguist of his era, a "genius" to many (Darnell 1990:x), who revolutionized the study of American Indian languages. He also shaped interdisciplinary studies of human relations and institutions and the field later known as "culture and personality." But the central anthropological theories that Sapir proposed regard the relationship between the individual and culture as dynamically shaped by language.

Sapir's name is linked with that of his student, Benjamin Whorf (1897–1941), in the famous Sapir-Whorf hypothesis, which posits a relationship between the categories of meaning found within a language and the mental categories speakers of that language use to describe and classify the world. The implications of this simple hypothesis are profound. It suggests that understanding meaning—in all its different dimensions—is as important as understanding phonetics, syntax, and grammar, the most common dimensions of linguistic analysis prior to Sapir's work.

The Sapir-Whorf hypothesis implies that different languages mark different systems of perception and the differences between societies' cultural behavior are communicated by and codified in the structure of linguistic meaning. The study of another culture's language is more than an investigation into how they speak; it's an inquiry into how cultural existence is created.

Sapir's contributions occurred in the context of an anthropological linguistics with long antecedents, but most immediately shaped through the work of Franz Boas. At a time when much ethnographic work was focused on elements of culture that did not require language mastery—such as trait studies of material culture or studies conducted through interpreters—Boas's emphasis on the importance of learning non-Western languages was innovative. In 1911 Boas wrote in his *Handbook of American Indian Languages*:

> A command of the language [of a tribe] is an indispensable means of obtaining accurate and thorough [ethnological] knowledge, because much information can be gained by listening to conversations of the natives and by taking part in their daily life, which, to the observer who has no command of the language, will remain entirely inaccessible. (1911:60)

This notion of language as a research tool was less important than the idea that language provided insights into other dimensions of culture, however. Boas particularly emphasized the importance of recording extended native language texts dictated by speakers. These texts could then be wrung of every drop of available information and correlated with other sources of information. The linguist Roman Jakobson describes the impact of Boas's idea:

> Language was considered by Boas not only as part of ethnological phenomena in general but even as "one of the most instructive fields of inquiry" and his motivation is thoroughly remarkable: "The great advantage that linguistics offers in this respect," Boas tells in his magnificent introduction to the *Handbook of American Indian Languages* (1911), "is the fact that, on the whole, the categories which are formed always remain unconscious and that for this reason the processes which lead to their formation can be followed without the misleading and

> disturbing factors of secondary explanations, which are so common in ethnology." (1966:129)

This "fertile and pathbreaking" idea, Jakobson continues, implies that

> among the various ethnological phenomena the linguistic processes (or rather operations) exemplify most strikingly and plainly the logic of the unconscious. For this reason—Boas insists—"the very fact of the unconsciousness of the linguistic processes helps us to gain a clear understanding of the ethnological phenomena, a point the importance of which cannot be underrated." The place of language with regard to the other social systems and the meaning of linguistics for a thorough insight into the diverse ethnological patterns had never been stated so precisely. (1966:130)

Literally, language reflects and shapes the world as it is perceived by humans, and understanding the organization of linguistic meaning illuminates the basic structures of culture. That essential concept, with its roots in Boas's approach to linguistics, was elaborated and refined in the works of Edward Sapir.

Background

Sapir, a Jew born in Prussia, arrived in New York with his parents when he was five years old, part of the great emigration from Europe that was funneled through Ellis Island. Growing up poor on the east side of New York, Sapir's intellectual gifts became obvious at an early age. He won scholarships to Columbia College, where he graduated in 1904 at the age of twenty, completing his undergraduate education in just three years (Darnell 1990:5). He immediately continued graduate studies at Columbia under Boas and in 1905 did fieldwork with the Wishram of the lower Columbia River valley; the resulting study was published in 1909. Sapir went to Oregon to study the Takelma language in 1906, research that formed the basis of his doctoral dissertation. The difficulties of the Takelma language make his dissertation quite remarkable; Benedict noted, "There was no period of apprenticeship in Sapir's linguistic work; his phonetic and morphological gifts are as apparent in this boyhood work as in that of a student of long and arduous experience" (1939:465). The same year Sapir finished his dissertation (1907) he also published two articles on Takelma ethnology in the *American Anthropologist* (1907a) and in the *Journal of American Folklore* (1907b).

Sapir was a research assistant at Berkeley in 1907–1908, working on the native Californian language Yana. Next he went to the University of Pennsylvania, which supported his research on the Southern Paiute, the first scientific study of a Shoshonean language. Working with Toni Tillohash, a Southern Paiute man employed by the University of Pennsylvania Museum, Sapir created a grammar of Southern Paiute that set new standards in its sensitivity to the native speaker's intuitive use of language (Darnell 1990:34–35).

In 1910 Sapir obtained his first permanent position as the chief of the Division of Anthropology, Geological Survey of Canada, based in Ottawa (Darnell 1990:65–79). From this post Sapir conducted research on the Nootka of British Columbia and a variety of Athabascan languages; this work led to the definition of Na-Dene, a linguistic stock consisting of Northwest Coast languages like Haida, Tlingit, and other Athabascan languages, including Navaho.

During his fifteen years in Ottawa, Sapir turned his attention to problems of historical linguistics. "Certain resemblances in vocabulary and phonetics are undoubtedly due to borrowing of one language from another," Sapir wrote in the 1929 *Enyclopedia Britannica*, "but the more deep-lying resemblances, such as can be demonstrated, for instance, for Shoshonean, Piman, and Nahuatl or for Athabaskan and Tlingit, must be due to a common origin now greatly obscured by the operation of phonetic laws, grammatical developments and losses, analogical disturbances, and borrowing of elements from sources" (1968a:171). To understand these historical connections, Sapir proposed a reclassification of American Indian languages. The classification proposed by Major John Wesley Powell—the great explorer, geologist, and ethnologist—posited some fifty-five different linguistic stocks for North America, treating each as fundamentally distinct. Sapir saw greater connections between American Indian languages and replaced Powell's scheme with a mere six linguistic stocks for North America: (1) Eskimo-Aleut, (2) Algonquian, (3) Dene, (4) Penutian, (5) Hokan, and (6) Aztec-Tanoan (today called Uto-Aztecan). Languages within such stocks might be mutually unintelligible but exhibit clear affinities and shared ancestry, as do English, German, Danish, Swedish, and Norwegian, for example. Sapir's six-unit classification of American Indian languages dominated American linguistics into the 1960s, and it remains an essential framework for organizing Native American languages (Darnell 1990:110).

Sapir's Ottawa period was a time of intellectual isolation. Ottawa was far from the centers of anthropology in New York, Berkeley, and Chicago. Sapir's position in the Geological Survey did not involve teaching, so he lacked the stimulation of exchanges with students. The letters exchanged during this time between Sapir and Ruth Benedict make his sense of isolation clear.

But the time in Ottawa was also marked by extreme creativity (Darnell 1990:87–88). Sapir had a wide-ranging intellect, seemingly captivated by everything to do with words, and his publications from the Ottawa period indicate an extraordinary productivity. In addition to his writings in ethnology and linguistics, Sapir also published poetry, book reviews, and essays on nonanthropological subjects. His twenty-six publications from 1922 include "The Fundamental Elements of Northern Yana" and "Athabaskan Tone," as well as reviews of poetry and novels that were published in *The New Republic*, *The Dial*, and *Canadian Bookman*; sixteen original poems; and translations of three French Canadian folksongs. Such versatile virtuosity is very rare.

In 1925 Sapir eagerly accepted a position at the University of Chicago where he could teach a group of appreciative graduate students and where he could develop his interests in the area of semantics—the study of meaning—and in personality and culture. This latter arena of interest led him to give central importance to the role of the individual in culture and marked a break with contemporary thinkers about the nature of culture.

Culture and the Individual

A recurrent aspect of early twentieth-century definitions of culture is their emphasis on the superorganic, supraindividual nature of culture. The notion of the superorganic is best developed in Kroeber's work (see pp. 69–73), in which he argued that culture had a superorganic property that varied independently of the individuals who composed it, and also that culture, society, and the individual were discrete, irreducible phenomena. Sapir's position was very different: he believed that broad generalizations about society were misplaced and that "there are as many cultures as there are individuals in a population" (quoted by Benedict 1939:407).

This idea forms the background of an article Sapir wrote in 1938 entitled "Why Cultural Anthropology Needs the Psychiatrist" (1968e:569–577). Sapir opens with a discussion of J. O. Dorsey's study of the Omaha Indians and the fact that after making several anthropological generalizations ("The Omaha believe . . .") Dorsey said at various points, "Two Crows denies this." Sapir admits to being shocked when he read this as a student, assuming that Dorsey had not fulfilled his anthropological responsibility of providing the reader with a seamless view of a different society, instead delegating to the reader the responsibility of weighing how Two Crows' different opinions fit into the general patterns of Omaha culture. But in retrospect, Sapir wrote,

> We see now that Dorsey was ahead of his age. Living as he did in close touch with the Omaha Indians [Dorsey was a missionary among the Omaha], he knew he was dealing, not with a society or with a specimen of primitive man nor with a cross section of the history of primitive culture, but with a finite, though indefinite, number of human beings, who gave themselves the privilege of differing from each other not only in matters generally considered as "one's own business" but even on questions which clearly transcended the private individual's concern and were, by the anthropologist's definition, implied in the conception of a definitely delimited society with a definitely discoverable culture. (1968e:570–571)

Sapir was tantalized by Two Crows' "contrariness" because he saw the implications for our understanding of other cultures. First, as a matter of method, the inquiry into variation can be extremely fruitful even in matters that may seem to be objective. For example, if all the other Omaha say there are eight clans, but Two Crows states there are seven clans, Sapir wonders, "How could this be?" (1968e:573–574). Well, it might be that one clan no longer exists in a practical sense, but that it is remembered by everyone except Two Crows. Perhaps the clan had a particular social or ceremonial function that makes its "existence" hard to overlook. Maybe Two Crows comes from a clan that detested the now extinct clan, making it easy for him to forget it and giving him "the perfectly honest conviction that one need speak of only seven clans in the tribe." Two Crows "had a special kind of rightness, which was partly factual, and partly personal." But more important than this is the fundamental implication of Two Crows' opinion:

> The truth of the matter is that if we think long enough about Two Crows and his persistent denials, we shall have to admit that in some sense Two Crows is never wrong. It may not be a very useful sense for social science but in a strict methodology of science in general it dare not be completely ignored. The fact that this rebel, Two Crows, can in turn bend others to his own view of fact or theory or to his own preference in action shows that his divergence from custom had, from the very beginning, the essential possibility of culturalized behavior. (Sapir 1968e:572)

Thus we arrive at a paradox, almost Zen-like in its counterintuitive simplicity, that normative and deviant behaviors are equally cultural behaviors, that "the world of socialized behavior is nothing more than consensus of opinion" (Sapir 1968e:572). Sapir's answer about the relationship between the individual and society is to simply point out that society consists of individuals, that culture is consensus, and that generalizations about cultural behavior are counterbalanced with individual, divergent behaviors. This is different from Benedict's approach, which presented the individual and culture as dichotomous and argued that those individuals who through experience and personality fit easily into their culture were successes, whereas those who did not were deviants (see pp. 84–85).

Sapir denied this implicit opposition between individual and culture:

> There is no real opposition, at last analysis, between the concept of the culture of the group and the concept of individual culture. The two are interdependent. A healthy national culture is never a passively accepted heritage from the past, but implies the creative participation of the members of the community. . . . It is just as true, however, that the individual is helpless without a cultural heritage to work on. (1968c:321)

Not surprisingly, Sapir extended this view of cultural behavior to that pure example of cultural practice, language:

> It is obvious that for the building up of society, its units and subdivisions, and the understandings which prevail between its members some processes of communication are needed. While we often speak of society as though it were a static structure defined by tradition, it is, in the more intimate sense, nothing of the kind, but a highly intricate network of partial or complete understandings between the members of organizational units of every degree of size and complexity. . . . It is only apparently a static sum of social institutions; actually it is being reanimated or creatively reaffirmed from day to day by particular acts of a communicative nature which obtain among individuals participating in it. (1968b:104)

On *Language*

In 1921 Sapir published *Language: An Introduction to the Study of Speech*, his only book for a general audience. Sapir's biographer, Regna Darnell, writes that *Language* was directed to a broad readership lacking in his own foundations in ethnology and linguistics. "Anthropologists knew about fieldwork but not about linguistic methods," Darnell observes. "Linguists knew about the methods but not about their application to a full range of human languages. The educated public knew neither" (1990:96). The literary origins and Indo-European focus of traditional linguistics and the methodological weakness and non-Western emphasis of anthropology meant that neither discipline agreed on a common ground. Darnell writes that "disciplinary boundaries had cut off recognition of the actual creativity of language, which was, in all cultures, a rich and precise vehicle for the expression of thought. Sapir set himself the challenge of producing a book that could be understood by any educated person with an open mind" (1990:96).

First, Sapir described the dynamic artificiality of human communication: "Language is a purely human and noninstinctive method of communicating ideas, emotions, and desires by means of a system of voluntarily produced symbols" (1921:8). Sapir then shows that words are not symbols of specific perceptions or even specific objects but always refer to concepts of objects, "a convenient capsule of thought that embraces thousands of distinct experiences and that is ready to take in thousands more" (1921:13). These capsules of thought not only express our thoughts, but in the process of learning language our thoughts are shaped by the concepts used to organize the perception of experience. That is true of even the most simple descriptive terms about the environment:

> The mere existence, for instance, of a certain type of animal in the physical environment of a people does not suffice to give rise to a linguistic symbol referring to it. It is necessary that the animal be known by the members of the group in common and that they have some interest, however slight, in it before the language of the community is called upon to make reference to this particular element of the physical environment. In other words, so far as language is concerned, all environmental influence reduces at last analysis to the influence of social environment. (Sapir 1968d:90)

Sapir cites numerous examples of the ways that language reflects the socially significant aspects of the environment; he lists, for example, eighteen topographic features used by the Shoshone Paiute to describe the landscape of their desert homeland, including canyon with creek, canyon without water, slope of mountain or canyon wall receiving sunlight, shaded mountain slope or canyon wall, and so on (1968d:91). In passing, Sapir points out that virtually any Native American hunter and gatherer would be shocked by the range of plants we would simply refer to as "weeds." But note, our linguistic impression does not merely reflect our lack of social interest in seed collecting—the words we employ and the conceptual categories they imply shape the way we perceive the world. We look into a vacant lot, and all we see are weeds. That basic truth is at the core of the Sapir-Whorf hypothesis, which links the categories of language and the cultural perception of the world.

The Sapir-Whorf Hypothesis

Benjamin Whorf was an amazing man who made significant contributions to linguistics in a scant dozen years before his early death in 1941 at the age of forty-four. Whorf was a peculiarly American type of genius (Chase 1956). He worked as a fire prevention engineer for the Hartford Fire Insurance Company for twenty-two years; his linguistic studies were done after work and during extended leaves from his company. Whorf's introduction to linguistics was circuitous, sparked by an interest in Aztec culture that led to an interest in Nahuatl, the Aztec language. His linguistic research was sufficiently impressive that in 1930 he was awarded a grant to study Nahuatl in Mexico. Whorf's contributions and achievements, all self-tutored, were very impressive.

But Whorf's linguistic career took a major change when he met Sapir. In the fall of 1931 Sapir left the University of Chicago for Yale, and Whorf immediately enrolled in Sapir's seminar. At Yale, Whorf's study on American Indian languages intensified, and he became a central member of a group of Yale graduate students—including Morris Swadesh, Charles Hockett, and Carl Voegelin—who made major contributions to American linguistics. Sapir was instrumental in directing Whorf toward a study of the Uto-Aztecan languages, and particularly Hopi, and the two men's interaction led to a fundamental model, the Sapir-Whorf hypothesis.

As discussed above (pp. 88–89), the Sapir-Whorf hypothesis proposes that linguistic categories structure and transmit culturally learned perceptions of existence. It is difficult to determine each man's contribution to the hypothesis about the relationship between language, culture, and perception. Whorf's ideas are clearly based on Sapir's writings and teachings, although Sapir died before most of Whorf's writings were published, and thus Sapir never commented directly on the Sapir-Whorf hypothesis (Darnell 1990:375).

In a paper titled "Linguistic Factors in the Terminology of Hopi Architecture," written in 1940 but not published until 1952, Whorf outlined the range of building terms and concepts associated with the Hopis' pueblo constructions and, more generally, their concepts of space. Whorf notes that Hopi architectural terms "all denote three-dimensional solids in the geometrical sense, solid and rigid masses, or definitely bounded areas on or penetrations through such solids"—these words included *te'k^{w}a* for a section of wall, unfinished wall, or walls of a ruin; *kí·?ạ̀mi* for roof; or *poksö* for a vent hole, unglazed window, or chimney (1956:200). What Whorf did not find was a diversity of words for three-dimensional spaces—corridor, hall, passage, cellar, loft, attic, storeroom, chamber, and room—like we have in English. It is not that Hopi is linguistically impoverished in its description of architecture, but that the spaces are described not in functional or nominative terms but in locational terms. Whorf writes,

> This is in line with the way Hopi and, in fact, most or all Uto-Aztecan languages represent location in space, or regions in space. They are not set up as entities that can function in a sentence like terms for people, animals, or masses of matter having characteristic form, or, again, human groups and human relations, but are treated as purely relations concepts, of an adverbial type. Thus hollow spaces like room, chamber, hall, are not really named as objects are, but are rather located; i.e. positions of other things are specified so as to show their location in such hollow spaces. (1956:202)

According to Whorf, the Hopi emphasize solid and constructional elements rather than enclosed spaces, and they describe the spaces in spatial reference to each other. This is a fundamentally different way of thinking about architectural space than we have in English, in which some architectural locators even incorporate functional elements ("Where is it?" "Upstairs").

The differences between the Hopi and English treatments of interior architectural spaces are paralleled in the terms applied to buildings as a whole. Whorf points out that in English we have a large vocabulary for buildings with different functions—as in "church," "chapel," "cathedral," "synagogue," "meeting house," "temple," "shrine," just to cite some religious structures—that does not exist in Hopi. Hopi has three words for structures, two of them minor—the word for shrine (*té·tèska*) and the word for tent (*mecávki*), an introduced item—and then *ki·he*, "building." Even though the Hopi have different "types" of buildings—residences, storehouses, piki-houses (used only for baking corn wafers [piki]), and the semisubterranean circular kivas used only for ceremonies—the language does not fuse structure and activity into functional sets. "They do not have . . . the pattern which is so natural to us," Whorf observes, "in which 'a church,' i.e. an institution, is a term that merges quite imperceptibly into 'a church' meaning a type of building used as a meeting place for this institution, with the distinction hardly felt until attention is drawn to it" (1956:204).

Such fundamental differences in the description of architectural space are paralleled by differences in basic classifications of the external world: colors, directions, weather phenomena, plant and animal classifications, kin relations, social obligations, and so on. These classifications reflect more than just different words applied to the same objects and concepts, but objects and concepts that are perceived and conceived of in fundamentally different ways.

Yet there are many critics of the Sapir-Whorf hypothesis, such as the linguist and cognitive scientist Steven Pinker (2000, 2002) who attacks the Sapir-Whorf hypothesis on several grounds. First, Pinker questions Whorf's actual mastery of Hopi and other Native American languages, citing the work of anthropologist Ekkehart Malotki (1983) who found verbal constructions in Hopi that Whorf contended were absent. Second, and more fundamentally, Pinker argues that Whorf mistook language for thought. It is a common mistake: thoughts are silent and internal, made known and public through words, and thus thought and language are easily confused (Pinker 2000:57). Yet, we regularly experience the disjuncture between thought and words:

> We have all had the experience of uttering or writing a sentence, then stopping and realizing that it wasn't exactly what we meant to say. To have that feeling, there has to be a "what we meant to say" that is different from what we said. . . . And if thoughts depended on words, how could a new word ever be coined? How could a child learn a word to begin with? How could translation from one language to another be possible? (Pinker 2000:57)

The independence of language and thought has been demonstrated in experiments with infants and nonhuman primates lacking language but employing conceptual categories (Pinker 2002:210). Further, the difference between language and thought is indicated by our personal experiences: we remember the gist of an argument (such as, the topics, the logical connections, the paradoxes) but not the individual words, and alternatively we change our language to describe new objects and concepts (e.g., house music, surf the web). Every language, Pinker writes, "far from being an immutable penitentiary, is constantly under revision" (2002:210).

So if the central tenet of the Sapir-Whorf hypothesis is suspect (that is, language shapes thought), what is its lasting value for anthropological theory? First is the undeniable historical impact of the hypothesis; the Sapir-Whorf hypothesis was one of the central concepts of cultural relativism and thus influenced anthropological research in the twentieth century. But perhaps a more subtle consequence was to focus anthropological attention on how members of different societies classify and describe the cultural worlds they inhabit. That, in turn, made the study of the cultural construction of meaning a central issue in anthropological theory.

Conclusion

Sapir and Whorf died within a few years of each other at the relatively young ages of fifty-four (Sapir) and forty-four (Whorf). It is impossible to know what more these men would have achieved had they lived as long as Alfred Kroeber. Apart from his linguistic analyses and polymath accomplishments, elements in Sapir's work have great importance for current anthropological thinking. The issue of meaning is central. Sapir's work shifted the focus of linguistic analysis from the word to its meaning, which immediately led to ideas about the cultural creation of meaning. If, as Two Crows seemed to demonstrate, the world of socialized behavior is simply, but significantly, nothing more than public consensus of opinion, then it follows that such a consensus is hammered out in argument, debate, gossip, rituals, and a whole array of symbolic interactions that anthropologists like Clifford Geertz (see chapter 19) would refer to as "discourse" (Geertz 1973:9–10).

Culture is not a chaotic tangle of individual opinions, however, in the views of Sapir and Whorf, because language itself imposes certain structures on perception. As members of a culture and speakers of a language we learn certain implicit classifications and consider those classifications to be accurate renderings of the world. And since those linguistic categories vary, different cultures, though made up of individuals who have the ability to disagree, also exhibit distinctive consensuses about the nature of existence.

References

Benedict, Ruth
1939 Edward Sapir. *American Anthropologist* 41:465–477.

Boas, Franz
1911 *Handbook of American Indian Languages*. Washington, D.C.: Government Printing Office.

Carroll, John
1966 Benjamin Lee Whorf. In *Portraits of Linguists: A Biographical Source Book for the History of Western Linguistics, 1746–1963*. Vol. 2. T. Sebeok, ed. Pp. 563–585. Bloomington: Indiana University Press.

Chase, Stuart
1956 Foreword. In *Language, Thought, and Reality: Selected Writings of Benjamin Lee Whorf*. J. Carroll, ed. Pp. v–x. Cambridge, Mass.: MIT Press.

Darnell, Regna
1990 *Edward Sapir: Linguist, Anthropologist, Humanist*. Berkeley: University of California Press.

Emmeneau, Murray
1966 Franz Boas as Linguist. In *Portraits of Linguists: A Biographical Source Book for the History of Western Linguistics, 1746–1963*. Vol. 2. T. Sebeok, ed. Pp. 122–127. Bloomington: Indiana University Press.

Geertz, Clifford
1973 *The Interpretation of Cultures*. New York: Basic Books.

Jakobson, Roman
1966 Franz Boas' Approach to Language. In *Portraits of Linguists: A Biographical Source Book for the History of Western Linguistics, 1746–1963*. Vol. 2. T. Sebeok, ed. Pp. 127–139. Bloomington: Indiana University Press.

Malotki, Ekkehart
1983 *Hopi Time: A Linguistic Analysis of Temporal Concepts in the Hopi Language*. Berlin: Mouton.

Mandelbaum, David
1968 Editor's Introduction. In *Selected Writings of Edward Sapir in Language, Culture and Personality*. Pp. v–xii. Berkeley: University of California Press.

Pinker, Steven
2000 *The Language Instinct: How the Mind Creates Language*. New York: Perennial Classics. [Originally published 1994.]
2002 *The Blank Slate: The Modern Denial of Human Nature*. New York: Viking Press.

Sapir, Edward
1907a Notes on the Takelma Indians of Southwestern Oregon. *American Anthropologist* 9:251–275.
1907b Religious Ideas of the Takelma Indians of Southwestern Oregon. *Journal of American Folklore* 20:33–49.
1909 *Takelma Texts*. Anthropological Publications of the University Museum 2(1):1–263. Philadelphia: University of Pennsylvania.
1921 *Language: An Introduction to the Study of Speech*. New York: Harcourt, Brace & World.
1968a Central and North American Languages. In *Selected Writings of Edward Sapir in Language, Culture and Personality*. D. Mandelbaum, ed. Pp. 169–178. Berkeley: University of California Press.
1968b Communication. In *Selected Writings of Edward Sapir in Language, Culture and Personality*. D. Mandelbaum, ed. Pp. 104–109. Berkeley: University of California Press.

1968c Culture, Genuine and Spurious. In *Selected Writings of Edward Sapir in Language, Culture and Personality*. D. Mandelbaum, ed. Pp. 308–331. Berkeley: University of California Press.

1968d Language and Environment. In *Selected Writings of Edward Sapir in Language, Culture and Personality*. D. Mandelbaum, ed. Pp. 89–103. Berkeley: University of California Press.

1968e Why Cultural Anthropology Needs the Psychiatrist. In *Selected Writings of Edward Sapir in Language, Culture and Personality*. D. Mandelbaum, ed. Pp. 569–577. Berkeley: University of California Press.

Voeglin, Carl

1966 Edward Sapir. In *Portraits of Linguists: A Biographical Source Book for the History of Western Linguistics, 1746–1963*. Vol. 2. T. Sebeok, ed. Pp. 489–492. Bloomington: Indiana University Press.

Whorf, Benjamin

1956 Linguistic Factors in the Terminology of Hopi Architecture. In *Language, Thought, and Reality: Selected Writings of Benjamin Lee Whorf*. J. Carroll, ed. Pp. 199–206. Cambridge, Mass.: MIT Press.

8

Margaret Mead

The Individual and Culture

When she died in November 1978, Margaret Mead was the most widely read anthropologist in America; she probably still is. Her first book, *Coming of Age in Samoa,* was published in 1928, became an instant classic, and remains the best selling of all anthropological books (Freeman 1983:xii). The book's vast popularity stemmed from its central question, a question humans find fascinating: why are we the way we are? Mead found the answer in three experiences that most people share—childhood, parenthood, and sex—and thus her work was immediately relevant to literally millions of people.

The wide interest in Mead's work and ideas is reflected by her numerous, diverse publications and availability in a variety of media, including records, tapes, films, and videos. As of 1976 her bibliography listed over fourteen hundred printed works: books, articles in scientific journals, book reviews, newspaper articles, statements entered as congressional testimony, conference reports, and a continuous stream of magazine articles (Gordon 1976). The magazine articles are interesting in their titles and venues: "South Sea Hints on Bringing up Children" appeared in the September 1929 issue of *Parents* magazine; the July 1948 *Mademoiselle* featured "Are Children Savages?"; and beginning in the 1960s Mead wrote a monthly column in *Redbook* magazine in which she would answer readers' questions: "Margaret Mead Answers: Questions about School Prayers, Happiness, Telepathy, etc." (February 1963), "Margaret Mead Answers: Is Housework Easier Than It Was 50 Years Ago? Was Shakespeare Really

Shakespeare? What Is the Fatal Fascination of Baseball?" (November 1964), and "Margaret Mead Answers: Questions about Jean-Paul Sartre, School Busing, Why People Like to Have Their Hair Stand on End, etc." (March 1965). This shows a certain daredevil flair, a bold willingness to write about almost anything. "Anthropology had attracted Mead in the first place because its borders were so flexible," Jane Howard writes, "but even it could not contain her" (1984:13).

Mead's motive was advocacy, her desire to speak to central issues about society and to reform social conditions based on comparative anthropological data. The fact that another society did not, for example, feed infants on a rigid schedule implied that to do so involved learned behavior, behavior that could be identified and changed if desired. The impacts of different child-rearing practices on adult personality could be assessed; different practices could be advocated and adopted; and society could be improved. "The process of inquiry," her daughter, Mary Catherine Bateson, writes about Mead's experimentation with her own child, "involving the life of a child, could have been pursued only in a context of advocacy, and advocacy, for Margaret, was never far behind" (1984:30).

Mead's insights into child rearing were widely felt in American society. Mead chose Dr. Benjamin Spock as her daughter's pediatrician because he had been psychoanalyzed (Bateson 1984:31), and Mary Catherine Bateson was the first breast-fed and demand-fed infant he had encountered. As an anthropologist, Mead recorded her infant's feeding demands, found patterns in the times, and then scheduled her teaching and writing commitments around those times. This had some influence on Dr. Spock's writings on infant care, and consequently for the rearing of the post–World War II baby boomers. For better or worse, many of us were raised or raise our children in a manner indirectly influenced by Margaret Mead. As her daughter writes, "The innovations that Margaret made as a parent were actually greater than they seem now because so many have been incorporated into patterns of society" (1984:33).

In spite of her prolific writings, or maybe because of them, Margaret Mead's influence on anthropology is diffuse. Unlike theoreticians like Sapir or Benedict whose core concepts can be neatly summarized and their implications derived, Margaret Mead's central idea—that differences between peoples are usually cultural differences imparted in childhood—does not lead to specific expectations but instead to a general shift in view, to a concern with how a human infant is transformed into an adult member of a particular society. And Mead's very public role as an advocate has raised questions about the accuracy of her anthropological research (Freeman 1983; Holmes 1987; Leacock 1993). Margaret Mead lived long, worked hard, and argued for combining social innovation and a respect for tradition in an effort to improve the human situation. The consequences of her life and work are deep and continuing.

Background

Margaret Mead was born in 1901 into an upper-middle-class, well-educated, and socially solid family (for a selection of Mead's letters, see Caffrey and Francis 2006). Her father was an economics professor and her mother a college-educated woman active in a variety of social causes—civil rights, women's suffrage, anti-fur—who imparted a sense of advocacy to her daughter. After a year at DePauw University, Mead transferred to Barnard College, the women's university associated with Columbia University in the heart of New York City. She thoroughly enjoyed herself at Barnard, forming lifelong friendships with other students and becoming swept up in the major theories, political issues, and controversies that flowed through academic circles with the development of modernism (Mead 1972).

As an English and psychology major, Mead took a course from Franz Boas in her senior year. She was captivated by Boas's lectures and after the first term attended every course and seminar he offered at Columbia. Mead was also fascinated by Boas's teaching assistant, Ruth Benedict, who convinced Mead to pursue anthropology as a graduate student. By the end of her senior year at Barnard, Mead was prepared to begin her studies in anthropology—and her first marriage to Luther Cressman, who went on to become a well-known archaeologist. She later married the anthropologist Reo Fortune, whose work

Sorcerers of Dobu is a classic ethnography discussed by Benedict in *Patterns of Culture* (see pp. 82–85), and finally Gregory Bateson, one of the most creative and iconoclastic social scientists of the twentieth century (Lipset 1980). Mead conducted fieldwork with Fortune and Bateson, and she and Bateson had a daughter, the anthropologist and writer Mary Catherine Bateson. Mead's anthropological research and her personal life were parallel explorations of the relationships between gender, childhood, and society.

Gender, Child Rearing, and Culture: Fieldwork and Theory

Mead's theoretical ideas evolved directly from her field investigations. Between 1925 and 1939 Mead participated in five field trips and studied eight different societies. Oddly, her own dissertation was not based on fieldwork but on library research about the material culture of Polynesia—a topic Boas assigned—and is described as detailed and competent by some (Thomas 1980) and lackluster by others (McDowell 1980:278). Mead's first field research was in Samoa where she spent eight months in the field in 1925. Her book, *Coming of Age in Samoa,* was the extremely popular outcome, and her results remain controversial (see discussion below, p. 110). After she returned from Samoa, Mead and Fortune worked on two field projects: a brief investigation of the Omaha during the summer of 1930 (her only work on a Native American group) and a much longer research project in New Guinea (1931–1933), a cross-cultural comparison described in her *Sex and Temperament in Three Primitive Societies* (1963). Later she conducted field research with Gregory Bateson in Bali in 1936–1938 and again in 1939 and among the Iatmul of New Guinea in 1938. The Balinese research is notable for its use of photography as a research tool, and it resulted in *Balinese Character* (Bateson and Mead 1942; for an excellent study, see Sullivan 1999).

These three phases of fieldwork capture the ethnographic basis of Mead's central contribution: that specific child-rearing practices shape personalities that in turn give specific societies their essential natures. In the introduction to *Coming of Age in Samoa*, Mead wrote,

> This tale of another way of life is mainly concerned with education, with the process by which the baby, arrived cultureless upon the human scene, becomes a full-fledged adult member of his or her society. The strongest light will fall upon the ways in which Samoan education, in its broadest sense, differs from our own. And from this contrast we may be able to turn, made newly and vividly self-conscious and self-critical, to judge anew and perhaps fashion differently the education we give our children. (1928:13)

Mead's profile of Samoan upbringing was based on a detailed study of sixty-eight girls between the ages of eight and twenty in three near-contiguous villages on the island of Ta'u, the largest of the three islands in the Manu'a group of easternmost islands in American Samoa. A sample record sheet (Mead 1928:284) indicates that Mead collected a variety of personal and family data on the ways Samoans evaluated each other (the most beautiful girl, the wisest man, the worst boy) and administered a set of basic psychological tests such as rote memory for numbers. "But," Mead admitted,

> this quantitative data represents the barest skeleton of the material which was gathered through months of observation of the individuals and of groups, alone, in their households, and at play. From these observations, the bulk of the conclusions are drawn concerning the attitudes of the children towards their families and towards each other, their religious interests or the lack of them, and the details of their sex lives. This information cannot be reduced to tables or statistical statements. (1928:264)

The basic conclusion was that adolescence in Samoa was not a stressful period for girls, because in general Samoan society lacked stresses:

> The Samoan background which makes growing up so easy, so simple a matter, is the general casualness of the whole society. For Samoa is a place where no one plays for very high stakes,

> no one pays very heavy prices, no one suffers for his convictions or fights to the death for special ends. Disagreements between parent and child are settled by the child's moving across the street, between a man and his village by the man's removal to the next village, between a husband and wife's seducer by a few fine mats. . . . And in personal relations, caring is slight. Love and hate, jealousy and revenge, sorrow and bereavement, are all matters of weeks. From the first months of its life, when a child is handed carelessly from one woman's hands to another's, the lesson is learned of not caring for one person greatly, not setting high hopes on any one relationship. (Mead 1928:199)

Mead cited a number of observations to support her conclusion. Samoan babies are nursed on demand until two or three, but other foods like mashed papaya and coconut milk are given to the infant during the first week. After weaning, toddlers are turned over to a girl who is six or seven years old; these older children watch over and are held responsible for their charges' misbehavior. The Samoan household is bilateral and often extended; household composition varies from nuclear families to households of fifteen to twenty people who may be related by marriage, blood, adoption, or friendship. This flexibility of residence allows a Samoan child to take up residence with another set of relatives when there are conflicts at home.

Mead described sexual relations as frequent and usually without consequence. Of the thirty postpubescent girls Mead studied, seventeen had heterosexual relations and twenty-two homosexual relations; most of the female virgins lived in the house of the Christian pastor. Liaisons occurred on the beach or when an intrepid lover crawled into the house; rape was infrequent in contrast to the "moetotolo, in which a man stealthily appropriates the favours which are meant for another" (Mead 1928:93; compare Freeman 1983). Abortions may end pregnancies, although there is no great fuss made over "illegitimate" children who are incorporated into the household.

This ease of transitions, the fluidity of status changes, Mead argued, characterized childhood and society in Samoa. It was not simply a matter of childhood shaping society or vice versa, but both. The implications of this research, and the discovery that adolescent turmoil was not an innate characteristic of the human condition, gave Mead's work great significance.

It is also a source of controversy fifty-five years later. In 1983 Derek Freeman published *Margaret Mead and Samoa: The Making and Unmasking of an Anthropological Myth* in which he argued that Mead systematically distorted Samoan society. Freeman, also a specialist on Samoa, contended that Mead "greatly underestimated the complexity of the culture, society, history, and psychology" of Samoans, assuming them to be "very simple" (1983:285). That simplicity, Freeman held, merely reflected Mead's lack of command of Samoan language, her ignorance of the complexities of Samoan status and political systems, and a naive euphoria over Samoa as a tropical Eden. But most damning, in Freeman's critique, was that Mead went to Samoa with the preconceived intention of showing that culture, not biology, determined human responses to life's transitions, like adolescence. This assumption, Freeman later asserted, predisposed Mead to uncritically accept Samoan girls' statements about sexual liaisons that were false hoaxes, "an example of the way in which a highly intelligent observer can be blinded to empirical reality by an uncritical commitment to a scientifically unsound assumption" (1999:212). Freeman writes,

> It is thus evident that her writings from this period, about Samoa as about other South Seas cultures, had the explicit aim of confuting biological explanations of human behavior and vindicating the doctrines of the Boasian school. . . . [T]here can be no doubt that Mead's fervent desire to demonstrate the validity of the doctrines she held in common with Benedict and Boas led her, in Samoa, to overlook evidence running counter to her beliefs. (1983:282)

Freeman's accusations touched off a howl of controversy, quite separate from the evaluation of the evidence, since he had had evidence contradicting Mead since the 1960s but only published it after her death. The debate, which was featured in the media, grew particularly vitriolic, because it touched a real nerve: the debasement of the best-known work of the best-known American anthropologist (see Holmes 1987; Leacock 1993; Orans 1996).

But long before the controversy, Mead's work in Samoa set the pattern for a series of detailed ethnographic studies conducted elsewhere in Oceania and Melanesia. *Sex and Temperament in Three Primitive Societies* presents the results of Mead's 1931–1933 work among three New Guinea societies. Her research examined a basic question about "the conditioning of the social personalities of the two sexes" (1963:xiv). Mead described her study as

> an account of how three primitive societies have grouped their social attitudes towards temperament about the very obvious facts of sex-difference. I studied this problem in simple societies because here we have the drama of civilization writ small, a social microcosm alike in kind, but different in size and magnitude, from the complex social structures. . . . Among the gentle mountain-dwelling Arapesh, the fierce cannibalistic Mundugumor, and the graceful headhunters of Tchambuli, I studied this question. Each of these tribes had, as has every human society, the point of sex-difference to use as one theme in the plot of social life, and each of these peoples has developed that theme differently. (1963:viii–ix)

These three groups lived within a one-hundred-mile radius of each other on the northern shore of Papua New Guinea, and yet their personalities were completely distinct. Of the Arapesh, Mead wrote,

> They regard both men and women as inherently gentle, responsive, and cooperative, able and willing to subordinate the self to the needs of those who are younger or weaker and to derive a major satisfaction from doing so. They have surrounded with delight that part of parenthood which we consider to be specially maternal, the minute, loving care for the little child and the selfless delight in that child's progress towards maturity. (1963:134)

Arapesh child-rearing responsibilities were so evenly divided between mother and father that "if one comments upon a middle-aged man as good-looking, the people answer, 'Good-looking? Y-e-s? But you should have seen him before he bore all those children'" (Mead 1963:39).

The Mundugumor could not be more different. Living in a society "based upon a theory of a natural hostility that exists between all members of the same sex," Mundugumor fathers and sons, and mothers and daughters, were adversaries. "The Mundugumor manchild is born into a hostile world," Mead wrote, "a world in which most of the members of his own sex will be his enemies, in which his major equipment for success must be a capacity for violence, for seeing and avenging insult" (1963:189). This hostile temperament was shared by men and women; the Mundugumor have

> no theory that women differ temperamentally from men. They are believed to be just as violent, just as aggressive, just as jealous. They simply are not quite as strong physically, although a woman can put up a very good fight and a husband who wishes to beat his wife takes care to arm himself with a crocodile jaw and to be sure that she is not armed. (Mead 1963:210)

Turning to the Tchambuli, Mead found another society where the principal themes of temperament and gender were differently defined:

> As the Arapesh made growing food and children the greatest adventure of their lives, and the Mundugumor found greatest satisfaction in fighting and competitive acquisition of women, the Tchambuli may be said to live principally for art. Every man is an artist and most men are skilled not in some one art alone, but in many: in dancing, carving, plaiting, painting and so on. Each man is chiefly concerned with his role upon the stage of his society, with the elaboration of his costume, the beauty of the masks that he owns, the skill of his own flute-playing, the finish and élan of his ceremonies, and upon other people's recognition and valuation of his performance. (Mead 1963:245)

And while Tchambuli men were preoccupied with art, women had the real power, controlling fishing and the most important manufactures, looking on their menfolk with "kindly tolerance and appreciation" (Mead 1963:255).

Sex and Temperament in Three Primitive Societies was important because at that time in the United States sex roles were viewed—

by men and women—as inevitable, natural characteristics of gender differences; Mead showed that these behavior patterns were actually extremely malleable and reflected cultural differences.

Mead and Gregory Bateson also explored the cultural bases of personality in their fieldwork in Bali in 1936 to 1938. Their goal was to "translate aspects of culture never successfully recorded by the scientist, although often caught by the artist, into some form of communication sufficiently clear and sufficiently unequivocal to satisfy the requirements of scientific enquiry" (Bateson and Mead 1942:xi). In the absence of a complex scientific vocabulary designed to express a culture's ethos, Mead had relied on ordinary English words—even though their meanings were specific to a cultural setting completely different from Balinese experience (Bateson and Mead 1942:xi). The way out of this dilemma was to combine traditional ethnography with a photographic record so that the observations could be recorded and communicated.

The result is a fascinating anthropological record. Based on their work in the mountain community of Bajoeng Gede, Mead and Bateson document a way of life that is based on orientation. "Orientation," Mead observes, "in time, space, and status are the essentials of social existence" (Bateson and Mead 1942:11). Mead writes that "each man's place in the social scheme of his village is known" (Bateson and Mead 1942:7). The status differences are reflected in space (the superior person should sleep on the eastern or inland side of the inferior person), vertical elevation (higher chairs for higher statuses), language (using polished language to speak to someone of a higher caste or status), posture, and gesture. In Bajoeng Gede, "space and time and social status form an orderly whole, with little stress or strain" and "within the fixed and complicated sets of regulations, obligations, and privileges, the people are relaxed and dreamy," and this spatiosocial orientation "is felt as a protection rather than a straitjacket and its loss provokes extreme anxiety" (Bateson and Mead 1942:10).

This cultural knowledge is literally transmitted at birth. Mead writes,

> When the Balinese baby is born, the midwife, even at the moment of lifting him in her arms, will put words in his mouth,

> commenting, "I am just a poor little new-born baby, and I don't know how to talk properly, but I am very grateful to you, honorable people, who have entered this pig sty of a house to see me born." And from that moment, all through babyhood, the child is fitted into a frame of behavior, of imputed speech and imputed thought and complex gesture, far beyond his skill and maturity. (Bateson and Mead 1942:13)

Gradually the child adopts these patterns of speech and behavior, a process that Mead describes in a fine metaphor, as "slip[ping] into speech, as into an old garment, worn before, but fitted on another hand" (Bateson and Mead 1942:13). "As with speech, so with posture and gesture," Mead writes, and it is in Bateson's photographs that we see mothers pose their children's hands in prayer, dance teachers extending children's arms to instruct by muscular rote, and a mother teasing her son by holding his younger sibling over his head and thus inverting proper relationships of age, status, and elevation.

In all Bateson shot some 22,000 feet of 16 mm film and 25,000 still photographs; combined with Mead's intensive ethnographic record, as Nancy McDowell observed, "they found themselves with a body of data, particularly photographic material, that was so detailed, extensive, and innovative that no other body of data existed with which they could compare it" (1980:297). It remains a masterpiece of documentation and analysis.

Conclusion

Balinese Character exemplifies a central theme in Mead's work—the relationship between individual and cultural pattern. It is an approach that became known as "culture and personality," and although it shares concerns with Benedict's approach of cultural patterns, Mead's work exhibits a more explicit use of psychological theory, methods of data collection, and a greater awareness of the dynamic between the individual and cultural ethos.

Culture is not just the individual writ large, Mead argued. The individual is a product of cultural behavior that shapes the person in common but unique manners that then are reinterpreted and reexpressed, relived as the infant becomes an adult, as the child becomes a parent. This interaction between individual and culture is the dynamic, complex process by which humans learn to be humans, but humans of very distinctive sorts.

Like her colleagues Kroeber, Benedict, and Sapir, Mead attempted to discover what it was that made cultures distinctive but coherent. How is it that human societies can be so incredibly different, not just on the surface but at their very cores, and yet within a particular society there can be such unanimity as to values and practice? For the Victorian evolutionists the answer was straightforward: societies were different because they represented stages in the "nearly uniform channels" of human progress. The Boasian critique demolished that easy answer yet put nothing in its place; the best Boas could suggest was to keep collecting good ethnographic data and someday, perhaps, the laws of human culture would become evident.

But that apparently did not satisfy Boas's students, at least not Kroeber, Sapir, Benedict, and Mead. Each sought a different way to explain the coherency of culture: Kroeber turned to the superorganic, Benedict to the core values of culture, Sapir and Whorf to the conceptual categories embedded in language, and Margaret Mead to the processes of human development: the way an infant is bathed, the shared intimacies of husband and wife, or the small gestures that teach a child its place in the world.

References

Bateson, Gregory, and Margaret Mead
1942 *Balinese Character: A Photographic Analysis.* New York: New York Academy of Sciences.

Bateson, Mary Catherine
1984 *With a Daughter's Eye: A Memoir of Margaret Mead and Gregory Bateson.* New York: William Morrow.

Caffrey, Margaret, and Patricia Francis
2006 *To Cherish the Life of the World: Selected Letters of Margaret Mead.* Cambridge, Mass.: Basic Books.

Freeman, Derek
1983 *Margaret Mead and Samoa: The Making and Unmasking of an Anthropological Myth.* Cambridge, Mass.: Harvard University Press.

1999 *The Fateful Hoaxing of Margaret Mead: A Historical Analysis of Her Samoan Research*. Boulder, Colo.: Westview Press.

Gordan, Joan, ed.

1976 *Margaret Mead: The Complete Bibliography, 1925–1975*. The Hague: Mouton.

Holmes, Lowell

1987 *Quest for the Real Samoa: The Mead/Freeman Controversy & Beyond*. South Hadley, Mass.: Bergin and Garvey.

Howard, Jane

1984 *Margaret Mead: A Life*. New York: Fawcett Columbine.

Leacock, Eleanor Burke

1993 The Problem of Youth in Contemporary Samoa. In *From Labrador to Samoa: The Theory and Practice of Eleanor Burke Leacock*. C. Sutton, ed. Pp. 115–130. Arlington, Va.: Association for Feminist Anthropology, American Anthropological Association.

Lipset, David

1980 *Gregory Bateson: The Legacy of a Scientist*. Englewood Cliffs, N.J.: Prentice Hall.

McDowell, Nancy

1980 The Oceanic Ethnography of Margaret Mead. *American Anthropologist* 82:278–303.

Mead, Margaret

1928 *Coming of Age in Samoa: A Psychological Study of Primitive Youth for Western Civilization*. New York: William Morrow.

1963 *Sex and Temperament in Three Primitive Societies*. New York: William Morrow. [Originally published 1935.]

1972 *Blackberry Winter: My Earlier Years*. New York: William Morrow.

Orans, Martin

1996 *Not Even Wrong: Margaret Mead, Derek Freeman, and the Samoans*. Novato, Calif.: Chandler and Sharp.

Sullivan, Gerald

1999 *Margaret Mead, Gregory Bateson, and Highland Bali: Fieldwork Photographs of Bayung Gedé, 1936–1939*. Chicago: University of Chicago Press.

Thomas, David H.

1980 Margaret Mead as a Museum Anthropologist. *American Anthropologist* 82:354–361.

III

THE NATURE OF SOCIETY

Beginning in 1920, a fundamental division occurred between American and British anthropology. In the United States, anthropology focused on culture as a set of ideas; in the United Kingdom, it focused on society as the consequence of action. For the American cultural anthropologists, explanation involved showing the relationship between values and cultural behavior. For the British social anthropologists, explanation required analyzing the different segments of society and the institutions that articulate them.

Ironically, British social anthropology has its origins in France. The emphasis on the segmentation and articulation of society was directly derived from Durkheim's discussions of mechanical and organic solidarity, and it was explicitly introduced into British anthropology by Radcliffe-Brown. The foundational trope is a recurrent metaphor in Western thought: the organic analogy which holds that society is like an organism. Just as living things have specific organs that perform certain tasks yet are articulated by nervous, circulatory, and respiratory systems, human societies have distinct subdivisions with different functions that are varyingly tied together through economic, political, and religious institutions. Therefore, explanation of a particular social pattern involves a description of the structure and analysis of its function. Explication of a general social pattern requires demonstrating the cross-cultural utility of its function. Thus, in 1899 Marcel Mauss and Henri Hubert wrote "Essay on the Nature and Function of Magic," marking an approach to social analysis that had no counterpart in America.

American cultural anthropology and British social anthropology developed along different trajectories. First, the nature of an explanation differed dramatically. For Boas, an explanation was a historical account, for his students an expression of shared mental constructs. For those operating in the Durkheimian tradition, an explanation was based on laws, statements of regularity about phenomena. This appeal to lawlike generalities was explicitly denied by Kroeber, who would write, "The findings of history can never be substantiated like proofs of natural science" (1952:79). And yet this is exactly what Malinowski and Radcliffe-Brown proposed.

They argued that functionalist explanations were scientific explanations and the word "science" figures prominently in their writings. The nexus of utility differed: for Malinowski, culture functioned to meet the cumulative social needs that originate in individual biological needs; for Radcliffe-Brown, culture functioned to maintain and reproduce society. But in either case, the cross-cultural occurrence of a specific cultural form resulted from its recurrent utility. The cross-cultural existence of sympathetic magic or Iroquois kinship systems or coil-made pottery was not the product of universal evolution or historical contexts or shared values. These cultural practices reoccur because they meet the same functions in different societies, and their reoccurrence can be characterized with the lawlike statements of science.

In addition to differing modes of explanation, British and American anthropology diverged in subject matter. British social anthropology produced an ethnography of societies, analyzing their institutions and operations. The individual social actor was characterized by role and status and shown to act within predetermined sets of behavior. Social forms operated to reinforce each other, ensuring the resolution of disruptive conflict and the perpetuation of social structure—in short, the continued functioning of society.

In contrast, American anthropology's emphasis on culture as values led to a greater interest in individuals, and particularly how cultural practices served to shape individual character. There was a tangent point with psychology, and between 1910 and 1950, particularly with Freudian psychology. This created a stream in American anthropology, culture and personality, that had no developed counterpart in Great Britain.

By the 1930s, American cultural anthropology and British social anthropology were on separate tracks, so distinct that anthropologists had difficulty communicating across the theoretical divide. As often occurs, the theoretical debates were enmeshed with personal conflicts, making the chance of understanding even more remote. The divide was partly bridged when Radcliffe-Brown and Malinowski began to lecture and teach in the United States, and a group of American functionalists grew in influence. Nevertheless, two distinct trends in anthropology persisted—one ideational, the other behavioral—and never really disappeared.

References

Kroeber, Alfred
1952 Historical Context, Reconstruction, and Interpretation. In *The Nature of Culture*. Pp. 79–84. Chicago: University of Chicago Press.

9

Marcel Mauss

Elemental Categories, Total Facts

"I cannot divorce myself from the work of a school," Marcel Mauss (1872–1950) wrote, musing that the common thread of his fifty years of research into the nature of human society was "the conviction that collaborating with others is a drive against isolation and the pretentious search for originality" (1983:139). Throughout his academic life, Mauss was tied to the sociological legacy of Durkheim, first as disciple and then as heir. An original member of the group of scholars who surrounded Durkheim and *L'Année sociologique,* Mauss spent much of his career working with other scholars or editing the posthumous works of Durkheim, Henri Hubert, and Robert Hertz. "I have perhaps worked too much in collaboration with others," Mauss wrote (1983:140). Indeed, it is difficult to disentangle Mauss's work or find its distinctive strand.

Marcel Mauss, however, is a pivotal figure in twentieth-century anthropology. As a teacher Mauss influenced an enormous number of students, including Maurice Leenhardt, Marcel Griaule, and most explicitly, Claude Lévi-Strauss (1987; see also Clifford 1982). In the United States, Mauss's work is unevenly known, largely due to the barrier of language (Nandan 1977:xiv).

Mauss was a prolific author, writing over 350 reviews and scores of articles on diverse topics, such as the origin of Australian magic, the notion of the self, Vedic literature, and Bolshevism (Besnard 1983; Leacock 1954:59; Nandan 1977:270–283). Before his works were collected in a three-volume set (Mauss 1968–1969), his writings were "disseminated in a notoriously fragmented form"

(Baker 1987:viii). Only a dozen of Mauss's writings have been translated into English, and his principal works have been available in English only since the 1960s (Durkheim and Mauss 1963; Hubert and Mauss 1964; Mauss 1967, 1979a, 1979b, 1979c).

Mauss's work touches numerous fields, including economic anthropology, cultural ecology, the history of religion, and the fundamentals of social organization. Though trained as a philosopher, Mauss emphasized the empirical basis for understanding the nature of humanity. "I have never lost sight," Mauss wrote, "of the only goal of the discipline to which I have dedicated myself: to show and specify the role played by social life in human life through the most precise and direct contact with facts" (1983:151).

Background

Marcel Mauss was born in 1872 into an orthodox Jewish family in Lorraine. Émile Durkheim (chapter 4) was Mauss's uncle and exerted a tremendous intellectual influence on the young student. Mauss went to the University of Bordeaux to study with Durkheim, who took enormous interest in his nephew's education; for example, he designed a course on the origins of religion simply to fit Mauss's intellectual goals. (For further details of Mauss's life, see Fournier's [2006] excellent biography.)

Mauss was the first of the group of young scholars who crystallized around Durkheim and established French sociology (Besnard 1983; Nandan 1977). Mauss (1983:140) described himself as a "recruiting agent" for Durkheim, bringing together students in such diverse fields as geography, law, philosophy, linguistics, and criminology to contribute their specialized knowledge to Durkheim's "science of society." In 1898 the first volume of *L'Année sociologique* was published, and it was "the symbol and organ of the Durkheimian School" (Nandan 1977:xxviii). Volume I contained Durkheim's article on the origins of incest, an article by Georg Simmel on the maintenance of social forms, and over 130 short notes and book reviews, a quarter of them written by Mauss. Mauss was instrumental in creating the dynamic group of bright scholars who surrounded

Durkheim not as "a school of blind disciples" but as a coterie of students attracted to Durkheim's science of society (Mauss 1983:140).

But World War I sliced through the young men of *L'Année* and marked even the survivors with tragedy. Robert Hertz, Durkheim's son Andre, and many others were killed on the battlefield, decimating the *Année* group and perhaps leading to Émile Durkheim's early death in 1917. The Durkheimian mantle fell to Mauss.

After World War I, Mauss edited two volumes of *L'Année sociologique* (1925–1927). It then failed for financial reasons but was reborn as the *Annales sociologiques* and was published from 1934 to 1942 until world war again suspended normal life.

Mauss's erudition is legendary, and his broad learning began at Bordeaux. Mauss wrote that his undergraduate studies "vacillated" between the study of law, the sociology of religions, and a series of studies in collaboration with Durkheim on the history of towns, human spatial organization, and suicide (1983:140, 144). But Mauss's principal focus was the study of religious phenomena, a field that forced him to combine extended studies in history and languages. Mauss's broad education included a command of English, German, Russian, Greek, Latin, Sanskrit, Celtic, and ancient Hebrew. He was willing to tackle ambitious research projects; thus he chose for one of his two thesis subjects "prayer in all its aspects," a subject he thought would require "a short period of philological studies" but instead led him on a five-year exploration of Vedic Sanskrit, the ancient Hebrew Talmud, and the Christian liturgy, among other topics (Mauss 1983:145). This polymath learning characterizes Mauss's career. For example, the footnotes to *The Gift* contain mini-essays on the evolution of money, ancient Sanskrit commercial vocabularies, nuances of Germanic law, and forms of Kwakiutl wealth. Active in politics and a committed socialist, Mauss was revered by his students, not only for his learning, but also because he was an affable, informal man (Clifford 1982:154). Mauss's students claimed, "Mauss knows all" (Clifford 1982:182).

Mauss spent his adult life in academic institutions. In 1895 he placed third in the national *agrégation* with a degree in philosophy and in 1900 joined the faculty of the École Practique des

Hautes Études at the University of Paris. In 1901 Mauss was appointed to the chair in the "History of the Religion of Noncivilized Peoples," a position he held until 1939 when the Nazi occupation of France forced Mauss to retire. In 1925 Mauss, Paul Rivet, and Lucien Lévy-Bruhl established the Institut d'Ethnologie at the University of Paris, which became the training ground for an entire generation of French anthropologists. In 1931 Mauss was elected to the chair in sociology in the exclusive Collège de France (Fournier 2006:270–283). Mauss was renowned as a teacher, and his course summaries indicate the stunning breadth and enormous detail that Mauss brought to his lectures on topics as diverse as "North American Kinship and Religion" (1905), "Primitive Forms of Religious Language" (1913), and "Australian Dramatic Poetry" (1924). James Clifford has written,

> From the perspective of today's intellectual regime, where publication is at a premium and where any idea of value tends to be guarded for the next article or monograph, it is astonishing, indeed moving, to note the tremendous energies that Mauss poured into his teaching at Hautes Études. (1988:123)

Although Mauss never engaged in ethnographic fieldwork, he emphasized the importance of intensive participant observation as the basis for anthropological knowledge. His instructions for making ethnographic observations, such as his *Manuel d'ethnographie* (1947) or his brief instruction on the study of "Body Techniques" (1979a), indicate an anthropologist concerned with concrete ethnographic details.

Mauss's greatest contribution to anthropology, however, was his exploration of the fundamental categories of cultural behavior. Mauss wrote that he had contributed to "a social history of the categories of the human mind" (1979b:59).

A Social History of Categories

Mauss's social history of cultural categories utilized a methodology employed by Durkheim—the search for elementary forms (see pp. 50–57). Ethnographic comparison could identify essential and primordial elements of human culture through the study of primitive cultures. This search for underlying structure is a recurrent theme in Mauss's research.

For example, in 1899 Mauss coauthored a study of sacrifice with Henri Hubert described as an attempt "to disentangle the simple and elementary forms of an institution" by comparing Hindu, Old Testament, Greek, and Latin sacrificial rites (Hubert and Mauss 1964:7). Hubert and Mauss identified a schema of sacrificial rites involving separation, consecration, sacrifice, and "exit" or reintegration (a model that anticipated Arnold van Gennep's [1960] insights into rites of passage; see p. 248). Arguing that such diverse rites were not derived from a single form of primitive ritual, Hubert and Mauss found the unity of sacrifice in two principles: that all sacrificial rituals establish "a means of communication between the sacred and profane worlds" via the agent of the victim, but by the same token those two realms are kept distinct because the victim—first consecrated, then killed—is of neither realm; the sacrifice of a victim separates the two realms "while uniting them" (Hubert and Mauss 1964: 97, 100). In the closing pages of their essay, Hubert and Mauss discuss the social origin and function of sacrifice, first contending that it consists of social facts rather than individual confusions about cause and effect (an extension of Durkheim's response to Tylor's and Müller's theories of the origins of religion, see pp. 55–56), then outlining the role of sacrifice in maintaining social norms, and finally concluding with a brief synopsis of nonreligious beliefs and practices organized around the sacrifice ritual. Sacrifice, in their analysis, is a primordial social category.

Hubert and Mauss's essay employs the central methods followed by Durkheim and his students: the use of comparative data, the search for elemental categories, and the assumption that primitive societies preserved fundamental social patterns lost in industrialized societies. As discussed in chapter 4, this rationale led Durkheim to analyze religious beliefs among the Australian aborigines since their beliefs—in Durkheim's view—were most "elementary." Durkheim and Mauss believed that this strategy was superior to philosophical musings about the origins of social concepts since it was based on ethnographic "facts."

Apparently, it never occurred to either Durkheim or Mauss that traditional societies like the Australian aborigines were other than semifossilized remnants of some prehistoric human condition. In *The Gift*, for example, Mauss describes the Trobrianders and other cases studied as "good representatives of the great neolithic stage of civilization" (1967:69). Such assumptions are not unique to Mauss or Durkheim; they are found in the writings of numerous anthropologists of different theoretical stripes. Mauss never justified his assumption, except to presume that cultural patterns changed from simple to complex and to assume that traditional societies were less complex than modern industrialized ones.

Overlooking this flaw, Mauss—solely and in collaboration with Durkheim and others—pursued bold lines of investigation. For example, in *Primitive Classification* Durkheim and Mauss explored the relationship between social systems and cosmological categories "to investigate the most rudimentary classifications made by mankind, in order to see with what elements they have been constructed" (1963:9). Arguing that systems of classification—categories of space, time, color, organisms, etc.—are too complex for spontaneous invention through individual observation and inference, Durkheim and Mauss conclude that all systems of classification are learned (1963:7–8). But what was the source or model of original, primitive classifications? Durkheim and Mauss contend that classifications are modeled on the categories of social life, a crucial point that reemerges in Mary Douglas's work (see pp. 278–84).

Turning first to the Australian aborigines, Durkheim and Mauss summarized social organization as based on moieties, dual social classifications that categorize clans into two equal units; all individuals of the tribe are members of a clan that, in turn, is subsumed by one moiety or the other. Durkheim and Mauss wrote, "*Now the classification of things reproduces this classification of men*" (1963:11, emphasis in the original), and they developed this argument with additional data from Australia, North America (Zuni, Sioux), and classical China. Durkheim and Mauss showed that the spatial arrangement of clans within the Zuni pueblo parallels the spatial division of the world, and they analyzed the complexities of Chinese cosmologies as shadowy reflections of ancient clan totems. Durkheim and Mauss concluded that different aspects of classification systems point to their social origins: the description of relatedness in kinship metaphors ("humans are members of the family Hominidae"); the hierarchical nature of categories mirroring the nested social units of subclan, clan, and moiety; and the spatial orderings of people and things. Primitive classifications are not based on the individual, Durkheim and Mauss asserted, but "society." They continue, "It is this that is objectified, not man" (1963:87).

In an introductory essay to his translation of *Primitive Classification*, Rodney Needham (1963) provides a detailed critique of the logic, method, and evidence employed by Durkheim and Mauss, exposing crippling faults in their essay. Yet, Needham concludes that the essay's great merit, and one that outweighs all its faults, is that it draws attention, for the first time in sociological inquiry, to a topic of fundamental importance in understanding human thought and social life (1963:xxxiv).

With his polymath brio, Mauss consistently raised key issues for the first time. His combination of insight and erudition characterizes his best-known work, *The Gift*.

The Gift, Total Prestations, and Total Phenomena

Mauss's *Essai sur le don*, as Evans-Pritchard (1967:ix) noted, is essential for understanding Mauss's significance as a scholar. Extending Durkheim's insights into social integration, Mauss "acknowledged that society is built on solidarity, but he believed it also requires reciprocity for survival" (Fournier 2006:3). *The Gift* is a cross-cultural assay of an institution that Mauss calls "total prestations": exchanges that may appear to be voluntary but in fact are obligatory and reinforced by recognized sanctions. Mauss situates *The Gift* within a larger study of contracts—economic and social—a theme that runs through French social theory to the Enlightenment and beyond (1967:3). Mauss contributes to this debate by grounding it in ethnographic detail.

Mauss contends that the "natural economy"—in which individuals compete in a free and open market with exchange value set solely by supply and demand—simply does not exist in traditional societies. Rather, Mauss argued, exchanges in "archaic" societies occurred between groups or representatives of groups (chiefs, clan leaders, groom's family to bride's family, and so on), not between socially isolated individuals.

Further, the exchanges were not only of goods and services, but also of "courtesies, entertainments, ritual, military assistance, women, children, dances, and feasts"; the exchange of wealth was only "one part of a wide and enduring contract" (Mauss 1967:3). Such exchanges, far from being voluntary, "take it or leave it" negotiations between individuals, were surrounded by socially recognized and sanctioned obligations. Although described in the voluntary language implied by the word "gift," such total prestations are defined by a triad of obligations: the obligation to give, the obligation to receive, and the obligation to repay (Mauss 1967:37–41). While not all exchanges take this form, total prestations are recurrent social phenomena.

In an exercise of extraordinary scholarship, Mauss documents total prestations in Oceania, Melanesia, the Northwest Coast, ancient Rome, classic Hindu law, and tribal Germany. For example, Mauss discusses the potlatch of the Northwest Coast, an economic institution in which vast amounts of wealth are accumulated and given away or even destroyed in elaborate ceremonial displays (see Drucker 1965; Piddocke 1969; Schneider 1974). Mauss analyzes the potlatch as a form of antagonistic prestation in which "consumption and destruction are virtually unlimited." The potlatch is "a war of wealth" (Mauss 1967:35).

To a Western economist, such destructive redistribution of wealth is senseless. Mauss argues that such exchanges are comprehensible only within a certain cultural context. But more importantly, Mauss shows that exchanges like the potlatch or the Kula ring are not solely economic transactions: they are total phenomena.

The potlatch is certainly an economic institution, but it is also a religious institution since the chief participants are viewed as incarnations of spirits and ancestors. The potlatch is also a social phenomena as different clans, families, and social groups come together, social ties are reestablished, and points of conflict reemerge. The potlatch provides the setting for movement up the social ladder for gift givers and their families. It is thus a pivotal institution in Northwest Coast society, bridging different elements of economic, social, religious, and legal life (Mauss 1967:31–37). Mauss's exploration of total prestations became a key text in the substantivist versus formalist debate in economic anthropology; it showed how the economy was "an embedded process" (Polanyi 1957), undivorceable from other realms of society.

Many American anthropologists approach *The Gift* as a contribution to economic anthropology (e.g., Schneider 1974), but Lévi-Strauss (1987) emphasized Mauss's discussion of total social phenomena. Put another way, American anthropologists consider the work to be a study on economy of which gift exchange is one form; Lévi-Strauss approached the work as a model analysis of total social phenomena using gift exchange as an example (see pp. 236–37).

For Lévi-Strauss, *Essai sur le don* is Mauss's masterwork, not because it introduced any new facts per se, but because in that work

> for the first time in the history of ethnological thinking . . . an effort was made to transcend empirical observation and to reach deeper realities. For the first time, the social ceases to belong to the domain of pure quality—anecdote, curiosity, material for moralising description or for scholarly comparison—and becomes a system, among whose parts connections, equivalencies and interdependent aspects can be discovered. (Lévi-Strauss 1987:38)

Mauss was aware of the importance of his concept, writing that nothing "is more urgent or promising than research into 'total' social phenomena" (1967:78). Mauss's concept was to link the individual and social, specific and general, structure and process.

> We are dealing then with something more than a set of themes, more than institutional elements, more than institutions, more even than systems of institutions divisible into legal, economic, religious and other parts. We are concerned with "wholes," with systems in their entirety. . . . It is only by considering them

> as wholes that we have been able to see their essence, their operation and their living aspect, and to catch the fleeting moment when the society and its members take emotional stock of themselves and their situation as regards others. (Mauss 1967:77–78)

Lévi-Strauss (1987:39–45) argues that Mauss stood on the verge of structuralism (see pp. 236–38), a contestable claim (Clifford 1988:128; Panoff 1970). Seth Leacock offered a more cautious assessment, arguing that Mauss's emphasis on the integration of social phenomena runs throughout his work (1954:67). Yet the concept of "total social facts" remains elusive; it is not clear whether all ethnographic facts are potentially total or if some facts are total and others are not. As James Clifford (1988:63–65) has pointed out, it is an ambiguous concept, indiscriminately validating different approaches to ethnographic research. The concept "offers no guidance as to which code, key, or luminous example is to be preferred," Clifford writes (1988:64). "Social reality and the moral world" are viewed "as constructed in many possible ways, none of which may be privileged" (Clifford 1988:64).

Perhaps, Mauss seems most modern at this point; his concerns are echoed in Clifford Geertz's discussion of "thick description" (see pp. 263–66); his emphasis on dynamic social phenomena anticipates Victor Turner's concept of social drama (see pp. 250–54); and Mauss's explorations of multiple alternatives suggest a postmodernism of the early twentieth century (pp. 295–97). But any such resonances remained undeveloped and were essentially unintentional. Mauss was primarily concerned with the analysis of diverse but concrete social phenomena.

Conclusion

A number of objections may be raised to Mauss's work. First, for all his scholarship, Mauss usually cited ethnographic data to support his ideas, not to test them. Mauss rarely accepted contradictory evidence as indicating an incorrect hypothesis; such inconvenient facts could frequently be explained, at least to Mauss's satisfaction.

Second, there is a maddening ambiguity and lack of development in Mauss's work. For example, it is unclear precisely what he meant by "social morphology," and his essay on "Body Techniques" (1979a:119) contains a section titled "Techniques of the Care of the Abnormal," which in total reads, "Massages, etc. But let us move on."

Third, Mauss's assumption that non-Western societies expressed archaic survivals of ancient social patterns was never closely scrutinized, an important oversight given the antievolutionary critiques of Boas (see pp. 40–42) and other Anglo-American anthropologists of whom Mauss was aware. And finally, one can only wonder how such a creative thinker would have been transformed by an extended period of fieldwork in a living society remote from the École Practique des Hautes Études.

Nevertheless, Mauss made enormous contributions to French sociology and ethnology as a teacher, editor, and scholar. His wide-ranging scholarship and engaging mind continue to provoke, and his work remains an essential starting point for inquiry into the fundamentals of social life.

References

Baker, Felicity

1987 Translator's Note. In *An Introduction to the Work of Marcel Mauss*. F. Baker, trans. Pp. viii–ix. London: Routledge & Kegan Paul.

Besnard, Philippe

1983 The "Année Sociologique" Team. In *The Sociological Domain: The Durkheimian School and the Founding of French Sociology*. P. Besnard, ed. Pp. 11–39. Cambridge: Cambridge University Press.

Besnard, Philippe, ed.

1983 *The Sociological Domain: The Durkheimian School and the Founding of French Sociology*. Cambridge: Cambridge University Press.

Clifford, James

1982 *Person and Myth: Maurice Leenhardt in the Melanesian World*. Berkeley: University of California Press.

1988 *The Predicament of Culture: Twentieth-Century Ethnography, Literature, and Art*. Cambridge, Mass.: Harvard University Press.

Derrida, Jacques
1992 *Given Time: I, Counterfeit Money*. P. Kamuf, trans. Chicago: University of Chicago Press.

Drucker, Philip
1965 *Cultures of the North Pacific Coast*. Scranton, Pa.: Chandler.

Durkheim, Émile, and Marcel Mauss
1963 *Primitive Classification*. R. Needham, trans. Chicago: University of Chicago Press. [Originally published in 1903 as "De quelques formes primitives de classification: Contribution l'étude des représentations collectives." *L'Année Sociologique* 6:1–72.]

Evans-Pritchard, E. E.
1967 Introduction. In *The Gift: Forms and Functions of Exchange in Archaic Societies*. I. Cunnison, trans. New York: Norton. [Originally published as *Essai sur le Don, Forme Archaique de l'Change*, 1925,]

Fournier, Marcel
2006 *Marcel Mauss: A Biography*. Princeton, N.J.: Princeton University Press.

Hubert, Henri, and Marcel Mauss
1964 *Sacrifice: Its Nature and Function*. W. Halls, trans. Chicago: University of Chicago Press. [Originally published in 1899 as "Essai sur la nature et la fonction du sacrifice." *L'Année Sociologique* 2:29–138.]

Leacock, Seth
1954 The Ethnological Theory of Marcel Mauss. *American Anthropologist* 56:58–73.

Lévi-Strauss, Claude
1987 *An Introduction to the Work of Marcel Mauss*. F. Baker, trans. London: Routledge & Kegan Paul. [Originally published 1950.]

Lukes, Steven
1968 Marcel Mauss. *International Encyclopedia of the Social Sciences*. Vol. 10. D. Sills, ed. P. 7882. New York: Macmillan and Free Press.

Mauss, Marcel
1947 *Manuel d'ethnographie*. Paris: Payot.
1967 *The Gift: Forms and Functions of Exchange in Archaic Societies*. I. Cunnison, trans. New York: W. W. Norton. [Originally published in 1925 as *Essai sur le don, forme archaique de l'change*.]
1968–1969 *Oeuvres*. 3 vols. Paris: Éditions de Minuit.
1979a Body Techniques. In *Sociology and Psychology: Essays*. B. Brewster, trans. Pp. 95–123. London: Routledge & Kegan Paul. [Originally published in 1935 in *Journal de Psychologie Normale et Pathogique* 35e année:271–293.]

1979b A Category of the Human Mind: The Notion of Person, the Notion of "Self." In *Sociology and Psychology: Essays*. B. Brewster, trans. Pp. 59–94. London: Routledge & Kegan Paul. [Originally published in 1938 as "Une catégoire de l'espirit humain: La notion de personne, celle de 'moi,' un plan de travail." *Journal of the Royal Anthropological Institute* 68:263–281.]

1979c *Seasonal Variations of the Eskimo: A Study in Social Morphology*. In collaboration with Henri Beuchat. J. Fox, trans. London: Routledge & Kegan Paul. [Originally published in 1950 as "Essai sur les variations saisonnières des sociétés Eskimos: Étude de morphologie sociale." In *Sociologie et anthropologie*. Pt. 7. Paris: Presses Universitaries de France.]

1983 An Intellectual Self-Portrait. In *The Sociological Domain: The Durkheimian School and the Founding of French Sociology*. P. Besnard, ed. Pp. 139–151. Cambridge: Cambridge University Press. [Originally published 1930.]

Nandan, Yash

1977 *The Durkheimian School: A Systematic and Comprehensive Bibliography*. Westport, Conn.: Greenwood Press.

Needham, Rodney

1963 Introduction. In *Primitive Classification*. By Émile Durkheim and Marcel Mauss. Chicago: University of Chicago Press.

Panoff, Michel

1970 Marcel Mauss's *The Gift* Revisited. *Man* 5:60–70.

Piddocke, Stuart

1969 The Potlatch System of the Southern Kwakiutl: A New Perspective. In *Environment and Cultural Behavior: Ecological Studies in Cultural Anthropology*. Andrew Vayda, ed. Pp. 130–56. New York: American Museum of Natural History.

Polanyi, Karl

1957 The Economy as Instituted Process. In *Trade and Markets in the Early Empires*. K. Polanyi, C. Arensberg, and H. Pearson, eds. Pp. 243–70. Glencoe, Ill.: The Free Press

Schnieder, Harold

1974 *Economic Man: The Anthropology of Economics*. New York: Free Press.

van Gennep, Arnold

1960 *The Rites of Passage*. Chicago: University of Chicago Press. [Originally published 1909.]

10

Bronislaw Malinowski

The Functions of Culture

Bronislaw Malinowski (1884–1942) inspired strong reactions from people, and it is clear he wanted it that way. There are no tepid accounts of Malinowski; they are either hot or cold. Anthropologists tend to evaluate Malinowski on three grounds—as a fieldworker, as a theoretician, or as a personality. As a fieldworker there is near unanimity: Malinowski set new standards for ethnographic research, influencing an entire generation of anthropologists. As a theoretician, opinions of Malinowski diverge. On one hand, the British social anthropologist Audrey I. Richards wrote, "Malinowski's concept of culture, as he first developed it, was one of his most stimulating contributions to the anthropological thought of his day," concluding that this contribution has been "considerably undervalued" (1957:15). At the other extreme, Edmund Leach contrasted Malinowski's valuable fieldwork with his theoretical contribution:

> Besides altering the whole mode and purpose of ethnographic inquiry Malinowski made numerous theoretical pronouncements of a general, abstract, sociological kind, which were supposed to be valid for all cultural situations, regardless of time or space. Here, I consider, he was a failure. For me, Malinowski talking about the Trobrianders is a stimulating genius; but Malinowski discoursing on Culture in general is often a platitudinous bore. (1957:119)

Remarkably, such different opinions appear in the same collection of symposium papers edited by one of Malinowski's first and most loyal former students, Raymond Firth. Writing ten years after his death, the contributors' different assessments of Malinowski's theoretical contributions to anthropology are broadly representative. But if response to his theories was mixed, Malinowski the man was either loved or hated. One supporter said, "He had a really creative mind, an international outlook and the approach and the imagination of an artist" (Karberry cited in Firth 1988:37). In contrast, the anthropologist Clyde Kluckhohn called him "a pretentious Messiah of the credulous"—and this in an obituary in the *Journal of American Folklore* (1943:208). Who was this man who inspired such different reactions?

Background

His life began in Kraków, but it blossomed in the South Seas. Born in 1884, the son of a distinguished professor of Slavic languages, Malinowski was descended from the aristocracy and raised among the intellectuals of Poland (Kubica 1988:88–89; Thorton and Skalnik 1993). His 1908 doctorate was in physics and mathematics; his thesis, titled "On the Principle of Economy of Thought," received the highest honor in the Austrian Empire and his Ph.D. was awarded in an elaborate ceremony with a flourish of trumpets (Flis 1988). But sickness and circumstances diverted him from a career in the physical sciences to the study of sociology and anthropology.

In 1910 Malinowski began postgraduate studies at the London School of Economics where he studied with C. G. Seligman. Seligman had been a member of the 1898–1899 Cambridge University expedition to the Torres Strait region, the island-dotted channel between northern Australia and New Guinea. As Kuper describes (1983:5–6), this was a period in which British anthropologists avidly sought to collect empirical data—similar to the "salvage ethnography" of Boas and Kroeber (see pp. 67–69); the Torres Strait expedition introduced systematic field research methods to British anthropology. The ethnographic data on Australia from the Torres expedition and the earlier work on central Australian tribes by Spencer and Gillen (1899) became the fuel for various sociological writers such as Durkheim and Freud. Similarly, Malinowski's first book, *The Family among the Australian*

Aborigines, was based on previously collected ethnographic data, as was his doctorate in anthropology (awarded in 1913). Nearly thirty, Bronislaw Malinowski had yet to do any fieldwork.

But by a fluke, an opportunity occurred: Malinowski was hired as secretary to the anthropologist R. G. Marett who, in his capacity as an officer of the British Association, was traveling to Australia. World War I broke out while they were there, and Malinowski, as an Austrian subject, was classified as an enemy alien. Marett and others intervened with the Australian authorities, and Malinowski was released and allowed to remain in Australian territories, including New Guinea, and carry out fieldwork. It was an opportunity that transformed his career.

Malinowski made three field trips to New Guinea: an initial six-month visit (September 1914 to March 1915) with the Mailu of Toulon Island and two visits with the Trobriand Islanders, first from June 1915 to May 1916 and then from October 1917 to October 1918 (Karberry 1957:77). It was a period of emotional despondency, sexual frustration, hard work, and intellectual excitement, partly recorded in Malinowski's diaries published twenty-five years after his death (Malinowski 1967); the diaries and personal letters (Wayne 1995) show a complex, flawed, but brilliant man (for an exhaustive biography of Malinowski's early years, see Young 2004).

Malinowski's writings also show an ethnographer very interested in the systematic collection of ethnographic data, a subject he discusses in the opening pages of his classic study of the Trobriand Islanders, *Argonauts of the Western Pacific*. Malinowski believed that the ethnographer had to consider

> the full extent of the phenomena in each aspect of tribal culture studied, making no difference between what is commonplace, or drab, or ordinary, and what strikes him as astonishing and out-of-the-way. At the same time, the whole area of tribal culture in all its aspects has to be gone over in research. The consistency, the law and order which obtain within each aspect make also for joining them into one coherent whole. (1922:11)

To achieve this, Malinowski advocated a three-part system. First, he took the idea of the kinship chart in which complex relations are shown schematically and devised "synoptic charts" to illustrate relationships in other dimensions of culture: economic transactions, exchanges, legal practices, magical ceremonies, rights to farming lands and fishing areas, and so on. Synoptic charts expressed relationships between ethnographic data, and supplemented with genealogies, maps, plans, and diagrams, they served to outline the framework of cultural actions.

But this only covered the bare bones of cultural existence; Malinowski, if nothing else, was always interested in the pulsing complexity of social life. These nuances of behavior and action Malinowski called the "imponderabilia of actual life" (1922:20). With that phrase, Malinowski wanted ethnographers to record the subjective dynamics of daily life as experienced by another group of human beings, not just the abstract structure of a primordial society. Arguing that the ethnographer should record the particular actors and spectators in a specific ceremony, Malinowski suggested that he should forget that he understands the stated purpose and structure of the ceremony and

> try to find himself only in the midst of an assembly of human beings, who behave seriously or jocularly, with earnest concentration or with bored frivolity, who are either in the same mood as he finds them every day, or else are screwed up to a high pitch of excitement, and so on and so on. (1922:21)

Although he realized that not every ethnographer could join into native life with equal ease—joking that "perhaps the Slavonic nature is more plastic and more naturally savage than that of Western Europeans" (1922:21)—Malinowski argued that the attempt was an important counterbalance to ethnographic abstractions about society, reminding the ethnographer that his subjects are living humans and not museum specimens. Even a sharp critic like Adam Kuper acknowledges, "Malinowski's greatness lay in his ability to penetrate the web of theories to the real man, boasting, hypocritical, earthy, reasonable" (1983:35).

Malinowski knew that not every motive could be reduced to synoptic charts or observed behaviors; one had to reconstruct the subjective mental states of another culture. This information could be derived from a body of "ethnographic statements, characteristic narratives, typical utterances, items of folk-lore and magical formulae . . . as documents of native mentality" (Malinowski 1922:24).

In this manner, Malinowski collected a body of data on the Trobriand Islanders that had deep effects on anthropology. His data on the social dimensions of long-distance exchange in the Kula ring influenced Marcel Mauss's *The Gift* (pp. 127–30) and was a key text in the development of the formalist versus substantive debate in economic anthropology. Malinowski's insights about the nature of magic and science led to greater interest in cognitive anthropology and also figured in the approaches of ecological anthropology that emerged in the 1960s and 1970s (e.g., Rappaport 1968). The Trobriand Islanders became one of the classic ethnographic case studies, and on the strength of that case study Malinowski returned to England to become a major figure in social anthropology.

Kuper (1983:10) contends that Malinowski turned his life story into a "messianic self-image" that served as a "mythical charter" for the new field of social anthropology: a brilliant Polish student diverted into anthropology and imprisoned in the wilderness of Melanesia through a fluke then returns to civilization to throw out the ignorant establishment, a battle waged with the assistance of his disciples (for more on Malinowski's self-myth see Firth 1988:31–32). But this caricature aside, Malinowski began publishing substantive ethnographic articles even before returning to England, and *Argonauts of the Western Pacific* was published in 1922. He taught at the University of London in the early 1920s and by 1927 held the chair in social anthropology, which allowed him to attract numerous students and increasing international recognition. By the 1930s Malinowski lectured widely in Europe and North America, and the outbreak of World War II found him in the United States where he remained until his death in 1942. He was fifty-eight years old.

Malinowski's works remain ethnographic classics, but his contribution to anthropological theory was debated during his lifetime and is still controversial. His ethnographic concerns were with how culture met the needs of the individual, and they conflicted with another viewpoint outlined by A. R. Radcliffe-Brown that emphasized how culture met the needs of society. The two men were labeled "functionalists," a term emphasizing their perspectives on how culture "functioned" to meet specific needs. From the early 1920s until the late 1930s, Radcliffe-Brown and Malinowski saw themselves as brothers in arms, advocating a new approach to cultures that emphasized them as functionally integrated wholes (Firth 1988:16–17). Yet each saw a different source of such needs—Malinowski emphasizing the individual, Radcliffe-Brown highlighting society—and a growing distance turned into mutual distaste heightened by a fundamental difference in personalities. But to understand this difference and to evaluate Malinowski's theoretical contribution, one must begin with his theory of needs.

Theory of Needs

Malinowski's theory of needs is central to his functional approach to culture; it is the theoretical statement linking the individual and society. It is a simple notion: culture exists to meet the basic biological, psychological, and social needs of the individual. But the theory seems unduly simplistic if we do not understand Malinowski's notions of function, the hierarchy of needs, and the role of symbolism, and if we ignore the intellectual context of Malinowski's thinking.

First, Malinowski viewed function in a physiological sense: "Function, in this simplest and most basic aspect of human behavior, can be defined as the satisfaction of an organic impulse by the appropriate act. Form and function, obviously, are inextricably related to one another" (1944:83). Malinowski developed the physiological analogy further. For example, he argued that if we were to describe how a normal lung operates we would be describing the form of the process, but if we attempt to explain why the lung is operating in a certain manner then we are concerned with its function. "We could say that the formal approach corresponds to the method of observation and documentation in the statement of a vital sequence," Malinowski wrote, "while function is the restatement of what has happened in terms of scientific principles . . . a full analysis of organic and environmental happenings" (1944:83). This has several implications. First, it means that societies are integrated wholes, requiring an anthropologist to examine the interconnections of different cultural domains. Second, those domains are linked by their complementary functions, and the only anthropological explanations that can be considered to explain those causal links must be functional explanations. Thus any anthropologist unconcerned with the functions of culture is, by definition, not engaged in science.

Malinowski recognized that cultural forms do not have simple or single functions, writing that "no [cultural] institution can be functionally related to one basic need, nor yet as a rule to a simple, cultural need. . . . Culture is not and can not be a replica in terms of specific responses to specific biological needs" (1944:112). Instead, Malinowski wrote that cultural institutions are integrated responses to a variety of needs, and to outline those needs he used a variant of his synoptic charts (1944:91):

Basic Needs	Cultural Responses
1. Metabolism	1. Commissariat
2. Reproduction	2. Kinship
3. Bodily Comforts	3. Shelter
4. Safety	4. Protection
5. Movement	5. Activities
6. Growth	6. Training
7. Health	7. Hygiene

Malinowski described each of these needs and cultural responses in detail, but a few examples illustrate his argument. The first human need, metabolism, refers to "the processes of food intake, digestion, the collateral secretions, the absorption of nutritive substances, and rejection of waste matter" (Malinowski 1944:91). The cultural response, dubbed "commissariat" (literally the military unit that supplies food to an army), included (1) how food was grown, prepared, and consumed; (2) where food was consumed and in what social units; (3) the economic and social organization of the distribution of foods (e.g., trade in canned salmon or reciprocal exchange of garden products); (4) the legal and customary rules that ensure the steady operation of food distribution; and (5) the authority that enforces those rules. The basic need, safety, simply "refers to the prevention of bodily injuries by mechanical accident, attack from animals or other human beings" (Malinowski 1944:92), but the cultural response, protection, may include such different behaviors as placing houses on pilings away from potential tidal waves, the organization of armed responses to aggression, or the magical recruitment of supernatural forces. And growth—which in humans is structured by the long dependency of infants—leads to the cultural response of training by which humans are taught language, other symbols, and appropriate behaviors for different stages and situations, and are instructed until they are socially and physiologically mature (Malinowski 1944:107).

Obviously Malinowski was not reducing complex cultural systems to simple biological needs: he did not argue that salmon canneries exist in Alaska because humans need to eat. Rather, cultural responses set new conditions—literally new environments—that elicit new cultural responses. "The problems set by man's nutritive, reproductive, and hygienic needs must be solved," Malinowski wrote, and the solution in turn produces "a new, secondary, or artificial environment. This environment, *which is neither more nor less than culture itself*, has to be permanently reproduced, maintained, and managed" (1944:37, emphasis added). The cultural responses to basic needs create new conditions, and "new needs appear and new imperatives or determinants are imposed on human behavior (Malinowski 1944:37). These new derived needs or cultural imperatives are "imposed on man by his own tendency to extend his safety and his comforts" (Malinowski 1944:120), but it would be wrong to think of derived needs as somehow dispensable. "Man does not," Malinowski writes,

> by biological determinism need to hunt with spears or bow and arrow; use poison darts; nor defend himself by stockades, by shelters, or by armor. But the moment that such devices have become adopted, in order to enhance human adaptability to the environment, they also become necessary conditions for survival. (1944:121)

Such items—and the systems of training, raw material exchange, cooperative labor, etc., they require—"are one and all as indispensable under the ultimate sanction of the biological imperative of self-preservation as are any purely physiologically determined elements" (Malinowski 1944:122). New cultural responses to primordial conditions create new situations, literally new environments, to which societies must respond.

Thus culture becomes an enormously complicated behavioral web responding to complex needs that can ultimately—but not always immediately—be traced to the individual. Malinowski summarized his theory of needs with two axioms: first "that every culture must satisfy the biological systems of needs" and second, "that every cultural achievement that implies the use of artifacts and symbolism is an instrumental enhancement of human anatomy, and refers directly or indirectly to the satisfaction of a bodily need" (1944:171). In sum, culture is utilitarian, adaptive, and functionally integrated, and the explanation of culture involves the delineation of function. A classic example of that type of explanation is Malinowski's approach to magic.

The Function of Magic

Magic may seem an improbable case for functional explanation, but it was an integral element in Malinowski's theory because magic was central to Trobriand life. Magic was used to kill enemies and prevent one being killed; it was used to ease the birth of a child, to enhance the beauty of dancers, to protect fishermen, or to ensure the harvest. Magic was never mere superstition or empty gesture. Rather, Malinowski argued,

> Magic, as the belief that by spell and rite results can be obtained, . . . always appears in those phases of human action where knowledge fails man. Primitive man cannot manipulate the weather. Experience teaches him that rain and sunshine, wind, heat and cold, cannot be produced by his own hands, however much he might think about or observe such phenomena. He therefore deals with them magically. (1944:198)

Malinowski hypothesized that limited "scientific" knowledge of illness and disease led "primitive" man to conclude that illnesses are caused by sorcery and countered by magic. Malinowski—a man in ill health much of his life—wrote, "The sick man, primitive or civilized, wants to feel that something can be done. He craves for miracles" (1944:199). Magic persists in societies because it appears to work; it functions. Beyond this apparent utility, Malinowski argued that magic has a profound function in exerting human control over those dimensions that are otherwise outside of our control.

> [Magic] is always strongest there, where vital interests are concerned; where violent passions or emotions are awakened; when mysterious forces are opposed to man's endeavours; and when he has to recognise that there is something which eludes his most careful calculations, his most conscientious preparations and efforts. (Malinowski 1922:395–396)

A classic example is the way that fishing magic is organized: when fishing occurs inside the protected coral reef where "it is possible to make a catch in weather and under conditions in which no other kind of fishing is practicable . . . no magic whatever is practiced in connection with this industry" (Malinowski 1965:17). In contrast, the magic associated with ocean fishing, sailing, and canoes is complex and pervasive, because the dangers and risks are greater.

Similarly, magic surrounding gardening is extensive and considered an indispensable part of cultivation. In terms of economic activity, "agriculture always takes precedence. The districts rich in produce are on the whole politically dominant as well as economically the most wealthy," Malinowski observed (1965:12). "Garden produce is the foundation of wealth throughout the area" (Malinowski 1965:12). Garden magic is public, direct, and extensive; the village garden magician is either the headman, his heir, or closest male relative, and therefore he is either the most important or next most important person in a community. Garden magic and garden work are distinct but inseparable. Malinowski wrote,

> Magic and practical work are, in native ideas, inseparable from each other, though they are not confused. Garden magic and garden work run in one intertwined series of consecutive effort, form one continuous story, and must be the subject matter of one narrative.
>
> To the natives, magic is as indispensable to the success of gardens as competent and effective husbandry. It is essential to the fertility of the soil: [they say] "The garden magic utters magic by mouth; the magical virtue enters the soil." Magic is to them an almost natural element in the growth of the gardens. I

> have often been asked: "What is the magic which is done in your country over gardens—is it like ours or is it different?" They did not seem at all to approve of our ways as I described them. (1965:62–63)

We lack the space to describe garden rituals; Malinowski devotes over 150 pages to the horticultural and magical activities associated with gardens and the crop cycle. But the role of magic in cultivation, Malinowski believed, captured its essential function—an attempt to extend control over uncontrollable elements of nature. In this sense, Malinowski's analysis of magic reflects his functional approach to culture.

Conclusion

Malinowski's work has been criticized on numerous grounds. First, there is the valid point that Malinowski extrapolated from the Trobriand case to traditional societies in general. It has been said that Malinowski's thought moved on two levels: the specific case of the Trobrianders and the abstract, general case of man and society, which bore a striking resemblance to the Trobrianders (Nadel 1957). Second, Malinowski's approach has been criticized because it relied on the ability of the anthropologist to perceive some function of a cultural behavior that could rarely be disproved and because it basically is a crude theory in which all sorts of behaviors are reduced to simplistic notions of utility (Kuper 1983:31). One could ask, "Don't societies do things that are counterproductive for the individual?" or "Aren't there cultural elements that are nonfunctional yet maintained because they are simply customary?" It is not certain that Malinowski developed a useful answer—as opposed to a scathing rebuke—to such questions (for example, see 1944:117–119).

Yet Malinowski has been very influential, particularly on lines of anthropological theory emphasizing the adaptive significance of culture. The ecological anthropology of the 1960s and 1970s took Malinowski's basic insights, recast them as hypotheses, and tested them with quantitative data, producing such classics as Roy Rappaport's (1968) study of the role of ritual in regulating subsistence activities. And sociobiology, although its roots are in Darwinian selection and ethology, shares with functionalism the notion that cultural behaviors either impart adaptive advantages, are neutral, or are eliminated.

The greatest point of departure between Malinowski's perspective and more recent anthropological theorists (for example, Ortner [chapter 22] or Wolf [chapter 24]) is the degree to which culture is a coherent, integrated system. Modern theorists tend to see culture as characterized by major disjunctures and schisms, rather than Malinowski's perspective of culture as an integrated body of adaptive responses. And so, somewhat ironically, Malinowski's most enduring contribution was his effort to understand the subjective experience of another culture through the immersive strategy of ethnographic research.

References

Firth, Raymond
1988 Malinowski in the History of Social Anthropology. In *Malinowski between Two Worlds: The Polish Roots of an Anthropological Tradition*. R. Ellen, E. Gellner, G. Kubica, and J. Mucha, eds. Pp. 12–42. Cambridge: Cambridge University Press.

Flis, Andrzej, ed.
1988 Bronislaw Malinowski's Cracow Doctorate. In *Malinowski between Two Worlds: The Polish Roots of an Anthropological Tradition*. R. Ellen, E. Gellner, G. Kubica, and J. Mucha, eds. Pp. 195–200. Cambridge: Cambridge University Press.

Karberry, Phyliss
1957 Malinowski's Contribution to Fieldwork Methods and the Writing of Ethnography. In *Man and Culture: An Evaluation of the Work of Bronislaw Malinowski*. R. Firth, ed. Pp. 71–91. New York: Humanities Press.

Kluckhohn, C.
1943 Bronislaw Malinowski, 1884–1942. *Journal of American Folklore* 56:208–219.

Kubica, Grazyna
1988 Malinowski's Years in Poland. In *Malinowski between Two Worlds: The Polish Roots of an Anthropological Tradition*. R. Ellen, E. Gellner, G. Kubica, and J. Mucha, eds. Pp. 88–104. Cambridge: Cambridge University Press.

Kuper, Adam
1983 *Anthropology and Anthropologists: The Modern British School*. London: Routledge & Kegan Paul.

Leach, Edmund
1957 The Epistemological Background to Malinowski's Empiricism. In *Man and Culture: An Evaluation of the Work of Bronislaw Malinowski.* R. Firth, ed. Pp. 119–138. New York: Humanities Press.

Malinowski, Bronislaw
1922 *Argonauts of the Western Pacific.* London: George Routledge & Sons.
1944 *A Scientific Theory of Culture and Other Essays.* Chapel Hill: University of North Carolina Press.
1965 *Coral Gardens and Their Magic.* Vol. 1: *Soil-Tilling and Agricultural Rites in the Trobriand Islands.* Bloomington: Indiana University Press.
1967 *A Diary in the Strict Sense of the Term.* New York: Harcourt, Brace & World.

Nadel, S. F.
1957 Malinowski on Magic and Religion. In *Man and Culture: An Evaluation of the Work of Bronislaw Malinowski.* R. Firth, ed. Pp. 189–208. New York: Humanities Press.

Piddington, Ralph
1957 Malinowski's Theory of Needs. In *Man and Culture: An Evaluation of the Work of Bronislaw Malinowski.* R. Firth, ed. Pp. 33–51. New York: Humanities Press.

Rappaport, Roy
1968 *Pigs for the Ancestors: Ritual in the Ecology of a New Guinea People.* New Haven, Conn.: Yale University Press.

Richards, Audrey
1957 The Concept of Culture in Malinowski's Work. In *Man and Culture: An Evaluation of the Work of Bronislaw Malinowski.* R. Firth, ed. Pp. 15–32. New York: Humanities Press.

Spencer, Baldwin, and F. J. Gillen
1899 *Native Tribes of Central Australia.* Cambridge, U.K: Cambridge University Press.

Thorton, Robert, and Peter Skalnik, eds.
1993 *The Early Writings of Bronislaw Malinowski.* Cambridge: Cambridge University Press.

Wayne, Helena, ed.
1995 *The Story of a Marriage: The Letters of Bronislaw Malinowski and Elsie Masson.* Vol. 1: *1916–1920.* London: Routledge.

Young, Michael
2004 *Malinowski: Odyssey of an Anthropologist, 1884–1920.* New Haven, Conn.: Yale University Press.

11

A. R. Radcliffe-Brown

The Structures of Society

A. R. Radcliffe-Brown (1881–1955), Adam Kuper has noted, "has come to stand for a phase of British social anthropology which is currently out of fashion" (1977:1). Kuper suggests that such judgments are only partly deserved and rest on caricatures of Radcliffe-Brown's positions. One such misjudgment yokes Malinowski and Radcliffe-Brown with the theoretical bond of functionalism, and thus, for example, Bohannan and Glazer note, "Seen from today's vantage, it is a little difficult to appreciate what the two were arguing about professionally" (1988:294). Yet when a 1948 article (Gregg and Williams 1948) placed Malinowski and Radcliffe-Brown in the same theoretical camp, Radcliffe-Brown responded with strident outrage:

> The authors arbitrarily apply the label functionalist to certain writers on anthropology and sociology . . . they build up an imaginary picture of something they call functionalism which they then present as a body of views held by all the persons they decided to call functionalists. All the canons of scholarly integrity are ignored.
>
> Malinowski has explained that he is the inventor of functionalism, to which he gave its name. His definition of it is clear; it is the theory or doctrine that every feature of culture of any people past or present is to be explained by reference to seven biological needs of individual human beings. . . . . I reject it entirely, regarding it as useless and worse. As a consistent opponent of Malinowski's functionalism, I may be called an anti-functionalist. (1949:320–321)

In the face of such strident opposition, it seems irresponsible to treat the theories of Malinowski and Radcliffe-Brown as minor variants on the functionalist theme.

Another criticism holds that Radcliffe-Brown conceived of social anthropology as an ahistorical inquiry resulting in a static view of societies unconcerned with diachronic change (White 1966). There is merit and confusion in such claims. On one hand, Radcliffe-Brown distanced himself from those anthropologists who, "thinking of their study as a kind of historical study, fall back on conjecture and imagination, and invent 'pseudo-historical' or 'pseudo-causal' explanations" (1977b:13). Radcliffe-Brown leaves these anthropologists unnamed, but Tylor's discussion of animism would fit this description (see pp. 55–56). Radcliffe-Brown's distinction between historical and scientific explanations was extended by his American students, including Robert Redfield who wrote that

> Radcliffe-Brown's signal contribution is . . . derived . . . from his emphasis on a strictly nonhistorical, sharply scientific method in anthropology. The objective of social anthropology is the formulation of general propositions as to society. The social anthropologist deals with classes of social phenomena; early [*sic*] he names the class with which he deals—sanctions, totemism, Omaha type of kinship system, or whatever; the particular society or institution with which he deals is then of significance only as it represents or modifies the class, type or declared general proposition. History, on the other hand has a logical nature essentially different; its nature [citing Kroeber] ". . . an endeavor at descriptive integration." (1962:xi)

This is an extraordinary statement for its time (1937), a clear contrast to the historical particularism of Boas, Kroeber, and others who considered explanation as primarily a historical reconstruction of specific cultural complexes. The notion that one could extract a concept—such as the Omaha type of kinship system—from its specific social context and make that abstraction the object of inquiry did not sit well with Boas or his students. Radcliffe-Brown observed, "My objection to conjectural history is not that it is historical but that it is conjectural" (1952c:50).

Elsewhere, Radcliffe-Brown condemns conjectural history as "worse than useless" but adds, "this does not in any way imply the rejection of historical explanation but quite the contrary" (1977b:13). Radcliffe-Brown's concern was to create a social anthropology that was generalizing and thus a science.

Kuper notes that Radcliffe-Brown has receded from the anthropological spotlight in Great Britain and the United States, although his influence on different anthropologists is evident (for example on Evans-Pritchard, chapter 12; Lévi-Strauss, chapter 17; and Turner, chapter 18, among others.) The repercussions of Radcliffe-Brown's approach are expressed by those who emulated him and those who vehemently disavow his work. Paradoxically, as Kuper notes, Radcliffe-Brown "remains influential, but, increasingly, indirectly" (1977:1).

Background

Born in 1881, Radcliffe-Brown was educated at Trinity College, Cambridge. The biographical sketches published after his death (Eggan and Warner 1956; Fortes 1956) contain scant information on Radcliffe-Brown's early years or personal life, possibly reflecting a "streak of aloofness" and somewhat reserved nature (Fortes 1956:153). Remembered as warm and gentle by his friends and students, he was considered condescending and pompous by others, particularly by Boas's students. This was complicated by Radcliffe-Brown's tendency to cite the work of his students and ignore the work of others—which effectively slighted all research conducted in America prior to his arrival at the University of Chicago in 1931. It is amazing how unpopular he was with American anthropologists. Mead called him insufferable, sulky, and rude. Benedict wrote, "He seemed to me impenetrably wrapped in his own conceit" (1973:327). Leslie White described "two traits of Radcliffe-Brown—the tendency to assume originality for himself, and to ignore or depreciate the work of others" (1966:32). These personal reactions may have limited Radcliffe-Brown's influence on some, but his contribution to the development of anthropology remains.

Under Haddon's direction, Radcliffe-Brown conducted fieldwork from 1906 to 1908 on the Andaman Islands, a chain of islands off the southern coast of Myanmar (Burma). Radcliffe-Brown finished his thesis in 1909, which was a descriptive account of traditional culture influenced by the work of Haddon and Rivers. In the year after completing his thesis, Radcliffe-Brown became aware of the work of Durkheim and Mauss and began rewriting his thesis to explore this newly found theoretical position. Although *The Andaman Islanders* was not published until 1922, it became the vehicle through which French comparative sociology shaped the course of British social anthropology.

Radcliffe-Brown conducted ethnographic research among the Kariera and other aboriginal groups in western Australia from 1910 to 1912. He then returned to England and became an overseas education officer during World War I. After the war, Radcliffe-Brown occupied a number of academic positions, frequently establishing new anthropology departments: University of Cape Town (1921–1926), University of Sydney (1926–1931), and the University of Chicago (1931–1937). Next he returned to Oxford where he remained until his retirement in 1946, after which he taught in Cairo and South Africa. Radcliffe-Brown died in England in 1955.

Radcliffe-Brown's impact is evident in the writings of his students. When he left the University of Chicago, his students presented Radcliffe-Brown with a volume titled *Social Anthropology of North American Tribes* (Eggan 1962). That group—including Fred Eggan, Morris Opler, and Sol Tax—all became important figures in American anthropology. Robert Redfield wrote in the introduction:

> Professor Radcliffe-Brown brought to this country a method for the study of society, well-defined and different enough from what prevailed here to require American anthropologists to reconsider the whole matter of method, to scrutinize their objectives, and to attend to new problems and new ways of looking at problems. (1962:ix)

Radcliffe-Brown called that approach "social anthropology."

Social Anthropology: Defining a Field

Radcliffe-Brown distinguished "social anthropology" from ethnology. In a 1951 lecture, Radcliffe-Brown pointed out that Boas had set two research objectives: (1) the reconstruction of the cultural history of a particular people or region, and (2) the "investigation of the laws governing social life" (1977a:54). Noting that Boas had referred synonymously to the field of inquiry as "ethnology" or "anthropology," Radcliffe-Brown proposed that the terms should mark different lines of inquiry, suggesting that anthropologists

> refer to those investigations that are concerned with the reconstruction of history as belonging to ethnology and to keep the term social anthropology for the study of discoverable regularities in the development of human society in so far as these can be illustrated or demonstrated by the study of primitive peoples. (1977a:54)

The observation of regularities and search for general laws characterizes Radcliffe-Brown's social anthropology. Although Boas recognized the potential existence of laws of human behavior, in fact most of Boas's efforts went to the explication of particular cultural developments. Radcliffe-Brown's 1951 lecture was a response, fifty-five years after the fact, to Boas's (1896) "The Limitations of the Comparative Method of Anthropology" in which Boas attacked the Victorian evolutionists (see pp. 40–42). Boas had argued that focused, intensive fieldwork was essential, not loose comparisons based on uneven published sources. Radcliffe-Brown responded that comparative studies were also necessary and that library research was useful when it supplemented ethnographic fieldwork. Radcliffe-Brown complained that the modern anthropology graduate student setting out for fieldwork "is told that he must consider any feature of social life in its context, in its relation to the other features of the particular social system in which it is found. But he is often not taught to look at it in the wider context of human societies in general" (1977a:54). This is what Radcliffe-Brown proposed to do.

Social anthropology was grounded in the comparative method; its goal was the elucidation of lawlike generalizations about human society. Radcliffe-Brown considered social anthropology to be a subdiscipline of comparative sociology—a discipline that he traced to the French social theorists such as Montesquieu and Comte, but most directly to Durkheim. Social anthropology differed from comparative sociology in scope but not in intent. Radcliffe-Brown wrote, "Comparative sociology, of which social anthropology is a branch, is here conceived as a theoretical or nomothetic study of which the aim is to provide acceptable generalisations. The theoretical understanding of a particular institution is its interpretation in the light of such generalisations" (1977b:13).

"Nomothetic"—from the Greek *nomos* for "law"—refers to the structure of scientific explanation. Scientific laws—like the law of gravity or the second law of thermodynamics—are generalizing propositions about the relationship between two or more factors. They are not idiographic explanations of a particular occurrence but are broadly relevant to all cases that express that relationship. Thus, Newton's law of gravity was not an explanation of why a particular apple fell out of a particular tree one day (to use the apocryphal example), but a statement about all bodies of matter characterized by mass and distance. Radcliffe-Brown envisioned an anthropology that could discover scientific laws about human society, cross-cultural regularities between "structure" and "function."

Structure and Function

Radcliffe-Brown's notion of social structure made his comparative approach possible; this was his unit of comparison. Social structures, Radcliffe-Brown argued, are the relations of association between individuals, and they exist independently of the individual members who might occupy those positions, much in the way that "hero," "heroine," and "villain" define a set of relationships in a melodrama regardless of the actors who play those roles. Social structures are not abstractions; unlike "culture," they exist and may be directly observed:

> We do not observe a "culture," since that word denotes, not any concrete reality, but an abstraction, and as it is commonly used a vague abstraction. But direct observation does reveal to us that . . . human beings are connected by a complex network of social relations. I use the term "social structure" to denote this network of actually existing relations. (Radcliffe-Brown 1952a:190)

Social structure includes all interpersonal relations, the differentiation of individuals and groups by their social roles, and the relationships between a particular group of humans and a larger network of connections. Although Radcliffe-Brown contends that social structures are concrete realities, they are not what an individual fieldworker observes in a specific society, which Radcliffe-Brown describes as "social forms."

This is confusing and an example is in order. If I am conducting a study of cooperative work groups in a peasant community, over the course of my fieldwork I will observe (hopefully) a number of cases of different groups of people getting together at various times to work in different people's fields. I will take notes on the participants, their efforts, and the interpersonal dynamics of the group. At that point, in Radcliffe-Brown's terminology, I would be describing social forms. But if I recorded "as precisely as possible the *general* or *normal* form of this relationship, abstracted from the variations of particular instances, though taking account of those variations" (Radcliffe-Brown 1952a:192, emphasis added), then I would be describing the social structure of corvée labor. We will sidestep the issue about whether, thus defined, social structure is a result of observation or an inferred creation; obviously, Radcliffe-Brown considered social structures to be empirically knowable and concrete.

This notion of structure, as Adam Kuper observes, "is perhaps the main contemporary stumbling-block to an understanding of what Radcliffe-Brown was saying" (1977:5). Part of the confusion stems from alternate uses of the word "structure," most notably in Claude Lévi-Strauss's structural anthropology (see chapter 17).

For Lévi-Strauss, "The term 'social structure' has nothing to do with empirical reality but with models which are built up after it" (1963:279). Radcliffe-Brown wrote to Lévi-Strauss:

> As you have recognized, I use the term "social structure" in a way so different from yours as to make discussion so difficult as to be unlikely to be profitable. While for you social structure has nothing to do with reality but in models which are built up, I regard the social structure as a reality. When I pick up a particular sea shell on the beach, I recognize it as having a particular structure. I may find other shells of the same species which have a similar structure so that I can say there is a form of structure characteristic of the species. (1977c:42)

Thus, we can identify certain social structures—exogamous moieties, joking relationships, corvée labor, cross-cousin marriage, and on and on—compare those structures as manifested in different societies, and then attempt to understand the underlying principles that account for these different social structures. Almost inevitably, Radcliffe-Brown's explanation of social structures leads to a consideration of function.

For Radcliffe-Brown, the function of cultural institutions was the role they played in maintaining society, not the satisfaction of individuals' needs as Malinowski argued. Like many theories of human society, the notion is based on the organic analogy, referring to activities meeting the needs of the structure. Extrapolated to the social realm,

> the continuity of structure is maintained by the process of social life, which consists of the activities and interactions of the individual human beings and of the organized groups into which they are united. The social life of the community is here defined as the *functioning* of the social structure. The *function* of a crime, or a funeral ceremony, is the part it plays in the social life as a whole and therefore the contribution it makes to the maintenance of structural continuity. (Radcliffe-Brown 1952b:180, emphasis in the original)

And,

> Such a view implies that a social system . . . has a certain kind of unity, which we may speak of as a functional unity. We may

> define it as a condition in which all parts of the system work together with a sufficient degree of harmony or internal consistency, i.e., without producing persistent conflicts which can neither be resolved nor regulated. (Radcliffe-Brown 1952b:181)

Such passages have led to the reasonable criticism of Radcliffe-Brown's view as overly static and synchronic. In a footnote to the above quotation, Radcliffe-Brown rather offhandedly comments, "Opposition, i.e., organised and regulated antagonism, is, of course, an essential feature of every social system," a scant recognition of social conflict. Radcliffe-Brown acknowledges the changes traditional societies underwent due to the imposition of European colonialism, but he did not actually analyze such postcolonial changes. Rather, Radcliffe-Brown laments the scarcity of unaltered traditional societies and the absence of precontact historical data and retreats into another attack on pseudohistory (1952b:183–184). Clearly diachronic study was not Radcliffe-Brown's preferred mode of inquiry; his contribution was in the analysis of social structures.

Eaglehawk, Crow, and the Cult of the Ancestors

Radcliffe-Brown observed that "the only really satisfactory way of explaining a method is by means of illustration" (1977a:54), and two examples make that clear—his analyses of exogamous moieties and of Andaman Islanders' ritual. Exogamous moieties are kin systems in which a population is divided into two social divisions and a man of one moiety must marry a woman of another moiety. Radcliffe-Brown began his analysis with the case of aboriginal groups in the interior of New South Wales in which moieties were matrilineal, exogamous, and the two divisions were named after their respective totems, the eaglehawk (Kilpara) and the crow (Makwara). How to explain this? Radcliffe-Brown argues that neither conjectural history nor diffusion provides satisfying explanations and turns to a comparison of social structures. Radcliffe-Brown examines other cases from Australia and finds many cases of exogamous moieties—some patrilineal, others matrilineal—named after birds. Further, other forms of dual organization (such as a system of alternating generational divisions in which you, your grandparents, and your grandchildren are members of a social group different from your parents', children's, and great-grandchildren's) are also named by pairs of birds. A search for more cases finds examples of moieties named by other pairs of animals (two species of kangaroos, for example). Radcliffe-Brown pursues a series of progressively broader questions, from "Why Eaglehawk vs. Crow?" to "Why all these birds?" to

> What is the principle by which such pairs as eaglehawk and crow, eagle and raven, coyote and wild cat are chosen as representing the moieties of a dual division? The reason for asking this question is not idle curiosity. We may, it can be held, suppose that an understanding of the principle in question will give us an important insight into the way in which the natives themselves think about the dual division as part of their social structure. (1977a:57)

Radcliffe-Brown analyzes stories about eaglehawk and crow and other moiety referents to gain insights into native thinking. It is a search for systems of classification similar to those discussed by Durkheim (chapter 4) and Mauss (chapter 9). The common element in all these tales may be distilled into a single theme: "The resemblances and differences of animal species are translated into terms of friendship and conflict, solidarity and opposition. In other words the world of animal life is represented in terms of social relations similar to those of human society" (Radcliffe-Brown 1977a:59). Eaglehawk and crow are both meat eaters, but eaglehawk hunts and crow steals. Other examples of oppositions between related entities are black cockatoo versus white cockatoo, coyote versus wildcat (in California), upstream versus downstream, and so on. They are all associated with exogamous moieties, leading Radcliffe-Brown to conclude that "wherever, in Australia, Melanesia or America, there exists a social structure of exogamous moieties, the moieties are thought of as being in a relation of what is here called 'opposition'" (1977a:61).

Radcliffe-Brown presented his analysis of exogamous moieties as an example of the comparative approach and the conceptual utility of social structure. Moving from the specific case to increasing levels of generalization, Radcliffe-Brown posed a series of interesting questions, not just about the societies of New South Wales, but about human societies in general.

Radcliffe-Brown's concern with society in general is clear from a 1945 lecture on "Religion and Society" in which he contrasted totemism and ancestor worship (1977d). He narrowly defines ancestor worship as the worship of a deceased ancestor or ancestors by an associated descent group such as a lineage or clan. Offerings of food and drink are made to the ancestors, which are usually conceived of as sharing a meal with the ancestors (Radcliffe-Brown 1977d:113–114). The rites of ancestor worship also reflect a sense of dependency between the worshiper and the ancestors—ancestors will give him children and well-being, provide blessings if propitiated, send illness and disaster if ignored (Radcliffe-Brown 1977d:125). Not surprisingly, ancestor worship is most developed among societies where unilineal descent is most important:

> In such a society what gives stability to the social structure is the solidarity and continuity of the lineage, and of the wider group (the clan) composed of related lineages. For the individual, his primary duties are those of lineage. These include duties to the members now living, but also to those who have died and to those who are not yet born. In the carrying out of these duties he is controlled and inspired by the complex systems of sentiments of which we may say . . . are centered [on] the lineage itself, past, present and future. It is primarily this system of sentiments that is expressed in the rites of the cult of the ancestors. The social function of the rites is obvious: by giving solemn and collective expression to them the rites reaffirm, renew and strengthen those sentiments on which the social solidarity depends. (Radcliffe-Brown 1977d:114)

Note that Radcliffe-Brown has done more than engage in idle speculation; he has proposed testable hypotheses: Does ancestor worship only occur in lineage-based societies? Are the sentiments expressed always those of dependency? Does ancestor worship diminish when traditional social forms weaken? He also produced a broader theoretical statement about "the social function of religions, i.e. the contribution they make to the formation and maintenance of a social order" (1977d:104).

Conclusion

Radcliffe-Brown's analysis of social structure and function redirected anthropological inquiry to the institutions of human life and to the role such institutions play in the maintenance and reproduction of society. Today these concerns are not as central as they were between 1930 and 1960 when British social anthropology was at its peak, and consequently Radcliffe-Brown's stature has declined (again, see Kuper 1977). An examination of the two principal social anthropology journals in the United Kingdom and the United States, *Journal of the Royal Anthropological Institute* (formerly *Man*) and *American Ethnologist*, respectively, shows that since 1995 Radcliffe-Brown was rarely cited, and only to be briefly acknowledged (Borneman 1996; Lipset 2004; Stasch 2002) or criticized (Dean 1995; Gupta 1995; Harrison 1995; Keen 1995). Over the last decade, Radcliffe-Brown tends to be cited either when a specific social dimension is discussed—like descent theory (Shapiro 1988) or brother-sister relationship (Joseph 1994)—or in matters relating to Australian kinship systems, for example, Cowlishaw's (1987:229–230) brief critical assessment of Radcliffe-Brown's contribution to studies of Australian aborigines.

Adam Kuper writes of Radcliffe-Brown, "The profound yet second-hand nature of his influence on modern anthropology may constitute a real difficulty for the contemporary reader" (1977:2). This suggests that the ideas of Radcliffe-Brown may deserve open-minded rereading.

References

Benedict, Ruth
1973 *An Anthropologist at Work: Writings of Ruth Benedict*. M. Mead, ed. Equinox Books: New York.

Boas, Franz
1896 The Limitations of the Comparative Method of Anthropology. *Science* 4:901–908.

Bohannan, Paul, and Mark Glazer, eds.
1988 *High Points in Anthropology*. New York: McGraw-Hill.

Borneman, John
1996 Until Death Do Us Part: Marriage/Death in Anthropological Discourse. *American Ethnologist* 23(3):215–238.

Cowlishaw, Gillian
1987 Colour, Culture and the Aboriginalists. *Man* 22(2):221–37.

Dean, Bartholomew
1995 Forbidden Fruit: Infidelity, Affinity, and Brideservice among the Urarina of Peruvian Amazonia. *Journal of the Royal Anthropological Institute* 1:87–110.

Eggan, Fred, ed.
1962 *Social Anthropology of North American Tribes*. 1937. Reprint, Chicago: University of Chicago Press.

Eggan, Fred, and W. Lloyd Warner
1956 Alfred Reginald Radcliffe-Brown. *American Anthropologist* 58:544–47.

Fortes, Meyer
1956 Alfred Reginald Radcliffe-Brown, F.B.P., 1881–1955: A Memoir. *Man* 41:149–53.

Gregg, D., and E. Williams
1948 The Dismal Science of Functionalism. *American Anthropologist* 50:594–611.

Gupta, Akil
1995 Blurred Boundaries: The Discourse of Corruption, the Culture of Politics and the Imagined State. *American Ethnologist* 22:335–402.

Harrison, Simon
1995 Four Types of Symbolic Conflict. *Journal of the Royal Anthropological Institute* 1:255–272.

Joseph, Suad
1994 Brother/Sister Relationships: Connectivity, Cousins and Power in the Reproduction of Patriarchy in Lebanon. *American Ethnologist* 21:50–73.

Keen, Ian
1995 Metaphor and Metalanguage: "Groups" in Northeast Arnhemland. *American Ethnologist* 22:502–527.

Kuper, Adam
1977 Preface. In *The Social Anthropology of Radcliffe-Brown*. A. Kuper, ed. Pp. 1–7. London: Routledge & Kegan Paul.

Lévi-Strauss, Claude
1963 *Structural Anthropology*. New York: Basic.

Lipset, David
2004 "The Trial": A Parody of the Law and the Mockery of Men in Post-Colonial Papua New Guinea. *Journal of the Royal Anthropological Institute* 10(1):63–89.

Radcliffe-Brown, A. R.
1922 *The Andaman Islanders*. Cambridge: Cambridge University Press.
1949 Functionalism: A Protest. *American Anthropologist* 51:320–322.
1952a On Social Structure. In *Structure and Function in Primitive Society*. E. Evans-Pritchard and F. Eggan, eds. Pp. 188–204. London: Cohen and West.
1952b On the Concept of Function in Social Science. In *Structure and Function in Primitive Society*. E. Evans-Pritchard and F. Eggan, eds. Pp. 178–187. London: Cohen and West.
1952c The Study of Kinship Systems. In *Structure and Function in Primitive Society*. E. Evans-Pritchard and F. Eggan, eds. Pp. 49–89. London: Cohen and West.
1977a The Comparative Method in Social Anthropology. In *The Social Anthropology of Radcliffe-Brown*. A. Kuper, ed. Pp. 53–69. London: Routledge & Kegan Paul.
1977b Introduction. In *The Social Anthropology of Radcliffe-Brown*. A. Kuper, ed. Pp. 11–24. London: Routledge & Kegan Paul.
1977c Letter to Lévi-Strauss. In *The Social Anthropology of Radcliffe-Brown*. A. Kuper, ed. P. 42. London: Routledge & Kegan Paul.
1977d Religion and Society. In *The Social Anthropology of Radcliffe-Brown*. A. Kuper, ed. Pp. 103–128. London: Routledge & Kegan Paul.

Redfield, Robert
1962 Introduction. In *Social Anthropology of North American Tribes*. F. Eggan, ed. Pp. ix–xiv. Chicago: University of Chicago Press. [Originally published 1937.]

Shapiro, Warren
1988 Ritual Kinship, Ritual Incorporation and the Denial of Death. *Man* 23:275–297.

Stasch, Rupert
2002 Joking Avoidance: A Korowai Pragmatics of Being Two. *American Ethnologist* 29(2):335–365.

White, Leslie
1966 The Social Organization of Ethnological Theory. *Rice University Studies* 52(4). Houston, Tex.: Rice University.

12

Edward Evans-Pritchard

Social Anthropology, Social History

Edward E. Evans-Pritchard (1902–1973) was the errant son of British social anthropology; he first followed its tenets, then attacked them. During the 1940s, Evans-Pritchard's theoretical outlook changed from a perspective essentially shaped by Radcliffe-Brown to an anthropological vision more attentive to social history and human agency. His early work included classic ethnographies like *Witchcraft, Oracles and Magic among the Azande* (1937), *The Nuer* (1940), *Kinship and Marriage among the Nuer* (1951), and he edited with Meyer Fortes and contributed to *African Political Systems* (Fortes and Evans-Pritchard 1940), a then "state-of-the-art" collection, all within the British social anthropology school of thought. Like Radcliffe-Brown, Evans-Pritchard's earlier works emphasize structure and function in social relationships. The articles in *African Political Systems* also tend to be synchronic and isolating, separating twentieth-century African societies from their historical past and colonial present. In reference to *African Political Systems*, Marvin Harris points out that 350 years of the slave trade followed by a century of direct European control created enormous cultural change: "Advancing before this scourge [of slavers] were shock waves of wars, migrations, political upheavals, and vast demographic changes. In such a context, restriction to an ethnographic present of the 1930s, in the name of empiricism, has little to commend it" (1968:536).

British social anthropology has fallen out of favor because of this ahistorical perspective, its emphasis on social stasis, and a tendency to reify society and to diminish the role of the individual. Evans-Pritchard's works prior to the 1950s are vulnerable to this criticism. For example, in *The Nuer* (1940) he documented the age-grade system of the Nuer in which every four years a new group of teenage boys underwent an initiation rite; this cohort formed an age-set, and as these males grew older, different behaviors would be expected of them. Evans-Pritchard called this progression "structural time," calendrical intervals marked by predictable changes in status.

> Seasonal and lunar changes repeat themselves year after year, so that a Nuer standing at any point of time has conceptual knowledge of what lies before him and can predict and organize his life accordingly. A man's structural future is likewise already fixed and ordered into different periods, so that the total changes in status a boy will undergo in his ordained passage through the social system, if he lives long enough, can be foreseen. (Evans-Pritchard 1940:94–95)

In this passage Evans-Pritchard makes even a person's life cycle static, reducing the individual to a staircase of status changes. This analysis is particularly intriguing given that it occurs in the best known work of an anthropologist who would later become famous for his emphasis on history and the importance of the individual.

Ten years after the publication of *The Nuer*, Evans-Pritchard argued a very different line distinctly at odds with the British social anthropology tradition: social anthropology should be recast into social history (Evans-Pritchard 1950). So what happened between 1940 and 1950? Why did Evans-Pritchard's ideas change? What core elements of his thought have been retained by contemporary anthropology?

Background

Evans-Pritchard's life and work were shaped by the British empire. Born in 1902, Evans-Pritchard studied history at Oxford, receiving his M.A. in modern history in 1924. He began his anthropological studies at the London School of Economics where he studied under C. G. Seligman, one of the members of the Torres Strait expedition directed by Haddon. According to Beidelman, "He left Oxford for London partly for a change of environment but mainly because he wanted to do field research and no one in Oxford had done that" (1974:1). He arrived at the London School of Economics the same term that Malinowski arrived to teach; in fact, Evans-Pritchard and Raymond Firth were Malinowski's first students. Evans-Pritchard was closer to Seligman, however, and apparently kept his distance from Malinowski.

In 1926 Seligman was contracted to provide an ethnographic survey of the indigenous groups of the Anglo-Egyptian Sudan. When Seligman became ill, he arranged for Evans-Pritchard to carry on the fieldwork. Nearly fifty years later Evans-Pritchard recalled his professors' advice before his first fieldwork experience:

> I first sought advice from Westermarck. All I got from him was "don't converse with an informant for more than twenty minutes because if you aren't bored by that time he will be." Very good advice, even if somewhat inadequate. I sought instruction from Haddon, a man foremost in field-research. He told me that it was really all quite simple; one should always behave as a gentleman. Also very good advice. My teacher, Seligman, told me to take ten grains of quinine every day and to keep off women. The famous Egyptologist, Sir Flinders Petrie, just told me not to bother about drinking dirty water as one soon became immune to it. Finally, I asked Malinowski and was told not to be a bloody fool. (1976:240)

There is an amateurish dash about all this, replete with "stiff upper lip–isms," but the Anglo-Egyptian government was paying for this ethnographic survey (and most of Evans-Pritchard's subsequent research) because the government had a serious objective.

The goal was empire. The British government wanted to assert imperial control over African peoples like the Azande and Nuer living in the watershed between the Nile and the Congo rivers. Initially British control was via indirect rule in which local political authorities were maintained but depended on colonial administrators, but in the early 1920s imperial authority was more directly applied. The traditional scattered Azande homesteads were forcibly resettled along new government roads. The expressed intent was to control sleeping sickness; the obvious consequence was to control the Azande (Gillies 1976:viii). In 1930 Evans-Pritchard began his work among the Nuer right after the British military had bloodily suppressed Nuer revolts (Evans-Pritchard 1940:11). He agreed to conduct the study with great hesitation, because, according to Douglas (1980:40), he felt responsible as an anthropologist to serve as a mediator between the Nuer and the government. "The Nuer would fight until they were destroyed." Evans-Pritchard recalled, "When I entered a [Nuer] cattle camp it was not only as a stranger but as an enemy, and they seldom tried to conceal their disgust at my presence, refusing to answer my greetings and even turning away when I addressed them" (1940:11).

Much of Evans-Pritchard's work was conducted under government auspices and was frequently written to inform British administrators (for example, 1937:3–4). Some of his investigations would raise ethical issues today that he and his contemporaries ignored. But Evans-Pritchard did not engage in espionage; he always made his intentions known to the people he studied and lived with and respected them.

Evans-Pritchard received his Ph.D. in 1927 by writing up the results of his first three months of fieldwork among the Azande for his thesis. Over the next three years he spent twenty months among the Azande. Between field trips he was lecturer in social anthropology at the London School of Economics, and in 1932 he became professor of sociology at Fuad I University in Cairo. He resigned that post to become a research lecturer in African sociology at Oxford, a position he held until the outbreak of World War II.

During the war, Evans-Pritchard led a guerrilla force along the Sudanese/Ethiopian border against the Italians, earning this headline in a London newspaper: "OXFORD DON GUERRILLA: LED ABYSSINIAN TRIBESMEN." He also served as an intelligence officer and political officer in Ethiopia, Sudan, Syria, and Libya. Referring to Evans-Pritchard's life, a colleague recalled, "Parts of his own life . . . had a fictional quality" (Lienhardt 1974:300).

He returned to England in 1945 and after a year at Cambridge, became professor of social anthropology at Oxford, succeeding Radcliffe-Brown. He remained at Oxford until he retired in 1970. Even after retirement, he remained very active. His bibliography lists twenty-one publications for 1970 alone, and although many are relatively brief reviews, prefaces, and notes, they range over topics like the sociology of Comte, witchcraft in Tudor and Stuart England, and nine different pieces about the Zande (Evans-Pritchard 1974a). He produced "one of the largest published ethnographic collections in social anthropology" (Lienhardt 1974:304).

But where are Evans-Pritchard's theories of human behavior in all of this ethnographic research? They are present but intentionally hidden. Douglas writes, "The relation of his ethnographic researches to contemporary speculations or theory was never spelled out in his big fieldwork monographs. As a matter of principle, these were written with practically no polemics, no controversies, no disputatious thrashing out of definitions" (1980:24). Instead, his ethnographic writing was a presentation of "a coherent story, omitting nothing, twisting nothing, and adding nothing that could not be justified. The theoretical burden would be found in the internal consistency of a large body of ethnographic analysis, in which other ethnographers would discern theoretical innovations" (Douglas 1980:24).

Evans-Pritchard believed that theories were inferred from local realities and that, therefore, general pronouncements should fade into the background. Evans-Pritchard's goal was to present a body of ethnographic work that was entire, coherent, and an accurate presentation of indigenous belief. Yet running through much of his work is an idea that Douglas calls Evans-Pritchard's "theory of accountability."

A Theory of Accountability

Mary Douglas has written brilliantly about Evans-Pritchard, placing his work within a larger theoretical debate (compare Gellner 1981:xv–xvi). Douglas writes, "One of the present crises in sociology comes from the criticisms of phenomenologists.

Maintaining that social understanding must start from the human experience of consciousness and reflection, they despair of truth in any so-called human science that ignores the distinctively human element" (1980:2).

Phenomenologists would dismiss theories proposed by White, Harris, and Radcliffe-Brown, for example, because their respective points of view argue that cultural life is knowable independently of the experience of its participants, holding that what informants think or perceive of reality is not necessarily the starting point for inquiry. Phenomenologists basically give explanatory priority to the informant's subjective view. Douglas continues,

> These critics have undermined confidence in the traditional methods and even in the traditional objectives of sociology. Consequently, many scholars sensitive to the criticism have been tempted to give up striving for objectivity and to shift their own writing into a mystical mode, indulgent to their own subjectivity. Others, who would still like to try for objective comparisons, find little alternative but to work on in the old framework of inquiry, and so tend to shirk these issues. In advance of this critical juncture Evans-Pritchard felt the dilemma keenly. (1980:2)

The dilemma is this: Where does culture exist other than in the perceptions, beliefs, and actions of individuals? This is the issue Sapir encountered when he read about the contrary Omaha, Two Crows (see pp. 93–94). How can we state, "The Nuer believe X," when we really need to list the opinions of each individual Nuer, as expressed at a particular time? And if culture only exists with the individual, how can comparisons between individuals—let alone between cultures—be made? And finally, and most problematically, how can an anthropologist's statement about another culture be anything more than her or his individual perception of another individual's expression, a flimsy bridge of communication across a chasm of cultural difference?

As Douglas suggests, one response to the dilemma is to say "The hell with it!" and focus on issues that do not require such epistemological turmoil. Another approach is to retreat into a co-

coon of hypersubjectivity in which ethnography and autobiography are not distinguished.

Evans-Pritchard, Douglas suggests, attempted to find a way through the dilemma:

> He taught that the essential point for comparison is that at which people meet misfortune. They may accuse others, they may accept responsibility. They count different kinds of misfortune as needing explanation. As they work their ideas of blame and compensation into their social institutions, they invoke existences and powers that are adapted to each particular accounting system. There are ways of getting valid evidence on these essential moral purposes as they surface from consciousness into action. (1980:3)

For example, how do we deal with misfortune in modern America? We litigate. If we spill scalding coffee on ourselves, we sue the restaurant that heated it. If we slip on ice and break a leg, we sue the store that should have shoveled the sidewalk. In American society, we appeal to the legal system to establish responsibility—even over "accidents"—and to assess penalties. An exploration of accountability in American society would readily identify major themes of a cultural life.

Similarly, Evans-Pritchard followed the threads of accountability in his classic studies of the Azande. He wrote, "I suppose that the simplest way of assessing an African people's way of looking at life is to ask to what they attribute misfortune, and for the Azande the answer is witchcraft" (1967:11).

Azande Witchcraft: The Allocation of Accountability

"Witchcraft is ubiquitous," Evans-Pritchard (1976:18) wrote,

> I had no difficulty in discovering what the Azande think about witchcraft, nor in observing what they do to combat it. These ideas and actions are on the surface of their life. . . . Mangu, witchcraft, was one of the first words I heard in Zandeland, and I heard it uttered day by day throughout the months. (1976:1)

Witchcraft may be the cause for misfortune in any element of Zande life:

> There is no niche or corner of Zande culture into which it does not twist itself. If blight seizes the ground-nut crop it is witchcraft; if the bush is vainly scoured for game it is witchcraft; if women laboriously bale water out of a pool and are rewarded with but a few small fish it is witchcraft; if termites do not rise when their swarming is due and a cold useless night is spent waiting for their flight it is witchcraft; if a wife is sulky and unresponsive to her husband it is witchcraft; if a prince is cold and distant with his subject it is witchcraft; if a magical rite fails to achieve its purpose it is witchcraft; if, in fact, any failure or misfortune falls upon anyone at any time and in relation to any of the manifold activities of his life it may be due to witchcraft. (Evans-Pritchard 1976:63–64)

This does not mean the Azande are unaware of other forms of causation—for example, incompetence or carelessness, breach of taboo or failure to observe a moral rule, or what we might call "natural processes," but witchcraft is an important explanatory link.

Evans-Pritchard's classic example of this is the case of the falling granary. Granaries are heavy structures of wattle and daub raised aboveground on wooden posts. Evans-Pritchard writes, "Sometimes a granary collapses. There is nothing remarkable in this. Every Zande knows that termites eat the supports in course of time and that even the hardest woods decay." In the heat of the summer the Azande will sit in the shade of the granary:

> Consequently it may happen that there are people sitting beneath the granary when it collapses and they are injured, for it is a heavy structure. . . . Now why should these particular people have been sitting under this particular granary at the particular moment when it collapsed? That it should collapse is easily intelligible, but why should have it collapsed at the particular moment when these particular people were sitting beneath it? Through years it might have collapsed, so why should it fall just when certain people sought its kindly shelter? Zande philosophy can supply the missing link. The Zande knows that the supports were undermined by termites and

> that people were sitting beneath the granary in order to escape the heat and glare of the sun. But he knows besides why these two events occurred at a precisely similar moment in time and space. It was due to the action of witchcraft. (Evans-Pritchard 1976:69–70)

Evans-Pritchard discusses Azande witchcraft in over five hundred pages impossible to summarize briefly. The Azande believe that witchcraft is located in an organ by the liver and is passed patrilineally from father to son, but that it is not present in the royal lineage. This genetic theory of witchcraft transmission, Douglas observes, "was adapted so that questions about transmission were directed away from those social relationships where claims could not be collected" (1980:55). Such selectivity in the organization of human thinking is one of the key points of Evans-Pritchard's theory of accountability. Douglas writes,

> Evans-Pritchard's implicit conception of human knowledge starts from three principles. First, rational thought is exercised only selectively over the possible field of attention. Second, the principle of selectivity depends on the social demand for accountability. Third, the social patterns of accountability which can be elicited by systematic observation provide a structured anchorage for a particular kind of reality, with its own array of beings invested with appropriate powers. In sum, each human society, insofar as its members expect to hold each other accountable, has its own locally selected reality anchored to agreement about moral objectives. (1980:132)

By focusing on the ways different segments of a society hold each other accountable, the structures linking individuals and institutions can be discerned. The identification of such local structures was one of Evans-Pritchard's goals in discussing social anthropology as a form of social history.

Social Anthropology as Social History

In the preface to *Witchcraft, Oracles and Magic among the Azande*, Evans-Pritchard wrote, "If I have paid no attention to Zande history this is not because I consider it unimportant but because I consider it so important that I desire to record it in detail elsewhere" (1937). In 1971 he published *The Azande: History and Political Institutions.* It is an incredibly complex description of Azande expansion during the 150 years before colonial subjugation, full of battles, royal intrigues, and struggles of succession. But in addition to the historical detail, Evans-Pritchard outlined why history was important for anthropology:

> Anthropological theory often rests on a basis of studies of primitive societies for which there is little recorded history. In the case of African kingdoms, such as those of the Azande, to leave out the historical dimension is to deprive ourselves of knowledge that is both ascertainable and necessary for an understanding of political organizations which have always, to a greater or lesser extent, been transformed by European rule before anthropologists have commenced their study of them, and which, furthermore, have been shaped by events that took place long before Europeans appeared on the scene. That the Azande had been expanding and . . . conquering and assimilating dozens of foreign peoples, as well as taking part in a long series of dynastic wars among themselves, for at least 150 years before Europeans imposed their administrations is surely a fact which cannot be left out of consideration in a study of their institutions and culture. (1971:267)

Such common sense struck at the heart of Radcliffe-Brown's form of social anthropology; it also formed the basis of Evans-Pritchard's later research agenda. Evans-Pritchard contended that social history could serve as a model for social anthropology. He argued that there are three levels of anthropological inquiry of increasing abstraction, each with direct parallels in historical methods (1950:122). First, the anthropologist attempts to understand another society and translate it to his own. The only difference between anthropology and history is that the anthropologist's data are produced from direct fieldwork experience while the historian relies upon the written record; this was merely "a technical, not a methodological, difference." Second, the anthropologist and historian attempt to make their subjects "sociologically intelligible." Evans-Pritchard writes,

> But even in a single ethnographic study the anthropologist seeks to do more than understand the thought and values of primitive people and translate them to his own culture. He seeks also to discover the structural order of the society, the patterns which, once established, enable him to see it as a whole, as a set of interrelated abstractions. Then the society is not only culturally intelligible, as it is, at the level of consciousness and action, for one of its members or for the foreigner who has learnt its mores and participates in its life, but also becomes sociologically intelligible. (1950:121)

And finally, "the anthropologist compares the social structures his analysis has revealed in a wide range of societies" (Evans-Pritchard 1950:122). Thus, Evans-Pritchard was not engaged in historical particularism, but based his comparison on social structures as documented from a historical perspective with abundant ethnographic detail.

Conclusion

Evans-Pritchard currently enjoys a level of respect that other British social anthropologists—Radcliffe-Brown most obviously—are denied. There are several reasons for this. First, in the later half of his career, Evans-Pritchard engaged in a virtual point-by-point refutation of Radcliffe-Brown's structural functionalism (Kuper 1977:129–135). Central to this was Evans-Pritchard's argument that anthropology should be modeled on social history rather than a science, and this call for a "humanistic" anthropology resonates with many anthropologists today. "It has seemed to me," Evans-Pritchard wrote in his last book, "that anthropologists (include me if you wish) have, in their writings about African societies, dehumanized the Africans into systems and structures and lost the flesh and blood" (1974b:9). Evans-Pritchard's stature derives from his attention to placing ethnographic accounts within their local logics, for example, embedding explanations within the specific cultural rationales of Zande culture. Unlike many scholars who articulated a singular view of human behavior, Evans-Pritchard was engaged in a living debate and did not create an

"Evans-Pritchardian position let alone dogma," as the late Ernst Gellner observed. E. E. Evans-Pritchard's relation to the anthropological tradition, Gellner wrote, was "not that of a prophet, but rather an intellectually restless, ever-questing, sceptical Hamlet" (1981:xv).

References

Beidelman, T. O.

1974 A Biographical Sketch. In *A Bibliography of the Writings of E. E. Evans-Pritchard*. E. E. Evans-Pritchard and T. Beidelman, eds. Pp. 1–13. London: Tavistock Publications.

Douglas, Mary

1980 *Edward Evans-Pritchard*. New York: Viking Press.

Evans-Pritchard, Edward

1937 *Witchcraft, Oracles and Magic among the Azande*. Oxford: Oxford University Press.

1940 *The Nuer: A Description of the Modes of Livelihood and Political Institutions of a Nilotic People*. Oxford: Oxford University Press.

1948 *The Divine Kingship of the Shilluk of the Nilotic Sudan*. Cambridge: Cambridge University Press.

1949 *The Sansusi of Cyrenaica*. Oxford: Clarendon Press.

1950 Social Anthropology: Past and Present. *Man* 198:118–124.

1951 *Kinship and Marriage among the Nuer*. Oxford: Oxford University Press.

1965 *Theories of Primitive Religion*. Oxford: Clarendon Press.

1971 *The Azande: History and Political Institutions*. Oxford: Oxford University Press.

1974a *A Bibliography of the Writings of E. E. Evans-Pritchard*. Compiled by E. E. Evans-Pritchard, amended and corrected by T. Beidelman. London: Tavistock Publications.

1974b *Man and Woman among the Azande*. New York: Free Press.

1976 *Witchcraft, Oracles, and Magic among the Azande*. Abridged with an introduction by E. Gillies. Oxford: Clarendon Press.

Evans-Pritchard, Edward, ed.

1967 *The Zande Trickster*. Oxford: Oxford University Press.

Fortes, Meyer, and E. E. Evans-Pritchard, eds.

1940 *African Political Systems*. Oxford: Oxford University Press.

Gellner, Ernst
1981 Introduction. In *A History of Anthropological Theory by E. E. Evans-Pritchard*. A. Singer, ed. Pp. xiii–xxxvi. New York: Basic Books.

Gillies, E.
1976 Introduction. In *Witchcraft, Oracles, and Magic among the Azande*. By E. E. Evans-Pritchard. Abridged with an introduction by E. Gillies. Oxford: Clarendon Press.

Harris, Marvin
1968 *The Rise of Anthropological Theory: A History of Theories of Culture*. New York: Thomas Y. Crowell.

Kuper, Adam
1983 *Anthropology and Anthropologists: The Modern British School*. London: Routledge & Kegan Paul.

Kuper, Adam, ed.
1977 *The Social Anthropology of Radcliffe-Brown*. London: Routledge & Kegan Paul.

Lienhardt, Geoffrey
1974 Evans-Pritchard: A Personal View. *Man* (n.s.) 9(2):299–304.

IV

EVOLUTIONARY, ADAPTATIONIST, AND MATERIALIST THEORIES

Evolution reemerges in American anthropology in the 1930s. It is explicitly anti-Boasian and only implicitly Marxist. In contrast to Boasian historical anthropology, the twentieth-century evolutionists—Leslie White, Julian Steward, Marvin Harris, and Eleanor Burke Leacock, among others—proposed a series of explicit, scientific laws linking cultural change to different spheres of material existence. Evolution's proponents revived the works of Morgan and Tylor, considered theoretically irrelevant by many, especially some of the hyper-particularistic followers of Boas. Due to reactionary politics within the United States, these scholars couldn't do more than implicitly address the contributions of Marx until the 1970s. In the 1920s and 1930s, Marxist ideas were commonplace in American universities; by the 1950s their espousal was cause for dismissal as the witch hunts of McCarthyism spread and the Cold War deepened.

As a consequence, American anthropologists disguised their indebtedness to Marx and Engels and emphasized their connection to Tylor and Morgan. This is not surprising given that red-baiting occurred in anthropological journals as well as before the House Un-American Activities Committee (Carneiro 1981). A classic example is Morris Opler's comment about the conceptual "tool kit" proposed by evolutionary anthropologists, that "its main contents seems to be a somewhat shopworn hammer and sickle" (1961:13). Such innuendo, labeling anthropologists as "communists," did no one's career any good.

White resisted numerous efforts to fire him during the McCarthy era; Steward distanced himself from Marxist approaches;

and Leacock carefully avoided mentioning Marx and Engels in her doctoral research even though she was a committed radical and active in politics. By the 1960s the reactionary movement in academia had slightly abated, but an openly Marxist anthropology would not emerge in the United States until the 1970s.

Evolutionary models became extremely important in America, much more so than in Great Britain where prehistorian V. Gordon Childe's evolutionary writings had broad impact in archaeology but not in social anthropology. In the United States, anthropologists tended to have a deeper diachronic perspective than advocated by the synchronic studies of British social anthropology. The idea of looking for systematic cultural changes through time fit better into American anthropology because it included archaeology. In spite of its reaction to anything tainted by Marxism, American anthropology saw an important role for examining general historical processes of change.

The twentieth-century evolutionists' signal contribution was a concern with the causes of change. Their causal explanations are materialist, in contrast to idealist or historical. Changes in the modes of production, whether caused by economic reorganizations or fluctuations in the environment, have consequences in other arenas of culture, and thus material factors have causal priority. Although claiming antecedents in Morgan and Tylor, or Marx and Engels, the so-called neo-evolutionists emphasized the importance of providing causal explanations rather than historical reconstructions.

For Leslie White, culture was humanity's means of adapting to the physical and social environments. Like any other organism, humans must capture energy in order to survive and reproduce, and those societies that capture more energy or use it most efficiently are at a competitive advantage over societies who do not. White contended that the history of human cultural evolution is essentially characterized by changes in quantity of energy and the efficiency of its use.

This adaptationist element is also found in the work of Steward and Harris, although it takes different forms. For Steward, cultures evolved as adaptations to the environment; similar cultural patterns reflect parallel adaptations to analogous environmental situations, not—as Morgan and Tylor argued—that all cultures have passed through similar evolutionary stages. Thus, Steward argues for a multilineal rather than a unilineal form of evolution.

Harris's concept, which he called cultural materialism, explains cultural patterns in terms of three sets of human life—infrastructure, structure, and superstructure—the most important being infrastructure. "Infrastructure" relates to the social control of production and reproduction, encompassing such aspects as technology, demography, subsistence, and environment—it is the cultural interface between humans and nature. Cultural materialism can serve to explain specific cultural practices and broad evolutionary trends, providing explanations rooted in material factors rather than ideological constructs.

Eleanor Burke Leacock's contributions are the most explicitly Marxist. For Leacock, changes in the mode of production (whatever their specific nature) are ultimately the source of social evolution. In that, Leacock directly follows Morgan, Engels, and Marx. Leacock's particular emphasis was to examine how changes in production relations caused by the expansion of capitalism affected traditional, egalitarian band societies, giving particular attention to the subjugation of women. Leacock's writings emulate those of Engels, both as a historical model and as a social critique.

These materialist explanations, which were linked at their roots, branched off in many directions. From 1960 to 1980 these ideas were central in American anthropology. Since the mid-1970s, materialist and idealist approaches have vied for popularity, a conflict within American anthropology that continues.

References

Carneiro, Robert
1981 Leslie White. In *Totems and Teachers: Perspectives on the History of Anthropology*. S. Silverman, ed. Pp. 209–251. New York: Columbia University Press.

Opler, Morris
1961 Cultural Evolutions, Southern Athapaskans, and Chronology in Theory. *Southwestern Journal of Anthropology* 17:1–20.

13

Leslie White

Evolution Emergent

In a variety of ways, Franz Boas cast a very large shadow over the development of American anthropology, but his influence threw theories of cultural evolution into pitch darkness. Boas's position—that cultural patterns were best explained by specific historical references rather than general cultural laws—had two effects. First, it erased most references to stages of cultural evolution or to lawlike generalizations from American anthropology, consigning to irrelevancy the nineteenth-century social evolutionists like Morgan, Tylor, and Karl Marx. Second, it refocused anthropological inquiry onto particular cultures—specific societies that exhibited a set of cultural behaviors at a certain place and time. The Boasian perspective prohibited—or at least inhibited—general theories about "culture." The antievolutionary and nongeneralizing influences of historical particularism were widespread in American anthropology from the early 1900s well into the 1950s. Berthold Laufer's glowing 1918 review of Robert Lowie's antievolutionary *Culture and Ethnology* characterized that perspective: "The theory of cultural evolution [is] to my mind the most inane, sterile, and pernicious theory ever conceived in the history of science" (cited in White 1959a:vii).

Leslie White's work ran headlong into this position on both scores. First, White advocated a theory of cultural evolution that, as he put it, "does not differ one whit in principle from that expressed in Tylor's *Anthropology* in 1881, although of course the development, expression and demonstration of the theory may—and does—differ at some points" (1959a:ix). Second, White advocated a general science of culture—not of cultures, but of Culture—that he called "culturology" (1949). White's theory of cultural evolution and his science of culture were not separate endeavors, but two prongs of the same general attack against historical particularism (see Service 1976:613). White, writing of himself in the third person, explained,

> The author absorbed the anti-evolutionist doctrines of the Boas school as a graduate student. But as he began to teach, he found, first, that he could not defend this point of view, and later that he could no longer hold it. . . . He has attacked the position of the anti-evolutionists in a number of articles. (1959a:ix)

It did not make him a popular man.

Background

Leslie White was born in 1900. He studied psychology at Columbia (B.A., 1923; M.A., 1924) and anthropology and sociology at the New School for Social Research under Alexander Goldenweiser, Thorstein Veblen, and John B. Watson. White began graduate work in anthropology at the University of Chicago, where he studied under Sapir and Fay Cooper-Cole. His 1927 Ph.D. was a study of medicine societies among the Southwest Indians. That same year White began teaching sociology and anthropology at the University of Rochester and the Buffalo Museum of Science. Fieldwork at the nearby Seneca reservations led to an interest in Morgan's work on the Iroquois (see chapter 2) and ultimately to White's reassessment of the Boasian critique (1937, 1942a, 1944, 1951, 1957, 1959b). In addition, every summer White conducted research in the American Southwest in the Native American communities of Acoma (1932a), the pueblo of San Felipe (1932b), the pueblo of Santo Domingo (1934), and the pueblo of Santa Ana (1942b). Each of these studies was a major ethnography, establishing White as an authority on the Southwest.

In 1930 White moved to the University of Michigan where, over the next forty years, he was instrumental in developing one of the best anthropology departments in the United States. Michigan produced a number of anthropologists who shared White's evolutionary interests, although White hired faculty who didn't necessarily share his views.

White's evolutionary interests were informed by his political commitment to socialism. During the Depression and thereafter, White contributed to the weekly paper of the Socialist Labor Party, writing under a pseudonym (Peace 2004:69–98). In these essays, White commented on the achievements of the Soviet Union, the inequities of American capitalism, and also developed his ideas of cultural evolution. David Peace writes, "It was White's political commitment to the Socialist Labor Party that shaped the corpus of the evolutionary work for which he is so well known" (2004:69).

White's evolutionary theories were so at odds with most anthropological thinking that they probably hampered his career. Anthropologist Elman Service (1976) suggests that White did not receive professional honors until late in life because he was unpopular with some anthropologists, and White's response to their critiques often strayed into personal vitriol (Peace 2004:111–129, 148–153). But if his ideas and polemics offended some scholars, they whipped certain elements of the public into a froth. His Michigan lectures emphasized how cultural patterns determined individual experience—in contrast to free will or deism—leading to attacks from irate parents. The Catholic Church lobbied state legislators against White and called for his dismissal from the University of Michigan (Peace 2004:135–157; Beardsley 1976; Service 1976). Yet White's lectures were well attended, his articles were extensively reprinted, he was interviewed on radio shows, and in a variety of ways his ideas were widely disseminated. After retiring from Michigan in 1970, he moved to the University of California, Santa Barbara, where he was visiting professor emeritus until his death in 1975.

What were White's provocative ideas about the evolution and science of culture? In order to understand them, we first need to recognize the functionalist core of White's approach to culture.

Evolution and the Functional Core

White's personal odyssey from historical particularism to cultural evolution is discussed below, but it is important to mention the similarities between White's theory of culture and Malinowski's functionalism (see pp. 138–44). Central to White's evolutionary theory is a functionalist conception of culture.

There are important differences between the two positions. Malinowski ultimately saw culture as functioning to meet individual needs, whereas White posited that culture met the needs of the species. This difference is not insignificant: Malinowski was interested in accounting for specific cultural patterns—usually exhibited by the Trobriand Islanders—while White was concerned with broader cultural developments exhibited by humanity, as White himself explained, "Man is unique: he is the only living species that has a culture. By culture we mean an extrasomatic, temporal continuum of things and events dependent upon symboling" (1959a:3). By extrasomatic—from the Greek *soma* for "body," therefore, literally, "external to the body"—White stipulated that culture had a "suprabiological character":

> Although culture is produced and perpetuated only by the human species, and therefore has its origins and basis in the biological make-up of man . . . after it has come into existence and become established as a tradition, culture exists and behaves and is related to man as if it were *nonbiological in character*. (1959a:12, emphasis in the original)

Culture exists separately from the individuals who are born and die in a society. A baby learns culture from other individuals; culture is not genetically transmitted. But this is not to suggest that culture has no biological functions; in fact, White writes, "The purpose and function of culture are to make life secure and enduring for the human species." In contrast to other, cultureless organisms:

> Man employs the extrasomatic tradition that we call culture in order to sustain and perpetuate his existence and give it full expression.

> Specifically, the functions of culture are to relate man to his environment—his terrestrial habitat and the circumambient cosmos—on the one hand, and to relate man to man, on the other. (White 1959a:8)

This functional notion is a key element in White's theory of evolution. It is a utilitarian notion that Elman Service has traced back to the nineteenth-century evolutionist Herbert Spencer. According to Service, White, by his own admission, borrowed this utilitarian notion "more or less unwittingly" (1976:614). Regardless of White's intent, the consequences of his emphasis on the functions of culture are diverse and profound in American anthropology. This is particularly true for American archaeology, which fully embraced that position from the mid-1960s until very recently.

This functionalist interpretation of culture was central to White's theory of evolution because it implied that the most important dimensions of culture were those that imparted adaptive, biological advantages. It logically followed that the most important cultural realm is the one that transforms energy and makes it available for human use—technology. And, by extension, the evolution of cultures could be measured by their relative capacities to obtain and divert energy. Those two concepts underlie White's theory of evolution.

Theory of Cultural Evolution

The first element in White's theory of cultural evolution is a division of culture into three subsystems: technological, sociological, and ideological.

> The technological system is composed of the material, mechanical, physical and chemical instruments, together with the techniques of their use, by means of which man, as an animal species, is articulated with his natural habitat. . . . The sociological system is made up of interpersonal relations expressed in patterns of behavior, collective as well as individual. The ideological system is composed of ideas, beliefs, knowledge, expressed in articulate speech or other symbolic form. (White 1949:362–363)

In a later work, White suggested four categories of culture: technological, sociological, ideological, and "sentimental or attitudinal" (1959a:6–7). The attitudinal category attempts to capture "the feelings or attitudes that constitute the subjective aspect." White did not really develop this category, it is almost an afterthought. He briefly refers to the culturally transmitted feelings about things—"loathing of milk, attitudes toward chastity, snakes, bats, death, etc."—a motley assortment of sentiments that reinforce the haphazard impression of this element of White's theory.

This reflects the firm priority that White gave to the technological realm of culture. White viewed the technological, sociological, and ideological systems as a three-part hierarchy of causation, with technology the foundation on which social and ideological systems are raised. White wrote,

> The technological system is basic and primary. Social systems are functions of technologies; and philosophies express technological forces and reflect social systems. The technological factor is therefore the determinant of a cultural system as a whole. . . . This is not to say, of course, that social systems do not condition the operation of technologies, or that social and technological systems are not affected by ideologies. They do and are. But to condition is one thing; to determine, quite another. (1949:366)

Why does technology—broadly defined—have a determinant role? Why does White posit that technology is the basis of cultural evolution? First, there is the obvious fact that all organisms must meet basic energy requirements, be protected from the elements, and defend themselves from enemies. These life-sustaining, life-perpetuating processes, White writes, "are technological in a broad, but valid, sense, i.e., they are carried on by material, mechanical, biophysical, and biochemical means" (1959a:19). By meeting these fundamental requisites of life, the technological dimensions allow other elements of culture to occur. "The technological system is therefore both primary and basic in importance: all human life and culture rest and depend upon it" (White 1949:365).

But more than technological potential, technology itself determines the nature of social and ideological systems:

> The social organization of a people is not only dependent upon their technology but is determined to a great extent, if not wholly, by it both in form and content. . . . The activities of hunting, fishing, gathering, farming, tending herds and flocks, mining, and all the processes by means of which raw materials are transformed and made ready for human consumption are not merely technological processes; they are social processes as well. (White 1959a:19–20)

And thus—to cite some of White's examples—a railroad workers' union is based on the technological fact of having a railroad and the social institutions formed by the existence of the railroad (White 1959a:21). Technology determines concepts of female beauty: "In cultures where technological control over food supply is slight and food is frequently scarce as a consequence, a fat woman is often regarded as beautiful. In cultures where food is abundant and women work little, obesity is likely to be regarded as unsightly[!]" (White 1959a:21).

We will object to the accuracy of such claims below, but for the moment it is more important to understand the logic behind White's theory: technology determines other aspects of culture. Thus White—echoing Malinowski's statements about the relationship between magic and science—suggests that as technological control increases, belief in the supernatural diminishes, stating, for example, that "where the ceramic art is well developed, a minimum of magic is employed" (1959a:23). Again, this may not be accurate, but the argument is clear.

By arguing that technological dimensions were primary factors, that technology was the bedrock of cultural development, White set the stage for his theory of cultural evolution. If technology was an attempt to solve the problems of survival and if this ultimately meant capturing enough energy and diverting it to human needs, then those societies that captured more energy and used it most efficiently were at an adaptive advantage; they were, in an evolutionary sense, more advanced. Note here that by energy White is thinking like a physicist, considering energy in all of its states: as human effort, as fossil fuel, as kilocalories stored in corn or other domesticated foods, as falling water, as explosives, and so on.

From White's perspective, "Culture thus confronts us as an elaborate thermodynamic, mechanical system. . . . The functioning of culture as a whole therefore rests upon and is determined by the amount of energy harnessed and by the way it is put to work" (1949:367–368).

This implied that the differences between cultures could be measured, not by some rough qualitative scale or "ethnical periods," but precisely in terms of horsepower or kilocalories or another unit of measure.

> The degree of cultural development, measured in terms of amount of human need-serving goods and services produced per capita, is determined by the amount of energy harnessed per capita and by the efficiency of the technological means with which it is put to work. We express this concisely and succinctly with the following formula: E X T→ C, in which C represents the degree of cultural development, E the amount of energy harnessed per capita per year, and T the quality of efficiency of the tools employed in the expenditure of energy. We can now formulate the basic law of cultural evolution: Other factors remaining constant, culture evolves as the amount of energy harnessed per capita per year is increased, or as the efficiency of the instrumental means of putting the energy to work is increased. Both factors may increase simultaneously of course. (White 1949:368–369)

With this elegant argument, White made thermodynamics into the bridging argument of cultural evolution, transforming intuitive classification of different societies into a series of propositions that were logical, testable, and lawlike. If, as Marvin Harris argues, White's law of evolution "is neither a law nor a definition but rather a statement of research strategy" (1968:636), it is worthwhile noting that previous evolutionary approaches lacked this predictive quality, instead being ex post facto classifications. White's statement was lawlike in a scientific sense, not a legal one: it stated a relationship between a set of observable phenomena that could be proven incorrect or falsified. This property of refutability sets scientific statements apart from other kinds of statements, and it suggests White's intentions when he outlined a science of culture.

The Science of Culture

Elman Service suggested that White's theories about the evolution of culture and the science of culture were two separate, completely independent bodies of theory: "Culturology, the science of culture as he presented it, is not the same thing as, nor does it even imply a connection to, his ideas about the evolution of culture" (1976:613). This may be slightly overstated because White's notions of the evolution of culture certainly exemplify what he thought a science of culture should contain: (1) it should be science; (2) it should be about culture, not cultures; and (3) it should be deterministic, i.e., denying appeals to free will, the individual, or to any cause other than Culture.

For White, humans had two ways of dealing with experience—science and art. "The purpose of science and art is one: to render experience intelligible," White wrote, but these two ways of knowing approached experience from different directions. "Art deals with universals in terms of particulars." In contrast, science was not merely a collection of facts and formulae, but a way of knowing by dealing with particulars from universals. "Art and science thus grasp a common experience, or reality, by opposite but inseparable poles," White concludes (1949:3).

Therefore, if we are interested in a science of culture, our task is to discover and delineate the universal principles that explain particular phenomena. Note that these phenomena exist independently of the subjective viewer; White approvingly cites Einstein's statement, "The belief in an external world independent of the perceiving subject is the basis of all natural science." Such phenomena—existing in space, time, and having particular formal properties—can be viewed from different frames of reference. Thus a raindrop may be viewed as one event in the evolution of the cosmos, as a mass changing its spatial relationship with other masses like the earth and clouds, or as a mass that changes form through time (White 1949:13). Although we define the different frames of reference, the reality exists separate from the viewer. Whereas some changes in form are repetitive and reversible—water may become ice and then melt again—the temporal order of events is not: "Only in *Through the Looking Glass* do Queens scream before they prick their fingers, or Alices pass the cake before they cut it. The evolutionary process, *being temporal as well as formal,* is likewise irreversible" (White 1949:13, emphasis added).

This developmental argument sets the stage for White's deterministic approach to cultural evolution. New cultural forms develop out of preceding cultural forms, regardless of the role of individuals. The theory of natural selection was discovered by Darwin and Alfred Russel Wallace; it was not created from thin air by either man but was a crystallization of previously existing, culturally expressed knowledge. Calculus was "invented" by both Leibnitz and Newton, but calculus would have been developed even if both men had died as infants. "The development of mathematics, like the development of technology or medicine, is an evolutionary process: new forms grow out of preceding forms" (White 1949:14). We may not be able to predict the name of an inventor or when another innovation will occur, but the fact that such an innovation will occur is predictable because of the inevitability of cultural evolution. White lavished great care on his article "Ikhnaton: The Great Man vs. the Culture Process," which considered the case of the pharaoh Ikhnaton who introduced monotheism to replace the multitude of gods in ancient Egypt in the fourteenth century B.C. Ikhnaton has been variously lauded as a seer or damned as a heretic but universally characterized as a "Great Man," a singular individual who brought about a truly original innovation. Not so, White argued: all the elements that made the acceptance of monotheism possible existed independently of Ikhnaton:

> In the process of cultural development, a Great Man is but the neural medium through which an important synthesis of culture takes place. Darwin, Newton, Beethoven, and Edison were men of this type. They were the neurological loci of important cultural events. To be sure, they were superior organisms. But had they been reared as swineherders, Greatness would not have found them. (1949:280)

A science of culture, White argued, is concerned with the general principles that define and predict relationships in cultural phenomena. It is not interested in defining specific cultural traits, but instead in understanding general cultural patterns.

> Particular cultures vary among themselves in specific form and content, but all are alike in general respects; i.e., all have tools, language, customs, beliefs, music, etc. And every cultural system functions as a means of relating man to the earth and cosmos, and as a means of relating man to man. *The science of culture will therefore concern itself with the structure and function of cultural systems.* (White 1959a:29, emphasis added)

Not only is such a science uninterested in particular cultures except as examples of universals, but it should consider culture as a realm of phenomena, "as if it had an existence of its own, independently of the human species" (White 1959a:16). Considered this way, a science of culture is one that posits generalizations about culture that are verifiable through the study of culture.

Conclusion

White's unsparingly deterministic view of human development led to criticisms of his work by church and state and by anthropologists as well. First, there is the notion that culture somehow exists independently of specific societies and thus is a phenomenon separate from its particular expressions. One may immediately ask, "Is this true, or are White's lawlike statements about Culture actually generalizations about some cultures to which other cultures are exceptions?" For example, White's contention that "in cultures where food is abundant and women work little, obesity is likely to be regarded as unsightly" (1959a:21)—presumably a reference to twentieth-century America and Europe—is only remotely valid if you classify "women's work" as not really work. It is also a very simplistic explanation of why anorexia and other eating disorders affect so many people—women and men of different ethnicities and classes around the world.

Second, White's three categories of culture—technological, sociological, and ideological—are not equivalent; technology has priority because, according to White's definition, it involves the capture and transformation of energy that is essential for life in all organisms; all other dimensions of culture are therefore based on technology. But, humans do not rely on instinctual means to obtain energy directly from the environment. For example, breast-feeding involves learned behavior on the part of both infant and mother. The infant is born with a sucking reflex, but it may take several days before she or he learns how to nurse; the new mother learns about breast-feeding from her relatives, her doctor, pages of advice, and the cries of her infant that she learns to distinguish between hunger, wetness, and tiredness. All of that is learned social and symbolic behavior. If breast-feeding—one of the most elementary energy transfers in human society—is learned behavior based on symbols, why isn't it that systems of meaning, rather than technology, constitute the fundamental cultural realm? White anticipated this point but simply denied it out of hand (1959a:19).

A final point concerns the definition of cultural development. The critique turns on the concept of tautology, a fallacious restatement about cause and effect. For example, "I am taller than other people because most people are shorter than I am" is a tautology. White's version of this tautology is to state:

> (1) Like all systems comprised of matter, culture is a "thermodynamic system" that requires the constant acquisition and transformation of energy (1959a:38).
>
> (2) Since it is fundamental that humans as organisms must capture and use energy, "it follows that this must be the basic function of culture also" (1959a:39). The basic purpose of cultural systems is to obtain and utilize energy.
>
> (3) Cultural systems vary in their effectiveness in harnessing and using energy; this effectiveness can be measured in terms of per capita horsepower, kilocalories, or some other measure of energy. And therefore:
>
> (4) "*Culture advances as the amount of energy harnessed per capita per year increases, or as the efficiency or economy of the means*

of controlling energy is increased, or both" (1959a:56, emphasis in the original).

Consider what happens to the logic if we substitute other desiderata for that of energy capture and efficiency. How would we evaluate cultures if energy conservation were the goal or to meet basic human needs with the minimum of effort or to have the maximum number of socially well-adjusted offspring? Couldn't we substitute any or all of these alternate goals for White's thermodynamic one? If we did, the entire logic of the argument would be reshaped.

White's theories of cultural evolution and culturology were extremely influential, and they form part of the backdrop to a current debate in American anthropology. White's adaptationist and utilitarian views of culture influenced a large school of American anthropology, particularly during the 1960s and 1970s when many of White's ideas about the energetics of cultural systems, the role of energy and structure in the organization of the state, and the notion that understanding past societies should be based on interpreting material remains as remnants of environmental, social, and ideological behaviors were pursued in fields such as ecological anthropology, comparative ethnology, and the New Archaeology (for example, Binford 1962). The last twenty years of debates in anthropology are partially a reaction to the theoretical positions inspired by White and others.

But perhaps White's most significant accomplishment was a more general one: the reintroduction of anthropological theories as legitimate topics of discussion. As Richard Beardsley concludes in his obituary of White:

> Even the many contemporary anthropologists to whom these subjects [about cultural evolution] are not matters of central concern share at least an indirect heritage from Leslie A. White. Their interests and ideas are possible in part because he fought successfully to restore to respectability a concern for grand theory. (1976:619–620)

Thus, White's contribution to anthropology was not only to propose a particular theory of culture, but to reintroduce theory building as a creative anthropological enterprise.

References

Beardsley, Richard

1976 An Appraisal of Leslie A. White's Scholarly Influence. *American Anthropologist* 78:617–620.

Binford, Lewis

1962 Archaeology as Anthropology. *American Antiquity* 28:217–225.

Harris, Marvin

1968 *The Rise of Anthropological Theory: A History of Theories of Culture.* New York: Thomas Y. Crowell.

Peace, William

2004 *Leslie White: Evolution and Revolution in Anthropology.* Lincoln: University of Nebraska Press.

Service, Elman

1976 Leslie Alvin White, 1900–1975. *American Anthropologist* 78:612–617.

White, Leslie

1932a *The Acoma Indians.* Bureau of American Ethnology, 47th Annual Report. Pp. 1–192. Washington, D.C.: Smithsonian Institution. [Reprinted 1973. Glorieta, N.M.: Rio Grande Press.]

1932b *The Pueblo of San Felipe.* American Anthropological Association, Memoir 38. [Reprinted 1964. New York: Krauss Reprint.]

1934 *The Pueblo of Santo Domingo.* American Anthropological Association, Memoir 43. [Reprinted 1964. New York: Krauss Reprint.]

1937 Extracts from the European Travel Journal of Lewis H. Morgan. *Rochester Historical Society Publications* 16:221–390.

1942a Lewis H. Morgan's Journal of a Trip to Southwestern Colorado and New Mexico, 1878. *American Antiquity* 8:1–26.

1942b *The Pueblo of Santa Ana, New Mexico.* Supplement to *American Anthropologist* 44(4), part 2. American Anthropological Association, Memoir 60. [Reprinted 1969. New York: Krauss Reprint.]

1944 Morgan's Attitude toward Religion and Science. *American Anthropologist* 46:218–230.

1949 *The Science of Culture: A Study of Man and Civilization.* New York: Grove Press.

1951 Lewis H. Morgan's Western Field Trips. *American Anthropologist* 53:11–18.

1957 How Morgan Came to Write *Systems of Consanguinity and Affinity. Papers of the Michigan Academy of Science, Arts, and Letters* 42:257–268.

1959a *The Evolution of Culture: The Development of Civilization to the Fall of Rome*. New York: McGraw-Hill.

1959b Lewis Henry Morgan: His Life and His Researches. In *The Indian Journals, 1859–62*. By Lewis Henry Morgan. L. White, ed. Pp. 3–12. Ann Arbor: University of Michigan Press.

14

Julian Steward

Cultural Ecology and Multilinear Evolution

The materialist approaches of Julian Steward (1902–1972) have been extremely influential in American anthropology, particularly in the 1950s and 1960s. His ideas were a bridge between the historical particularism of Boas and Kroeber and the cultural evolution of Leslie White. On the one hand, Steward criticized the particularist approaches as nonexplanatory, arguing that clear similarities between different cultures could be explained as parallel adaptations to structurally similar natural environments. On the other hand, he contended that not all societies passed through similar stages of cultural development and that unilineal models of evolution were, therefore, too sweeping to be interesting.

Steward's ideas had a crucial impact on American archaeology, shifting archaeological focus from cultural history to cultural evolution. During the 1960s and 1970s, the changing conception of archaeology—dubbed the New Archaeology—relied heavily on his ideas. Steward's work was relevant to archaeology because it considered the relationship between human society and environment and because it focused on social changes through time. Both were issues archaeologists could address with their data.

Steward's contributions to anthropology were diverse. He was a major figure in the development of area studies programs, in turning anthropological inquiry to problems of culture change and Third World development, and in leading large research projects with teams of investigators. He also made a major contribution to anthropological theory with two significant concepts: cultural ecology and multilinear evolution.

Background

Born in Washington, D.C., in 1902, Julian Haynes Steward's most important formative years were spent in the American West. (For an extended discussion, see Kerns's [2003] outstanding biography of Steward.) At the age of sixteen Steward went to a preparatory school in Owens Valley, California, on the western margin of the Great Basin, a region to which he would return for his first sustained anthropological fieldwork as a graduate student and which would remain an area of research interest throughout his life (Clemmer, Myers, and Rudden 1999). After spending his freshman year at the University of California–Berkeley where he was exposed to the teachings of Alfred Kroeber and Robert Lowie, Steward transferred east to Cornell University to complete his B.A. in 1925. He returned to Berkeley for graduate training. Under Kroeber and Lowie, Berkeley graduate students primarily studied North American Indian groups, and Steward was no exception. His 1929 dissertation, "The Ceremonial Buffoon of the American Indian," was based on library research, which was a common practice at the time; ethnographic fieldwork was presented in descriptive monographs and comparative studies, and dissertations were based on published materials (Murphy 1977:4). A study of role reversal and cross-cultural patterns of social humor and ritual clowning, Steward's dissertation exhibits no obvious connection to his subsequent research (for a synopsis, see Steward 1977a).

Steward became a professional anthropologist as the Great Depression began. In 1928 he was one of the first anthropology instructors at the University of Michigan; in 1930 he moved to the University of Utah where he established a program of research and instruction, conducting archaeological excavations at Pueblo sites (Manners 1973:889; Murphy 1977:4–5). But Steward's research was not sharply focused until he resumed his ethnographic investigations in the Great Basin. He returned to Berkeley as a lecturer for the 1933–1934 academic year and then began a two-year research project focusing on Shoshone and Northern Paiute communities in eastern California, Nevada, Utah, and Idaho.

The Shoshone and Northern Paiute were to Julian Steward what the Trobriand Islanders were to Bronislaw Malinowski (see pp. 136–38): a pivotal ethnographic case that exemplified broad cultural patterns. For Steward, the fundamental pattern of Shoshonean society was derived from the fact that "pursuits concerned with the problems of daily existence dominated their activities to an extraordinary degree and limited and conditioned their [social] institutions" (1938:1–2). As Steward documented the limited natural resources, simple technology, and seasonal movements of Great Basin food collectors from arid basins to alpine piñon groves, a general model of hunting and gathering societies emerged. This model emphasized the egalitarianism and social fluidity of bands (Steward 1938:258–260; 1977b). Anthropologist Robert Murphy writes,

> Living in a forbidding country of high desert and harsh landscape, the single dominant fact of their lives was the necessity to eke out subsistence through the seasons of the year. Given the simple technology at their disposal, the environment offered few alternatives to the ways in which they lived, and their very patterns of social life had to be understood as an adjustment to bleak physical reality. Steward grasped and developed this essential truth of Shoshoni [*sic*] society and made it into a general theory. (1977:6)

Steward's early research on band society outlined parallels between such scattered societies as the Shoshone, Australian Aborigines, the San and other so-called Bushmen groups of southern Africa, and the Semang of Malaysia. He argued that they exhibited similar adaptations shaped by low population density, reliance on foot transportation, and hunting of scattered and nonmigratory game (1936). Today Steward's ideas are accepted as basic anthropological insights, so it is somewhat surprising to realize his early article on the topic was rejected by American anthropological journals as too speculative (Manners 1973:890).

The cool response to Steward's early work stems from three innovations that ran counter to American anthropology in the 1930s. First, he conducted ethnographic fieldwork that focused on a specific problem rather than attempted to "complete" a description of another culture. Just as descriptive ethnography and comparative ethnology were separated when Julian Steward was a graduate student, many anthropologists viewed problem-oriented fieldwork as somehow preconceived and biased. Second, Steward was not interested in cultural traits, styles, or norms—common concerns of American anthropologists—but instead in the adaptive relationships between humans and their environments. Finally, he proposed that regular patterns existed in human adaptations, between groups like the Australian aborigines and the Great Basin Shoshone who had never been in contact. Steward emphasized cultural parallels due to adaptation rather than historical diffusion or migration. This made his work suspect to many American anthropologists but also produced, in Marvin Harris's phrase, "the first coherent statement of how the interaction between culture and environment could be studied in causal terms" (1968:666). That search for causal relationships would occupy the balance of Steward's career.

In 1935 Steward joined the Bureau of American Ethnology of the Smithsonian Institution where he remained until 1946. The most successful of a number of large research projects he headed at the Smithsonian was a program of library and field research on the native peoples of South America. The multivolume *Handbook of South American Indians* employed almost every ethnographer and archaeologist who had worked in South America: Alfred Kroeber, Robert Lowie, Alfred Métraux, Claude Lévi-Strauss, Gordon Willey, John Rowe, Paul Kirchoff, John Murra, Luis Valcárcel, Wendell Bennett, and W. D. Strong, among many others. Fifty years after its publication, the *Handbook of South American Indians* remains a major resource for anthropologists (Steward 1946–1950). Its organization and emphasis on the cultural developments of native South American societies reflect the research interests of Julian Steward.

In 1946 Steward left the Smithsonian and joined the Department of Anthropology at Columbia University where the graduate program had swelled as postwar students entered school on the GI Bill; Steward chaired thirty-five doctoral dissertations in the six years he was at Columbia, a staggering quantity of work. His students included Stanley Diamond, Eric Wolf, Robert Murphy, and Sidney Mintz, among others. Steward also initiated a large research program in Puerto Rico (Steward et al.

1956) coordinating the investigations of five graduate students and establishing one of the first area studies of a complex society and its historical context.

In 1952 Steward accepted a research professorship at the University of Illinois, Urbana-Champaign, where he remained until his retirement in 1968. Freed of all teaching responsibilities—except for seminars he chose to offer—Steward initiated yet another large research project, focusing on social and economic changes in twentieth-century traditional societies. Eleven fieldworkers investigated traditional societies and documented patterns of culture change in Third World countries on four continents (Steward 1967). Steward also published prolifically during his time at Illinois: he wrote *Theory of Culture Change: The Method of Multilinear Evolution* (1973b); a biographical sketch of Alfred Kroeber (1973a); a major synthesis entitled *Native Peoples of South America* (Steward and Faron 1959); and a stream of articles and reviews on cultural evolution, irrigation agriculture, and native societies in the Great Basin. Until the end of his life, Julian Steward maintained an active interest in diverse areas of research, but these were bound together by two central, unifying concepts: cultural ecology and multilinear evolution.

Cultural Ecology

"Cultural ecology," Steward wrote, "is the study of the processes by which a society adapts to its environment. Its principal problem is to determine whether these adaptations initiate internal social transformations of evolutionary change" (1968:337). Like biological ecology, which analyzes adaptation to the complex interconnections that make up an environment, cultural ecology is a view of "man in the web of life" (Steward 1973b:31). That web consisted of both natural and cultural realities:

> Cultural ecology is broadly similar to biological ecology in its method of examining the interactions of all social and natural phenomena within an area, but it does not equate social features with biological species or assume that competition is the major process. It distinguishes different kinds of sociocultural systems and institutions, it recognizes both cooperation and

> competition as processes of interaction, and it postulates that environmental adaptations depend on the technology, needs and structure of the society and on the nature of the environment. It includes analysis of adaptation to the social environment. (Steward 1968:337)

The web of life of a human group "may extend far beyond the immediate physical environment and biotic assemblage. In states, nations, and empires, the nature of the local group may be determined by these larger institutions no less than by its local adaptation" (Steward 1973b:32). Steward argued that the links between environment and culture were particularly clear in societies like the Shoshone where the margins of survival were slim. In contrast, in societies that "have adequately solved subsistence problems, the effect of ecology becomes more difficult to ascertain. In complex societies certain components of the social superstructure rather than ecology seem increasingly to be determinants of further developments. With greater cultural complexity analysis becomes increasingly difficult" (Steward 1938:262).

Steward viewed cultural ecology as a research agenda rather than a religious dogma; other processes of cultural change—for example, diffusion or innovation—were not precluded by the culture ecological approach. And cultural ecology provided a key advantage: cross-cultural parallels in social patterns could be explained as adaptations to similar environments.

That interest in causes distinguished cultural ecology from the historical particularism of Boas and his students. Relying on mechanisms of diffusion, innovation, and migration, cultural-historical "explanations," Steward argued, were not really explanations since they relied on the inexplicable tendency "of societies to develop in unlike ways" (1973b:35). The explanations of historical particularism were actually reconstructed accounts of the "divergences in culture history," with the cause of diversity remaining mysterious.

Further, Steward wrote, in cultural-historical explanations, the environment was relegated to a secondary role in explaining cultural differences (1973b:35). Ironically, cultural-historical explanations relied on the "culture area" concept, a scheme used by Clark Wissler and Alfred Kroeber to subdivide culture patterns—such as the American Southwest or the Great Plains—based on shared cultural traits exhibited in similar environments. If, Steward asked, there were such clear patterns between environment and culture, how could environment be ignored?

Steward outlined three basic steps for a cultural-ecological investigation. "First, the interrelationship of exploitative or productive technology and environment must be analyzed," that is, the relationship between material culture and natural resources. "Second, the behavior patterns involved in the exploitation of a particular area by means of a particular technology must be analyzed" (Steward 1973b:40–42). For example, certain animals are best stalked by individual hunters while other game can be captured in communal hunts; different social behaviors are involved in the exploitation of different resources. The third step in the analysis is to determine how "behavior patterns entailed in exploiting the environment affect other aspects of culture" (Steward 1973b:41). This three-step empirical analysis identifies the cultural core, "the constellation of features which are most closely related to subsistence activities and economic arrangements" (Steward 1973b:37).

Cultural ecology was not a form of unilineal evolution, but an attempt "to explain the origin of particular cultural features and patterns which characterize different areas rather than to derive general principles applicable to any cultural-environmental area" (Steward 1973b:36). Although it differed from the nineteenth-century unilineal evolutionary theories of Tylor (chapter 1), Morgan (chapter 2), or Marx and Engels, and lacked the broad, generalizing character of the twentieth-century theories of Leslie White (chapter 13) and Marvin Harris (chapter 15), cultural ecology was, nevertheless, a clear materialist strategy. Marvin Harris wrote,

> The essence of cultural materialism is that it directs attention to the interaction between behavior and environment as mediated by the human organism and its cultural apparatus. It does so as an order of priority with the prediction that group structure and ideology are responsive to these classes of material conditions. Turning to Steward's statement of the research strategy of cultural ecology [as summarized above], we find all of these attributes of cultural materialism clearly delineated. (1968:659)

By emphasizing human adaptation and the varying relationships between human societies and natural resources, cultural ecology provided both the analytical focus and the empirical bases for Steward's theory of culture change—multilinear evolution.

Multilinear Evolution

Steward's concept of cultural evolution rested on two key concepts: "First, it postulates that genuine parallels of form and function develop in historically independent sequences or cultural traditions. Second, it explains these parallels by the independent operation of identical causality in each case" (Steward 1973b:14). Thus, understanding cultural evolution involved discovering "parallels and similarities which recur cross-culturally" and proposing "lawlike" statements about the causes of such parallels (Steward 1973b:14). Steward's approach was to find and explain similarities between societies without assuming that all societies passed through identical stages of development. Multilinear evolution, he wrote, "deals only with those limited parallels of form, function, and sequence which have empirical validity. What is lost in universality will be gained in concreteness and specificity" (1973b:19).

For example, Steward compared the prehistoric patterns of developments in five independent centers of ancient civilization—Mesopotamia, Egypt, China, Mesoamerica, and the Andes. These centers shared "parallels of form, function, and sequence" based on having developed in arid and semiarid environments in which the economic basis was irrigation and floodwater agriculture. Agriculture created food surpluses that allowed for nonsubsistence activities and population growth. When population growth reached the limits of agricultural productivity, competition over natural resources intensified, warfare ensued, and political leadership shifted from temple priest to warrior king. As some communities prospered and others suffered, empires were forged that instituted strong political controls over vast regions (Steward 1973b:206–208).

Steward traced the evolutionary similarities in the five ancient civilizations. Although the chronology of events differed, Steward argued that there were striking parallels in the pattern of cultural evolution, not because there were universal stages of cultural development or due to the diffusion of civilization between regions, but because these five cultural traditions emerged in similar arid and semiarid environments where agriculture had been able to flourish. This development of agrarian civilizations in arid and semiarid environments was one "line" of the multilinear evolution that Steward proposed. Thus, Steward's multilinear evolution intentionally avoided sweeping statements about culture in general, applying more limited models to specific sets of cultures.

Conclusion

Julian Steward's theory of multilinear evolution has fallen out of favor among many anthropologists, but some of his insights are the anthropological equivalent of gospel. Steward's basic insights about the organization of band societies, the importance of cultural ecology, and the search for cross-cultural similarities are all firmly embedded in anthropological thought and practice. Steward's form of materialism emphasized (1) the central relationship between environment and culture and its implications for other aspects of social life, (2) the search for patterned regularities and similarities between societies, and (3) the importance of causal explanations of parallel developments over historical reconstructions. These central tenets of Steward's thought are recurrent themes in a body of work that was written over thirty years and originated in the arid landscape of the American West.

References

Clemmer, Richard, L. Daniel Myers, and Mary Rudden, eds.
1999 *Julian Steward and the Great Basin: The Making of an Anthropologist.* Salt Lake City: University of Utah Press.

Harris, Marvin
1968 *The Rise of Anthropological Theory: A History of Theories of Culture.* New York: Thomas Crowell.

Kerns, Virginia

2003 *Scenes from the High Desert: Julian Steward's Life and Theory*. Urbana: University of Illinois Press.

Leone, Mark, ed.

1972 *Contemporary Archaeology: A Guide to Theory and Contributions*. Carbondale: Southern Illinois University Press.

Manners, Robert

1973 Julian Haynes Steward, 1902–1972. *American Anthropologist* 75:886–903.

Murphy, Robert

1977 The Anthropological Theories of Julian Steward. In *Evolution and Ecology: Essays on Social Transformation*. J. Steward and R. Murphy, eds. Pp. 1–39. Urbana: University of Illinois Press.

Steward, Julian

1938 *Basin-Plateau Aboriginal Sociopolitical Groups*. Bureau of American Ethnology, Bulletin 120. Washington, D.C.: Smithsonian Institution.

1968 Cultural Ecology. In *International Encyclopedia of the Social Sciences*. Vol. 4. D. Sills, ed. Pp. 337–344. New York: Macmillan.

1973a *Alfred Kroeber*. New York: Columbia University Press.

1973b *Theory of Culture Change: The Methodology of Multilinear Evolution*. Urbana: University of Illinois Press.

1977a The Ceremonial Buffoon of the American Indian. In *Evolution and Ecology: Essays on Social Transformation*. J. Steward and R. Murphy, eds. Pp. 347–365. Urbana: University of Illinois Press.

1977b The Foundations of Basin-Plateau Society. In *Evolution and Ecology: Essays on Social Transformation*. J. Steward and R. Murphy, eds. Pp. 366–406. Urbana: University of Illinois Press.

Steward, Julian, ed.

1946–1950 *Handbook of South American Indians*. Bureau of American Ethnology, Bulletin 143. Vols. 1–6. Washington, D.C.: Smithsonian Institution.

1967 *Contemporary Change in Traditional Societies*. Urbana: University of Illinois Press.

Steward, Julian, and Louis Faron

1959 *Native Peoples of South America*. New York: Columbia University Press.

Steward, Julian, Robert Manners, Eric Wolf, Elena Padilla Seda, Sidney Mintz, and Raymond Scheele

1956 *The People of Puerto Rico: A Study in Social Anthropology*. Urbana: University of Illinois Press.

15

Marvin Harris

Cultural Materialism

The work of Marvin Harris (1927–2001) is solidly identified with the notion of cultural materialism, which, as he put it, "is based on the simple premise that human social life is a response to the practical problems of earthly existence" (1979:ix). It is a point of view thoroughly associated with Harris; as he said, "Although I did not invent 'cultural materialism,' I am responsible for giving it its name" (1979:x). Though intellectually indebted to Marx and Engels, Harris outlined a distinctive materialist approach to culture. In his numerous provocative and often provoking writings, Harris developed a coherent body of anthropological theory (Kuznar and Sanderson 2007).

Background

Harris received his Ph.D. in 1953 from Columbia University, where he taught until 1981, at which time he moved to the University of Florida, retiring as graduate research professor in 2000 (Margolis and Kottack 2003). Harris's ethnographic research and theoretical concerns are clearly connected. His research focused on Latin America, primarily Brazil, which led him to study Angola and Mozambique, former African colonies of Portugal. His first book, *Town and Country in Brazil* (1956), was based on fieldwork in Minas Velhas—literally "Old Mines" in Portuguese—located in the state of Bahia, Brazil. A straightforward ethnography, *Town and Country in Brazil* describes the growth of an isolated gold rush settlement that quickly became a regional center, but then faded in glory as the mines were worked out. Surrounding regions with more secure economies grew in importance, and Minas Velhas settled into a genteel oblivion distant from national life. Harris questioned classifying Brazil as a "rural" developing nation because many of its rural areas cannot be understood at all except in relation to hundreds of deeply entrenched urban nuclei like Minas Velhas spawned by the odd economics of mining.

Town and Country in Brazil is an early introduction to Harris's research agenda and his emphasis on infrastructure, which he later defines as the "technological, economic, demographic, and environmental activities and conditions directly related to sustaining health and well-being through the social control of production and reproduction" (1992:297). In his first book, Harris documented economic pursuits, the public economy, and class and race, but the distinctive factors in Minas Velhas were its establishment as a mining community and the importance of an urban ethos, a "complex of interconnected values" emphasizing the "preference for living in a town rather than in the country" (Harris 1956:279–280). It might seem that Harris had lapsed into idealism, but he quickly observed that there are "dynamic, functional factors which account for the persistence of these traits" and that once societies reach "the stage of technology and social organization in which a large number of people can be freed from food-producing activities and occupational specialization becomes feasible on a large scale, there is little likelihood of reverting to more homogeneous arrangements" (1956:283). The urban ethos of Minas Velhas reproduced and reinforced a social arrangement initially defined by infrastructure.

Harris's work in Brazil led to issues of race, as discussed in *Minorities in the New World* (1958), which he coauthored with Charles Wagley, and his later book, *Patterns of Race in the Americas* (1964). *Patterns of Race in the Americas* is a brief (ninety-nine pages), densely packed discussion of the roots of racism in the Americas, and it was published during the civil rights movement—the march on Selma, the freedom riders, and the inspiring oratory of Dr. Martin Luther King Jr. Harris contributed a powerful analysis of the economic origins of racism, constantly comparing the history of racism in Latin America and the United States. He traced the varying contours of unequal race relations between American Indians, Africans, and Europeans in the Americas to the differing impositions of economic systems of plantations, haciendas, or small farm holdings. It is interesting that in the 1960s, at a time in the United States when racism was considered a matter of unequal rights, Harris argued that it had an economic basis—an analysis that remains current.

But again, Harris gives explanatory priority to infrastructure, and that emphasis is fundamental in his 1968 magnum opus, *The Rise of Anthropological Theory*. If *Patterns of Race in the Americas* is a marvel of compression, *The Rise of Anthropological Theory* is a sprawling critique of Western thinking about the nature of culture and its evolution. Harris assessed the contributions of thinkers—from Plato to Montesquieu to Hegel—and anthropological schools—from culture and personality to structuralism to cultural evolution. In the process, he expressed an opinion, frequently negative, on almost every social thinker since the Enlightenment. Although Harris apologized in advance for his severe attacks on anthropologists past and present, he felt justified because "at this particular moment in the development of anthropological theory . . . critical judgments deserve priority over polite ones" (1968:7). Harris attacked the "dubious factual foundation on which [Ruth] Benedict reared her psychologistic portraits" (1968:404), accused Alfred Kroeber of making statements about changes in style and artistic achievement based on "the effete standards of salon gossip" (1968:331), and suggested that Claude Lévi-Strauss—far from plumbing the hidden structures of another culture—"may not even understand what's going on in his own head" (1968:511).

But why was Marvin Harris so mad? Harris's agenda had two tasks. First, he attacked the atheoretical legacy of Boas, arguing that historical particularism, far from being a neutral presentation of "just the facts," was a theoretical position characterized by a misinterpretation of nineteenth-century evolutionary social theorists and a murky view of science. Harris argued for the importance of anthropological theory in general and against a current of American anthropology in which "hypothesis" was used as a synonym for "guess" and "theory" for vague supposition.

Second, Harris advanced his own theoretical point of view, distinguishing it from other theories and claiming its greater logical utility. He dubbed that theory "cultural materialism."

Cultural Materialism

In the introduction of *The Rise of Anthropological Theory*, Harris described cultural materialism as the sociocultural analogue of Darwinian selection and immediately identifies it as nonidealist and evolutionary. There will be no appeal to human nature, to the utter uniqueness of different cultures, or to such intangibles as core values, superorganic configurations, or deep structures. Instead, Harris developed

> the principle of techno-environmental and techno-economic determinism. This principle holds that similar technologies applied to similar environments tend to produce similar arrangements of labor in production and distribution, and that these in turn call forth similar kinds of social groupings, which justify and co-ordinate their activities by means of similar systems of values and beliefs. Translated into a research strategy, the principle of techno-environmental, techno-economic determinism assigns priority to the study of the material conditions of sociocultural life, much as the principle of natural selection assigns priority to the study of differential reproductive success. (Harris 1968:4)

Harris distinguished his position, "cultural materialism," from philosophical materialism (such as, questions of the priority of matter or mind) and from dialectical materialism (the body of concepts formulated by Marx and Engels). He considered philosophical materialism irrelevant to considerations of sociocultural phenomena and subsumed dialectical materialism as a subset of cultural materialism. In the opening pages of *The Rise of Anthropological Theory*, Harris states, "I shall demonstrate that the failure to apply the cultural-materialist strategy resulted not from any reasonable program of oriented research, but from the covert pressures of the sociocultural milieu in which anthropology has achieved its disciplinary identity" (1968:5). With that, the challenge has been made.

Harris's most concise and also complete presentation of his theory is *Cultural Materialism: The Struggle for a Science of Culture* (1979). It begins by outlining the epistemological basis for cultural materialism, considering how scientific knowledge

> can be acquired. Alone among the things and organisms studied by science, the human "object" is also a subject; the "objects" have well-developed thoughts about their own and other people's thoughts and behaviors.
>
> No aspect of a research strategy more decisively characterizes it than the way in which it treats the relationship between what people say and think as subjects and what they say and think and do as objects of scientific inquiry. (Harris 1979:29)

Harris insisted that the relevant question is not "the reality" of the actions versus the ideas of people, or of sociocultural phenomena as observed versus sociocultural phenomena as experienced. Instead, Harris asserted, we must make two sets of distinctions: "First, the distinction between mental and behavioral events, and second, between emic and etic events." Behavioral events are simply "all the body motions and environmental effects produced by such motions, large and small, of all the human beings who ever lived." Mental events, on the other hand, "are all the thoughts and feelings that we humans experience within our minds" (Harris 1979:31–32). The second set of distinctions is between emic and etic. Emic perspectives convey a participant's point of view; etic perspectives are from an observer's point of view. These two ways of knowing imply different research approaches and agendas:

> Emic operations have as their hallmark the elevation of the native informant to the status of ultimate judge of the adequacy of the observer's descriptions and analyses. The test of the adequacy of emic analyses is their ability to generate statements the native accepts as real, meaningful, or appropriate.
>
> Etic operations have as their hallmark the elevation of observers to the status of ultimate judges of the categories and concepts used in descriptions and analyses. The test of the adequacy of etic accounts is simply their ability to generate sci-

> entifically productive theories about the causes of sociocultural differences and similarities. Rather than employ concepts that are necessarily real, meaningful, and appropriate from the native point of view, the observer is free to use alien categories and rules derived from the data language of science. Frequently, etic operations involve the measurement and juxtaposition of activities and events that native informants may find inappropriate or meaningless. (Harris 1979:32)

These distinctions lead to specific categories of human actions and thoughts. First are those relating to the needs of meeting subsistence requirements, the etic behavioral mode of production. Second are the actions taken to ensure the existence of the population, the etic behavioral mode of reproduction. Third are actions taken by each society to maintain "secure and orderly behavioral relationships among its constituent groups and with other societies," and because this is a principal area of discord, an associated set of behaviors are "the economic processes which allocate labor and the material products of labor to individuals and groups" (Harris 1979:51). Therefore, we are concerned with the etic behavioral domestic economies and etic behavioral political economies. A final etic category, behavioral superstructure, consists of acts related to the importance of symbolic processes for the human psyche—from art to advertising, ritual to sport. Harris then lumps—for no clear reason—modes of production and reproduction under the rubric "infrastructure" and domestic and political economies under the name "structure." When "behavioral superstructure" is added to these two categories, voilà—a tripartite scheme of etic behavior emerges: infrastructure, structure, and superstructure. Although Harris briefly sketched a parallel tripartite scheme for mental and emic components, he was uninterested in the effort and collapsed the framework as soon as it was constructed, leaving us with infrastructure, structure, and superstructure (all etic categories) and the fourth catchall, mental and emic superstructure (1979:54).

This is a circuitous route to arrive at a foregone destination, the principle of infrastructural determinism. "Infrastructure," Harris wrote, "is the principal interface between culture and nature, the boundary across which the ecological, chemical, and physical restraints to which human action is subject interact with the principal sociocultural practices aimed at overcoming or modifying those restraints" (1979:57).

Harris argued that studies focused on infrastructure have a "strategic priority" for anthropological research (and funding), justifying this claim on two points. First, if the goal of science is to create an ordered body of knowledge based on lawlike generalizations, then one should begin with those sociocultural arenas "under the greatest direct restraints from the givens of nature" (Harris 1979:57). Second, innovations in infrastructure tend to produce greater systemic changes since their reverberations are felt in the other arenas of structure, superstructure and mental/emic superstructure (Harris 1979:71–73). This does not mean that structure and superstructure "are insignificant, epiphenomenal reflexes of infrastructural factors" (Harris 1979:72). Rather, such dimensions often serve as regulating mechanisms that may counteract changes or enhance and amplify them. Innovations, Harris wrote,

> are unlikely to be propagated and amplified if they are functionally incompatible with the existing modes of production and reproduction—more unlikely than in the reverse. . . . This is what cultural materialists mean when they say that in the long run and in the largest number of cases, etic behavioral infrastructure determines the nature of structure and superstructure. (1979:73)

In short, understanding cultural patterns first requires explaining phenomena in terms of infrastructure—the culture/nature interface, as expressed by such dimensions as subsistence, settlement, population, demography, and so on—and then understanding how such changes reshape structure and superstructure. Harris employed this strategy in an evolutionary sketch of world history (1979:79–113), but also uses it to explain specific, contemporary social phenomena (1974, 1977, 1985), like the sacred cows of India and the collapse of the Soviet empire.

Sacred Cows and the End of Empire

Harris's cultural materialist approach is exemplified in analyses that explain perplexing social patterns by examining the nature of infrastructure. Two examples are "Why are there so many sacred cows in India?" and "Why did the Soviet Union collapse?"

To someone from the meat-eating West, the notion of cows wandering freely in India while people starve is a paradoxical waste of protein (Harris 1985). The Hindu ban on the slaughter of cattle and the consumption of beef would seem nonadaptive, a case where cultural rules run roughshod over common sense and, by extension, an illustration that mental superstructure, and not infrastructure, is causally prior.

The religious, symbolic, and political regulations associated with sacred cattle in India are well known. There are laws regulating the slaughter of cows in India's constitution, all but two states' laws forbid the slaughter of India's native humpbacked zebu cow, and a complete ban on cow slaughter is a common flash point of political agitation. In Hindu sacred literature, the god Krishna is described as a cowherd and protector of cows. Milk, butter, curds, urine, and dung are blended into a sacred nectar used to anoint religious statues and worshippers. Cows are decorated with flowers, placed in animal shelters when they are old and sick, in short, venerated and worshipped. The worship of cows is associated with the adoration of human motherhood. It is a major theme in political life; a constant friction between Muslims and Hindus is that Muslims eat beef. Similarly, British beef-eating was a rallying cause during India's independence movement, and one source of Mohandas Gandhi's political support was his ardent belief in the sacredness of the cow.

Consequently, India has more cows than any other nation in the world—an estimated 180 million plus 50 million water buffalo—a seeming waste created by illogical religious belief. Not surprisingly, Harris disagrees.

> Both politics and religion obviously play a role in reinforcing and perpetuating the beef and slaughter taboos, but neither politics nor religion explains why cattle slaughter and beef eating have achieved symbolic prominence. Why the cow and not the pig, horse, or camel? I do not doubt the symbolic power of the sacred cow. What I doubt is that the investment of symbolic power in one particular kind of animal and one particular kind of meat results from an arbitrary and capricious mental choice

> rather than from a definite set of practical constraints. Religion has affected India's foodways, but India's foodways have affected India's religion even more. (Harris 1985:51)

How has infrastructure produced the sacred cow? Harris's detailed answer can be distilled to a simple point—the need for oxen. Harris cites Vedic texts describing a beef-eating past (before 600 B.C.) when cattle were slaughtered for communal, carnivorous feasts. But as the human population increased and grazing lands were converted to farmlands, beef became too expensive and eventually was limited only to privileged castes. Beginning in the fifth century B.C., religions (Buddhism and Jainism) developed that banned killing, and during subsequent centuries milk, not meat, became the ritual food, and cow worship became part of Hinduism.

But the need for oxen as plow animals meant that cows were always necessary. Draft animals are needed on small farms. Today tractors are only more efficient on larger farms, and they break down and are expensive to repair. The poorest of India's farmers are the real owners of the supposedly stray animals wandering in the landscape; with no pasturage, the cows scavenge food from roadside vegetation, food stands, and garbage heaps. Producing little milk and only an occasional ox, the cow is nonetheless cost-efficient—sufficient reason for protection from slaughter:

> Not only did she give milk but she was the mother of the cheapest and most efficient traction animal for India's soils and climate. In return for Hindu safeguards against the reemergence of energetically costly and socially divisive beef-eating foodways, she made it possible for the land to teem with human life. (Harris 1985:66)

This is the interface between nature and culture: infrastructure pure and simple.

A second case is Harris's (1992) analysis of the demise of the Soviet Union. The deterioration of Soviet state Communism was not, as some contend, due to the triumph of capitalism, the unforeseen consequences of perestroika, or the political foresight of

American foreign policy. Instead, Harris argues that the Soviet Union collapsed because of infrastructural devolution.

On the eve of perestroika, per capita economic growth in the Soviet Union was at zero or less, grain production was unchanged over the previous decade in spite of heavy investments, and between 1970 and 1987 output per unit of input declined at the rate of 1 percent per year. Factories, agricultural equipment, generation plants, and transmission systems were worn and antiquated. The diffusion of technological innovations took three times longer in the Soviet economy than it did in the Western economies. Inadequate distribution systems meant that 20 percent to 50 percent of the wheat, potato, sugar beet, and fruit harvests were lost between farm and store. A broad range of pollution—from the radiation of Chernobyl to the poisoning of the Baltic, Black, and Caspian seas—was a further index of decline, as was the decrease in life expectancy for Soviet males (Harris 1992:298).

Such problems at the level of infrastructure were compounded by impediments at the structural level of the Soviet command economy. State-owned factories' budgets were allocated based on the number of employees rather than on the efficiency of production, creating payrolls of unneeded workers. Production quotas were stated in terms of output without quality control. "This meant that the penalties for inefficient and irrational management, such as excessive inventory, over-employment, and excess investment, were minimal and did not lead to the extinction of the enterprise" (Harris 1992:299). The command economy unevenly distributed the trickle of resulting production. Thus the interminable queues and unpredictable shortages that people endured in Moscow were paralleled by inequities between the republics. Russia gained more from the other republics than it redistributed. Harris points out that in the 1970s–1980s infant mortality increased in Kazakhstan by 14 percent, Turkmenistan by 22 percent, and in Uzbekistan by 48 percent (1992:300). The perception that Russia was benefiting at the expense of the other republics intensified nationalistic movements. "The collapse of state communism and the Soviet empire," Harris concluded, was "a case of selection against a political economy that increasingly impeded and degraded the performance of its infrastructure" (1992:300).

Harris's analysis of the Soviet Empire was presented as a distinguished lecture to the American Anthropological Association, and he directed a number of comments to his fellow anthropologists. He notes that

> infrastructural, structural and symbolic-ideational features are equally necessary components of human social life. It is no more possible to imagine a human society without a symbolic-ideational or structural sector than it is possible to imagine one without a mode of production and reproduction. Nonetheless, these sectors do not play a symmetrical role in influencing the retention or extinction of sociocultural innovations. (1992:297)

Rather, the realm of infrastructure is determinant. Innovations in the realm of infrastructure will tend to change structural and symbolic-ideational systems, while innovations in structural and symbolic-ideational systems that reduce the efficiency of the infrastructure, as measured "by the efficiency of productive and reproductive processes that sustain [human] health and well-being," will be selected against (Harris 1992:297). And that, Harris argued, is what happened to the Soviet Union.

Conclusion

As noted above, Harris gave causal priority to infrastructure in explanations of sociocultural innovations; he does not suggest that structural or symbolic-ideational realms are irrelevant or unimportant for understanding cultural change. There is a simply greater probability that innovations in infrastructure will cause changes in other realms than there is the reverse: symbolic-ideational innovations will not cause innovations if they are fundamentally incompatible with the infrastructure.

In his address to the American Anthropological Association, Harris pointed out that the causal primacy of infrastructure does not

> diminish our freedom to intervene and direct the selection of alternate futures. For along with the restraints come opportunities—opportunities that can deepen the benefits of social life

> for all of humankind. Recognition of the primacy of infrastructure does not diminish the importance of conscious human agency. Rather, it merely increases the importance of having robust theories of history that can guide conscious human choice. (1992:302)

But what does this tell us about other dimensions of culture? How do aspects of culture without direct adaptive consequences develop, spread, or get maintained? Let us grant, for the sake of argument, that Harris is correct that the infrastructural domain is likely to be regulated by laws. Why does that make other aspects of culture uninteresting? Harris's argument is this: anthropology is a science, science is based on laws, infrastructure is (most likely) governed by laws, therefore anthropology should focus on infrastructure. But what if anthropology is not a search for lawlike generalizations? What if it is a humanistic discipline, as Evans-Pritchard argued (see pp. 169–71), or one that "is not an experimental science in search of law, but an interpretive one in search of meaning," as Clifford Geertz (1973:5) stated (see pp. 263–66)?

Finally, how can we be so dismissive of the informant's emic viewpoint if culture is rooted in values and meanings held by individuals? Why should we give research priority to etic research focused on infrastructure when as anthropologists we are interested in the rich diversity of human cultures? Doesn't cultural materialism reduce human culture to mere matters of eating and breeding? These are some of the issues that emerged in the 1970s and later as American anthropology split into two major camps: those who argued for an anthropology grounded in the humanities and those—such as Marvin Harris—who advocated an anthropology modeled on natural science.

References

Geertz, Clifford
1973 *The Interpretation of Cultures*. New York: Basic Books.

Harris, Marvin
1956 *Town and Country in Brazil*. New York: Columbia University Press.
1964 *Patterns of Race in the Americas*. New York: Walker.

1968 *The Rise of Anthropological Theory: A History of Theories of Culture.* New York: Thomas Y. Crowell.

1974 *Cows, Pigs, Wars and Witches: The Riddles of Culture.* New York: Random House.

1977 *Cannibals and Kings: The Origins of Cultures.* New York: Random House.

1979 *Cultural Materialism: The Struggle for a Science of Culture.* New York: Random House.

1985 *Good to Eat: Riddles of Food and Culture.* New York: Simon and Schuster.

1992 Distinguished Lecture: Anthropology and the Theoretical and Paradigmatic Significance of the Collapse of Soviet and East European Communism. *American Anthropologist* 94:295–305.

Harris, Marvin, and Charles Wagley

1958 *Minorities in the New World.* New York: Columbia University Press.

Kuznar, Lawrence, and Stephen Sanderson, eds.

2007 *Studying Societies and Cultures: Marvin Harris's Cultural Materialism and Its Legacy.* Boulder, Colo.: Paradigm.

Margolis, Maxine, and Conrad Kottack

2003 Marvin Harris (1927–2001). *American Anthropologist* 105:685–688.

16

Eleanor Burke Leacock

Feminism, Marxism, and History

Eleanor Burke Leacock (1922–1987) was the leading Marxist feminist in American anthropology, and her contributions to the field were wide and profound. Her field research spanned forty years and covered such diverse topics as hunter-gatherer economies of Labrador, child rearing in Europe, educational ethnography in urban America and rural Zambia, the ethnohistory of the North American fur trade, and the problems of urban adolescents in Samoa. Leacock was a radical and leading exponent of Marxist analyses of human society, producing critical essays on Engels's *The Origins of the Family, Private Property, and the State* and on Morgan's *Ancient Society* (Leacock 1963, 1972, 1981a, 1981b). A central focus to Leacock's work was her argument that the subordination of women was the consequence of capitalism, not an innate reflection of gender differences. This argument was documented with rich ethnohistoric detail in her earliest writings and remained a central theme throughout her life (Leacock 1954, 1978, 1981c, 1982b).

Leacock's theoretical contributions were fundamental: she was one of the first American anthropologists to apply an explicitly Marxist approach to understanding ethnographic realities, particularly the historical transformation of women's status (Gailey 1993). She contributed to the postwar reemergence of evolutionary thinking in American anthropology but advocated a materialist approach markedly different from those of White, Steward, or Harris (Leacock 1958, 1982a). Lauded for her detailed research (Grumet 1993), her dissertation was published as a memoir of the American Anthropological Association (Leacock 1954)—a clear recognition of her scholarly contribution and academic promise.

Yet, Leacock was excluded from academic anthropology, marginalized by a discipline to which she contributed so much. She obtained her first tenure track position fifteen years after completing her Ph.D. at Columbia. In contrast, her male contemporaries at Columbia—including fellow radicals Elman Service, Morton Fried, and Stanley Diamond—were quickly hired by universities. In the pages of the *International Dictionary of Anthropologists* (Winter 1981), there is not even a brief mention of Eleanor Burke Leacock.

Why did this occur? Simply because, as Stanley Diamond writes, "being an honest scholar, a radical and a feminist, the going was rough" (1993:114). But the most difficult barrier Leacock faced was simply being a woman in American society.

Background

Eleanor Burke was born into a family enmeshed in radical and literary politics. Her father was the critic and writer Kenneth Burke, and her mother, Lily, was trained as a mathematician. In the early 1920s, Kenneth Burke became a full-time freelance critic, and as a biographer notes, "He began to earn enough to live in poverty" (Jay 1988:6). The family lived a mobile lifestyle, spending Easter to Thanksgiving on a rustic farm in northern New Jersey where the family gardened, cut wood, and hauled water and then moving to Greenwich Village each winter (Leacock 1993). It was an unconventional lifestyle, but it led Eleanor Burke to absorb values that "mixed the respect for manual work that characterized the marginal farming community . . . with the high esteem for intellectual integrity and independence that characterized the Bohemian circle of writers and artists in Greenwich Village" (Leacock 1993:5).

Burke began college at Radcliffe where she was exposed to the books of evolutionary archaeologist V. Gordon Childe and to the misogyny of Mayanist Alfred Tozzer, who announced to his class of Radcliffe women "bluntly and unsympathetically, that they should not go into anthropology unless they had independent incomes, because they would never get jobs" (Leacock 1993:7). Burke absorbed anthropology courses, participated in radical student groups, and in 1941 married Richard Leacock, a filmmaker who would work with Robert Flaherty and later direct the film studies program at the Massachusetts Institute of Technology.

Leacock returned to New York to complete her undergraduate education at Barnard and began graduate studies at Columbia, where she was influenced by Gene Weltfish and William Duncan Strong. Weltfish lectured on the political consequences of anthropological research, a concern Leacock took to heart (Leacock 1993:13–14). Strong's influence was also formative. An archaeologist and ethnologist who worked throughout the Americas (Solecki and Wagley 1963), Strong had conducted ethnographic research in Labrador in 1927–1928 (Leacock and Rothschild 1993) and was marginally involved in an anthropological debate over the social and economic organization of the Montagnais-Naskapi of the Labrador peninsula. Unlike many academic squabbles, this debate had content and consequence.

Property, Colonialism, and the Montagnais-Naskapi

In 1915 the anthropologist Frank Speck had documented that the Montagnais-Naskapi bands of Labrador held territory, essentially showing that private property ownership existed among hunters and gatherers and arguing that this was an aboriginal, precontact economic pattern (Speck 1915, 1923; Speck and Eiseley 1939). Speck's evidence for private land ownership countered claims by Morgan, Marx, and Engels that collective, not private, ownership was fundamental to hunting and gathering societies. Speck's study became more than an ethnographic obscurity when it was whipped into a "disproof" of Morgan, Marx, and Engels by antievolutionists like Robert Lowie (1920, 1927).

Sparked by Strong's unpublished data from Labrador (Leacock 1993:15; Leacock and Rothschild 1993), Leacock studied the early Jesuit accounts about Labrador at the Bibliothèque nationale in Paris and examined other historical sources for the sixteenth to nineteenth centuries. A basic point emerged from her ethnohistoric research: Montagnais-Naskapi social life had been dramatically restructured due to the fur trade.

In 1950 Leacock went to Labrador to conduct ethnographic research with the Montagnais-Naskapi. By collecting genealogies and mapping hunting territories, she was able to reconstruct the historical transformations of the hunting economy and Montagnais-Naskapi property relations. The combination of ethnohistoric and ethnographic sources deepened Leacock's knowledge of the Montagnais-Naskapi and the historical changes they had experienced. Individual ownership resulted from the changes in property relationships triggered by the fur trade; it was not, as Speck argued, an aboriginal economic institution. In her tightly documented monograph, *The Montagnais "Hunting Territory" and the Fur Trade*, Leacock (1954) carefully builds the argument. Speck had argued that the fur trade was relatively recent (since the 1700s) and its impacts too short-lived to create completely new property relations. Leacock shows how indirect trade began in the early 1500s and was of major importance by the early 1600s (1954:10–12). Citing historical accounts, Leacock documents (1) that prior to the eighteenth century hunting bands were fluid social groups freely ranging over large territories, (2) that individual ownership emerged in the eighteenth century, (3) that even in the twentieth century property rules distinguished between hunting for food and trapping for sale, and (4) that Jesuits, Hudson's Bay factors, and government officials had been actively changing Montagnais-Naskapi social and economic structures for four hundred years (Leacock 1954). Leacock concludes,

> It is becoming increasingly evident that Indian tribal life as recorded in the nineteenth and even late eighteenth centuries reflected important changes which had already come about as a result of the Indians taking an active part in the world-wide growth of trade and commerce. . . . The present study has taken the position that the [Montagnais-Naskapi] are no exception. Their apparent "primitivity" is deceptive. In order to reconstruct their aboriginal culture, one cannot simply record their recent life and subtract those traits that are of obvious European origin. One must work from the understanding that fun-

> damental socioeconomic changes have been taking place in some parts of their area for over three hundred years, one aspect of which is the development of the family hunting territory. (1954:43)

Apart from its substantive merits, Leacock's monograph contained two important, if tangential, points. First, the historical changes of the Montagnais-Naskapi showed that traditional, non-Western societies are not static—they change. This seems like an obvious point today—and it is central to the ideas of Eric Wolf (see pp. 350–56)—but it was not so clear to anthropology prior to 1950 when "primitive" cultures frequently were characterized as conservative and stable rather than innovative and dynamic. Thus, Tylor could view non-Western societies as fossilized representatives of earlier stages of human progress (see pp. 9–12), Radcliffe-Brown could view social structures as expressions of the stabilizing forces that maintain society (see pp. 154–55), and Benedict could view the Native American worldview as representing stable cultural configurations (see pp. 81–85).

Second, Leacock's emphasis on the transformations caused by the fur trade highlighted two dimensions of change: changing concepts of property and gender relations. Although sparked by an interest in primitive communism, Leacock intentionally camouflaged her interests in Marxism and evolution. Writing her dissertation at the height of the McCarthy era, Leacock buried her theoretical interests in dense ethnographic detail. Years later she wrote that when she discussed the historical transformations of production in Montagnais-Naskapi society, "I cited, not Marx as I should have, but a chance statement of the far-from-Marxist [Melville] Herskovits" (1982b:255). In 1954 it was simply too dangerous to admit to an interest in Marxism. Over the next twenty years the situation would change, and Eleanor Leacock emerged as a leading Marxist anthropologist.

Marxism and Feminism

In a personal reflection Leacock (1993) traced her radical roots to her upbringing and political experiences, but her personal outlook found support in the works of Lewis Henry Morgan and Friedrich Engels. Leacock wrote that her appreciation of Morgan "is born out of a perverse reaction to the virtually universal criticism of Morgan encountered in my student days, and reinforced both by my field experience and by the recognition that far more of Morgan's theory is already incorporated into the science of anthropology than is generally conceded" (1981b:106).

Christine Gailey notes that from the early 1960s Eleanor Leacock "would focus on the transformation of societies through colonially catalyzed class and state formation," giving particular attention to "the imposition or encouragement of capitalist development in the postcolonial period" and to consequent changes in women's authority and autonomy (1993:68).

Leacock's central argument stemmed directly from her field experience in Labrador. First, band-organized hunting and gathering societies tend to be characterized by communal ownership (particularly of land), egalitarian social relations, and nonhierarchical gender relationships (Leacock 1982a). Second, the evolution of class societies and the development of capitalism also produced changes from (1) kin-based societies that hold property communally and unify societies as collectivities, into (2) social systems that define groups which compete for resources and control of labor—an argument advanced by Morgan (Leacock 1982b:247; see pp. 26–29). In particular, the expansion of capitalist systems and the creation of commodity production and exchange resulted in the restructuring of social control over production and products—a point made by Marx (Leacock 1981a:14).

Finally, the subordination of women is an inevitable outcome of these economic changes. In her Labrador research, Leacock analyzed a very explicit program of economic and social changes implemented by the seventeenth-century Jesuit Paul le Jeune, who, as superior of the Jesuit mission of Quebec, studied Montagnais culture in order to convert and "civilize" the Indians (Leacock 1980, 1981c). This program involved several steps: the establishment of permanent settlements instead of traditional, mobile camps; the creation of chiefs; the introduction of corporal punishment, particularly of children; and finally the imposition of Catholic family values based on patriarchy, monogamy, female sexual fidelity, and the abolition of divorce.

How could such different cultural values be successfully imposed on the Montagnais? "The answer," Leacock wrote, "is that the Jesuits and their teachings arrived in New France a full century after the economic basis for unquestioned cooperation, reciprocity, and respect for individual autonomy had been undercut by the trading of furs for European goods" (1980:38). With the spread of the fur trade and the expansion of capitalism, women progressively were deprived of control over their labor, although the Montagnais retained a higher degree of respect and autonomy between the sexes than is found in other societies (Leacock 1980:40–41).

Leacock expanded her analysis beyond Labrador. In an extremely influential article, "Women's Status in Egalitarian Society: Implications for Social Evolution," Leacock (1978) showed how anthropologists' assumption that women had inferior status in most traditional societies reflected poor ethnographic research and the extension of biases inherent in the anthropologists' own class societies. Too many anthropologists had dealt with women's roles in other societies "with brief remarks about food preparation and child care" and comments on the sexual division of labor (Leacock 1978:247). Anthropologists had overlooked the degree of autonomy women in egalitarian societies have over their lives and activities, assuming that separate was unequal. Consequently, anthropologists, extrapolating from their own class-based societies, found women everywhere of lower status and then contended that female inferiority was cross-cultural. Leacock argued that this was false. (For an alternative view by Ortner, see pp. 311–15.)

Leacock's feminist anthropology, as Rapp argues, insisted "on the importance of locating family forms in evolutionary and historical processes, and on the explicitly political nature of monogamy, patriarchy, private property, and class relations" (1993:90). Thus Leacock's theoretical approach directly stems from Morgan, Engels, and Marx, but her ethnographic analyses are so richly documented and tightly argued that they read more like the writings of Franz Boas.

For Leacock, feminist anthropology was a principal element of a broader radical critique, one grounded in detailed attention to historical processes. Although colonialism and capitalism had common consequences, the ethnographic situations had to be understood based on specific, well-documented historical cases. Leacock wrote,

> Colonization characteristically brought disruption and devastation to foraging peoples and it is necessary to point this out. However, for ethical and political as well as scientific reasons, it is equally necessary to note and to document the resiliency and creativity with which different peoples moved to survive in, cope with, and take what advantage they could of new situations in which they found themselves. . . . They evolved new cultural forms which, although much changed from aboriginal times, continued to be distinctively theirs. (1978:168)

Conclusion

Eleanor Burke Leacock's work covered many different topics, but they shared a common set of themes. First, Leacock argued that the subordination of women was a product of history, not a universal condition (Sutton and Lee 1990:137). Second, Leacock emphasized the historical transformations caused by the development of class societies and the expansion of Western capitalism, causing anthropologists to be cautious in their assumptions about the "aboriginal" patterns in other societies. Finally, Leacock merged the Boasian tradition of establishing the historical context of cultural patterns with a Marxist tradition of engagement, creating a unique body of scholarship and activism.

References

Diamond, Stanley
1993 Eleanor Leacock's Political Vision. In *From Labrador to Samoa: The Theory and Practice of Eleanor Burke Leacock*. C. Sutton, ed. Pp. 111–114. Arlington, Va.: Association for Feminist Anthropology, American Anthropological Association.

Gailey, Christine

1993 Egalitarian and Class Societies: Transitions and Transformations. In *From Labrador to Samoa: The Theory and Practice of Eleanor Burke Leacock*. C. Sutton, ed. Pp. 67–76. Arlington, Va.: Association for Feminist Anthropology, American Anthropological Association.

Grumet, Robert

1993 Contributions to Native North American Studies. In *From Labrador to Samoa: The Theory and Practice of Eleanor Burke Leacock*. C. Sutton, ed. Pp. 47–55. Arlington, Va.: Association for Feminist Anthropology, American Anthropological Association.

Jay, Paul

1988 Introduction: Part One. In *The Selected Correspondence of Kenneth Burke and Malcolm Cowley, 1915–1981*. P. Jay, ed. Pp. 3–7. New York: Viking Press.

Leacock, Eleanor Burke

1954 *The Montagnais "Hunting Territory" and the Fur Trade. American Anthropologist* 56(5), part 2. American Anthropological Association, Memoir 78. Washington, D.C.: American Anthropological Association.

1955 Matrilocality in a Simple Hunting Economy (Montagnais-Naskapi). *Southwestern Journal of Anthropology* 11(1):31–47.

1958 Social Stratification and Evolutionary Theory: Introduction to a Symposium. *Ethnohistory* 3:193–199.

1963 Introduction. In *Ancient Society*. By Lewis Henry Morgan. New York: World.

1972 Introduction. In *The Origin of the Family, Private Property, and the State*. By Friedrich Engels. Pp. 7–67. New York: International.

1978 Women's Status in Egalitarian Society: Implications for Social Evolution. *Current Anthropology* 19(2):247–275.

1980 Montagnais Women and the Jesuit Program for Colonization. In *Women and Colonization: Anthropological Perspectives*. M. Etienne and E. Leacock, eds. Pp. 25–42. New York: Praeger.

1981a Introduction: Engels and the History of Women's Oppression. In *Myths of Male Dominance*. Collected by E. Leacock. Pp. 13–29. New York: Monthly Review Press.

1981b Introduction to Lewis Henry Morgan, *Ancient Society*, Parts I, II, III, IV. In *Myths of Male Dominance*. Collected by E. Leacock. Pp. 85–132. New York: Monthly Review Press.

1981c Seventeenth-Century Montagnais Social Relations and Values. In *Handbook of North American Indians*. Vol. 6: *Subarctic*. J. Helm, ed. Pp. 190–195. Washington, D.C.: Smithsonian Institution.

1982a Marxism and Anthropology. In *The Left Academy: Marxist Scholarship on American Campuses.* B. Ollman and E. Vernoff, eds. Pp. 242–276. New York: McGraw-Hill.

1982b Relations of Production in Band Society. In *Politics and History in Band Societies.* E. Leacock and R. Lee, eds. Pp. 159–170. Cambridge: Cambridge University Press.

1993 On Being an Anthropologist. In *From Labrador to Samoa: The Theory and Practice of Eleanor Burke Leacock.* C. Sutton, ed. Pp. 1–31. Arlington, Va.: Association for Feminist Anthropology, American Anthropological Association.

Leacock, Eleanor, and Nan Rothschild, eds.

1993 *William Duncan Strong's Labrador Winter.* Washington, D.C.: Smithsonian Institution.

Lowie, Robert

1920 *Primitive Society.* New York: Boni and Liveright.

1927 *The Origin of the State.* New York: Harcourt, Brace.

Rapp, Rayna

1993 Eleanor Leacock's Contributions to the Anthropological Study of Gender. In *From Labrador to Samoa: The Theory and Practice of Eleanor Burke Leacock.* C. Sutton, ed. Pp. 87–94. Arlington, Va.: Association for Feminist Anthropology, American Anthropological Association.

Solecki, R., and C. Wagley

1963 William Duncan Strong, 1899–1962. *American Anthropologist* 65:1102–1111.

Speck, Frank

1915 The Family Hunting Band as the Basis of Algonkian Social Organization. *American Anthropologist* 17:289–305.

1923 Mistassini Hunting Territories in the Labrador Peninsula. *American Anthropologist* 25:452–471.

Speck, Frank, and Loren Eiseley

1939 The Significance of the Hunting Territory Systems of the Algonkian in Social Theory. *American Anthropologist* 41:269–280.

Sutton, Constance, and Richard Lee

1990 Eleanor Burke Leacock (1922–1987). *American Anthropologist* 92:201–5.

Winter, Christopher, ed.

1981 *International Dictionary of Anthropologists.* New York: Garland.

V

STRUCTURES, SYMBOLS, AND MEANING

Beginning in the 1960s anthropological theory has been characterized by divergence. Unlike previous periods when a few theoretical positions dominated the field, the last decades have been characterized by a multiplicity of unreconcilable theoretical points of view. As anthropologist Sherry Ortner wrote in 1984,

> The field appears to be a thing of shreds and patches, of individuals and small coteries pursuing disjunctive investigations and talking mainly to themselves. We do not even hear stirring arguments any more. Although anthropology was never actually unified in the sense of adopting a single shared paradigm, there was at least a period when there were a few large categories of theoretical affiliation, a set of identifiable camps or schools, and a few simple epithets one could hurl at one's opponents. (1984:126–127)

Yet, certain themes run through anthropological theories since the 1960s, and they point to the idealist nature of current explanations. There has been a general movement away from materialist theories, such as those discussed in the previous section, that treat culture as humanity's principal means of adaptation to the physical and social environment. In addition, there is an increased emphasis on the way in which individual actions creatively shape culture and, by extension, a diminished effort to reify culture as somehow separable from the individual, as Kroeber argued (see chapter 5).

Finally, the symbolic nature of culture has come to dominate definitions of culture, and this has had several consequences. A symbolic approach to culture means that ethnographic studies that emphasize ecological, economic, or other materialist concerns have fallen into disfavor in some anthropological circles.

Perhaps more importantly, a symbolic approach to culture inevitably leads to a concern with meanings: If culture is symbolic, then it follows that it is used to create and convey meanings since that is the purpose of symbols. If meanings are the end products of culture, then understanding culture requires understanding the meanings of its creators and users. And if that is true, then culture is unknowable to the etic observer, since the meanings are only obtainable from the emic insider's point of view.

And this shift has led to a subtle atomization of theoretical models. As theoretical definitions have highlighted culture's symbolic aspects, explanations of cultural patterns have become increasingly localized. If, for example, culture is the creation of symbolic meanings and these meanings differ even among the individuals involved in a single cultural exchange (such as a ritual, a conversation, or a coronation), then there can be, to recall Edward Sapir's phrase, "as many cultures as there are individuals in a population." And since symbols contain multiple layers of meaning, explaining cultural behavior becomes an interpretive task in which the anthropologist unravels tangled skeins of significances as seen from the insiders' points of view.

The shifting points of view discernible in the works of Claude Lévi-Strauss, Victor Turner, Clifford Geertz, and Mary Douglas are a long way from the simple definition of culture used by Edward Tylor. For Lévi-Strauss, culture involves a variety of communicative exchanges in the domains of kinship, myth, and language. For all their superficial variety, these exchanges follow a relatively small set of basic forms or "deep structures." These structures reflect a universal grammar of culture that is rooted in the subconscious properties of the human mind and exposes the principles by which humans classify. With a legacy in the Durkheimian concern with representations, Lévi-Strauss's structuralism views culture as the symbolic expression of the human mind.

The works of Victor Turner equally emphasized the symbolic nature of culture but place its explanation within the dynamics of social life. Symbols are used and meanings are created in public, social exchanges. Symbols have specific properties: they are powerful concentrates of meaning, their meanings are multiple, and the meanings vary for different members of a society. Understanding cultural life requires isolating symbols, identifying their meanings, and showing how symbols resonate within a specific, dynamic cultural context.

Clifford Geertz shared this interest in the symbolic basis of culture. For Geertz, culture involved the acting out of worldview, values, and ethos—the particular "core values," to use Benedict's phrase—that give societies their distinctive styles. This process, however, is extremely complex because the use of symbols and the creation of meaning inevitably involve misunderstandings, differences of opinions about meaning, and conflicts between individuals in their use of symbols. Thus, one cannot make global statements about "Culture X believes . . . ," which are common in earlier ethnographies. Explication involves situating an event in a particular cultural actor(s)' motives, values, and intentions. In turn, the anthropologist's role is not to explain a cultural event within an overarching, universal framework, but to interpret it within a specific code of meanings.

In her ethnographic works, Mary Douglas explored the social categories of cultural meanings. Extending a line of analysis that clearly originates in the ideas of Durkheim and Mauss, Douglas examined the ways in which cultural statements about symbolic purity and contamination—food taboos, behavioral prohibitions, avoidance rules—are restatements of ideas about society. Douglas analyzes how humans articulate symbolic systems and social institutions to make meaningful and unique assertions about who they are.

As anthropological theories have shifted, there has been increasing attention on the role of the anthropological observer. If culture is the creation of meanings and explanation is their interpretation, then how does the anthropologist influence meaning? How can these different experiences be translated faithfully and how can veracity be measured? Is the anthropologist writing an account of another culture always and inevitably writing autobiography? How do the genres we use to describe another society shape understanding? If we treat others as subjects described in a scientific format, are we dehumanizing them?

Anthropologists rarely worried about such issues before 1960, or if they did, they kept it to themselves. But the increasing emphasis on the symbolic nature of culture and the interpretive basis of explanation leads almost inevitably to these concerns that influence ongoing debates in anthropological theory.

Reference

Ortner, Sherry

1984 Theory in Anthropology since the Sixties. *Comparative Studies in Society and History* 26:126–166.

17

Claude Lévi-Strauss

Structuralism

The anthropologist Claude Lévi-Strauss (b. 1908) occupies a unique position in the development of anthropological theory and the intellectual life of the twentieth century. In anthropology Lévi-Strauss is known as the founder of structuralism, an approach that emerged uniquely in his work. The ideas of Lévi-Strauss seemed fully developed and utterly original at first sight, yet the importance of his anthropological ideas were recognized belatedly in the United States, similar to American anthropologists' treatment of Émile Durkheim. The anthropologist Robert Murphy wrote that *Les structures élémentaires de la parenté* was read "by most French anthropologists, many English anthropologists, and few American anthropologists—a gradient that reflected facility with French rather than doctrinal schisms" (1970:165).

The cultural critic George Steiner wrote that the relevance of Lévi-Strauss's "work on the notion of culture, on our understanding of language and mental process, on our interpretation of history is so direct and novel that an awareness of Lévi-Strauss' thought is part of cultural literacy" (1977:241). And the essayist and novelist Susan Sontag, describing the modern search for moral place, wrote, "The anthropologist is thus not only the mourner of the cold world of the primitives, but its custodian as well. Lamenting among the shadows, struggling to distinguish the archaic from the pseudoarchaic, he acts out a heroic, diligent, and complex modern pessimism" (1966:69–81). Claude Lévi-Strauss was, in Sontag's well-known phrase, "the anthropologist as hero."

The ascent of Lévi-Strauss to such pinnacles of esteem has confounded any number of commentators and the heroic anthropologist himself. Lévi-Strauss's popularity was the French intellectual's equivalent of the hula hoop, as Sanche de Gramont observed (1970:8). Steiner wondered if those who invoked "Lévi-Strauss" and "structuralism" like the words of a magic spell had actually read his works (1977:239). And Robert Murphy groused that Lévi-Strauss's "vogue has spread throughout the United States . . . making him as unavoidable at cocktail parties as the cheese dip" (1970:165).

Even Lévi-Strauss was mystified by the intense popularity of structuralism in the 1960s and 1970s. Part of the intensity was created by the verbal jousting between Lévi-Strauss and Jean-Paul Sartre, a debate that began in the last chapter of *The Savage Mind* (Lévi-Strauss 1966) but quickly spilled into the pages of intellectual journals and personified the conflicts between existentialism and structuralism as reigning systems of thought.

Yet four decades later, as Robert Deliège observes, "One would have to go a long way to find a structuralist anthropologist today. This movement, which held many intellectuals in thrall for decades, has now fallen so far out of fashion that it might seem like one of the eccentricities of a by-gone era" (2004:1). Lévi-Strauss commented on the fadish popularity of structuralism:

> The educated public in France is bulimic. For a while, it fed on structuralism. People thought it carried a message. That fashion has passed. A fashion lasts for five or ten years. . . . That's how things go in Paris. I have neither nostalgia nor regret. (Lévi-Strauss and Eribon 1991:91–92)

But beyond mere fad, Lévi-Strauss achieved this intense interest among the reading public because of the depth of his insights and the breadth of his prose. Anthropologist Bob Scholte describes him as "a French savant par excellence, a man of extraordinary sensitivity and human wisdom, an encompassing mode of considerable erudition and philosophical scope, a deliberate stylist with profound convictions and convincing arguments" (1970:146). Claude Lévi-Strauss is an institution in French intellectual life and a lifelong Parisian; his central experience was to encounter that "single, awe-inspiring presence: the New World" (Lévi-Strauss 1974:80).

Background

Claude Lévi-Strauss was born in 1908. The son of a painter whose fortunes diminished with the waning tastes for the Belle Epoque, Lévi-Strauss was raised in a household that was very rich intellectually but not without "struggles with material difficulties" (Lévi-Strauss and Eribon 1991:5). After graduating from the Sorbonne in 1932 with degrees in philosophy and law, Lévi-Strauss taught at a lycée for the next two years and was active in socialist politics. Tiring of teaching, Lévi-Strauss returned to the university to pursue postgraduate studies in sociology, which was still very much Durkheim's science of society (and incorporated anthropology).

In 1935 he got the chance to join a French educational mission involved in establishing the University of Sao Paulo, Brazil, which only had a few dozen students. Lévi-Strauss developed his interest in anthropology and at the end of his first academic year began fieldwork among the Indian tribes of the Mato Grosso in western Brazil. He wrote of his first encounter with a group of Tibagy, a group of enculturated Native Americans, who had been contacted by the Brazilian Indian Protection Service and then thrown back on their own resources:

> So, to my great disappointment, the Tibagy Indians were neither completely "true Indians," nor what was more important, "savages." But, by removing the poetry from my naive vision of what experiences lay ahead, they taught me, as a beginner in anthropology, a lesson in prudence and objectivity. Although I had found them to be less unspoiled than I had hoped, I was to discover that they were more mysterious than their external appearance might lead one to believe. (1974:154)

In 1936 Lévi-Strauss published his first anthropological article, "Contribution . . . l'étude de l'organisation sociale des Indiens Bororo" in the *Journal de la Société des Américanistes*, and soon his work was known by Americanists like Robert Lowie, Curt

Nimuendaju, and Alfred Métraux. Over the next few years Lévi-Strauss made brief trips into the interior of Brazil, but in 1938 he obtained French support for a longer expedition. He traveled to the far northwestern corner of Brazil, along the border with Bolivia, where he carried out research among the Nambikwara and Tupi-Kawahib, an experience beautifully described in *Tristes tropiques.* In the beginning of 1939, however, Lévi-Strauss returned to Europe where he hoped to organize his collections, prepare a thesis, and reenter academic life in France.

World War II made that impossible. After a few months of military service, Lévi-Strauss, along with the rest of the French army except for de Gaulle's Free French, was demobilized by the Vichy government. For a brief period he returned to teaching until the imposition of racial laws ended his job. Though his parents did not practice their Judaism, Lévi-Strauss's maternal grandfather was a rabbi; his Jewish heritage made him an obvious target when the Nazis occupied France in 1940. Fortunately, it was still possible to leave Vichy France, and Lowie and Métraux were able to obtain a position for Lévi-Strauss at the New School of Social Research in New York. The Rockefeller Foundation was actively involved in rescuing European intellectuals at risk from the Nazis, and New York became a vast expatriate community of artists and scholars.

After a squalid sea voyage in a ship crammed with refugees, Lévi-Strauss arrived in New York. He taught at the New School from 1942 to 1945, interacting with anthropologists at Columbia (Boas, Linton, Benedict, Mead) and other scholars such as Kroeber and Lowie who visited New York. This personal exposure to American cultural anthropology with its emphasis on values and ethos influenced Lévi-Strauss and complemented his concerns with classifications and representations derived from Durkheim and Mauss.

During his exile in New York, Lévi-Strauss began work on his first major book, *The Elementary Structures of Kinship* (1969a). At the end of the war, Lévi-Strauss was assigned the position of cultural counselor to the French embassy; his duties kept him in New York, and he continued to write. He returned to France in 1947 where he presented *Les structures élémentaires de la parenté* as a doctoral thesis at the Sorbonne, receiving his Doctorat ès lettres in 1948. He served as assistant curator of ethnology at the Musée de l'Homme and was then elected to a chair at the École des Hautes Études, the same position that Marcel Mauss once held.

With the publication of *Les structures élémentaires de la parenté* in 1949, *Tristes tropiques* in 1955, and *Anthropologie structurale* (volume 1) in 1958 (volume 2 appeared in 1973), Lévi-Strauss became very well known in French letters. His books were widely reviewed in leading intellectual journals, he participated in international organizations, and after two unsuccessful nominations, he was made a member of the illustrious Collège de France in 1959 where he taught until 1982. The pinnacle of French academia, the Collège consists of fifty elite professors, each elected by fellow faculty, whose responsibilities are to teach one course annually, but each on a new topic (Lévi-Strauss 1987:1–3). Those courses were the testing ground for Lévi-Strauss's ideas on structural anthropology, which appeared in such works such as *The Savage Mind* (1966) and *Totemism* (1963b), and his monumental studies of the nature of myth, which resulted in the publication of four volumes in his Mythologiques series: *The Raw and the Cooked* (1969b), *From Honey to Ashes* (1973), *The Origin of Table Manners* (1978), and *The Naked Man* (1981). It represents a prodigious creation and analysis. These are difficult, demanding writings in which logical constructs are devised only to be dismantled by new tacks of analysis. Sanche de Gramont wrote, "His books are possibly the greatest collection of riddles since the Sphinx" (1970:16).

In retirement Lévi-Strauss has continued to work, writing the *The View from Afar* (1985) and *The Jealous Potter* (1988), publishing a collection of photographs from his ethnographic explorations in the Matto Grosso (1995), and writing a brilliant collection of essays on art, literature, and music—*Look, Listen, Read* (1997). In all these works, anthropology frames his personal perspectives. Lévi-Strauss has written deeply on his personal attraction to anthropology:

> Anthropology affords me intellectual satisfaction: as a form of history, linking up at opposite ends with world history and my own history, it thus reveals the rationale common to both. In proposing the study of mankind, anthropology frees me from

> doubt, since it examines those differences and changes in mankind which have a meaning for all men, and excludes those peculiar to a single civilization, which dissolve into nothingness under the gaze of an outside observer. Lastly it appeases that restless and destructive appetite [for new knowledge and intellectual challenges] I have already referred to, by ensuring me a virtually inexhaustible supply of material, thanks to the diversity of manners, customs and institutions. It allows me to reconcile my character with my life. (1974:58–59)

That restless process of reconciliation has led to one of the great intellectual searches of the twentieth century: the search for structures of the unconscious that shape the forms of cultural life.

Structural Anthropology

Lévi-Strauss argues that "social anthropology is devoted especially to the study of institutions considered as systems of representations" (1963a:3). Lévi-Strauss uses "representations" as Durkheim did, to refer to beliefs, sentiments, norms, values, attitudes, and meanings. Those institutions are cultural expressions that are usually unexamined by their users; in that narrow but fundamental sense anthropology examines the unconscious foundations of social life: "Anthropology draws its originality from the unconscious nature of collective phenomena" (Lévi-Strauss 1963a:18). This search for the underlying structures of social life led Lévi-Strauss to explore three principal areas: systems of classification, kinship theory, and the logic of myth.

Edmund Leach, not usually sympathetic to Lévi-Strauss, provides a handy paraphrase of the basic argument of structuralism:

> The general argument runs something like this: what we know about the external world we apprehend through our senses. The phenomena which we perceive have the characteristics which we attribute to them because of the way our senses operate and the way the human brain is designed to order and interpret the stimuli which are fed into it. One very important

> feature of this ordering process is that we cut up the continua of space and time with which we are surrounded into segments so that we are predisposed to think of the environment as consisting of vast numbers of separate things belonging to named classes, and to think of the passage of time as consisting of sequences of separate events. Correspondingly, when, as men, we construct artificial things (artifacts of all kinds), or devise ceremonials, or write histories of the past, we imitate our apprehension of Nature: the products of our Culture are segmented and ordered in the same way as we suppose the products of Nature to be segmented and ordered. (1970:21)

The segmentation and imposition of form on inherently formless phenomena (like space or time) reflect deeply held structures from the bedrock of humanness. At this point, the theoretical parallels between linguistics and the study of language and anthropology and the study of culture become important. Structuralism is not a mere restatement of the Sapir-Whorf hypothesis; Lévi-Strauss does not argue that language shapes cultural perceptions in that direct manner (1963a:73, 85). Rather, there are parallels between language and certain aspects of culture such as kinship, exchange, and myths, because they are all forms of communication:

> In any society, communication operates on three different levels: communication of women, communication of goods and services, communication of messages. Therefore kinship studies, economics, and linguistics approach the same kinds of problems on different strategic [that is, methodological] levels and really pertain to the same field. (Lévi-Strauss 1963a:296)

The path of analysis had been blazed by the development of structural linguistics, which Lévi-Strauss was introduced to by the linguist and Slavic specialist Roman Jakobson during their shared exile in New York. Lévi-Strauss states, "At the time I was a kind of naive structuralist, a structuralist without knowing it" (Lévi-Strauss and Eribon 1991:41), but learning of the advances in linguistics was "a revelation." According to Lévi-Strauss, the revolutionary aspects of these developments were (1) the shift of linguistic focus from conscious behavior to unconscious structure, (2) the new focus on the relations between terms rather than on terms, (3) the importance of proving the concrete existence of systems of relationships of meaning, and (4) the goal of discovering general laws (1963a:33). Those became Lévi-Strauss's analytical objectives as he turned to examinations of kinship, exchange, art, ritual, and myth—all of which are forms of communication analogous to language (Lévi-Strauss 1963a:83–84).

Phonemes are the minimal units of sound that a group of speakers consider distinct; for example, the aspirated /t^h/ in "top" and the unaspirated /t/ in "stop" are considered to be the same sound "t" in English but are different sounds in Thai. Lévi-Strauss argues that phonemes and kinship terms are both elements of meaning, although meaningful only in reference to systems that "are built by the mind on the level of unconscious thought" (1963a:34). A kinship system, like language, "exists only in human consciousness; it is an arbitrary system of representations," but representations whose organizations reflect unconscious structures (Lévi-Strauss 1963a:50). Consequently, Lévi-Strauss holds that

> the unconscious activity of the mind consists in imposing forms upon content, and if these forms are fundamentally the same for all minds—ancient and modern, primitive and civilized (as the study of the symbolic function, expressed in language, so strikingly indicates)—it is necessary and sufficient to grasp the unconscious structure underlying each institution and custom. (1963a:21)

A Structural Approach to Kinship: Analysis of the Avunculate

In *The Elementary Structures of Kinship,* Lévi-Strauss provides an encyclopedic summary of kinship systems but focuses on a central theme: kinship systems are about the exchange of women, defining the categories of potential spouses and prohibited mates. "Marriage is thus a dramatic encounter between nature and culture, between alliance and kinship. . . . [M]arriage is an arbitration between two loves, parental and conjugal" (Lévi-Strauss 1969a:489). The value of this way of seeing kin relationships is demonstrated by his analysis of the relationship between a young man (Ego) and his mother's brother, an institution called the avunculate.

The avunculate is a recurrent problem in kinship literature. Kin systems that recognized a special bond between Ego and his maternal uncle—often expressed in a joking relationship—had been interpreted as remnants of matrilineal systems, until they were shown to exist in patrilineal systems as well. Yet the avunculate relationship expresses not only a system of kin terminology but also a system of attitudes, and Lévi-Strauss, following Radcliffe-Brown, argued that the "avunculate covers two antithetical systems of attitudes": one in which the uncle is feared and respected and one in which the relationship is easy and familiar (1963a:40). Further, there is an inverse relationship in the attitudes between Ego and his maternal uncle (mother's brother) and Ego and his father; when the relationship between Ego and mother's brother is familiar, the relationship between Ego and Father is formal, and vice versa.

Even more interesting is that these relationships (Ego:Father and Ego:Mother's Brother) are linked to other relationships, namely between Ego's father and mother or husband and wife (Father:Mother) and between brother and sister, in this case Ego's mother and Ego's mother's brother (Mother:Mother's Brother). The relationship between Ego and his maternal uncle fits into a set of relationships in which (1) the relationships between Ego and Father and Ego and Maternal Uncle are inversely correlated, and (2) the relationships between Father and Mother (or husband and wife) and Mother and Mother's Brother (or brother and sister) also are inversely correlated. This produces the possible arrangements shown in the diagram.

	A	B	C	D
Ego and Father	+	+	−	−
Ego and Mother's Brother	−	−	+	+
Father and Mother	+	−	−	+
Mother and Mother's Brother	−	+	+	−

+ = familiar relationship; − = formal or hostile relationship

The avunculate only makes sense as one relationship within a system, a structure in which there are attitudinal oppositions between generations and between husband and wife and brother/sister, constituting "the most elementary form of kinship that can exist. It is properly speaking, the unit of kinship" (Lévi-Strauss 1963a:46). It expresses the fundamental relationships of consanguinity, affinity, and descent in a formal, structured manner. That same search for structure led Lévi-Strauss to another domain of cultural phenomena—the study of myth.

Structural Approach to Myth: The Story of Asdiwal

Lévi-Strauss expanded his search for structure by turning to the study of myth because "the elements of mythical thought . . . lie half-way between precepts and concepts" (1966:18), relying on both concrete situations and the notions to which they refer. Mythical thought "builds up structured sets, not directly with other structured sets," but by using the odds and ends of experience, building "ideological castles out of the debris of what once was a social discourse" (Lévi-Strauss 1966:21–22). Thus, "the myth is certainly related to given facts, but not as a representation of them. The relationship is of a dialectic kind, and the [social] institutions described in the myths can be the very opposite of the real institutions" (Lévi-Strauss 1976:172). It is, therefore, incorrect to see myths as reflections of social reality; rather, they are created transformations of social existence. "The conception of the relation of myth to reality," Lévi-Strauss writes, "no doubt limits the use of the former as a documentary source. But it opens the way for other possibilities; for, in abandoning the search for a constantly accurate picture of ethnographic reality in the myth, we gain, on occasions, a means of unconscious categories" (1976:173).

In *The Raw and the Cooked*, Lévi-Strauss lays out his hypothesis explicitly:

> Mythology has no obvious practical function: unlike the phenomena previously studied, it is not directly linked with a different kind of reality, which is endowed with a higher degree of objectivity than its own and whose injunctions it might

> therefore transmit to minds that seem perfectly free to indulge their creative spontaneity. And so, if it were possible to prove in this instance too [as in the case with kinship classifications] that the apparent arbitrariness of the mind, its supposedly spontaneous flow of inspiration, and its seemingly uncontrolled inventiveness imply the existence of laws operating at a deeper level, we would inevitably be forced to conclude that when the mind is left to commune with itself and no longer has to come to term with objects, *it is in a sense reduced to imitating itself as an object.* (1969b:10, emphasis added)

If basic unconscious structures were found in myth, then that might reflect the existence of fundamental mental structures that provide the organizing categories of cultural phenomena.

Mythology was the subject of four volumes in his series of Mythologiques (literally "logics of myth"): *The Raw and the Cooked, From Honey to Ashes, The Origin of Table Manners,* and *The Naked Man.* The series, as Lévi-Strauss points out, progressively expands its geographic focus, beginning with myths from central and eastern Brazil and then expanding to much of South America and moving north to focus on North America. In a parallel manner, the studies treat progressively more complex problems considered by different myths (Lévi-Strauss and Eribon 1991:135). Lévi-Strauss also addressed the complex problems reflected by myth throughout his writings.

One example is his analysis of the story of Asdiwal, a myth Boas had recorded among the Tsimshian of British Columbia. "The Story of Asdiwal" is Lévi-Strauss's most commonly reprinted analysis of myth, published in the second volume of *Structural Anthropology* (1976) and in several edited collections (Bohannan and Glazer 1988; Dundes 1984; Leach 1967). It is a complex story, and the reader is urged to examine the detailed synopsis that Lévi-Strauss provides in his article. Doing little justice to the myth, it can be summarized in the following schematic form:

> (1) During the famine of winter, a mother and daughter, both widowed, leave their respective villages and meet on the banks of the Skeena River where they suffer, finding only a single rotten berry to eat.

(2) The women are visited by a mysterious stranger, Hatsenas, the bird of good omen. They begin to find food, Hatsenas sires a son with the younger woman, and the culture hero Asdiwal is born.

(3) After Hastenas's disappearance and the older woman's death, Asdiwal and his mother head west to the mother's native village. There Asdiwal hunts a white she-bear that leads him up a ladder into the heavens where the she-bear is transformed into the beautiful girl Evening-Star, who successfully lures Asdiwal to the house of her father, the Sun. Asdiwal and Evening-Star marry, but only after a series of trials does Asdiwal win the Sun's approval.

(4) Asdiwal longs to see his mother and to return to earth, which he does with four inexhaustible baskets of food. Asdiwal commits adultery with a woman from his home village, the marriage with Evening-Star ends, and Asdiwal's mother dies. Loose of all social bonds, he sets off downstream.

(5) Asdiwal arrives at a downstream village, marries a woman there, then antagonizes his new wife's brothers who break camp, taking Asdiwal's wife with them. Asdiwal meets another band, marries a woman from that band, enjoys fortune, but then, bragging that he can hunt sea lions better than his newest set of brothers-in-law, Asdiwal is stranded on a reef as a large storm occurs. Fortunately, Hastenas appears and Asdiwal is transformed into a bird that can hover above the waves.

(6) Asdiwal falls asleep exhausted when the storm finally ends, but a mouse wakes him and leads him to the subterranean lair of the sea lion that Asdiwal has wounded. Since Asdiwal's arrows are magic and invisible, the sea lions think they are dying from an epidemic and are grateful to Asdiwal when he cures them by extracting the arrows. In repayment, the king of the sea lions helps Asdiwal reach land. There Asdiwal carves wooden killer whales that come to life and attack the boats of his brothers-in-law, avenging Asdiwal for their treachery.

(7) After a long and eventful life, Asdiwal goes on a winter hunting trip when he becomes lost. Asdiwal is transformed into stone where he may be seen on a peak on the Skeena River. (Lévi-Strauss 1976:149–152)

Lévi-Strauss identifies four levels of representations within this myth: geographic, techno-economic, sociological, and cosmological. The myth describes rivers, place-names, famines, postmarital residence patterns, and relationships between affinal kin; these descriptions are not distorted reflections of reality, but a multilayered model of structural relationships. Lévi-Strauss proposes that there are two aspects in the construction of the myth: the sequence of events that form the apparent content of what happened and the schemata of the myth, which represent the different planes of abstraction on which the sequence is organized (1976:161–165). On the geographic level, there is the basic opposition between east and west, while on the cosmological level, there are oppositions of the highest heaven and the subterranean world. There are integration schema such as water/land and sea hunting/land hunting that cross geographic and cosmological schema. There are sociological schema, such as the changes in postmarital residence patterns from patrilocal to neolocal to matrilocal (for example, Asdiwal's mother and grandmother leave their husbands' villages and establish a new settlement, and then in the next generation Asdiwal settles in Evening-Star's village). Structural analysis clarifies the multiple levels of meanings in the story of Asdiwal:

> Asdiwal's two journeys—from east to west and from west to east—were correlated with types of residence, matrilocal and patrilocal, respectively. But in fact the Tsimshian have patrilocal residence, and from this we can . . . draw the conclusion that one of the orientations corresponds to the direction implicit in a real-life "reading" of their institutions, the other to the opposite direction. (Lévi-Strauss 1976:173)

Lévi-Strauss views the east-west axis as the structural parallel between imaginary and real, and therefore Imaginary/Real, Matrilocal/Patrilocal, Journey West/Journey East, Sea/Land, and Sea Hunting/Land Hunting form parallel oppositions on the different schematic planes of the story of Asdiwal.

The oppositions do not exist in Tsimshian society, "but rather with its inherent possibilities and its latent potentialities. Such speculations . . . do not seek to depict what is real, but to justify the shortcomings of reality, since the extreme positions are only *imagined* in order to show that they are *untenable*" (Lévi-Strauss 1976:173). Yet, these different considerations all reflect a similar underlying structure that shapes the substratum of consciousness.

Conclusion

The work of Lévi-Strauss has been criticized intensely on varying levels; a bibliography (Nordquist 1987) lists over one hundred critical writings in English alone. Structuralism, once, as Hénaff rather exuberantly proclaims, "a triumphant theory," has been attacked as reductionistic and unnuanced; if its influence has waned it is not because "it has been fulfilled so completely" (Hénaff 1998:1). Yet, even those who criticize his work acknowledge the impact Lévi-Strauss has had on the way we think about culture and consciousness. Mary Douglas, who has attacked his analysis of the story of Asdiwal, nonetheless considers Lévi-Strauss to be one of three twentieth-century thinkers—along with Piaget and Chomsky—who have changed our way of viewing the nature of human thought processes (1980:129). The British social anthropologist Edmund Leach, with grudging respect, has written that social anthropology

> would not exist in its present form if it had not, in recent years, developed a dialectical relationship with the work of Claude Lévi-Strauss. I know of no British social anthropologist who has ever declared an unqualified enthusiasm for structuralist anthropology of a Lévi-Straussian sort, but likewise there is today no British social anthropologist who has not been deeply influenced by Lévi-Strauss' work. (1983:10)

References

Bohannan, Paul, and Mark Glazer, eds.
1988 *High Points in Anthropology*. New York: Knopf.

de Gramont, Sanche
1970 There Are No Superior Societies. In *Claude Levi-Strauss: The Anthropologist as Hero*. E. Hayes and T. Hayes, eds. Pp. 3–21. Cambridge, Mass.: MIT Press.

Deliège, Robert

2004 *Lévi-Strauss Today: An Introduction to Structural Anthropology*. Oxford: Berg.

Douglas, Mary

1980 *Edward Evans-Pritchard*. New York: Viking Press.

Dundes, Alan, ed.

1984 *Sacred Narrative, Readings in the Theory of Myth*. Berkeley: University of California Press.

Hénaff, Marcel

1998 *Claude Lévi-Strauss and the Making of Structural Anthropology*. Minneapolis: University of Minnesota Press.

Leach, Edmund

1967 *The Structural Study of Myth and Totemism*. London: Tavistock Press.

1970 *Lévi-Strauss*. London: Fontana/Collins.

1983 Roman Jakobson and Social Anthropology. In *A Tribute to Roman Jakobson*. P. Gray, ed. Pp. 10–16. Berlin: Mouton.

Lévi-Strauss, Claude

1963a *Structural Anthropology*. Vol. 1. New York: Basic Books. [Originally published 1958 as *Anthropologie structurale*.]

1963b *Totemism*. New York: Basic Books. [Originally published 1962 as *Le totemisme aujourd'hi*.]

1966 *The Savage Mind*. Chicago: University of Chicago Press. [Originally published 1962 as *La pensée sauvage*.]

1969a *The Elementary Structures of Kinship*. Boston: Beacon Press. [Originally published 1949 as *Les structures élémentaires de la parenté*.]

1969b *The Raw and the Cooked*. New York: Harper & Row. [Originally published 1964 as *Le cru et le cuit*.]

1973 *From Honey to Ashes*. New York: Harper & Row. [Originally published 1967 as *Du miel aux cendres*.]

1974 *Tristes tropiques*. New York: Atheneum. [Originally published 1955.]

1976 *Structural Anthropology*. Vol. 2. New York: Basic Books. [Originally published 1973.]

1978 *The Origin of Table Manners*. New York: Harper & Row. [Originally published 1968 as *L'Origine des manieres de table*.]

1981 *The Naked Man*. New York: Harper & Row. [Originally published 1971 as *L'Homme nu*.]

1985 *The View from Afar*. New York: Basic Books. [Originally published 1983 as *Le regard eloigne*.]

1987 *Anthropology and Myth, Lectures, 1951–1982*. Oxford: Basil Blackwell.

1988 *The Jealous Potter*. Chicago: University of Chicago Press. [Originally published 1985 as *La potiere jalouse*.]

1995 *Saudades do Brasil: A Photographic Memoir*. Seattle: University of Washington Press.

1997 *Look, Listen, Read*. New York: Basic Books. [Originally published 1993 as *Regarer, écouter, lire*.]

Lévi-Strauss, Claude, and Didier Eribon

1991 *Conversations with Lévi-Strauss*. Chicago: University of Chicago Press.

Murphy, Robert

1970 Connaissez-vous Lévi-Strauss? In *Claude Levi-Strauss: The Anthropologist as Hero*. E. Hayes and T. Hayes, eds. Pp. 164–169. Cambridge, Mass.: MIT Press.

Nordquist, Joan

1987 *Claude Lévi-Strauss: A Bibliography*. Santa Cruz, Calif.: Reference and Research Services.

Pace, David

1983 *Claude Lévi-Strauss: The Bearer of Ashes*. Boston: Routledge & Kegan Paul.

Scholte, Bob

1970 Epistemic Paradigms: Some Problems in Cross-Cultural Research on Social Anthropological History and Theory. In *Claude Lévi-Strauss: The Anthropologist as Hero*. E. Hayes and T. Hayes, eds. Pp. 108–22. Cambridge, Mass.: MIT Press.

Sontag, Susan

1966 The Anthropologist as Hero. In *Against Interpretation, and Other Essays*. Pp. 69–81. New York: Farrar, Straus & Giroux.

Steiner, George

1977 Orpheus with His Myths: Claude Lévi-Strauss. In *Language and Silence: Essays on Language, Literature and the Inhuman*. Pp. 239–250. New York: Atheneum.

18

Victor Turner

Symbols, Pilgrims, and Drama

Victor Turner (1920–1983) was one of the most creative thinkers in British-American social anthropology. As a developer of new anthropological insights, Turner had few peers. And only rarely have anthropologists achieved the dazzling quality of Turner's writings, which are marked by global knowledge, captivating prose, and stubborn common sense. Take, for example, Turner's explanation of his term *communitas*, which refers to a transitional state experienced during out-of-the-ordinary situations like rites of passage or pilgrimages:

> Communitas is almost always thought of or portrayed by actors as a timeless condition, an eternal now, as "a moment in and out of time," or as a state to which the structural view of time is not applicable. Such is frequently the character of at least parts of the seclusion periods found in many protracted initiation rites. Such is the character, too, I have found, of pilgrimage journeys in several religions. In ritual seclusion, for example, one day replicates another for many weeks. The novices in tribal initiations waken and rest at fixed hours, often at sunrise and sunset, as in the monastic life in Christianity and Buddhism. They receive instruction in tribal lore, or in singing and dancing from the same elders or adepts at the same time. At other set times they may hunt or perform routine tasks under the eyes of the elders. Every day is, in a sense, the same day, writ large or repeated. (1974:238–239)

Turner's work is filled with paragraphs like this one, which illustrates the breadth of his knowledge: he alludes to his ethnographic research on ritual among the Ndembu of Zambia and on pilgrimages in Mexico and to historical research into major religions. The basic idea—that one element of communitas is its existence outside of structured time—is, as far as I know, Turner's unique insight. The poetry is evident throughout, but particularly in the last sentence. His commonsense nature is also in evidence: Turner does not become a captive of his own metaphors.

It is curious how frequently anthropological theorists have turned to key metaphors to explain their insights (for example, the organic analogy), and then have treated those metaphors as if they had a social rather than only a heuristic existence. The unexamined metamorphosis from metaphor to scientific law occurs frequently among anthropological theorists, but Victor Turner avoided that pitfall—a remarkable accomplishment considering that Turner's work is full of metaphors, analogies, and striking images. Turner clearly states when he is speaking metaphorically and when he is speaking literally (see, for example, Turner 1974:21–32). For example, when he develops van Gennep's division of rites of passage into preliminal, liminal, and postliminal states—a metaphor based on *limen*, Latin for "threshold," and applied to stages of separation, transition, and reintegration of social statuses—it is clear that Turner is speaking metaphorically. It is equally clear that when Turner writes of rituals as social dramas, he means it quite literally: they are performances; he is not saying "rituals are like performances" (Turner 1985a:180–181). That precision adds enormously to Turner's writing.

Victor Turner's work is dense, complex, and of enormous value. Turner's theoretical contribution has three major nuclei: the nature of symbols, the social process of pilgrimage, and analysis of social performance. It is a body of theory with its origins in British social anthropology, but it is uniquely the creation of Victor Turner.

Background

Born in Glasgow in 1920, Turner studied at the University of London, where he took courses from Radcliffe-Brown, Meyer

Fortes, Edmund Leach, and Raymond Firth before continuing his graduate studies at Manchester University under Max Gluckman (Babcock 1984). Turner's education was interrupted by World War II in which he served as a conscientious objector digging up unexploded bombs (E. Turner 1985:1). Turner found Mead's *Coming of Age in Samoa* and Radcliffe-Brown's *The Andaman Islanders* in the local library and after reading them said, as his wife recalled, "I'm going to be an anthropologist." Turner married Edith Davis in 1943, and for the next forty years they shared a very creative life of fieldwork, writing, and family, coauthoring *Image and Pilgrimage in Christian Culture: Anthropological Perspectives* (1978). (See Edith Turner's fascinating and charming autobiography [2006].)

Gluckman arranged a grant for Turner with the Rhodes-Livingstone Institute, and Turner carried out fieldwork from 1950 to 1954 among the Ndembu of northwestern Zambia on the border between Zaire and Angola. A community of some seventeen thousand people with matrilineal descent and virilocal residence, the Ndembu had a high level of personal mobility, particularly due to marriage, divorce, and remarriage, "each of which normally entails a change of domicile." Paradoxically, even though "the majority of local groups in Ndembu society are relatively transient and unstable," Turner wrote, "the organizational principles on which they are formed and reformed are enduring" (1981:10). Ndembu social organization was the subject of *Schism and Continuity in an African Society* (Turner 1957), which Gluckman decreed would be the subject of Turner's dissertation. "Until you've mastered that, you're in no position to analyze ritual," Gluckman admonished (E. Turner 1985:4). The topic implied the need to analyze social organization within a functionalist framework, but Turner was disenchanted with a view of society predicated on the organic analogy. Turner recalled that when he began fieldwork, the "normal science of British social anthropology tried to present a unified theory of order and change based on a biological metaphor." In this conception, the nature of change is hidden but present in the social structure, and "the simple, like the grain of mustard seed, grows into the complex, through various preordained stages" (Turner

1974:31). Writing about the Ndembu of Zambia, Turner found that

> it was quite useful to think "biologically" about "village life-cycles," and "domestic cycles," the "origin," "growth," and "decay" of villages, families and lineages, but not too helpful to think about change as immanent in the structure of Ndembu society, when there was clearly "a wind of change," economic, political, social, religious, legal, and so on, sweeping the whole of central Africa and originating outside all village societies. (1974:31–32)

Buffeted by external forces, it was nonsense to think that change was immanent in social structure or that it was cyclical or repetitive.

> With my conviction as to the dynamic nature of social relations I saw movement as much as structure, persistence as much as change, indeed, persistence as a striking aspect of change. I saw people interacting, and, as day succeeded day, the consequence of their interactions. I then began to perceive a form in the process of social time. This form was essentially dramatic. (Turner 1974:3)

Edith Turner (1985:5) recalls how Turner and a colleague, both writing their dissertations, went out to commiserate over beers in a pub. Turner was concerned with how to analyze the extended Ndembu conflicts that were serious perturbations in an otherwise smoothly operating social system. The phrase "social drama" came to Turner, and that night he wrote out his paper for Gluckman's seminar. It analyzed conflict surrounding the sorcerer Sandombu:

> With controlled excitement he read the story of Sandombu; and he analyzed its stages—breach, crisis, redress, reintegration—the social drama as the window into Ndembu social organization and values. Now you see the living heart. Max sat, his hands folded on top of his bowed bald head. When it was over, he raised his head, his eyes burning. "You've got it! That's it." (E. Turner 1985:5)

It is ironic, but appropriate, that the story of the conceptual birth of social drama would itself have the elements of breach, crisis, redress, and reintegration. But beyond that, Turner argued, "When the interests and attitudes of groups and individuals stood in obvious opposition, social dramas did seem to me to constitute isolable and minutely describable units of social process" (1974:33).

The social drama becomes a potential unit of analysis because it has a beginning, a middle, and an end. Social dramas also possess "a regularly recurring 'processional form' or 'diachronic profile'—in other words, crisis situations tended to have a regular series of phases" (Turner 1985b:74). Drawing on his Ndembu research, Turner plotted how conflict began with a breach of a rule or norm that would rapidly escalate and oppose the maximal level of social groups involved in the conflict. Some procedures of adjustment or redress would then occur, "ranging from informal arbitration to elaborate rituals, that result either in healing the breach or public recognition of its irremediable character" (Turner 1985b:74). Not all social processes are dramatic; for example, Turner describes "social enterprises" that are based on cooperative efforts and have different profiles (1974:34). But social dramas were recurrent units of social life, and although "each society's social drama could be expected to have its own 'style'" (Turner 1985b:74), there were sufficient similarities for comparison without erasing social actors, eliminating temporal depth, or making the organic assumptions of Radcliffe-Brown. "I felt that I had to bring the 'humanistic coefficient' into my model if I was to make sense of human social process," Turner wrote (1974:33). He clearly did.

Turner's analysis of social dramas led him from the Ndembu (1967, 1969), to a study of Icelandic sagas (1985a), to an analysis of social dramas in the 1810 Mexican Revolution. It eventually led him to theater:

> Theater is one of the many inheritors of that great multifaceted system of preindustrial ritual which embraces ideas and images of cosmos and chaos, interdigitates clowns and their foolery with gods and their solemnity, and uses all the sensory codes to produce symphonies in more than music: the intertwining of

> dance, body languages of many kinds, song, chant, architectural forms (temples, amphitheaters), incense, burnt offerings, ritualized feastings and drinking, painting, body painting, body marking of many kinds, including circumcision and scarification, the application of lotions and the drinking of potions, the enacting of mythic and heroic plots drawn from oral traditions. (Turner 1985c:295)

It is writing like this—vivid, dense with thought, and provocative—that makes Victor Turner such a major figure in anthropological theory. It embodies his emphasis on process—dynamic, communicative, and cultural—an emphasis also represented in his approach to symbols.

Symbols

It is worth recalling that anthropologists of very different theoretical stripes agree that symbols mark the threshold of culture. For example, an arch-materialist like Leslie White writes, "The symbol is the universe of humanity" (1949:22). Yet relatively few anthropologists were concerned with how symbols mean. Sapir, for example, distinguished between primary symbols, which directly mimic an object—the picture of a dog that means "dog"—and secondary symbols, in which "a connection is no longer directly traceable between words, or combinations of words, and what they refer to," as in the sentence, "The red, white, and blue stands for freedom" (1929:211). Turner's contribution—and an example of his sophisticated common sense—was to consider symbols within specific fields of social action. In analyzing Ndembu ritual, Turner wrote,

> I found I could not analyze ritual symbols without studying them in a time series in relation to other "events," for symbols are essentially involved in social processes. I came to see performances of ritual as distinct phases in social processes whereby groups become adjusted to internal changes and adapted to their external environment. From this standpoint the ritual symbol becomes a factor in social action, a positive force in an activity field. The symbol becomes associated with human interests, purposes, ends, and means, whether these

> are explicitly formulated or have to be inferred from the observed behavior. The structure and properties of a symbol become those of a dynamic entity, at least within its appropriate context of action. (1967:20)

Thus, the symbol of the American flag takes on different meanings if it is flapping on a flag post in a schoolyard, hanging in the back of a Chevrolet van, or draped across the casket of a slain soldier. The image is the same, but the meanings associated with it are different in kind and intensity.

Turner considers cultural symbols, including ritual symbols, "as originating in and sustaining processes involving temporal changes in social relations, and not as timeless entities" (1974:55). Symbols have some basic properties in common. They are powerful condensations of meaning: "Many things and actions are represented in a single formation" (Turner 1967:28). For example, Turner analyzes the meanings associated with the *chishing'a,* a Ndembu hunting shrine consisting of only a forked stick placed in the ground, a piece of earth from a termite hill trimmed into a rectangle and placed at the base of the branch, and a braid of grass. The associated meanings include social relationships between hunters and nonhunters, the hunter's immediate family and matrikin, toughness of mind and body, piety toward the hunter's ancestors, fertility, skill in the use of weapons, and fairness in the distribution of meat—some fifteen different meanings directly associated with this shrine. "This is but a single example of the mighty synthesizing and focusing capacity of ritual symbolism," Turner observes; "It might almost be said that the greater the symbol, the simpler its form" (1967:298). A moment's reflection on the evocative nature of the Christian cross—simply two perpendicular pieces of wood of unequal length—suggests the truth of Turner's observation. Therefore, symbols are "'multivocal,' susceptible of many meanings" (Turner 1974:55), though their meanings tend to cluster around two extremes of a continuum; at one end, there is often a cluster of meanings around physiological and natural phenomena, and at the other, another cluster of meanings about social relationships. For example, the red in the American flag is sometimes explained as representing the blood of those who have died in defense of freedom, the stripes as the original thirteen colonies, and the entire symbol as evoking values of patriotism and respect.

But the important point is that symbols, condensed and multivocal, may speak to different people in different ways; the construction and reconstruction of meaning occurs with specific, dynamic contexts of social process. This has profound theoretical implications. If, as so many anthropologists have argued, symbols are the key to cultural life, and if, as Turner suggests, symbols are dynamic social creations—with the potential for contradictory, but coexisting, interpretations—then how can a cultural trait or a social structure be abstracted from its dynamic context? Why should one believe that cultural patterns serve to create social stability (Radcliffe-Brown) or meet discernible human needs (Malinowski) when the very nature of cultural life is fluid, contradictory, and dynamic as opposed to stable, congruent, and static?

Turner's insights into symbols touch a central nerve in twentieth-century anthropological thought. Culture exists as experience; it only occurs insofar as it is practiced. This leads to an anthropology of performance and a concern with praxis (literally, "action" or "practice," as in the performance of an art or skill), rather than an anthropology of social structure. Turner pursued this approach in a variety of investigations, but one particularly intriguing investigation focused on pilgrimages.

Liminality, Communitas, and Pilgrimage

As noted above, Turner borrowed van Gennep's concept of liminality and expanded it into a conceptual tool for understanding special phases in social life when transition is the dominant theme. "If our basic model of society," Turner wrote, "is that of a 'structure of positions,' we must regard the period of margin or 'liminality' as an interstructural situation" (1967:93). Periods of transition during rites of passage or other rituals or during pilgrimages are similar in that they

> are neither here nor there; they are betwixt and between the positions assigned and arrayed by law, custom, convention, and ceremonial. As such, their ambiguous and indeterminate

> attributes are expressed by a rich variety of symbols in the many societies that ritualize social and cultural transitions. (Turner 1969:95)

Liminal periods fascinated Turner because they frequently are characterized by changes in and suspension of normal social relationships. Liminal periods are not just in and out of time but are also "in and out of social structure" (Turner 1969:96), suggesting the existence of two major models of human relationships:

> The first is of society as a structured, differentiated, and often hierarchical system of politico-legal-economic positions with many types of evaluation, separating men in terms of "more" or "less." The second, which emerges recognizably in the liminal period, is of society as an unstructured or rudimentarily structured and relatively undifferentiated communitas, community, or even communion of equal individuals who submit together to the general authority of the ritual elders. (Turner 1969:96)

Turner lists a number of binary oppositions that parallel the associated properties of communitas versus structure: transition/state, equality/inequality, anonymity/systems of nomenclature, silence/speech, absence of status/status, and so on (1969:106–107). Such properties are part of rites of passage in traditional societies, but they also characterize moments in the major religions, particularly during pilgrimages.

The imagery of pilgrimage underscores its transitional nature; it is a recurrent metaphor in Christian literature, such as in the most famous pilgrimage in English literature, Chaucer's *The Canterbury Tales*:

> This world nis but a thrughfare ful of wo
> And we ben pilgrims, passinge to and fro;
> Death is an end of every worldy soore

and this nineteenth-century American hymn:

> This world is not my home,
> I'm just a passin' through.
> My treasures are laid up
> Somewhere beyond the blue.

Christian imagery emphasizes the liminal nature of pilgrimage. After all, Christ was born while in transition, his human existence a brief separation from his true nature.

Outside the Christian tradition, pilgrimages are liminal phenomena exhibiting the quality of communitas in their social relations (Turner 1974:166–167). Such liminality may be communicated by removing the outward symbols of social differences. Turner comments on

> the bond that exists between communitas, liminality, and lowermost status. It is often believed that the lowest castes and classes in stratified societies exhibit the greatest immediacy and involuntariness of behavior. This may or not be empirically true, but it is at any rate a persistent belief. . . . Those who would maximize communitas often begin by minimizing or even eliminating the outward signs of rank as, for example, Tolstoy and Gandhi tried to do in their own persons. In other words, they approximate in dress and behavior the condition of the poor. (1974:243)

Pilgrimages are a type of social process with basic properties: they are liminal social relations characterized by communitas, and they employ symbols emphasizing the merger or inversion of normal social rankings. Shrines, the objects of pilgrimages, may create a ritual topography in which paramount shrines, related shrines, and the paths between them mark a network of social process. Pilgrimages touched on Turner's basic theoretical interests as he listed them: "the study of 'processual units,' 'anti-structure,' and the semantics of ritual symbols. All these interests converge on pilgrimage processes" (1974:166).

Conclusion

A brief sketch of Turner's key concepts does not do justice to his vigorous intellect and energetic exploration of such different ideas as the process approach to political anthropology (Swartz et al. 1966) and a study of Noh drama (Turner 1984). Edith Turner recalls that during the early 1960s, "it was as if, as his thought progressed, there would come a stage when it was time for him to take a new tack, like a sailboat beating upwind" (1985:8). Turner articulated how his varied interests formed part of a basic research agenda:

> My work as an anthropologist has been the study of cumulative interactions over time in human groups of varying span and different cultures. These interactions, I found, tend to amass toward the emergence of sustained public action, and given my Western background, it was difficult to characterize these as other than "dramatic." (1984:19)

References

Babcock, Barbara A.
1984 Obituary: Victor W. Turner (1920–1983). *American Journal of Folklore* 97:461–464.

Sapir, Edward
1929 The Status of Linguistics as a Science. *Language* 5(4):207–214.

Swartz, Marc, Victor Turner, and Arthur Tuden, eds.
1966 *Political Anthropology*. Chicago: Aldine.

Turner, Edith
1985 From the Ndembu to Broadway. In *On the Edge of the Bush*. E. Turner, ed. Pp. 1–15. Tucson: University of Arizona Press.
2006 *Heart of Lightness: The Life Story of an Anthropologist*. New York: Berghan Books.

Turner, Victor
1957 *Schism and Continuity in an African Society*. Manchester: Manchester University Press.
1967 *The Forest of Symbols: Aspects of Ndembu Ritual*. Ithaca: Cornell University Press.
1969 *The Ritual Process: Structure and Anti-Structure*. New York: Aldine.
1974 *Dramas, Fields, and Metaphors: Symbolic Action in Human Society*. Ithaca: Cornell University Press.
1981 *The Drums of Affliction: A Survey of Religious Process among the Ndembu of Zambia*. 1968. Reprint, Ithaca, N.Y.: Cornell University Press.
1984 Liminality and the Performative Genres. In *Rite, Drama, Festival, Spectacle: Rehearsals toward a Theory of Cultural Performance*. J. MacAloon, ed. Pp. 19–41. Philadelphia: Institute for the Study of Human Issues.

1985a An Anthropological Approach to the Icelandic Saga. In *On the Edge of the Bush*. E. Turner, ed. Pp. 71–93. Tucson: University of Arizona Press.

1985b The Anthropology of Performance. In *On the Edge of the Bush*. E. Turner, ed. Pp. 177–204. Tucson: University of Arizona Press.

1985c Are There Universals of Performance in Ritual, Myth, and Drama? In *On the Edge of the Bush*. E. Turner, ed. Pp. 291–301. Tucson: University of Arizona Press.

Turner, Victor, and Edith Turner

1978 *Image and Pilgrimage in Christian Culture: Anthropological Perspectives*. New York: Columbia University Press.

White, Leslie

1949 *The Science of Culture*. New York: Farrar, Straus & Giroux.

19

Clifford Geertz

An Interpretive Anthropology

At the close of his career of more than fifty years, Clifford Geertz (1926–2006) was the subject of radically different assessments by his peers. On the one hand, Richard Shweder claimed, "For three decades Clifford Geertz has been the single most influential cultural anthropologist in the United States" (2005:1). In contrast, Lionel Tiger, in a brief note published soon after Geertz's death, wrote that Geertz's "influence and impact were real but fundamentally unfortunate in the social sciences. He was a major contributor to the willfully fuzzy logic which continues to plague the social sciences" (2006:A12). Geertz's influence had the "dolorous result of turning much of what well-meaning anthropologists do into a lame and confused form of literary scholarship" (Tiger 2006:A12).

Ironically, Geertz offered a more balanced assessment of his career than either his supporters or detractors. In an autobiographical essay, Geertz placed his anthropological career in the contexts of four major phases of American anthropology since World War II (2002). The first phase (1946–1960) was characterized by "postwar exuberance" and an optimism that anthropology and the other social sciences would improve human life. The second phase (from 1960 to the mid-1970s) was dominated by the Cold War and "the romances and disappointments of Third-Worldism" (Geertz 2002:2). This was followed by a period of "increasing uncertainty, self-doubt, and self-examination, both within anthropology and Western culture generally" that characterized the various theoretical strands (postmodernist, poststructuralist, and so on) articulated between 1975 and 1989 (Geertz 2002:2). The current era, beginning in the 1990s, is marked by fragmentation and dispersion, as anthropology—and the rest of humanity—has been roiled by globalization, transnationalism, ethnic conflict, and, paradoxically, "the simultaneous increase in cosmopolitanism and parochialism" (Geertz 2002:14).

Geertz's approach to culture was based on the idea that understanding another culture is always an act of interpretation, an inquiry that involves placing a cultural act—a ritual, a game, a political campaign, and so on—into the specific and local contexts in which the act is meaningful. Those ideas, first articulated in *The Interpretation of Cultures* (1973), were a catalyst for a debate in American anthropology that turned on key issues such as, What is the nature of culture? How is it distinct from social structure? How is culture understood? What is the relationship between observer and observed?

These anthropological issues arose against the backdrop of a changing world and worldview. Unlike earlier ethnographers, Geertz and his contemporaries conducted their research in the new Third World nations that emerged after World War II. As independence movements transformed former colonial subjects into new national citizens, intergroup conflicts intensified as power was reconfigured and new governments exerted their control. In the face of such change, the idea of functionally integrated societies was difficult to maintain since there were no isolated societies and little evidence of equilibrium.

The anthropologist's role had changed as well; instead of studying an isolated society for a year or two and returning to be "the expert" on those people, anthropologists were working in communities and institutions in the United States, Europe, and developing countries among people who had their own stories to tell and the means to tell them (see cases discussed in Brettell 1993). The relationships between anthropologists and informants also changed, sparking a self-examination of the nature of anthropological inquiry. The works of Clifford Geertz contributed to that examination, and the changes in anthropology are reflected in his own career.

Background

Clifford Geertz was born in 1926 in San Francisco and served in the U.S. Navy during World War II. After the war, he went to Antioch College, pursuing interests in English and philosophy (Geertz 2000:4–7). Except for a couple of economics courses, he did not study the social sciences before receiving his B.A. in 1950. Geertz recalls that "the [philosophical] problems I was concerned with—values and so on—seemed to me to be in need of empirical study" (Johnson and Ross 1991:150), and that led him to anthropology. He enrolled in Harvard's Department of Social Relations and in late 1951 joined a research project in Indonesia (Geertz 1995:100, 2002:3–7). From 1952 to 1954 Geertz was one of a team of social scientists who worked in Modjokuto, Java, on a project funded by the Ford Foundation (Geertz 1963b:vii). The objective of that research was understanding a "Third World" nation, with the explicit goal of improving economic growth (Higgins 1963). The Modjokuto Project was one of the earliest efforts by anthropologists "to adapt themselves and their tribes-and-islands discipline to the study of large-scale societies with written histories, established governments, and composite cultures—nations, states, civilizations" (Geertz 2002:6–7).

Geertz's works from this period differ from his later writings. His book *The Religion of Java* (1960) is an example of classic ethnography; Evans-Pritchard could have written it. Another book, *Agricultural Involution* (1963a), is a cultural ecological study of Indonesia, an archipelago comprised of the inner islands (Java, Bali, and Lombok), where 9 percent of the landmass supported 65 percent of the population, and the outer islands (Sumatra and Borneo, for example), where 90 percent of the landmass was home to 30 percent of the population. *Agricultural Involution* contrasted the agrosystems of wet-rice, labor intensive, paddy agriculture and dry-rice, land extensive, swidden agriculture and showed how the spatial distribution of those different agrosystems affected local economies, their colonial economic histories, and their future paths of development. *Peddlers and Princes* (1963b) profiled the very different Indonesian towns of Modjokuto, Java, and Tabanan, Bali, with the goal of understanding the ways local cultural patterns may affect economic development plans. At a time when development projects often ignored local realities for top-down socioeconomic engineering, Geertz argued that "over-all developmental policies need to be much more delicately attuned to the particularities of local social and cultural organization"(1963b:154). Geertz continued his analysis of Modjokuto in *The Social History of an Indonesian Town* (1965), a synthesis of political and economic development in the community from its mid-nineteenth-century establishment to the late 1950s.

These studies are solid anthropological contributions that advanced scientific knowledge, international policy, and Geertz's career. After a fellowship at the Center for Advanced Study in the Behavioral Sciences at Stanford (1958–1959) and a year as an assistant professor at the University of California, Berkeley, Geertz went to the University of Chicago in 1960, where he became full professor in 1964 and remained until 1970. In 1970 Geertz left Chicago to establish the School of Social Science at the Institute for Advanced Study in Princeton, N.J., the research institute established in 1930 whose faculty had included Albert Einstein, art historian Erwin Panofsky, and other major intellectuals. Geertz spent the next thirty-six years at the Institute for Advanced Study where he was professor emeritus at his death in 2006 (Geertz 1995:120–126, 2002:13; Institute for Advanced Study 2006).

In the course of his career, Geertz authored, coauthored, or edited seventeen books. A prolific author, his writings included ethnographies and several collections of essays. His prose style was distinctive, marked by a "list-laden vernacular discursivity" (Boon 2003:30). Geertz's *Works and Lives* was the 1989 winner of the National Book Critics Circle Award for literary criticism, a recognition of the clarity of his prose and its accessibility to educated readers outside the field of anthropology, a discipline not known for its prose stylists. Geertz's essays were published in the *New York Review of Books*, *Dædalus*, *American Scholar*, and other intellectual journals (for example, Geertz 2003).

Geertz's first books did not break with traditional anthropological theory, although some interesting cracks were beginning to show. For example, in *Agricultural Involution* Geertz invoked the cultural ecology of Julian Steward and adopted a systems approach shaped by functionalism, although he denied the privileged explanatory role for cultural ecology, arguing that it is important but not all-encompassing (1963a:10–11). The final chapter of *The Social History of an Indonesian Town* introduces an approach called "the document method" (following Harold Garfinkel), which Geertz develops in his subsequent work:

> In this approach a single naturally coherent social phenomenon, a found event of some sort, is interpreted not so much as an index of a particular underlying pattern, as in most quantitative work, nor yet again as the immediate substance of that pattern itself, as in most ethnographic work, but rather as a unique, individual, peculiarly eloquent actualization—an epitome—of it.
>
> The document (which might better be called the "example" or as this method is often referred to as clinical, the "case") is seen as a particular embodiment, a specific manifestation of a more comprehensive pattern which has a very large, in some cases virtually infinite, number of such embodiments and manifestations, the one at hand simply being regarded as particularly telling in the fullness, clarity, and the elegance with which it exhibits the general pattern. In it the paradigm is made flesh: the ineradicable specificity of actual events and the elusive generality of meaningful form render one another intelligible. (1965:153–154)

With that, Geertz turns to an examination of a bitterly contested election in Modjokuto in a section titled "A Village Election as a Social Document." It is that approach to culture as text, first broached in *The Social History of an Indonesian Town*, that marked Geertz's subsequent work.

Thick Description and Culture as Text

The course of Geertz's approach was set out in "Thick Description: Toward an Interpretive Theory of Culture," the introductory essay to the collection, *The Interpretation of Cultures*. The essay clearly and forcefully outlines Geertz's view of culture and the nature of anthropological insights. After reviewing the multiple definitions of the word "culture," Geertz states his own position:

> The concept of culture I espouse, and whose utility the essays below attempt to demonstrate, is essentially a semiotic one. Believing, with Max Weber, that man is an animal suspended in webs of significance he himself has spun, I take culture to be those webs, and the analysis of it to be therefore not an experimental science in search of law but an interpretive one in search of meaning. (1973:5)

This is a key, widely quoted passage (for example, Barrett 1991) with a complex series of implications. In a 1990 interview Geertz said, "That's exactly what I still think. It's just that I didn't know exactly what I was getting myself into by thinking it" (Johnson and Ross 1991:151).

Semiotics is the analysis of signs and symbols, and Geertz argues that cultural behavior is the interactive creation of meaning with signs: "Human behavior is seen as . . . symbolic action—action which, like phonation in speech, pigment in painting, line in writing, or sonance in music, signifies" (1973:10). The relevant questions concern the meanings of such signs, as Geertz contends,

> Doing ethnography is like trying to read (in the sense of "construct a reading of") a manuscript—foreign, faded, full of ellipses, incoherencies, suspicious emendations, and tendentious commentaries, but written not in conventionalized graphs of sound but in transient examples of shaped behavior. (1973:10)

In *The Interpretation of Cultures,* Geertz outlined the notion of thick description, which draws on the work of Gilbert Ryle, especially his "winking" analogy. Ryle used a seemingly silly example—the difference between a twitching eyelid and a winking eye—to show that these similar behaviors were different because the wink communicated meaning and the twitch did not. Building on that difference, Ryle points out that one could see parodies of winks, practice parodies of winks, fake winks, and so on, producing multiple possibilities with even such a simple form of communication; unraveling and identifying those contexts and meanings requires "thick description."

Geertz argued that this is precisely what ethnographic writing does, except most of the time we are unaware of it. To make that point, Geertz reproduced an account from his Moroccan field notes, which, quoted raw, is readable but cannot be understood until it is interpreted:

> In finished anthropological writings . . . this fact—that what we call our data are really our own constructions of other people's constructions of what they and their compatriots are up to—is obscured because most of what we need to comprehend a particular event, ritual, custom, idea, or whatever is insinuated as background information before the thing itself is directly examined. (Even to reveal that this little drama [from his field notes] took place in the highlands of central Morocco in 1912—and was recounted there in 1968—is to determine much of our understanding of it.) There is nothing particularly wrong with this, and it is in any case inevitable. But it does lead to a view of anthropological research as rather more of an observational and rather less of an interpretive activity than it really is. (1973:9)

Asserting that "culture, this acted document, thus is public," Geertz argued that debates over whether culture is materialist or idealist, subjective or objective are misconceived: culture consists of created signs that are behaviors, and anthropology's task is "sorting out the structures of signification" in order to determine "their social ground and import" (1973:9–10). What makes other cultures different is "a lack of familiarity with the imaginative universe within which their acts are signs," and the goal of anthropological analysis is to make those signs interpretable (Geertz 1973:13).

Geertz distinguished this point of view from other conceptions of culture. Obviously, a semiotic emphasis does not give priority to technology or infrastructure or any other conception of the nature/culture interface as do materialists like White or Harris. Equally, culture does not exist in some superorganic realm subject to forces and objectives of its own as Kroeber suggested; culture cannot be reified. Neither is culture "brute behavior" or "mental construct" subject to schematic analyses or reducible to ethnographic algorithms. Just as a Beethoven quartet is not the same as the score, the knowledge of it, the understanding of a group of musicians, a particular performance of it, or a transcendent force, but rather is irreducibly a piece of music, culture consists of "socially established structures of meaning" with which people communicate (Geertz 1973:11–12); it is inseparable from symbolic social discourse.

Javanese Funeral

The implications of interpretation are exemplified in Geertz's analysis of a funeral in Java, a case of social discourse in which shifting political divisions and their symbolic expressions affected core rituals and emotions surrounding death (1973). Geertz first outlined a critique of functionalism, focusing on its inability to deal with social change, and then sketched the distinction between culture and social system, "the former as an ordered system of meaning and of symbols, in terms of which social interaction takes place; and to see the latter as the pattern of social interaction itself" (1973:144).

> Culture is the fabric of meaning in terms of which human beings interpret their experience and guide their action; social structure is the form that action takes, the actually existing network of social relations. Culture and social structure are then but different abstractions from the same phenomena. (Geertz 1973:145)

But these two different abstractions are integrated, Geertz argued, in very different ways. Social structure is bound together based on "causal-functional integration," the articulation of different segments that interact and maintain the system. Culture, in contrast, is characterized by logico-meaningful integration, "a unity of style, of logical implication, of meaning and value." It is the sort of coherent unit "one finds in a Bach fugue, in Catholic dogma, or in the general theory of relativity" (Geertz 1973:145). Such distinctions become important in the Javanese funeral when changing associations between symbols and political parties create dissonance in the integration of culture and disrupt the organization of society.

To oversimplify, peasant religion in Java had been a syncretic mix of Islam and Hinduism overlain on an indigenous Southeast Asian animism. "The result," Geertz wrote, "was a balanced syncretism of myth and ritual in which Hindu gods and goddesses, Moslem prophets and saints, and local spirits and demons all found a proper place" (1973:147). This balance has been upset increasingly during the twentieth century as conservative Islamic religious nationalism crystallized in opposition to a secular, Marxist nationalism that appealed to pre-Islamic, Hinduist-animist "indigenous" religions. Those positions became sufficiently distinct that the difference between the self-conscious Muslim and self-conscious "nativist" (combining Hindu and native elements with Marxism) became polarized as types of people, *santri* and *abangnan*. In postindependence Indonesia, political parties formed along these dividing lines: Masjumi became the conservative Islamic party and Permai, the anti-Islamic mix of Marxism and nativism. These differences were epitomized at a specific Javanese funeral.

"The mood of a Javanese funeral is not one of hysterical bereavement, unrestrained sobbing, or even of formalized cries of grief for the deceased's departure," Geertz observed. "Rather it is a calm, undemonstrative, almost languid letting go, a brief ritualized relinquishment of a relationship no longer possible" (Geertz 1973:154). This willed serenity and detachment, *iklas*, depends on the smooth execution of a proper ceremony that seamlessly combines Islamic, Hindu, and indigenous beliefs and rituals. Javanese believe that it is the suddenness of emotional turmoil that causes damage—"It is 'shock' not the suffering itself which is feared" (Geertz 1973:154)—and that the funeral procedure should smoothly and quickly mark the end of life.

But in this particular case, the deceased was a boy was from a household loosely affiliated with the Permai party, and when the Islamic village religious leader was called to direct the ceremony, he refused, citing the presence of a Permai political poster on the door and arguing that it was inappropriate for him to perform the ceremony of "another" religion. At that moment, iklas—the self-willed and culturally defined composure surrounding the death—unraveled.

Geertz describes the emotional chaos that ensued, tracing its roots to a central ambiguity: religious symbols had become political symbols and vice versa, which combined sacred and profane and created "an incongruity between the cultural framework of meaning and the patterning of social interaction" (1973:169). Not only is this an interesting point about the dynamic uses of religious and political symbols, but it is a fine example of thick description. Nothing about this case—its selection, its historical background, the political dimension, the cultural expectations, the motives of distraught family and neighbors—none of it can be explained except by exposing "a multiplicity of conceptual structures, many of them superimposed upon or knotted into one another, which are at once strange, irregular, and inexplicit, and which [the anthropologist] must contrive somehow first to grasp and then to render" (Geertz 1973:10).

Conclusion

"Theory," Geertz wrote, "grows out of particular circumstances and, however abstract, is validated by its power to order them in their full particularity, not by stripping that particularity away (2000:138). The process of interpreting those particular circumstances, Geertz argued, is the essence of ethnography. Once ethnography moves beyond simple listing, interpretation is involved as the ethnographer provides a gloss of the gloss that informants provide. Geertz distinguished the experience-near "native point of view" from the experience-distant realm of social theorists and argues that the ethnographer's task is to explicate the links between the two:

> To grasp concepts that, for another people, are experience-near, and to do so well enough to place them in illuminating connection with experience-distant concepts theorists have fashioned to capture the general features of social life, is clearly a task at least as delicate, if a bit less magical, than putting oneself into someone else's skin. The trick is not to get yourself

> into some inner correspondence of spirit with your informants. Preferring, like the rest of us, to call their souls their own, they are not going to be altogether keen about such an effort anyhow. The trick is to figure out what the devil they think they are up to. (1983:58)

And that requires interpretation, distinct from either description or invention. Discerning the connections between multilayered cultural phenomena is not the same as inventing those connections (Geertz 1988:140). The presentation of ethnographic interpretations as observed facts simply reflects the selection of a genre, not an epistemological reality.

Geertz's works, ethnographies and essays, exemplify this kind of self-cognizant balancing act between literal and literary. It is a body of work that draws on developments in neighboring disciplines and speaks to thinkers in other fields (see, for example, Bruner 2003; Davis 2003). It has also raised some sharp debates about verification: if ethnography is interpretation, then how can we know if the interpretation is correct? Most of us cannot go to Modjokuto or northern Morocco and check the interpretations; we need some other ways to evaluate the ethnographer's claims, but how? In traditional ethnographies we could search for various validating points: Is the ethnographer fluent in the local language? Did she live in the culture for an extended period? Was he methodical or biased in his observations? Were the informants "representative" of a larger culture?

But if cultural knowledge is inherently interpretive, how can we invalidate the "truth" of an interpretation since there are potentially as many "true" interpretations as there are members of a culture? And, to extend this logic, if all such claims are equally valid, then the most anthropology can hope for is to create a rich documentary of multiple interpretations, none denied and none privileged. This means that anthropology cannot be a science since it cannot generalize from truth statements or test the statements against empirical data; the nature of culture precludes this. Geertz argued,

> Human beings, gifted with language and living in history, are, for better or worse, possessed of intentions, visions, hopes, and moods, as well as of passions and judgments, and these have more than a little to do with what they do and why they do it.

> An attempt to understand their social and cultural life in terms of forces, mechanisms, and drives alone, objectivized variables set in systems of closed causality, seems unlikely of success. (1995:127)

For anthropology, Clifford Geertz's major contribution was to force anthropologists to become aware of the cultural texts they interpret and the ethnographic texts they create. He also touched off a major debate within anthropology about the fundamental nature of the field (see "Postscript: Current Controversies"). Geertz's "evocative metaphor of interpretation as the reading of texts both by the observer and the observed," Marcus and Fischer write, "has led to the present dominant interest within interpretive anthropology about how interpretations are constructed by the anthropologist, who works in turn from the interpretations of his informants" (1986:26). That key point has triggered a profound rethinking of the anthropological enterprise.

References

Barrett, Richard
1991 *Culture and Conduct: An Excursion in Anthropology*. Belmont, Calif.: Wadsworth.

Boon, James
2003 Geertz's Style: A Moral Matter. In *Clifford Geertz by His Colleagues*. R. Shweder and B. Good, eds. Pp. 28–37. Chicago: University of Chicago Press.
2007 Clifford James Geertz. *Anthropology News* 48(1):34–35

Brettell, Caroline, ed.
1993 *When They Read What We Write: The Politics of Ethnography*. Westport, Conn.: Bergin and Garvey.

Bruner, Jerome
2003 Celebrating Geertzian Interpretivisim. In *Clifford Geertz by His Colleagues*. R. Shweder and B. Good, eds. Pp. 20–23. Chicago: University of Chicago Press.

Davis, Natalie Zemon
2003 Clifford Geertz on Time and Change. In *Clifford Geertz by His Colleagues*. R. Shweder and B. Good, eds. Pp. 38–44. Chicago: University of Chicago Press.

Geertz, Clifford

1960 *The Religion of Java*. New York: Free Press.

1963a *Agricultural Involution: The Process of Ecological Change in Indonesia*. Berkeley: University of California Press.

1963b *Peddlers and Princes: Social Change and Economic Modernization in Two Indonesian Towns*. Chicago: University of Chicago Press.

1965 *The Social History of an Indonesian Town*. Cambridge, Mass.: MIT Press.

1973 *The Interpretation of Cultures*. New York: Basic Books.

1983 *Local Knowledge: Further Essays in Interpretive Anthropology*. New York: Basic Books.

1988 *Works and Lives: The Anthropologist as Author*. Stanford, Calif.: Stanford University Press.

1995 *After the Fact: Two Countries, Four Decades, One Anthropologist*. Cambridge, Mass.: Harvard University Press.

2000 *Available Light: Anthropological Reflections on Philosophical Topics*. Princeton, N.J.: Princeton University Press.

2002 An Inconstant Profession: The Anthropological Life in Interesting Times. *Annual Review of Anthropology* 31:1–19.

2003 Which Way to Mecca? *New York Review of Books*, June 12, 2003, vol. L, no. 10, pp. 27–30.

Higgins, Benjamin

1963 Preface. In *Agricultural Involution: The Process of Ecological Change in Indonesia*. By Clifford Geertz. Berkeley: University of California Press.

Institute for Advanced Study

2006 Clifford Geertz, 1926–2006. Press release, October 31. Accessed at www.ias.edu/newsroom/announcements/view/geertz-1926-2006.html.

Johnson, A., and W. Ross

1991 Clifford Geertz. *Contemporary Authors, New Revision Series* 36:148–154.

Marcus, George E., and Michael M. J. Fischer

1986 *Anthropology as Cultural Critique: An Experimental Moment in the Human Sciences*. Chicago: University of Chicago Press.

Shweder, Richard A.

2005 Cliff Notes: The Pluralisms of Clifford Geertz. In *Clifford Geertz by His Colleagues*. R. Shweder and B. Good, eds. Pp. 1–9. Chicago: University of Chicago Press.

Tiger, Lionel

2006 "Fuzz, Fuzz . . . It Was Covered in Fuzz." *Wall Street Journal*, November 7, 2006, A12.

20

Mary Douglas

Symbols and Structures, Pollution and Purity

In a modest self-assessment, Mary Douglas (1921–2007) once said, "I am primarily interested in cross-cultural comparison" (Locher 1981:144); in fact, her works created an important anthropological approach to symbolic classifications and their social contexts. It has been written that "Douglas has been of inspiration to hundreds of social scientists who have felt the need to grasp the symbolic world more effectively" (Wuthnow et al. 1984:13). Douglas's contributions were recognized in honorary doctorates from universities in Sweden, the United Kingdom, and the United States; in 1992 she was named a Commander, Order of the British Empire, and made Dame Commander shortly before her death in May 2007 (Fardon 2007). Her ideas are presented in fifteen books and scores of articles characterized by probing intellect, modest tone, and sly wit.

Two theoretical traditions are entwined in Douglas's thought. First, she extended Durkheim's search for systems of classification and the bases of social experience. Like Durkheim, Douglas argued that systems of knowledge are social systems and that their definitional categories express social realities. While Durkheim's point of entry was the nature of the totem, Douglas entered through a commonplace, yet marvelously complex, subject: dirt. If we want to make a cross-culturally relevant definition of dirt, Douglas wrote,

> we are left with the old definition of dirt as matter out of place. This is a very suggestive approach. It implies two conditions: a set of ordered relations and a contravention of that order. Dirt

> then, is never a unique, isolated event. Where there is dirt there is system. Dirt is the by-product of a systematic ordering and classification of matter. (1966:35)

From that deceptively ordinary starting point, Douglas enlarged her analysis into the broader problems of purity and pollution and their classification.

Second, Douglas employed a comparative method derived from Evans-Pritchard. In her fine study of Evans-Pritchard's work (Douglas 1980; see chapter 12), Douglas discussed how his exploration of accountability provided a comparative angle that was sensitive to local realities yet recurrent in all human societies. Similarly, Douglas examined two experiences common to all societies: (1) To what extent is a bounded social unit experienced? and (2) To what extent are there specific rules relating one person to another as individuals? These two variables—which Douglas called "group" and "grid"—are variously found in all societies and thus are a basis for cross-cultural analysis, but they also reflect local realities. In this way, Douglas balanced objectivity with attention to local knowledge, simultaneously avoiding uncontextualized comparison and hypersubjectivity. In her studies of the social bases of knowledge and the comparison of social groups, Douglas produced a corpus of extremely stimulating ideas.

Background

Mary Douglas (née Tew) was born in Italy in 1921 and raised and educated in Great Britain (see Richard Fardon's [1999] excellent intellectual biography of Douglas). After serving as a civil servant in the Belgian Congo during World War II, she returned to Oxford in 1946 to study anthropology under Edward Evans-Pritchard. She received her doctorate in 1951, the same year she began her fifty-three years of marriage to James Douglas (1919–2004), an economic researcher for Britain's Conservative Party. From 1949 to 1950 and again in 1953, Mary Douglas conducted ethnographic fieldwork among the Lele of Zaire. Characterizing her monograph, *The Lele of Kasai* (1963), as "a study of authority—or rather its failure," Douglas described the existence of aristocratic clans who do not rule or lead, of village headmen "who did not govern, allocate resources [or] adjudicate disputes," and of clans that "had no corporate character whatsoever" (1963:68–85, 202). With its minimal emphasis on overt theoretical statements, *The Lele of Kasai* is clearly influenced by Evans-Pritchard. Most of the book examines the institutions of Lele society and only briefly touches on the issues of pollution that would become prominent in Douglas's later work.

After a brief stint as a lecturer at Oxford, Douglas began teaching at University College London where she advanced from lecturer to professor between 1951 and 1977. A spate of articles discussed various aspects of her Lele research (e.g., 1951, 1952, 1955, 1957, 1960), and at various points they presage some of her later interests. For example, an article on Lele social and religious symbolism (1955; reprinted 1975) showed how social form and symbolic systems are linked in Lele culture.

In the mid-1960s Douglas expanded her insights about the Lele into a broader cross-cultural program, considering wider theoretical problems in books such as *Purity and Danger: An Analysis of Concepts of Pollution and Taboo* (1966), *Natural Symbols: Explorations in Cosmology* (1970), and in essays in her edited volume *Rules and Meanings: The Anthropology of Everyday Knowledge* (1973).

Rules and Meanings collects articles by such diverse authors as philosopher Ludwig Wittgenstein, composer John Cage, novelist Tom Wolfe, the anthropologists Evans-Pritchard and Stanley Tambiah, and Mrs. Humphry, the Victorian author of *Manners for Women* (1897). The collection is a fascinating, though indirect, statement of Douglas's intellectual intentions, as indicated by her selections and brief essays. She prepared the collection for a course taught under the various titles of "Cognitive Anthropology," "Symbolism," or "Religion and Morals," and she admitted, "The book expounds more of what this editor believes ought to be accepted in anthropology than what is actually accepted" (1973:9). The collection expresses a recurrent line of intellectual concerns that began among late-nineteenth-century social thinkers—most prominently Durkheim and Mauss—who shared

> a common concern with problems of commitment, solidarity, and alienation. They knew only too well that there can be rules without meaning. They also assumed that there can be no meaning without rules. They drove the study of meaning straight to the study of social relations. Formal analysis would reveal the formal properties of a communication system, as a vehicle for meaning: the meanings conveyed would be uncovered only through social analysis. (Douglas 1973:9)

Despite this promising start, the cross-disciplinary conversation splintered into specialists' musings, and consequently, Douglas argued, "our knowledge of social conventions which make understanding possible remains scarcely advanced from that beginning" (1973:9). The advancement of understanding of social conventions has been the primary aim of Mary Douglas's work.

Purity and Pollution

"Holiness means keeping distinct the categories of creation," Douglas wrote (1966:53), and the social bases of symbolic classifications are central to her work. At the core of religious classifications are the concepts of pollution and purity.

Douglas's interest in pollution and purity had two sources. First, these concepts are discussed by early anthropologists of religion such as Tylor, Frazer, Robertson Smith, and Durkheim, as well as by her own teachers, Evans-Pritchard and Franz Steiner (Douglas 1966:vii, 10–28, 1968b). Second, and perhaps more important, the Lele were deeply concerned with pollution (Douglas 1966:vii, 1955). *Buhonyi* is the virtue of propriety expressed in shyness, modesty, and shame. Buhonyi imbues all status relationships and personal functions. In contrast, all bodily dirt (*hama*) is shameful, the material antithesis of buhonyi. The Lele say that insulting a man is like rubbing excrement (*tebe*) in his face (Douglas 1975:9–13). The avoidance of hama extends to corpses, blood, excrement, maggots, used clothing, and sexual intercourse. The Lele are horrified by milk drinking and egg eating, since milk and eggs are body products and thus hama.

By extension, Lele "rules of cleanliness largely amount to an attempt to separate food from dirt" (Douglas 1975:13), and the classification of edible and disgusting foods is referenced to the contrast between buhonyi and hama. Carnivores, dirty feeders, rats, snakes, and smelly animals like jackals are hama. Women will eat most types of monkeys, except for one species that eats the secretions of palm trees; since vegetable secretions, like animal excrement, are called tebe, that one species of monkey is also hama (Douglas 1975:13–15).

Obviously, Lele symbolism is not about hygiene. It is a system of symbolic classifications that literally distinguish clean/dirty, human/animal, male/female, village/forest, upstream/downstream, and so on, classifications spanning both secular and religious symbols.

What is true of the Lele is broadly true of other human societies, even though the symbols and systems are differently configured. As Douglas wrote,

> Lord Chesterfield defined dirt as matter out of place. This implies only two conditions, a set of ordered relations and a contravention of that order. Thus the idea of dirt implies a structure of idea. For us dirt is a kind of compendium category for all events which blur, smudge, contradict, or otherwise confuse classifications. The underlying feeling is that a system of values which is habitually expressed in a given arrangement of things has been violated. (1968b:338)

In an often reprinted chapter, Douglas examined the best-known system of pollution in the West: the abominations of Leviticus. These Old Testament dietary rules distinguish between what is edible and inedible:

> These are the living things which you may eat among all the beasts that are on the earth. Whatever parts the hoof and is cloven-footed and chews the cud among the animals, you may eat. Nevertheless among those that chew the cud or part the hoof, you shall not eat these: The camel, because it chews the cud but does not part the hoof, is unclean to you. (Leviticus 11:2–4)

The biblical dietary laws define dozens of unclean animals. Varyingly interpreted as designed to discipline the Jews in their search for holiness or as a primitive avoidance of nonhygienic foodstuffs, Douglas argued that the dietary laws are founded on a model of God as One, Complete, and Whole. "To be holy is to be whole, to be one: holiness is unity, integrity, perfection of the individual and of the kind" (Douglas 1966:64). Unclean animals combine elements of different realms: the things that live in the water but lack both fins and scales (eels, shellfish), the birds of the air that live in the water (pelicans, gulls), and any land animal that lacks both characteristics of the paragon of domestication—the cow—chewing the cud and the cloven hoof. "By rules of avoidance holiness was given a physical expression in every encounter with the animal kingdom and at every meal" (1966:57). (Not surprisingly, Douglas's interpretation of Old Testament food taboos differs dramatically from one proposed by Marvin Harris [1974; see chapter 15] who argued that the food taboos served an adaptive purpose.)

In *Purity and Danger*, Douglas traced the convoluted lines of magic, taboo, mana, and contamination and in the process provided a masterful commentary on anthropological approaches to ritual and religion. But in the last half of *Purity and Danger*, Douglas focused on the relationships between ritual and social systems. For example, Douglas argued that there is a recurrent parallel between the human body and the body politic; rituals designed to protect the human body from outside contamination are mirrored in ceremonies designed to protect the external boundaries of society (1966:114–128). Other rituals concern relationships within society. Whether we discuss mana in Polynesia, witchcraft among the Azande, or the curative power of the Royal Touch, "beliefs which attribute spiritual power to individuals are never neutral or free of the dominant patterns of social structure" (Douglas 1966:112). Douglas outlined a clear hypothesis:

> Where the social system explicitly recognises positions of authority, those holding such positions are endowed with explicit spiritual power, controlled, conscious, external and approved—powers to bless or curse. Where the social system requires people to hold dangerously ambiguous roles, these persons are credited with uncontrolled, unconscious, dangerous, disapproved powers—such as witchcraft and evil eye.
>
> In other words, where the social system is well-articulated, I look for articulate powers vested in the points of authority;

> where the social system is ill-articulated, I look for inarticulate powers vested in those who are a source of disorder. (1966:99)

Douglas's interest in the links between symbolic classifications and social systems led to her most ambitious theoretical contribution (Wuthnow et al. 1984:78), a cross-cultural inquiry into group and grid.

Group and Grid, Society and Symbol

Douglas proposed two concepts to frame her cross-cultural inquiry into societies: group and grid. The concepts are simple: "Group is obvious—the experience of a bounded social unit. Grid refers to rules which relate one person to others on an ego-centred basis" (1970:viii). Group and grid are independent variables. Group and grid also are continuous variables; for example, one could imagine a "group" as a sliding scale, varying from "no sense of a bounded social unit" to "some sense of bounded social unit" to "well-developed sense of bounded social unit." In Douglas's initial explanations, however, grid and group are simplified as nominal variables—you live in either a "weak-group" or "strong-group" society—and their relationships can be presented in a simple 2 x 2 table:

		GROUP	
		–	+
GRID	+	B	C
	–	A	D

When a society experiences grid and group (Cell C), "the quality of relations is ordered and clearly bounded. If group is found by itself (Cell D), or grid is found without group (Cell B), the quality of relations is different" (Douglas 1970:viii). Douglas further explained the two categories:

> The group itself is defined in terms of the claims it makes over its constituent members, the boundary it draws around them, the rights it confers on them to use its name and other protec-

> tions, and the levies and constraints it applies. . . . The term grid suggests the cross-hatch of rules to which individuals are subject in the course of their interaction. As a dimension, it shows a progressive change in the mode of control. At the strong end there are visible rules about space and time related to social roles; at the other end, near zero, the formal classifications fade, and finally vanish. (1982a:191–192)

As an example of a strong-grid society, we can recall (see pp. 113–14) the traditional society of Bajoeng Gede, Bali, as described by Bateson and Mead (1942). In Bali, Mead wrote about the complex rules concerning personal interactions, in which a "fixed and complicated set of regulations, obligations, and privileges" produces a grid in which "space and time and social status form an orderly whole" (1942:10). In contrast to the Balinese strong-grid society, in weak-grid societies social "boundaries begin to be arbitrated. Individuals, deciding to transact across them, weaken the classifications" (Douglas 1982a:192). Paradoxically, as grid weakens and as individuals more freely engage in social transactions, the rules governing such transactions may become more explicit, legalistic, and increase in number. For example, one might argue that modern American society is a weak-grid society since we elevate the individual and celebrate free choice in economic and social realms, yet we regulate the behaviors and expectations of interactions through our legal system.

Up to this point in her analysis, Douglas's ideas are interesting but not really unique: numerous schemes have been used to classify societies. What is significant is the way Douglas links grid and group to other dimensions of culture, such as the economic and political expressions of differing social contexts; symbolic structures relating to the human body and society; and cosmological statements regarding nature, time, human nature, and social behavior (1970, 1982a, 1982b).

In situations with strong-grid/strong-group (Cell C), the individual's social experience is defined first by the social boundary maintained between the group and outsiders and second by the clear rules of behavior between group members. Individual behavior is regulated in the name of the group. Within the group, clearly defined social sectors exist (such as classes, castes, age-grades, and so on) that may have specialized roles and unequal access to resources, and a variety of solutions will be used to resolve conflicts between those groups. Strong grid/strong group societies will tend to be larger than other societies and last longer without internal fissioning. Since their members perceive the possibility of "persisting as a group into the future," strong group/strong grid societies can make levies of their members (taxes, corvée, military service) to invest in their continued existence.

Strong group/weak grid societies (Cell D) also emphasize the definition and authority of the group, but because of their low-grid conditions they will lack formalized internal divisions or segregated social sectors. Consequently, relationships between individuals are ambiguous and the resolution of conflicts more difficult. In the face of conflicts, the only penalty for internal disputes is expulsion from the group or the fissioning of the group. This has several consequences: "disagreement is driven underground" since mechanisms for resolution are ill-developed. Covert factions develop, and group members committed to the maintenance of society will argue for stronger group boundaries to control admission and strengthen the group. Consequently, strong group/weak grid societies will tend to be small and subject to internal divisions (Douglas 1982a:205–206).

The two remaining possibilities, strong-grid/weak-group and weak-grid/weak-group, have very different social outcomes. In extreme cases of strong-grid/weak-group societies (Cell B), the individual is tightly regulated by social rules and individual autonomy is minimized, but so is the individual's affiliation with any social groups, since those groups—by definition—do not exist. The individual's role and behavior are unambiguously defined by powers that are remote, impersonal, and insulating (Douglas 1982a:207).

In weak-grid/weak-group societies, "the social experience of the individual is not constrained by any external boundary" and is unregulated by ascribed status classifications (Douglas 1982a:207). All social classifications are potentially negotiable; the relationships between individuals are ambiguous and their mutual obligations implicit. Individuals can transact freely. However, there will be an opposing tendency to regulate individual behaviors that violate social contracts, such as laws prohibiting breach of contracts, rules protecting the free exercise of rights, and legislation defending religious minorities. In such societies, rewards go to innovators, economic activities specialize and expand, and the market is controlled by alliances. Nothing succeeds like success in weak-grid/weak-group societies, and success is measured by the size of one's following, whether these are customers, political supporters, or fans (Douglas 1982a:207–208).

An analysis of grid and group is linked to broader issues of symbolism. In essence Douglas asked, "If symbols mark systems of classifications, and if classification systems are reflections of social systems, then what types of classifications are associated with which types of societies?" She argued that

> the most important determinant of ritualism is the experience of closed social groups. The man who has that experience associates boundaries with power and danger. The better defined and the more significant the social boundaries, the more bias I would expect in favour of ritual. If the social groups are weakly structured and their membership weak and fluctuating, then I would expect low value to be set on symbolic performance. (1970:14)

In strong-group/weak-grid societies, humanity is divided into insiders and outsiders, and nature is similarly classified into two classes: the lovable, vulnerable, cuddly part of nature and the threatening, dangerous, untamable part of nature. The parallel dualities in humanity and nature are more than the extension of metaphors but reflect "the use made of nature in moral justifications" (Douglas 1982a:210). Outside the village edge, beyond the border of society, evil forces lurk waiting to penetrate the human realm. Within the community, one must find the contaminated agent of evil, drive him out, and purify the realm of humanity again.

In strong-group/strong-grid societies, the same emphasis on society's borders is present, but it is modified by the presence of strong grid. The explicit rules about the interrelations between group members are justified by a "transcendental metaphysics which seeks to make an explicit match between civilization and the purposes of God and nature" (Douglas

1982a:210). When social relations are confirmed by ritual, the laws of nature are used for moral justification. In strong group/strong grid societies, theoretical models are elaborated, divine sacrifice is highly developed, and social contexts are justified by appeals to "natural law" and cosmological analyses (Douglas 1982a:210–211).

In weak-group/strong-grid societies, theoretical notions of society and the cosmos are undeveloped, and cosmologies are incoherent and eclectic "things of shreds and patches" (Douglas 1982a:211). Finally, in weak-group/weak-grid societies, the unrelenting competition and selection exercised by individuals is expressed in cosmologies that convey the "excitement and rewards of competition" (Douglas 1982a:212).

In addition, since success is measured by the size of one's following in weak-group/weak-grid cases, society is a source of constant concern because approval, once granted, also may be withdrawn. Because following is based on performance, there is intense demand for high standards: our movie stars can never make a flop, our presidents cannot be adulterers.

Nature stands in contrast to the competition of weak-grid/weak-group society. Outside the realm of humanity and an oasis of innocence, nature is not cited to justify social relations since nature and society are separate realms. Yet "a wistful sense of alienation from nature never wins against the excitement and rewards of competition" (Douglas 1982a:212).

Building on the framework shaped by group and grid, Douglas offered an amazing list of predictions about such different topics as cookery ("In D the classification of edible foods is likely to assert the prohibition against eating carnivores"), gardening ("D will not be specially interested in gardening as a cultural activity, whereas C is likely to use this medium to justify and expand its view of society as hierarchized, trained and compartmentalized"), monuments ("though it has nothing much to raise public monuments to, B respects the burial places of its private dead"), and attitudes about youth and old age, death, personal abnormalities and handicaps, punishment, and justice (1982a:214–226).

But if we accept Douglas's predictions as plausible, how do we decide where Society X fits on the grid/group diagram?

First, grid/group analysis assumes that society is the product of interactions between the individual and her/his environment, the environment consisting of "all the other interacting individuals and their choices." A group does not exist "independently of the volition of its independent members. Their investment of time and energy quickens its life and marks its boundaries" (Douglas 1982a:198). Alternately, as appeals are made to "an ethic of individual value," grid diminishes in force.

Second, the analysis of grid/group occurs at the level "at which people find it necessary to explain to each other why they behave as they do" (Douglas 1982a:201). This level—"the social accounting level, the level of justification and explanation"—can be observed and investigated by the anthropologist (Douglas 1982a:201). For example, if an individual conducts the varying facets of life—residence, work, shared resources, marriage, and kinship—within a common social set, then group is strong. If I spend the early morning as a member of my family, my day as an employee, then return to my family most evenings except for the one night a month I join a poker party and the other evenings I spend as a member of a homeowners' association, as a seminar participant, as a PTA member, and other socially disconnected networks, then group is weak. Similarly, if I justify my actions by appeals to the rights of the individual or, alternately, to my expected roles as a member of a particular social unit, then grid is varyingly weak or strong. None of this requires anthropologists to restructure their basic methods, and it produces tantalizing lines of inquiry.

Fundamentally, Douglas outlined an approach in which "most values and beliefs can be analyzed as part of society instead of as a separate cultural sphere" (1982b:7). Group/grid analysis, Douglas wrote,

> is a method of identifying cultural bias, of finding an array of beliefs locked together into relational patterns. The beliefs must be treated as part of the action, and not separated from it as in so many theories of social action. The action or social context, is placed on a two-dimensional map with moral judgements, excuses, complaints and shifts of interest reckoned as the spoken justifications by individuals of the action they feel required to take. As their subjective perception of the scene

> and its moral implications emanates from each of them individually, it constitutes a collective moral consciousness about man and his place in the universe. (1982a:199–200)

Conclusion

In the late 1970s Douglas moved to the United States where she was director of research at the Russell Sage Foundation in New York, a private nonprofit organization sponsoring research in the social sciences. During her time at the Sage Foundation (1977–1981), Douglas coauthored and edited volumes that applied group/grid analysis to modern industrialized societies (1982a) and explored the ways those societies perceived risk (1985; Douglas and Wildavsky 1982). In 1981 Douglas became Avalon Foundation Professor of the Humanities at Northwestern University where she was professor emerita in 1985. After two years as visiting professor at Princeton, Douglas returned to England in 1988. Beginning in the late 1980s and after her professional "retirement," Douglas's interest in religion dominated her writings (Fardon 1999:199–205), including the books, *In the Wilderness: The Doctrine of Defilement in the Book of Numbers* (1993), *Leviticus as Literature* (1999), and *Jacob's Tears: The Priestly Work of Reconciliation* (2004). Douglas observed that her study of Leviticus would have never occurred "if during African fieldwork I had not been confronted by local dietary rules," which in turn led her to focus on "the class of unclassifiable things" (1999:vi). Douglas approached another set of unclassifiable things in her final book, *Thinking in Circles: An Essay on Ring Composition* (2007). Douglas observed that certain types of myths, epic poems, novels, and sacred texts—including the Old Testament's Book of Numbers—are considered by Western readers to be disorderly and unstructured (2007:43). In fact, Douglas contended, such works have an nonlinear, circular structure, in which parallel sections are opposed and balanced, the ring characterized by "its symmetry, its completeness, and its patterned cross-referencing (2007:13–14). Rather than unreadable or disordered, Douglas found ring composition in literatures from diverse cultures and epochs, leading her to suggest that "its robustness over thousands of years supports the theory that something in the brain preserves it, and yet we know that it can fade out so completely that new readers miss it altogether" (2007:12). And yet a modern reader's "blindness" to ring structures reflects other social realities. Living in a postmodern era of multiple traditions and a multiplicity of truths and in a culture "heavily against boundaries, rules, and closures as such, the ring shape would seem too formal, artificial, mechanical" (Douglas 2007:146). When societies undergo dramatic changes—wars, social upheavals, rapid technological changes—traditions become unstable, notions of grid and group are reassessed, and bounded and stable aesthetics lose favor (Douglas 2007:144–48).

Thus, for the entirety of her long intellectual career, Mary Douglas pursued the "study of meaning straight to the study of social relations" (1982c:ix–x). Rather than view meanings and social rules as constraints mechanically applied to passive members of human cultures, Douglas argued that humans "holding each other responsible in their dealings . . . attribute to each other voluntary, intended agency" (1982c:ix). Her view of culture sought the ways "people make statements about their life," an analytical stance that listened for "the active voice" rather than a passive one.

References

Bateson, Gregory, and Margaret Mead

1942 *Balinese Character: A Photographic Analysis.* New York: New York Academy of Sciences.

Douglas, Mary

1950 *Peoples of the Lake Nyasa Region.* London: Oxford University Press. (Published under maiden name Mary Tew.)

1951 A Form of Polyandry among the Lele of the Kasai. *Africa* 21(1):1–12.

1952 Alternate Generations among the Lele of the Kasai. *Africa* 22(1):59–65.

1955 Social and Religious Symbolism of the Lele of the Kasai. *Zaire* 9(4):385–402.

1957 Animals in Lele Religious Symbolism. *Africa* 27(1):46–58.

1960 Blood Debts among the Lele. *Journal of the Royal Anthropological Institute* 90(1):1–28.

1963 *The Lele of Kasai*. London: Oxford University Press.
1966 *Purity and Danger: An Analysis of Concepts of Pollution and Taboo*. New York: Praeger.
1968a Dogon Culture: Profane and Arcane. *Africa* 38:16–25.
1968b Pollution. In *International Encyclopedia of the Social Sciences*. Vol. 12. D. Sills, ed. Pp. 336–342. San Francisco: Macmillan and Free Press. [Reprinted 1975 in *Implicit Meanings: Essays in Anthropology*. Pp. 47–59. London: Routledge & Kegan Paul.]
1968c The Social Control of Cognition: Some Factors in Joke Perception. *Man* (n.s.) 3:361–375.
1970 *Natural Symbols: Explorations in Cosmology*. New York: Pantheon Books.
1971 Do Dogs Laugh? Cross-Cultural Approach to Body Symbolism. *Journal of Psychosomatic Research* 15:387–390.
1975 *Implicit Meanings: Essays in Anthropology*. London: Routledge & Kegan Paul.
1980 *Edward Evans-Pritchard*. New York: Viking Press.
1982a Cultural Bias. In *In the Active Voice*. M. Douglas, ed. Pp. 183–254. London: Routledge & Kegan Paul.
1982b Introduction to Group/Grid Analysis. In *Essays in the Sociology of Perception*. M. Douglas, ed. Pp. 1–8. London: Routledge & Kegan Paul.
1982c Preface. In *In the Active Voice*. M. Douglas, ed. Pp. vii–xi. London: Routledge & Kegan Paul.
1985 *Risk Acceptability According to the Social Sciences*. Occasional Reports on Current Topics, 11. New York: Russell Sage Foundation.
1986 *How Institutions Think*. Syracuse, N.Y.: Syracuse University Press.
1993 *In the Wilderness: The Doctrine of Defilement in the Book of Numbers*. Sheffield: JSOT Press.
1996 *Thought Styles: Critical Essays on Good Taste*. London: Sage.
1999 *Leviticus as Literature*. Oxford: Oxford University Press.
2004 *Jacob's Tears: The Priestly Work of Reconcilation*. Oxford: Oxford University Press.
2007 *Thinking in Circles: An Essay on Ring Composition*. New Haven, Conn.: Yale University Press.

Douglas, Mary, ed.
1973 *Rules and Meanings: The Anthropology of Everyday Knowledge—Selected Readings*. Harmondsworth: Penguin Books.

Douglas, Mary, and Aaron Wildavsky
1982 *Risk and Culture: An Essay on the Selection of Technical and Environmental Dangers*. Berkeley: University of California Press.

Fardon, Richard
1999 *Mary Douglas: An Intellectual Biography*. London: Routledge.
2007 Obituary: Dame Mary Douglas. *Guardian*, May 18, 2007. Online at education.guardian.co.uk/obituary/story/0,2082786,00.html.

Harris, Marvin
1974 *Cows, Pigs, Wars and Witches: The Riddles of Culture*. New York: Random House.

Locher, Frances, ed.
1981 Douglas, Mary (Tew), 1921–. In *Contemporary Authors* 97–100:143–144.

Wuthnow, Robert, James D. Hunter, Albert Bergesen, and Edith Kurzweil
1984 *Cultural Analysis: The Work of Peter L. Berger, Mary Douglas, Michel Foucault, and Jürgen Habermas*. Boston: Routledge & Kegan Paul.

VI

STRUCTURES, PRACTICE, AGENCY, POWER

By the late 1970s, major theoretical crevasses emerged within the field of anthropology, divides that widened to nearly unbridgeable chasms. The "four-fields approach" in American anthropology, rooted in the optimistic and polymath vision of Franz Boas, began to appear less a description than a dream. As Clifford Geertz observed,

> The initial difficulty in describing anthropology as a coherent enterprise is that it consists, most especially in the United States, but to a significant extent elsewhere in the world as well, of a collection of quite differently conceived sciences rather accidentally thrown together. . . . The "Four Fields" ideology, proclaimed in addresses and enshrined in departments, has held together an uncentered discipline of disparate visions, ill-connected researches, and improbable allies: a triumph, and a genuine one, of life over logic. (2000:90)

To some extent, the different fields of anthropology have diverged as they have become more sophisticated, often drawing on concepts and techniques from fields outside of anthropology: linguistics with cognitive sciences, physical anthropology with genetics and neurophysiology, archaeology with paleoecology, and so on. A given biological anthropologist may have more in common with a genetics researcher across campus in the school of medicine than with an ethnographer in her own department; the ethnographer may share greater interests with his colleagues in the humanities. Yet, the issues are deeper than mere disciplinary affiliation.

Two broad and intersecting sources of unease infuse anthropology, beginning in the mid-1970s, and become broadly recognized by the end of the twentieth century: a gradual rejection of a unitary notion of culture and the growing concern about how anthropological paradigms and frameworks shape or distort understanding the social experiences of others. Interestingly, these issues surface in the works of quite different anthropologists, such as James Fernandez, Pierre Bourdieu, Sherry Ortner, Eric Wolf, and Marshall Sahlins.

The notion that a culture formed some kind of integrated unit permeated twentieth-century anthropology: a culture consists of a group of people with a shared set of learned values, worldviews, classifications, vocabularies, and so on. This perspective is evident in anthropologists operating from divergent theoretical positions. Margaret Mead (chapter 8) contrasted the gentle culture of the Arapesh with the fierce culture of the Mundugumor. Evans-Pritchard described the social determinations of Nuer culture (chapter 12). Marvin Harris (chapter 15) wrote of a sociocultural system as consisting of *a* population, *a* society, and *a* culture. In each of these perspectives, the anthropologist contends (or assumes) that there is something "out there" in human experience that one may call "a culture." Further, the anthropologists asserted that these different cultures—Dobuan or Kwakiutl, Arapesh or Mundugumor—exhibited a discernible coherence that distinguished them from other cultures. The distinctiveness of different cultures remained even when individual members disagreed with the social canons of appropriate thought and behavior, attributing such variations to incomplete socialization, the uneven mastery of the informant's own culture, or social deviancy. But despite these variant explanations, a central theme reoccurs—a culture consists of a set of knowledge learned and shared by a specific group of humans, and different human groups learn and share different sets of knowledge.

A related corollary is this: such different sets of knowledge are "out there" ready for the anthropologist to discover and describe. Discovery and description were never easy, but they were possible given a variety of factors: mastering the native language, finding a good informant, pursuing the logics of kinship, deciphering the structure of a myth, and so on. The locals may be uncooperative, wars and typhoons may drive the anthropologist from the field, and any number of accidents and challenges may prohibit the successful completion of one's fieldwork—but these were all extraneous factors, not inherent to the anthropological enterprise. Culture existed and it could be known.

In the late twentieth century these two fundamental assumptions crumbled. A growing sense of unease crystallized around two objections: cultures are not unitary, and the anthropological inquiry is itself a cultural construction influencing the outcome of the inquiry. Various factors contributed to this intellectual disquiet. First, the world changed, simultaneously becoming more fragmented and interconnected. As Geertz has observed, after World War II as "even putative social isolates . . . grew fewer in number, and anthropologists turned their attention toward vaster, more mixed-up, iridescent objects, India, Japan, France, Brazil, Nigeria, the Soviet Union, the United States," the unitary view of culture "became, in turn, strained, imprecise, unwieldly, and hard to credit" (2000:249). Within the postwar emergent nation-states of Europe, Asia, Africa, and Latin America, it was obvious that specific groups—ethnicities, religious groups, tribes—could not be viewed as cultural isolates, but had to be seen within a larger, dynamic perspective. This obvious fact led to a less-evident implication: if such groupings existed, it was because a certain group of people viewed themselves as having something in common and/or their neighbors saw them as having some shared identity. As Geertz put it, "What makes Serbs Serbs, Sinhalese Sinhalese, French Canadians French Canadians, or anybody anybody, is that they and the rest of the world have come, for the moment and to a degree, for certain purposes and in certain contexts, to view them as contrastive to what is around them" (2000:249).

This view of cultures is conceptually distant from Kroeber's cultural elements lists or Benedict's configurational approach. Mapping a region, delineating a culture area, shading the regions in distinctive colors ("Nuer territory," "Hmong villages"), distorted reality because the cultural differences were conditional, not permanent, and shifting, not clear-cut. And yet, there were distinctive differences between Serbs and Nuer, Sinhalese and French Canadians. What makes them different?

The second unease stemmed from a concern with the anthropological inquiry. After World War II anthropologists became increasingly aware that their assumptions and methods were influenced by their own history and culture. This growing awareness of the philosophy and practice of science is marked by the 1962 publication of Thomas Kuhn's *The Structure of Scientific Revolutions*, which argued that science changed when its fundamental frameworks were reordered, not by the gradual accumulation of scientific facts. Such paradigm shifts, as Kuhn called them, partially were products of scientific breakthroughs, but also the consequences of new and rather generalized visions of human existence originating outside the realm of science: the challenge to divine authority, the idea of progress, the call for revolution, and so on. New scientific models could not be divorced from their surrounding intellectual, social, and political milieus. This broad awareness had specific implications for anthropologists: if anthropologists' inquiries are shaped by our intellectual, social, and political milieus, then do our inquiries necessarily distort or incompletely render the cultural experiences of others?

The pervasiveness of these concerns is evidenced by their presence in the divergent theories of five anthropologists: James Fernandez, Sherry Ortner, Pierre Bourdieu, Eric Wolf, and Marshall Sahlins. Fernandez's position (chapter 21) is broadly "postmodernist," contending that the cultural experience is fragmentary and shifting and that ethnography should document but not reduce or ignore the mutabilities of meaning. Whatever coherencies occur, Fernandez argues, derive from the individuals elaborating on various cultural themes, what he calls "tropes."

Ortner's perspective (chapter 22) is related but distinct. Ortner would agree with Fernandez that cultural experience is shifting but insist that it tends to pivot around discernible sets of symbols, what she refers to as key scenarios. Key scenarios are culturally defined "models of" social conceptions and "models for" social action. Further, key scenarios tend to cluster around the dimensions and contradictions of social life, such as differences based on gender, class, and ethnicity.

Pierre Bourdieu outlined a "theory of practice" in which cultural rules and the actions of individual social agents are constantly reordered but never separable (chapter 23). Cultural experience is neither the acting out of learned rules of behavior nor the chaos of idiosyncratic actions. The realm of practice, Bourdieu argued, is like a game in which the rules, possible strategies, and individual performance *all* comprise the game. In turn, the anthropologist brings to ethnographic inquiry another set of practices, and Bourdieu called for a careful self-scrutiny of the distortions inherent in anthropological practice.

Eric Wolf (chapter 24) approached these issues from another perspective, one informed by a Marxist concern with the structures of power. Arguing that cultures are not integrated wholes or static expressions of shared values, Wolf argued that every society contained groups and factions with differential access to power. Such structures of power, in essence, delineate the field for individual social action. In turn, the configurations of power within a given society are not only expressions of internal order, but also depend on the historical connections with other societies. Wolf argued that an anthropological perspective that saw cultures as ahistorical, stable, and uniform was inherently flawed.

Marshall Sahlins (chapter 25) has examined the intersections of cultural structures and historical processes and contingencies that are engaged through human actions. In a series of studies of specific historical cases, Sahlins argues that culture, history, and agency are indivisibly linked. Sahlins has articulated, as Ortner observes, "an explicitly historical form of practice theory" in which the collective symbolic structures relevant in a specific culture are put into play by the intentions and actions of individuals, but that "while people act in the world according to their own cultural conceptions, the world is under no compulsion to conform to those conceptions" (2006:9–10). Therefore, the meanings of culture may either be reconfirmed or restructured through specific and historically contingent practice.

Thus, in the early twenty-first century, anthropological theories exhibit a set of common concerns—the need to examine both shared patterns and individual practices, the essential requirement to look at the different groups and positions within a culture, the imperative to view the connections between cultures, and the scrutiny of anthropological inquiry. A final, diffuse conclusion emerged: understanding culture was infinitely more complex than it had once seemed.

References

Geertz, Clifford
2000 *Available Light: Anthropological Reflections on Philosophical Topics.* Princeton, N.J.: Princeton University Press.

Kuhn, Thomas
1962 *The Structure of Scientific Revolutions.* Chicago: University of Chicago Press.

21

James Fernandez

The Play of Tropes

In many ways the works of James W. Fernandez (b. 1930) exemplify a postmodernist approach to anthropology. "Postmodern" is an extremely diffuse concept—perhaps intentionally and inherently so—eluding easy definition. One attempt to distinguish modernism and postmodernism was a schematic list of thirty-two paired opposites describing "modernism" and "postmodernism," respectively: purpose/play, design/chance, hierarchy/anarchy, selection/combination, and so on (Hassan 1985). Many concepts in the list distinguished the universalizing and authoritative aspects of modernism from the fragmentary, creative, and competitive mosaic of postmodernism. Harvey writes that the most startling aspect of postmodernism is "its total acceptance of the ephemerality, fragmentation, discontinuity, and the chaotic." Rather than try to transcend, reverse, or reduce that mosaic, the movement revels in "the deep chaos of modern life" (1989:44). In the humanities and social sciences, postmodernism is frequently associated with thinkers such as Jacques Derrida, Michel Foucault, and Jean François Lyotard, who share a common emphasis on the progressive unraveling of multiple layers of language and meaning, an intellectual process that highlights the shifting nature of truth and truths.

Fernandez's writings are an example of a distinctively anthropological context of postmodernist thought. The postmodern influence in anthropology has had a variety of consequences, but the most central is on the nature of ethnography. Rather than present other cultures as set examples of an overarching theory of functionalism or cultural materialism or structuralism, the objective of anthropological research becomes an ethnography of experience that is deeply emic and may require new forms of experiments in writing about another culture. "These experiments," Marcus and Fischer suggest, "are asking, centrally, what is a life for their subjects, and how do they conceive it to be experienced in various social contexts" (1986:46).

Such concerns are at the heart of James Fernandez's work and were explicitly connected with broader themes in the late twentieth century:

> There is just now an especially pronounced awareness that what is done in human affairs is not simply to be taken literally, at face value as it were, but that many such doings, like metaphor itself, stand for something else, so that our sober-minded constructions have obligatorily to be reconstructed. For another thing, we are living at a time when the referential value of language, its ability to provide us with an accurate, transparent view through to and mapping of the reality of things . . . is profoundly questioned. (Fernandez 1991:10)

So the slipperiness of meaning in human affairs requires us to question our views of social life. Our perspectives are not pure reflections of reality—"immaculate perceptions" in Fernandez's term—but are instead refracted through our own, often unrecognized frames of reference. And if this is true as we try to understand our own society, then the distortions are intensified as our gaze turns to another culture.

It is hard to imagine Radcliffe-Brown, Malinowski, Marvin Harris, or Julian Steward worrying about such matters. This is not to suggest that these anthropologists believed understanding another culture was easy, but there is no hint in their works that such difficulties stemmed from the inherent nature of culture. Over the past hundred years, most anthropologists have assumed that understanding another culture—as a coherent set of values, behaviors, and symbols shared by a specific group of humans—was the basis of anthropology. While there was debate whether anthropology was to be modeled after the natural sciences, like biology, or the humanities, like history, there was a recurrent consensus that "the truth" about another culture could be obtained.

Postmodern anthropology severely questions that assumption. First, it argues that there is never one truth, but always several. Second, postmodern anthropologists scrutinize anthropological models as reflecting their proponents' usually Western, often male-dominated, developed societies rather than being pure images of other cultures. The postmodernist critique often analyzes such models as extensions of domination. Thus, Radcliffe-Brown's portrayal of non-Western societies as "ahistorical" is seen as a not-so-subtle justification of the superiority of British culture—and thus imperialism—which prides itself on its tradition and written history.

Finally, the opaque meanings of language and behaviors require that anthropologists find an entrée into the way people create and order their own cultural meanings. Rather than reduce reality to imposed, all-encompassing models, the goal is to identify significant concepts that members of a particular society deem relevant.

These issues intersect in Fernandez's work. In 1986 he wrote, "Over the last decade and a half . . . I have been trying to do an anthropology that is alert to the arguments that lie at the heart of our human experience in culture" (1986:vii). But even earlier, Fernandez was concerned with the meaningful construction of culture, a process exemplified by the heated discussions in the men's council house of the Fang of northern and central Gabon.

Background

Fernandez traces his intellectual genealogy to a group of anthropologists—Malinowski, Benedict, and Evans-Pritchard, among others—who are distinguished by "their embeddedness in the local idiom, their skillful presentation of local points of view" (1982:xx). Born in 1930, Fernandez received a B.A. at Amherst College in 1952 and then went to Northwestern University, where he studied under the wide-ranging Africanist Melville Herskovits. As a graduate student, Fernandez initiated preliminary research in Spain (a research area he would return to), but in the mid-1950s Africa increasingly dominated his interests. From 1958 to 1961 Fernandez conducted twenty-four months of fieldwork in Gabon, a Francophone nation on the Atlantic coast of equatorial Africa. After choosing a village, Assok Ening, in the rain forest of northern Gabon as his study area, Fernandez asked permission to stay in the community, a request that triggered a very public debate.

> The room was full. Everyone was anxious to know why a European (ntangen) wished to live among them. The speculation was particularly intense because it was said I had come to establish a commerce. Some had heard that I was a mwan amerika (a child of America), and since this phrase was often used for Protestant missionaries, some thought I might be intending to set up a mission station. When, as it turned out, I wanted only to live among them to learn their way of life, there was evident disappointment, and some drifted away. (Fernandez 1982:28)

Fernandez's study of Fang religion and syncretism was the basis of a 1962 dissertation and his book *Bwiti: An Ethnography of the Religious Imagination in Africa,* published twenty years later and discussed in detail below. While finishing his dissertation Fernandez started teaching at Smith College where he remained until 1964, at which time he moved to Dartmouth.

Over the next decade Fernandez published widely on the Fang, African religious movements, and the concept of metaphor in cultural analysis. His interest in the cultural ordering of symbols is expressed in articles on Fang aesthetics (1966a, 1970, 1972) and architectural design (1977a, 1979) and recordings of Fang music (1973). From 1975 to 1986 Fernandez taught at Princeton and after that at the University of Chicago, where he retired as professor in 2000. A fellow of the American Academy of Arts and Sciences, Fernandez has been visiting professor at universities and institutes in Spain, Great Britain, Sweden, and the United States.

Beginning in the early 1970s, Fernandez resumed his research in northern Spain. His research on culture change in the mountain province of Asturias continues to the present. Fernandez has discussed his research among the miners and cattle herders of Asturias in over a score of articles, each of which takes a specific ethnographic event—boys' schoolyard games, a folklore parade, or a ribald exchange between men and women on a bus—and holds the event up to an analytical light, turning it over like an artifact, examining it from different points of view. From these "revelatory incidents" Fernandez's intention is to "expose the importance of the analysis of metaphors in anthropological inquiry" and the way that such metaphors become adopted by human actors (1986:6). That is the play of tropes.

The Play of Tropes

According to the *Oxford English Dictionary*, a trope is literally "a figure of speech which consists in the use of a word or phrase in a sense other than that which is proper to it." Fernandez expands the notion to cover "the metaphoric assertions men make about themselves or about others," assertions that influence action (1986:24). For example, in American society we commonly employ the trope of "the competitive race": "Life's a rat race," "The race for the presidency," "With hard work you can get ahead," "Whoever ends up with the most toys wins," and so on. Life isn't really a race, yet not only do Americans use this trope to describe our lives, but we shape our actions based on this conception. (In this regard, the concept of trope is very similar to the notion of a key scenario discussed by Ortner [chaper 22].) The trope is thus a bridge between metaphor and act, and this creates the opening for anthropological insight. Although understanding is not obtained by the simple observation of behavior, neither is Fernandez primarily interested in metaphors as philosophical or linguistic structures. "I am more interested in what tropes do," Fernandez writes, "than in what they are" (1986:ix). Arguing that anthropology is "essentially a pragmatic and not a platonic or idealist enterprise," Fernandez states,

> It is the kind of study primarily concerned with how humans in real situations get things done such as living together with some sense of fulfillment and satisfaction; mastering an environment, providing food, clothing, and shelter; creating some sense of ultimate meaning to life as well as some sense of humor; bringing up the next generation. (1986:ix)

At that point, Fernandez's argument sounds similar to Marvin Harris's statement that "human social life is a response to the practical problems of earthly existence" (1979:ix; see p. 204), but Fernandez is obviously not a cultural materialist. Fernandez states that his specific concern is how humans create "identities through the argument of images and the play of tropes" (1986:ix).

Fernandez frequently refers to the "movement" in this process, transitions from an ill-defined or vague status to one that is concrete and specific. That movement from the ill-defined to the specific characterizes semantic metaphors ("My love is a red, red rose") and also social metaphors ("Men are dirty pigs"). Movement from the vague to the concrete also characterizes symbolic actions, particularly during ritual. Fernandez argues that rituals should be analyzed "as a series of organizing images or metaphors put into operation by a series of superordinate and subordinate ceremonial scenes" (1982:43). Thus ritual becomes an acted, public discourse in which meanings are created, referred to, and juxtaposed in actions and words that always stand for something else.

In a very basic sense, that is the play of tropes. But that simple starting point requires enormous ethnographic effort: ceremonial scenes must be described, their relative significances determined, and the polyvalent web of the metaphors' referents untangled. Fernandez outlines a research design to achieve this. Broadly, the research must be based on participant observation, a method that provides "as none other, an awareness of the many different domains of experience in a culture" (1986:60–61).

Specifically, the research should focus on the way metaphor and metonymy are used to transform vague, socially inchoate individuals into specific, well-defined occupants of particular positions in the social sphere. This process of definition calls on specific sets of signs and symbols ("sign-images") that form a cultural lexicon unique to a particular culture. Rituals that mark such transitions are constructed from that cultural lexicon and refer to a limited number of themes or tropes "to bring about significant conversions in themselves" (Fernandez 1986:61).

Like most anthropologists, Fernandez has arrived at his theoretical position in the process of understanding another cultural reality. The idea of the "play of tropes" emerged directly from Fernandez's efforts to understand the complex meanings of a cult of transformation: Bwiti.

Bwiti

Fernandez's introduction to Bwiti was dramatic: late one night, a loud knock, and a man stood at the door wearing a long flowing robe belted with a red cord. He said, "You do not know me but I am no stranger. I am a child of this village just returned from a long spiritual journey. I have been following the truth!" The night visitor went on, "You must come to the Bwiti Chapel in my father's house," then grabbing Fernandez's left arm, the man pointed at freckles and said,

> "These are your sins! You have heard the harp at night? While all these villagers are asleep we dance and journey far. They go nowhere here. They wander around in confusion. They don't know where to go. But we go far." He took hold of the red-woven cord around his waist. "You see this cord? This is the Path of Birth and Death. We follow this path. We know life. We know death." (Fernandez 1982:292)

Bwiti is a revitalization movement that developed after World War I, as Fang society experienced the twin pressures of French colonialism and Protestant missionary activity. "The invention and diffusion of religious cults for purposes of protection and revitalization in Africa," Fernandez writes, "is . . . a very old phenomenon antedating European contact. But the pressures of colonial domination and missionary evangelization coupled with the relative inertia, the ennui, that came to prevail among such a previously turbulent people as Fang created particular needs for revitalization" (1982:292). Referring to the "malaise and increasing isolation of parts of Fang culture," Fernandez argues that the Fang "achieve some assuagement and reconciliation in Bwiti" (1982:6). But Fernandez's point is not a Malinowskian reduction of cultural complexes to individual psychological needs. Rather, Fernandez situates Fang cultural malaise and Bwiti's response within specific, local explanations.

In so doing he reveals—and revels in—the complexities of the particular ethnographic situation.

The Fang experienced a garbled, uncertain social order. "Social realities had collapsed while a lexicon persisted" that described categories of social life that no longer existed (Fernandez 1982:87). An egalitarian society lacking specialized genealogists or cosmographers who could establish opinion, the Fang expressed vocal disagreements about the lost meanings of social concepts. "And the Fang were discomfited by these differences. Terminological evidence that clan organization was formerly greater, coupled with present ambiguities about the application of terms, convinced many that their social affairs were in a vestigial state" (Fernandez 1982:87).

Bwiti creates movement from chaos to unity, from divisiveness to common purpose. Intriguingly, it achieves this by multiplying symbolic options rather than reducing them "by offering them extension into a variety of realms of being" (Fernandez 1982:301).

In the first half of his book (part I), Fernandez outlines the history of Fang–European contacts and Fang conceptions of the past, time, social and built space, social structure, and worldview. He reviews the historical and modern Fang, with particular attention to the aspects of folklore, religion, and legend that had become disarticulated, conflicted, and controversial. It is these elements of collapse that Bwiti reunifies. "In Fang lore we see the roots of Bwiti," Fernandez writes, "but it is a significantly new composition" (1982:73). In his own composition, Fernandez is intent on placing our knowledge of the Fang within their specific cultural frame. Fernandez organizes his ethnography into conceptual sets that are uniquely Fang (for example, "Compositions of the Past") rather than into the common chapter titles found in ethnographies (such as "Historical Background," "Subsistence," or "Social Structure"). Fernandez uses two other devices to emphasize local knowledge. First, each chapter begins with an ethnographic vignette in which a conversation, an encounter, or a remembered myth opens the discussion of a set of themes. Second, Fernandez consistently provides the Fang word for a concept in English, as in, "The overall transformation is from the state of despair (*engôngôl*) to a state of grace (*abora*)" (1982:309). Since relatively few readers understand Fang, this intratextual commentary serves two implicit goals: it bolsters confidence in Fernandez's understanding of Fang culture, and it constantly nudges the reader's attention to the ethnographic detail, to the specifically Fang reality. Fernandez writes, "Our interpretation of Bwiti, it should be remarked, has its center of gravity in Fang culture itself" (1982:6).

Bwiti is expressed in a complex all-night ceremony (*engosie*) that travels the path between life and death, from despair to tranquility, and from isolation to "one-heartedness" (for a description of the liturgical cycle, see Fernandez 1982:436–469). Small doses of a psychotropic plant, *eboga,* which induces "euphoric insomnia," are taken as communion during the engosie. Much larger doses are consumed by initiates, and the resulting visions are designed to "break open the head" of new converts (*banzie*) to Bwiti (Fernandez 1982:470–493). Satisfying eboga visions are extensions "into the unseen, the death realm, of the path of birth and death which the all-night ceremonies evoke and follow. Most visions are a following of that path. What the liturgy can only suggest, the taking of eboga actualizes" (Fernandez 1982:485).

Midway through the engosie, a brief sermon from the *évangile*—often less than fifteen minutes long—is dense with polyvalent meanings. The sermons edify, as Fernandez points out (1982:529), but are not didactic or expository. Rather, the sermons create a multilayered "edification by puzzlement" in which "one obtains . . . as indeed one obtains in the architectonic of Bwiti life and in the ritual drama of their celebrations, a sense of reverberation, resonance between levels and domains of interest." In that manner, "we are forced to extend ourselves to larger integrities in wider contexts" (Fernandez 1982:530).

Bwiti is not a set of rules, Fernandez argues, but "a set of projected qualities" (1982:310). Through the combination of dance and action, sermon and vision, Bwiti seeks to move the Fang from despair to grace, from corporeality to spirituality, from sloth to industry, from sexual indulgence to sexual purity, from bad body to clean body, from worthlessness to worthiness—toward the promise of becoming one-hearted (Fernandez 1982:309). Bwiti is movement.

> To search for the Bwiti order in codified form, although it may gratify a Western need for abstractions of that kind, yet misses

> the Bwiti moral order where it reposes: in the images and actions of Bwiti myths and legends, in the night-long rituals and accompanying song cycle, in the architectonics of the cult house, and in the midnight "évangiles" of cult leaders. The moral order is more acted out than spelled out, more ritualistic than didactic. . . . It is as much as anything a kinesthetic order that is gradually exposed to the membership in the process of their worship. (Fernandez 1982:303–304)

In the process of the Bwiti rituals, actions are based on key sets of metaphor, emphasizing shared communal experience and motivating action. These "performative metaphors" are used in Bwiti to unify, motivate, inspire, and to create "an overarching sense of solidarity in the sacred society of Bwiti" (Fernandez 1982:563).

Conclusion

In his introduction to *Bwiti*, Fernandez previews his idea of explanation, calling it "basically genetic and semantic" (1982:8). His basic assumptions are that, first, historical experiences create the expectations for revitalization and, second, that revitalization is created from "the residue of these experiences" (1982:8). Necessarily this implies that all explanations are based on local knowledge, framed by specific historical circumstances, and formed by particular social creators.

Of course this is not enough to make James Fernandez a postmodern anthropologist; Franz Boas's notion of explanation was very similar. But Fernandez's emphasis on local knowledge, the existence of parallel truths (1982:29–73), relations between power and knowledge (e.g., 1986:172–173), and a stubborn insistence on the irreducibility of meaning mark the postmodernist themes in the anthropology of James W. Fernandez.

References

Fernandez, James

1962 Redistributive Acculturation and Ritual Reintegration in Fang Culture. Ph.D. dissertation, Northwestern University.

1964 African Religious Movements—Types and Dynamics. *Journal of Modern African Studies* 3:428–446.

1965 Symbolic Consensus in a Fang Reformative Cult. *American Anthropologist* 67:902–927.

1966a Principles of Opposition and Vitality in Fang Aesthetics. *Journal of Aesthetics and Art Criticism* 25:53–64.

1966b Unbelievably Subtle Words: Representation and Integration in the Sermons of an African Reformative Cult. *Journal of the History of Religions* 6:43–69.

1969 *Microcosmogony and Modernization in African Religious Movements*. Occasional Paper Series, no. 3. Pp. 1–34. Montreal: Centre for Developing-Area Studies, McGill University.

1970 Rededication and Prophetism in Ghana. *Cahiers d'Etudes Africaines* 10(38):228–305.

1972 Tabernanthe Eboga and the Work of the Ancestors. In *The Flesh of the Gods: The Ritual Use of Hallucinogens*. P. Furst, ed. Pp. 237–260. New York: Praeger.

1973 *Music from an Equatorial Microcosm: Fang Bwiti Music (with Mbiri Selections)*. New York: Folkways Records.

1975a On Reading the Sacred into the Profane: The Dramatic Fallacy in the Work of Victor Turner. *Journal for the Scientific Study of Religion* 14:191–197.

1975b On the Concept of the Symbol. *Current Anthropology* 16(4):652–654.

1977a *Fang Architectonics*. Working Papers in the Traditional Arts, no. 1. Philadelphia: Institute for the Study of Human Issues.

1977b The Performance of Ritual Metaphors. In *The Social Uses of Metaphor*. J. Sapir and C. Crocker, eds. Pp. 100–131. Philadelphia: University of Pennsylvania Press.

1978 African Religious Movements. *Annual Review of Anthropology* 7:195–234.

1982 *Bwiti: An Ethnography of the Religious Imagination in Africa*. Princeton, N.J.: Princeton University Press.

1986 *Persuasions and Performances: The Play of Tropes in Culture*. Bloomington: Indiana University Press.

1991 Introduction: Confluents of Inquiry. In *Beyond Metaphor: The Theory of Tropes in Anthropology*. J. Fernandez, ed. Pp. 1–13. Stanford, Calif.: Stanford University Press.

Harris, Marvin

1979 *Cultural Materialism: The Struggle for a Science of Culture*. New York: Random House.

Harvey, David

1989 *The Condition of Postmodernity: An Enquiry into the Origins of Cultural Change*. Cambridge, Mass.: Blackwell.

Hassan, I.
1985 The Culture of Post-Modernism. *Theory, Culture and Society* 2(3):119–132.

Marcus, George E., and Michael M. J. Fischer
1986 *Anthropology as Cultural Critique: An Experimental Moment in the Human Sciences*. Chicago: University of Chicago Press.

22

Sherry Ortner

Symbols, Gender, Practice

Sherry Ortner (b. 1941) is an extremely influential anthropologist, whose research and writings explore a recurrent theme: the cultural dynamic between symbolic meaning and social inequalities based on gender, status, ethnicity, and wealth. Initially, Ortner's writings occupied distinct nodes—Sherpa ethnography (1973b, 1978), studies of symbolism (1973a, 1975), and feminist anthropology (1996a)—but these gradually have fused into a coherent scholarly project (e.g., Ortner 1989, 1997, 1999). The increasing unification of this research marks Ortner's theoretical migration from an emphasis on nature of symbols to a concern with issues of practice and power (1984, 1989, 1996b). In a still-expanding corpus of work, Sherry Ortner's central contribution is to bridge the realms of human ideas and human action via the analysis of symbolic schemes and social practice.

Background

Sherry Ortner was born in a middle-class, Jewish section of Newark, New Jersey. She studied anthropology as an undergraduate at Bryn Mawr College, graduating in 1962. She went to graduate school at the University of Chicago and began fieldwork with the Sherpas, an ethnic group living in northeastern Nepal. Ortner worked in Nepal for fourteen months in 1966–1968, fieldwork that was the basis of her 1970 dissertation (completed under Clifford Geertz's supervision), early articles

(1973a, 1973b), and the book *Sherpas through Their Rituals* (1978). After a couple of years as a lecturer at Princeton, Ortner began teaching at Sarah Lawrence College in 1971 where she remained until 1977. As an undergraduate, Ortner had participated in the social protests of the 1960s, and after returning to the United States in 1968, Ortner resumed her involvement in antiwar and civil rights protests and the emergent feminist movement (Duda 2002:54–55). Ortner recalled that in 1971 she and other anthropologists were invited to contribute to a volume on "the anthropology of women" to be edited by Michelle Rosaldo and Louise Lamphere. Rosaldo and Lamphere organized an informal meeting at a hotel room at the American Anthropological Association annual conference. "I can still picture the scene," Ortner recalled twenty-five years later, "people sitting on beds and on the floor and standing along the walls. And I said it sounds like a good idea, but I don't know anything about women, and Shelly [Rosaldo] said, neither does anyone else" (1996a:216). In the early 1970s "women's issues" were not viewed as major anthropological topics, and Ortner was determined to gain professional approval and status by studying "big" topics, and religion and symbolism were big. "Questions of gender were not for the most part on the table in academia," Ortner recalled; "the feminist revolution had yet to break" (1996c:226).

Ortner went to the University of Michigan in 1977 where she taught in the anthropology and women's studies departments. During her seventeen years at Michigan, Ortner gained national recognition for her research and critical writings. She returned to Nepal for additional fieldwork in 1976 and 1979 and conducted interviews with urban Sherpas living in Katmandu in 1990. She received prestigious fellowships and awards, she was elected to the American Academy of Arts and Sciences (1992), and in 1990 Ortner received a five-year MacArthur Fellowship (the "genius grants") for her research. From 1992 she held an endowed professorship in anthropology and women's studies at Michigan until her 1994 departure to the University of California, Berkeley. In 1996 Ortner went to Columbia University where she taught until 2004 when she became Distinguished Professor at the University of California, Los Angeles. During her career, Ortner has contributed to anthropological theory in several arenas: the anthropological approaches to symbols, feminist anthropology, and a theory of practice emphasizing relationships of gender, ethnicity, and power.

Symbols and Symbolic Schemes

Ortner's early work focused on Sherpa symbolism. Influenced by Geertz's ideas, Ortner argued that symbolic systems serve as "a guide, or program, or plan for human action in relation to certain irreducible and recurrent themes or problems of the human condition as conceptualized in particular cultures" (1973b:49–50). Geertz had argued that symbolic systems were simultaneously "models of" social existence at a given historical moment and also "models for" appropriate action (Ortner 1975:134–135). In her article "Sherpa Purity," Ortner argued that the array of polluting items and behaviors in Sherpa culture (dirt, sexual intercourse, adultery, birth, illness, death, "bad smells" and "dirty food," crowds, and lower castes, to list a few)—reflects a larger, more coherent symbolic system (1973b:50–58). Humans are fallen gods, the Sherpas believe; humanity's initial purity was destroyed by contamination with polluting things. The Sherpa symbolic system is delineated by three conceptual nodes—"spiritual," "physical," and "demonic"—represented by gods, domestic animals, and demons. The Sherpa symbolic strategy is to avoid animal-like or demonlike things and behaviors. Since the gods are "totally incorporeal, wholly spiritual, and wholly blissful" (Ortner 1973b:58), the search for purity requires the rejection of the physical, the earthy, and the demonic. Therefore all human excretions—feces, urine, semen, blood, mucus—are polluting because they are animal-like, except for tears, which are only shed by humans. Rather than a reflection of social order as Durkheim (chapter 4) or Douglas (chapter 20) argue or of deep structures as Lévi-Strauss (chapter 17) might contend, Ortner views "a system of symbols . . . as encoding a program for action *vis-à-vis* certain problems of the human condition" (1973b:55). In Sherpa culture a central paradox is the fact of bodily existence and the incorporeity of divinity: humans have bodies, gods do not, so how can a human become godlike? The answer, Ortner argues, is provided by the symbolic system: avoid natural and polluting things. Thus the Sherpa symbolic system is both a "model of" a specific conception of reality and a "model for" human action.

In the same volume of *American Anthropologist*, Ortner (1973a) published another article, a programmatic overview of "key symbols"—phrases, behaviors, signs, or entire events that seem pivotal for understanding another culture. Ortner notes that anthropologists distinguish key symbols from other, less fundamental symbols in several ways. Informants may state that the symbol is important, expressing interest in or avoiding it. The symbol may occur in different circumstances or be surrounded by elaborated explanations, cultural practices, or prohibitions. A society may have multiple key symbols. A partial list of American key symbols might include the American flag, the Statue of Liberty, Abraham Lincoln, Martin Luther King Jr., the "rags-to-riches" story, the family home, and so on. One could distinguish these from "non-key" symbols—a STOP sign or the cartoon convention of a lightbulb over someone's head signifying an idea, for example—because these latter symbols do not provide a profound entry into the heart of American culture. An account of the significance of Martin Luther King Jr., for example, requires a depth of explanation (e.g., regarding the history of slavery and discrimination, the civil rights struggle, violence in the United States, and the tragedy of martyrdom) that the STOP sign does not.

Key symbols can be organized along a continuum between *summarizing symbols* and *elaborating symbols*. Summarizing symbols bring together disparate meanings in "an emotionally powerful and relatively undifferentiated way" (Ortner 1973a:1339). Elaborating symbols sort out "complex and undifferentiated feelings and ideas, making them comprehensible to oneself, communicable to others, and translatable into orderly action" (Ortner 1973a:1340). Thus, if the American flag, as a summarizing symbol, brings together "a conglomerate of ideas" (Ortner 1973a:1340) about patriotism, democracy, freedom, and national superiority, then the Horatio Alger "rags-to-riches" story serves as an elaborating symbol, outlining a course of action—energetic, hard work to gain wealth and power and thus climb from one's original status. Elaborating symbols may be root metaphors or key scenarios. Root metaphors—life is a race, society is like an organism, and so on—serve "to sort out experience, to place it in cultural categories, and to help us think about how it all hangs together" (Ortner 1973a:1341). Key scenarios "both formulate appropriate goals and suggest effective action for achieving them; which formulate, in other words, key cultural strategies" (Ortner 1973a:1341).

"Sherpa Purity" and "On Key Symbols" are very different articles, and yet they overlap at an important point: in both articles, Ortner views symbolic systems as the basis for action. Symbols are not reflections of deep structures or social orders but provide statements about and models for cultural actions. Ortner is interested in how key scenarios provide a rationale and route for cultural behavior. Her explanations stay very close to the action; not surprisingly, Ortner will become a sympathetic (though not uncritical) advocate of a theory of practice, drawing on the ideas of Pierre Bourdieu (see chapter 23).

These articles are also relevant to Ortner's early feminist anthropological writings. For example, in "Sherpa Purity" she discusses the sources of pollution and they are generally linked to two domains—nature and women. The natural realm is polluting, which, Ortner observes, makes sense in Sherpa culture as the physical is rejected in the search for purity. But the female realm is also polluting. Menstruation and childbirth are polluting. Sexual intercourse is polluting, although it "weakens" men more than women. If sexual intercourse is polluting, sex between Sherpas and lower caste Nepalis is even more polluting, but it is more contaminating for a Sherpa woman to have sex with a lower caste male than for a Sherpa man to have sex with a lower caste woman. Although not the major theme in "Sherpa Purity," Ortner alludes to the gendered imbalances of purity and pollution, an issue central to her feminist anthropology.

Feminist Anthropology: Female/Male, Nature/Culture

Feminist anthropology is extremely broad, centered by its concern with the human consequences of gender and illuminated from various theoretical points of view (for a review, see Mascia-Lees and Black 2000). Feminist anthropology is a multifaceted exploration of what Simone de Beauvoir in *The Second Sex* referred to as one of the central issues of human existence—the gendered responses to the natural limits of being human. "One is not born, but rather becomes, a woman" Beauvoir wrote (1953:267). The biological facts of gender result in a body that is "not a thing, it is a situation . . . it is the instrument of our grasp upon the world, a limiting factor for our projects" (Beauvoir 1953:84). For Beauvoir, Jean-Paul Sartre, and other existentialists, "project" was a pivotal concept, connoting a purposeful vision and active creation of the self. Yet, Beauvoir cautioned, the individual's project was restricted by gendered differences, which—while rooted in and often justified by the biology of sex—are defined and elaborated by social codes:

> [A human society's] ways and customs cannot be deduced from biology, for the individuals that compose the society are never abandoned to the dictates of their nature; they are subject to that second nature which is custom and in which are reflected the desires and the fears that express their essential nature. It is not merely as a body, but rather as a body subject to taboos, to laws, that the subject is conscious of himself [*sic*] and attains fulfillment—it is with reference to certain values that he evaluates himself. And once again, it is not upon physiology that values can be based; rather, the facts of biology take on the values that the existent bestows upon them. (Beauvoir 1953:36)

This leads to a cluster of fundamental questions. Sexual differences are universal—all humans are born female or male—but gender distinctions vary . . . or do they? Are women subordinate in all societies? Do gender roles vary with social or biological evolution? What is the correlation between gendered relations and other dimensions of social distinction such as access to property and power? And what does a feminist anthropology imply (for an excellent review of these and related issues, see Mascia-Lees and Black 2000)?

One of Ortner's first professional papers was also one of her most controversial and well known, "Is Female to Male as Nature is to Culture?" (1996a). Building on Beauvoir's ideas (Ortner 1996b:14) and employing a pair of structuralist homologies, Ortner contended that women are universally devalued, in some degree considered inferior to men in all cultures (Ortner 1996a:23–24). Ortner seemingly contradicted both feminist aspirations and an uneven anthropological literature. Some feminists reacted that universality implied that the devaluation of women was biologically inevitable, a point that Ortner dismissed. On the other hand, some anthropologists had contended that women were dominant in non-Western societies. Margaret Mead had argued that gender-based differences were extremely varied, for example contending that women held the real power among the Tchambuli of New Guinea (see p. 112). Even earlier, Morgan (chapter 2) had argued that matrilineal kinship systems echoed the existence of matriclans under conditions of savagery, patterns that changed with the development of agriculture and property. Friedrich Engels in his 1884 *Origins of the Family, Private Property and the State* argued that women were supreme in early communal societies in which property and sexual partners were shared, but over centuries men instituted monogamy so property would pass to their heirs, subjugating women in the first historical example of class domination. Morgan and Engels contended that female subjugation was a historical development and not a universal human condition, a contention resurrected by Eleanor Leacock (for an extended discussion, see pp. 221–24).

Ortner argued that any "evidence" for elevated female status in societies always faces a universal fact: women are ultimately subordinated to men. Clearly influenced by Beauvoir, Ortner contended that universal subordination of women is not due to nature nor because "biological facts are irrelevant, or that men and women are not different, but that the facts and differences only take on significance of superior/inferior within the framework of culturally defined value systems" (1996a:24).

Ortner's explanation is that every culture attempts to transcend natural existence. Social groups universally distinguish the human realm from the natural realm and usually, although not always, accord greater prestige to culture. Women are associated with nature and thus are universally devalued. Women are seen as closer to nature in reference to three dimensions: (1)

women's bodies are seen as more natural since they are more involved with the species' life; (2) a woman's social roles are viewed as closer to nature, specifically confining her to the domestic realm; and (3) social perceptions of female psyche or personality portray women as closer to nature. Note, these cultural constructs place women as *closer to* nature not *as* nature. This intermediate role means that women's position, while always viewed as subordinate, may be given different sets of meanings depending on how a society views the culture/nature dichotomy. Women may be seen as intermediate and "lower" and/or intermediate between culture and nature and thus mediating and ambiguous (Ortner 1996a:38–41). Despite such variations, Ortner argues, women are universally devalued because "culture (still equated relatively unambiguously with men) recognizes that women are active participants in its special processes, but at the same time sees them as being more rooted in, or having more direct affinity with, nature" (1996a:27).

Nothing about this is inevitable. Ortner discusses how changes in human society require activism directed to both institutional limits and cultural values. In the final analysis—and this is important—"it must be stressed again that the whole scheme is a construct of culture rather than a fact of nature" (Ortner 1996a:41). Women are no more or less "natural" than are men; we are equally mortal, conscious organisms. But starting with the biological facts of gender differences, human societies universally create a "(sadly) efficient feedback system: various aspects of woman's situations (physical, social, psychological) contribute to her being seen as closer to nature, while the view of her as closer to nature is in turn embodied in institutional forms that reproduce her situation" (Ortner 1996a:41).

In a retrospective essay, Ortner (1996c) assesses her early article in light of subsequent criticism and her own thoughts, and she suggests several correctives and revisions. First, Ortner admits that gender equality is more difficult to assess than she originally thought because cultures are more "disjunctive, contradictory, and inconsistent" than she had assumed (1996c:175). Second, Ortner acknowledges, the nature/culture dichotomy is not universally structured with "culture" being superior to "nature," but the distinction is very widespread. Nature may be a place of tranquility and beauty and culture a realm of anxiety and pollution—but the dichotomy remains, and it is usually (but not always) the case that women are more associated with nature than culture. In essence, Ortner would accept some loosening and revision of her thesis—but not its complete abandonment.

Finally, Ortner notes that her interests had shifted from a concern with universals to trying to understand the dynamics of how such symbolic systems are enacted.

> While I do think there are such things as structures . . . , large existential questions that all human beings everywhere must cope with, I also think that the linkage between such structures and any set of social categories—like female/male—is a culturally and politically constructed phenomenon. From early on after the publication of "Is Female to Male . . . ," my interests lay much more in understanding the politics of the construction of such linkages, than in the static parallelism of the categories. (Ortner 1996c:180)

Himalayan Ethnographies

Ortner's evolving theoretical concerns are explored in three major ethnographic studies of Sherpa culture. In *Sherpas through Their Rituals* (1978), Ortner summarizes four sets of Sherpa rituals, organizing her analysis by the distinctive problems each ritual encounters. "Rituals do not begin with eternal verities," Ortner writes,

> but arrive at them. They begin with some cultural problem (or several at once), stated or unstated, and then work various operations upon it, arriving at "solutions"—reorganizations and reinterpretations of the elements that produce a newly meaningful whole. The solutions (and the means of arriving at them) embody the fundamental cultural assumptions and orientations with which we are partly concerned. (1978:2–3)

Sherpas through Their Rituals is very tightly focused on the specific ethnographic case, but it touches on issues and strategies that Ortner develops in later works. First is her emphasis on ritual as "first and foremost a system of meanings—goals, values, concerns, visions, world constructions" (Ortner 1978:5). Second is her consideration of rituals as providing a strategy for action, "a matter of shaping actors in such a way that they wind up appropriating cultural meaning as personally held orientations" (Ortner 1978:5). At the same time, ritual is reshaped by the actualities of social life. Ritual is a "a sort of two-way transformer" modifying an individual's conscience in reference to cultural meanings but in turn reshaped to align with the realities of everyday life (Ortner 1978:5). Third, Ortner notes that the Sherpa and other societies contain central contradictions that are rarely eliminated but usually mediated through rituals. In sum, culture is symbolic and meaningful, symbolic systems provide guidelines for action, and the action is often directed to the central contradictions of social life (see below, pp. 317–19). Rituals are a class of symbolic systems. These themes are developed in later books.

In her most recent Himalayan ethnography, *Life and Death on Mt. Everest: Sherpas and Himalayan Mountaineering* (1999), Ortner examined the complex relationships between Western high altitude climbers and the Sherpas. Initially Sherpas were employed as porters on foreign expeditions and then became high altitude climbers and trekking entrepreneurs. Expeditions originally were all male, but Western and Sherpa women became increasingly involved in climbing. Accompanying these changes were variations in the climbing ethos. The large postwar military-style expeditions—with tons of gear, hundreds of porters, hierarchical command, and the goal of "conquering" the mountain—gave way to smaller expeditions whose counterculture members sought equality among themselves and with the Sherpas. The emergence of all-women expeditions, commercialization and the appearance of "yuppie climbers," and the development of identity politics all shaped the social dynamics of climbing on Mount Everest. In this the mountain becomes an extremely prominent microcosm to understand how human social life is shaped by complexities of power relationships, the patterns and contradictions of social forms, and the way humans employ symbolic systems to resolve (without eliminating) those contradictions.

Ortner's third Himalayan ethnography, *High Religion: A Cultural and Political History of Sherpa Buddhism* (1989), examines the establishment of Buddhist monasteries of celibate monks in the early twentieth century but also treats a central issue in anthropological theory regarding symbols, structure, and practice in the Himalayas—and in human culture in general.

Structure, Symbols, and Practice in the Himalayas

The idea that there are patterns in culture runs throughout anthropological theory—from Benedict's modal personalities (chapter 6) to Fernandez's play of tropes (chapter 21)—but there are equally recurrent suspicions that cultural patterns are imposed by the ethnographer or that such patterns are less important than other fundamental forces, such as environmental factors, individual self-interest, or the internal forces of social forms. Ortner (1989:198–202) contends that neither position is absolutely correct and argues for a "loosely structured" social actor "who is prepared—but no more than that—to find most of his or her culture intelligible and meaningful, but who does not necessarily find all parts of it equally meaningful in all times and places" (1989:198). Different actors have varying relationships to their culture, even when they employ the same symbols from a cultural repertoire. Further, those relationships change as new social configurations emerge and people attempt to "to find meaning where one did not find it before (or indeed changing or losing meaning as well)" (Ortner 1989:199). The problem is not whether cultural meanings are irrelevant or embedded, but rather to understand "how people react to, cope with, or actively appropriate external phenomena, on the basis of the social and cultural dynamics that both constrain and enable their responses" (Ortner 1989:200).

Those responses are enabled and constrained by key scenarios (which Ortner also calls "cultural schemes"). Key scenarios/cultural schemes are

> preorganized schemes of action, symbolic programs for the staging and playing out of standard social interactions in a

> particular culture. . . . [E]very culture contains not just bundles of symbols, and not even just bundles of larger propositions about the universe ("ideologies"), but organized schemas for enacting (culturally typical) relations and situations. (Ortner 1989:60)

Ortner contends that such key scenarios or cultural schemas frequently crystallize around a society's internal contradictions. Ortner's rich Himalayan ethnography illustrates this point and anchors its theoretical implications, but an example from American society might clarify issues before turning to the Sherpa case.

The United States, for example, is often described as a nation where "anyone can grow up to become president" despite the historical reality that every American president has been a white "Christian" male. This is an obvious contradiction. If asked to explain this contradiction, we do not attempt to "solve" the contradiction nor do we stop repeating the phrase, but rather we appeal to key scenarios. We might say that America is "a place of change" and that "the day will come" when a person of color, a Jew, or a woman will be elected president of the United States. We "explain" the contradiction by appealing to a scenario, one that makes cultural sense and describes a course of action ("work hard, and you *can* become president").

Interestingly, cultural schemas are not restricted to a single domain of social life but achieve "a degree of generality and transferability across a variety of somewhat disparate social adaptations" (Ortner 1989:60). Thus, the American cultural scenario "work hard, and you can become president" outlines a course of action extrapolated to other domains—"study hard, and you can get into Harvard," "practice the violin, and you can play Carnegie Hall," or "work on your jump shot and you can make the NBA." The reason we can generalize a cultural scenario is because it illuminates recurrent contradictions in American society (e.g., all citizens have equal rights but unequal opportunities, or all people are created equal, but some are more accomplished than others). Cultural schemas are durable because "they depict actors responding to, and resolving (from their point of view), the central contradictions of the culture" (Ortner 1989:61).

Perhaps all societies contain such contradictions, and Ortner discusses several contradictions in Sherpa society that are resolved by appeals to key scenarios. For example, Ortner examines the intersection of the problem of egalitarianism and hierarchy and the social efficacy of symbolic schemes. For the Sherpa, egalitarianism is problematic because equality among males is viewed as natural and desirable, yet hierarchy is seen as equally inevitable and favorable (Ortner 1989:19). These two opposed dimensions "constantly destabilize one another, making equality fragile and subject to hierarchical manipulation . . . and making hierarchy weak and subject to challenge" (Ortner 1989:125). In traditional Sherpa society, brothers are equals and should inherit family lands equally, yet there is "natural" hierarchy in which older brothers have greater authority and higher status over younger brothers. This internal contradiction has pragmatic consequences as the Sherpa population exceeded the carrying capacity of arable land and some brothers inherit farmland while others do not. Fraternal equality and hierarchy are in conflict in Sherpa culture. This inherent conflict is explained by reference to key scenarios, as encoded in legends, oral histories, and vocabularies that deal with competition, hierarchy, and inequality (Ortner 1989:32–35). These key scenarios do not eliminate this central contradiction in Sherpa society—any more than the key scenario "in America anyone can grow up and become president" has resulted in a nonwhite, non-Christian, or female president. Rather, humans weave various key scenarios into larger social discourses and practices. Ortner writes,

> The general contradiction, and its specific variants within specific relational contexts, are at once reflected in, mediated by, and constituted through meaningful cultural forms. . . . The contradictions and the schema together constitute a hegemony, a mutually sustaining universe of social experience and symbolic representation through which Sherpa actors would tend to understand themselves, their relationships, and their historical circumstances. (1989:125)

Ortner concludes with a theory of practice, one that builds from her early discussion of key scenarios and is also indebted to

Bourdieu's concepts of praxis and habitus (see chapter 23). What gives a society its distinctiveness and coherence is the repertoire of key scenarios available to people to explain their lives, their actions, and their cosmos. Such scenarios are culturally and historically contingent (the scenario "in America anyone can grow up to become president" made no sense before 1790 when the U.S. Constitution was ratified), and they are clearly not universal. Even when the thematics of a key scenario appear universal—the distinctions between nature/culture or female/male—the scenarios are nevertheless rooted in specific social experiences. Neither are key scenarios invariant cultural codes that individuals perform. Key scenarios may be internally inconsistent or a given key scenario may be contradicted by another key scenario. Most importantly, key scenarios are not invariant codes because they are employed by social actors who—sometimes in a calculated fashion, other times unthinkingly—may emphasize some cultural schemes, downplay others, or actively modify the key scenarios. This entire dynamic realm comprises practice. Ortner writes,

> A theory of practice is a theory of history. It is a theory of how social beings, with their diverse motives and their diverse intentions, make and transform the world in which they live. It is a theory for answering the simplest-seeming, and yet largest, questions that social science seeks to answer: Why does a given society have a particular form at a particular moment—that form and not some other? And how do people whose very selves are part of that social form nonetheless sometimes transform themselves and their society? It is a theory that allows social and cultural analysts to put all their various methodological tools to work—ethnographic and historical research; structural, interpretive, and "objectivist" analytic approaches—in ways that enhance and enrich the effectiveness of each. (1989:193)

Conclusion

Since Sherry Ortner continues to conduct ethnographic research and to contribute to conceptual debates within anthropology, any assessment of her contribution to anthropological theory is necessarily incomplete. Although she continues to draw on her ethnographic research among the Sherpa, in the late 1980s Ortner began investigating her own culture (Duda 2002:57) and is currently engaged in a research project focused on Hollywood (Ortner 2007a, 2007b). In her book *New Jersey Dreaming: Capital, Culture, and the Class of '58* (2003), Ortner shifted her ethnographic focus not only to her own society, but to her own, predominantly Jewish, high school graduating class. Following the lives of the 1958 graduates of Weequahic High School, Newark, New Jersey, Ortner examines the dynamic relationships between structure and agency in American society. On the one hand, the class of '58 experienced the boundaries, limits, and potentials that framed American society in the late twentieth century: the connections between class, race, and gender; the upward social mobility and "middle-classing" of postwar America and the shrinking middle class of late capitalism (Ortner 2003:28–33, 265–274); and the emergence of identity politics such as the civil rights movement and feminism (Ortner 2003:205–209). On the other hand, individual actors—Ortner and her classmates—either internalized or rejected such parameters, and rather than passively occupy socioeconomic positions, they were engaged in class-based "projects" (to recall Beauvoir and Sartre's concept discussed previously [p. 312]). "We may think of class as something people are in or possess, or as a place in which people find themselves or are assigned, but we may also think of it as a project, as something that is always being made or kept or defended, feared or desired" (Ortner 2003:14). The theoretical fulcrum of *New Jersey Dreaming* is Ortner's insistence on this "two-way relationship, fully active in both directions between actors' perceptions/imaginings and objective locations" (2003:13).

Ortner explores this two-way relationship in her revelatory ethnography. Given that it is "hard to overstate the significance of high school for the American cultural imagination," Ortner argues that "high schools as social systems attempt to 'force' identities" (2003:90–91). These identities are neither simple nor innocent. During the twentieth century, these identities were expressed in the "amazingly constant" and "remarkably durable" categories of "popular kids," "jocks," "nerds/geeks," "cheerleaders," "sluts," and "nobodies" (Ortner 2003:92). Just as the social distinctions of gender are "explained" in reference to natural differences, as previously discussed (pp. 312–14), the differences between jocks and nerds/geeks, for example, are presented as "social types based on seemingly natural, and thus seemingly randomly distributed, characteristics (beauty, "personality," athletic prowess) which are neither natural nor random, and which always carry . . . a heavy load of class baggage" (Ortner 2003:91). While some individuals resist these categories, and most people are never completely caught in their implications, "this often cruel system of categories" remains extremely powerful (Ortner 2003:92).

Ortner's study is filled with illuminating ethnographic detail. Ortner writes of the geographies of high schools and neighborhoods as a proxy for class distinctions in a supposedly "class-less" American society (2003:56–65). She discusses the powerful key symbol of *success*, which among the class of '58 meant making a lot of money, as in "[her] father has been *very successful* and her brother is *very, very successful*" (2003:1989, emphasis in the original). From observations on her cohort's "visceral response to doo-wop music" (2003:173) to the impacts of globalization on the disappearance of the American working class (2003:265–274), Ortner consistently returns to "the simple, yet very complex, idea that history makes people but people make history" (2003:277).

In sum, the most consistent dimension of Ortner's research is the contradictions between cultural patterns (or structures or schemas or order) and human agency. Ortner summarized her theoretical interest in "the ways the cultural categories both facilitated and constrained agency, and at the ways in which agents faithfully enacted or radically stretched the cultural categories" (Ortner 1996c:227). Arguing that the practice of ethnography produces a body of knowledge that is usually more solid than that of casual observers—"fieldwork makes a difference," Ortner asserts (1999:203)—and thus illuminates the contradiction of cultural pattern and human agency, she writes,

> I could never let go of the idea that, however profoundly power, violence, and sheer difference may form and deform the world, people still try, wherever they are and whatever they are doing, to construct meaningful worlds from their own

point of view. The strongest kind of anthropology today, in my view, is the kind that attempts to keep walking the tightrope between the two perspectives. (Ortner 1999:293)

References

Beauvoir, Simone de
1953 *The Second Sex*. H. Parshley, trans. and ed. New York: Alfred A. Knopf.

Duda, Karen
2002 Sherry B. Ortner. *Current Biography* (November):54–58.

Mascia-Lees, Frances, and Nancy Johnson Black
2000 *Gender and Anthropology*. Prospect Heights, Ill.: Waveland.

Ortner, Sherry
1970 Food for Thought: A Key Symbol in Sherpa Culture. Ph.D. dissertation, University of Chicago.
1973a On Key Symbols. *American Anthropologist* 75:1338–1346.
1973b Sherpa Purity. *American Anthropologist* 75:49–63.
1975 Gods' Bodies, Gods' Food: A Symbolic Analysis of a Sherpa Ritual. In *The Interpretation of Symbolism*. R. Willis, ed. Pp. 133–169. New York: John Wiley and Sons.
1978 *Sherpas through Their Rituals*. Cambridge: Cambridge University Press.
1984 Theory in Anthropology since the Sixties. *Comparative Studies in Science and History* 26(1):126–166.
1989 *High Religion: A Cultural and Political History of Sherpa Buddhism*. Princeton, N.J.: Princeton University Press.
1996a Is Female to Male as Nature Is to Culture? In *Making Gender: The Politics and Erotics of Culture*. Pp. 21–42, 215–217. Boston: Beacon Press. [Originally published 1972 in *Feminist Studies* 1(2):5–31.]
1996b Making Gender: Toward a Feminist, Minority, Postcolonial, Subaltern, etc., Theory of Practice. In *Making Gender: The Politics and Erotics of Culture*. Pp. 1–20. Boston: Beacon Press.
1996c The Problem of "Women" as an Analytic Category. In *Making Gender: The Politics and Erotics of Culture*. Pp. 116–138, 226–230. Boston: Beacon Press.
1997 Thick Resistance: Death and the Cultural Construction of Agency in Himalayan Mountaineering. *Representations* 59:135–162.
1999 *Life and Death on Mt. Everest: Sherpas and Himalayan Mountaineering*. Princeton, N.J.: Princeton University Press.

2003 *New Jersey Dreaming: Capital, Culture and the Class of '58*. Durham, N.C.: Duke University Press.
2006 *Anthropology and Social Theory: Culture, Power, and the Acting Subject*. Durham, N.C.: Duke University Press.
2007a Notes from Hollywood: *Little Miss Sunshine* Finds Its Way. *Anthropology News* 48(7):22–23.
2007b Notes from Hollywood: The Indie Movement. *Anthropology News* 48(6):27–28.

23

Pierre Bourdieu

An Anthropology of Practice

Sometimes it seems that anthropology oscillates with equal certainty between two diametrically opposite theoretical positions. At one extreme is the idea that self-aware individuals, who employ free will, construct the social universe, and the explanation of their behavior is found in their own accounts of reality. The opposite position contends that the social universe is regulated by general principles separate from individual choice and consciousness. These positions imply divergent anthropological goals. In the first position, the measure of an accurate ethnographic account is its fealty to "native" experience and its ability to translate that experience to an outsider. The opposite position considers an ethnographic analysis valuable if it illuminates patterned regularities or explains social behavior in terms of underlying codes or variables, which may or may not be recognized by an informant. This dichotomy appears in varying guises. For example, Kroeber argued that the superorganic of culture held sway over individual choice (see pp. 70–73), while Sapir insisted that culture was the cumulative expressions of self-aware individuals (see pp. 93–95). Harris distinguished between the emic insiders' accounts versus the etic outsiders' scientific hypotheses—and clearly preferred the latter (see pp. 208–9). Lévi-Strauss argued that cultural classifications reflect innate, deep structures of the human mind (see p. 238), while Geertz would argue that any such reduction distorts the very essence of culture, "this acted public document" (see pp. 264–65). "Humanistic" anthropologists deride scientific colleagues as reductionists. "Scientific" anthropologists attack their humanistic colleagues as unrigorous. And on it goes.

The French social scientist Pierre Bourdieu (1930–2002) attempted an analytical exit from this endless dichotomy and posited an alternative position, a theory of practice (praxis). Bourdieu argues that culture is neither the exclusive product of free will nor of underlying principles, but is actively constructed by social actors from cultural dispositions and structured by previous events. The sociologist Craig Calhoun (2000) offers a useful analogy to introduce Bourdieu's concept of practice. When someone is adept at playing a sport, they simultaneously do several things. First, they know the rules of the game: the formal statements about points and penalties, the composition of teams, the game's objectives, the limits of play, and so on. Every player is also aware of her or his performance—the sprint to the finish line, the diving catch in center field, or the left-handed punch that came from nowhere. The rules of the game and the player's performance are linked by strategy: walking a power hitter to first base, running down the time on the shot clock, waiting for a key moment to cycle ahead of the pack. All these domains indivisibly comprise the "game." The game is not the rules. The game is not the individual player's actions. The game is not solely strategy since strategy relies on using the rules and employing specific players to achieve a goal. The game is all of these things, and players move between rules, individual behavior, and strategy without confusion. And finally, the outcome of a specific game—though limited by rules, performed by individuals, and realized via strategy—is not at all predetermined.

The social universe of practice, Bourdieu argued, is gamelike in its stubborn fusion of rules, individual behavior, and strategy. The anthropologist must attend to all these dimensions. But further, just as we attempt to understand the practice of others, social scientists must inquire into their own practice, clarifying assumptions and hidden operations. In this Bourdieu proposes not so much a theory of society as a theory of social genesis and a methodology for understanding the social universe (Wacquant 1992:5).

Background

"Nothing is more misleading than the illusion created by hindsight," Bourdieu wrote, "in which all the traces of a life . . . appear as the realization of an essence that seems to pre-exist them" (1990:55). Yet, there are important connections between Bourdieu's life and ideas. Bourdieu was born in a province in southwestern France to a family of modest means, and even after he was recognized as France's leading intellectual in the late twentieth century, he remained uncomfortable in the universe of French academia. "In France," Bourdieu said in an interview, "to come from a distant province, to be born South of the Loire, endows you with a number of properties that are not without parallel in the colonial situation. It gives you a sort of objective and subjective externality" (Bourdieu and Wacquant 1992:209). This sense of outsiderhood runs through his studies (Calhoun and Wacquant 2002).

After obtaining a philosophy degree from the École Normale Supérieure—"the central institution for consecration of French intellectuals" (Calhoun and Wacquant 2002)—Bourdieu was sent to Algeria for his military service in 1955. He remained to teach at the University of Algiers and to conduct research among the rural Kabyle and with Berber-speaking migrants to Algiers, research further discussed below. Returning to France in the early 1960s, he moved to Paris where at the École Practique des Hautes Études he organized a group of scholars examining European educational systems. Throughout his life, Bourdieu's interests were wide ranging. He decried "the effects of the premature division of labour [that] separate anthropology from sociology" (1984:xiv), and he published on photography and television, the role of art museums in European public life, on how elite schools—like the École Normal Supérieure he attended—create the state "nobility," as well as a number of critical analyses of academic life (for bibliographies see Bourdieu and Wacquant 1992 and the "HyperBourdieu" website at www.iwp.uni-linz.ac.at/sektktf/bb/HyperBourdieu.html).

A stream of publications in the 1970s secured Bourdieu's position in French academia, and his impact in the United States was enhanced by the translations of his works. In 1981 he was elected to the College of France (see p. 235), holding the chair in sociology. As he continued investigations of the relationships between culture and power in some twenty-five books and numerous articles, Bourdieu became increasingly involved in political efforts. Beginning in the 1990s Bourdieu was involved in the antiglobalization movement, describing his position as "to the left of the left" (Riding 2002). The announcement of his death in January 2002 on the front page of the French newspaper *Le Monde* was accompanied by statements from leading figures, including an assessment of President Jacques Chirac: "Famous philosopher and scientist, Pierre Bourdieu lived sociology as a science inseparable from engagement" (*Le Monde,* January 25, 2002).

Bourdieu's ideas resonate among different intellectual fields—art history and criticism, educational research, cultural studies, philosophy—but his investigations resulted in a more integrated corpus than is often recognized. Several commentators (e.g., Postone, LiPuma, and Calhoun 1993; Wacquant 1992, 1993) observe that Bourdieu's readers tended to overlook the connections between his different works, as if Bourdieu pursued three disarticulated nodes of interest: one centered on education (Bourdieu 1988; Bourdieu and Passeron 1979, 1990; for an overview see Collins 1993), another on the sociology of aesthetics and class (Bourdieu 1984, 1993b, 1998; Bourdieu and Schnapper 1990), and a third concerned with North African ethnography and the theory of practice (Bourdieu 1963, 1977, 1990). The following discussion, however, is limited to Bourdieu's impact on two central concepts: the theory of practice and its implications for ethnographic research. And to understand them one must understand the context and impact of Bourdieu's original ethnographic research in Algeria.

Algeria and North African Ethnography

France annexed Algeria in the 1830s and over the next fifty years extended its control from coastal cities to the interior. In the process, Algerians were dispossessed, revolts were brutally suppressed, and Muslim Algerians never received rights equal to those of Europeans. After World War II, the Algerian independence movement became increasingly violent. Guerillas attacked military targets and civilians; the French responded by sending some four hundred thousand troops. Both sides committed atrocities. During eight years of fighting, some one hundred thousand French and one million Algerians were killed. The French government was increasingly pressured to solve the conflict, and after a series of referendums, revolts, and counterrevolts, Algeria gained independence in 1962.

Bourdieu began his ethnographic research in the midst of this violence. "In the Algeria of the late fifties and early sixties, then struggling for its independence," Bourdieu would later write, "to work towards a scientific analysis of Algerian society meant trying to understand and explain the real foundations and objectives of that struggle" (1990:2). Any ethnographic research in Algeria required understanding the war. This recognition, Bourdieu admitted, did not require "exceptional epistemological lucidity or outstanding ethical or political vigilance" (1990:3). During that tragic war, it was impossible to think of Algerian peasant villages as "timeless" or "closed communities," a realization similar to that made by other anthropologists working in other regions after World War II, such as Turner in Africa (chapter 18) or Wolf in Latin America (chapter 24).

Yet, other less obvious forces shaped the ethnography of North Africa. Lévi-Strauss's structuralism was an enormous influence and with it the search for oppositions (earth/sky, land/water, upper moiety/lower moiety, and so on) and homologies (sunrise is to sunset as birth is to death) that expressed hidden structures (see pp. 240–44). Initially, Bourdieu's research followed a structuralist agenda, but as he tried to organize ethnographic data, Bourdieu gradually came to two conclusions. First, the methods and devices of organizing ethnographic data—synoptic charts, kinship diagrams, maps, and tables—assumed logical models that were learned by the anthropologist as part of her or his own scientific culture. Second, what the ethnographer observed in Algerian society—or anywhere else—was not the acting out of implicit rules, but the products of a more fluid and often contradictory social experience. For example, Bourdieu spent hours attempting to depict the "agricultural calendar" in a single diagram but "encountered countless contradictions as soon as I endeavoured to fix simultaneously more than a certain number of fundamental oppositions, of whatever kind" (1990:10). In his studies of ritual he arrived at the same irreducibly contradictory results, and yet he continued "to seek perfect coherence in the system" (1990:10), a search reinforced by structuralist assumptions rather than ethnographic data.

Another conclusion emerged from Bourdieu's ethnographic study: culture is the dynamic outcome of interactions. In an early article on "The Sentiment of Honour in Kabyle Society" (1966), Bourdieu explored not only the rules of honor and shame, but also the strategies of outrage and riposte. Kabyle honor cannot be reduced to a simple set of rules. A specific insult is defined by the scale of the response, and the severity of a counterresponse is carefully weighed by one's kinfolk or community. In summarizing this point, Bourdieu hints at an incipient theory of practice:

> The sentiment of honour is the common and intimate code with reference to which the Kabyle judges his actions and those of others. But are the values of honour really the ideal norms that every one accepts and feels bound to respect? Or are they on the contrary unconscious models of behaviour that govern one's conduct and regulate one's attitudes without clearly rising to consciousness, and which colour one's attitudes without ever being formulated? *In practice the system of the values of honour is lived rather than clearly conceived.* (1966:231, emphasis added)

Such observations led Bourdieu away from the view of culture as the "acting out" of rules and into the midst of practice.

A Theory of Practice

Bourdieu developed his theory of practice in two books, the *Outline of a Theory of Practice* (original 1972, English translation 1977) and *The Logic of Practice* (original 1980, English translation 1990), whose publication history obscures their tight conceptual connections (see Bourdieu 1990:284n1). Neither book is an easy read, and *Outline of a Theory of Practice* revels in paradoxes, parentheses, and lengthy sentences that coil down the page. As discussed above, Bourdieu constructs a theoretical bridge between two long-held oppositions in anthropology and other social analyses: the "subjective" experience of the native and the "objective" perspective of the social scientist. In the early 1960s this durable dichotomy was recast into two dominant positions within the French intelligentsia (Postone, LiPuma, and Calhoun 1993:7–8). Jean-Paul Sartre's existentialism emphasized the priority of the individual, in which "existence precedes essence"; the human condition is created through free choice and its attendant problems, and human behavior is not predetermined. In contrast, Lévi-Strauss's structuralism contended that apparently diverse realms of human behavior—kinship, exchange, and myths—were actually shaped by universally held deep structures reflecting the innate organizational constructs of the human brain, and not by individual free will.

Since most anthropologists study cultures other than their own and are "excluded from the real play of social activities" (Bourdieu 1977:1), the anthropologist usually opts for the analytical pose of an observer intent on decoding behavior—whether speech, ceremonies, or any other interpersonal exchange. The anthropologist's distanced, objectivist stance involves deciphering the code that structures human action (Bourdieu 1977:22–27). In turn, this code may be divided into component subsystems—kinship systems, economic strategies, conventionalized speech, and so on—that contain their own codes. The explanation of another social universe proceeds, first by observation and then by analysis, from behavior to the rules that they express—whether they are rules about social solidarity, rational cost-benefit analysis, or grammatical constructions.

Such an approach, Bourdieu insists, overlooks several problems. First, it ignores that the objectivist stance is itself a culturally defined way of knowing that shapes the outcome of analysis. By adopting "a point of view on the action, withdrawing from it in order to observe it from above and from a distance," the objectivist inevitably sees social behavior "as an object of *observation and analysis, a representation*" of the hidden codes of social life (Bourdieu 1977:2, emphasis in the original). And yet, when we carefully consider the social universe, we recognize it is more than the acting out of preset codes.

For example, language involves more than linguistic structure, and once one becomes interested in how real speakers use actual language, then the linguistic code gives an imperfect representation of what is occurring. Language relies on additional factors—the status relationships between speakers, the formality or casualness of their relationships, their mutual comfort or antagonistic competitiveness, the setting in which speech occurs, and on and on—that are not coded in grammar or syntax but are nonetheless essential to speech. Bourdieu argues that to confuse language with linguistic codes neglects "the functional properties the message derives from its use in a determinate situation and, more precisely, in a socially structured interaction" (1977:25).

If this is true of language, it is equally true of kinship "systems." If a social anthropologist determines that members of Society X prefer patrilateral parallel-cousin marriage, for example, then the anthropologist has a difficult time explaining why deviations from the rule occur. Was the rule poorly understood, incorrectly followed, or were there are not enough "right" mates to go around? This misses the point, Bourdieu argues; what has occurred is the anthropologist has confused the stated *rules* of behavior for the actual *practice* of making kin relationships. The confusion stems from several sources. The anthropologist may have confused "official kinship" with "practical kinship." Official kinship relates to abstract statements that are publicly articulated and socially formalized, their positions occupied by generic agents in specific roles. Practical kinship is kinship in practice, the strategies and resources employed by an individual or a group. Kin relations cannot be reduced to underlying rules or a code. Kin relations are "something people *make,* and with which they *do* something" (Bourdieu 1977:35, emphasis in the original).

To cite another example, Mauss (chapter 9) famously delineated "gift exchange" as the totalizing prestations that are described as if they are voluntary, good-willed, and between individuals but are in fact obligatory, calculated, and between groups. Gift exchange is surrounded by three obligations: the obligation to give, the obligation to accept, and the obligation to repay. But can gift exchange be reduced to these rules? Absolutely not, Bourdieu answers (1977:5–8), and we know this from thinking about how gift exchange is "played." We realize that the gifts must be different objects or "exchange" would become "swapping." There must be a suitable interval between the exchanges of gift and counter-gift: the interval allows for the fiction that the exchange is voluntary, and timing allows for "the collectively maintained and approved self-deception" (Bourdieu 1977:6). These considerations are not just additional rules; they are strategies built upon rules but given existence through individuals' actions.

We could amplify these examples, but they illustrate Bourdieu's point: the social universe is not reducible to a series of rules or a code. This critical point slashes across a broad field of twentieth-century anthropological thought. Are we therefore limited to simply recording the natives' responses? Absolutely not, Bourdieu argues; the proper focus is the realm of *practice*. Instead of an outsider's view, Bourdieu insists that a theory of practice must examine the "objective structures" that anthropologists have long identified, the motives and actions of individuals, *and* the strategies and functioning of practical knowledge (Bourdieu 1977:4). The anthropologist must be alert to the connections between "objective structures" (e.g., patrilateral parallel-cousin marriage) and the acted-out strategies of social life ("this will be a prestigious marriage").

The theory of practice leads the anthropologist to a critical self-recognition: the anthropologist brings her or his own practice to every study. Like all scientists—like all humans—anthropologists are "part and product of their social universe" (Postone, LiPuma, and Calhoun 1993:3). Just like every other field of social life, anthropologists contend with forces that shape their position (e.g., granting agencies, peer reviewers, tenure), matching strategy against structure. Anthropologists create conceptions and misconceptions of social reality. For example, the scientific credo of "the pursuit of knowledge for knowledge's sake" may be as misconceived as the social pretense that gift exchange is "individual, voluntary, and disinterested." A theory of practice requires that anthropologists examine their own practice.

To summarize Bourdieu's argument, the subjectivist/objectivist dichotomy misleads anthropologists to think they can either accept informants' accounts or search for the rules underlying social behavior. Yet, to view social behavior as the acting out of cultural rules overlooks several key points: individual agents as creating their own social universe, the practical strategies of social life, and the anthropologists' own practice. But is there any internal order to practice? Is practice whatever a group of individuals does? If so, what is the common origin of the practices that are shared by members of a particular group—and distinct from those of another group? The answer, Bourdieu suggests, is found in the concept of habitus.

Habitus, *Doxa*, and Practice

A society's members draw upon sets of generative schemes that Bourdieu calls habitus. These schemes are the products of historical antecedents. Habitus has "an endless capacity to engender products—thoughts, expressions, actions—whose limits are set by the historically and socially situated conditions of its production" (Bourdieu 1977:95). Habitus is not the objectivist's rules or roles under another name. Habitus, to use a jazz analogy, is like a thematic riff that jazz musicians improvise upon, produce countermelodies against, or restate in a different key, but it is not a precoded musical score. It provides a coherent thread to the musicians' play, but they are active creators of a previously unheard cultural experience. And the resulting music cannot be reduced to a score, a recording of the improvisation made by an onlooker, the individual players, or their instruments. The music *is* the jazz—it is the *practice*—created by a group of musicians who elaborate upon a theme (habitus), known to all and thus available for modification.

> Thus, because habitus is, as its name suggests, a product of a history, the instruments of construction of the social that it invests in practical knowledge [i.e., knowledge employed in

> practice] of the world and in action are socially constructed, in other words structured by the world that they structure. It follows from this that practical knowledge is doubly informed by the world it informs: it is constrained by the objective structure of the configuration of properties that the world presents it; and it is also structured through the schemes, resulting from incorporation of the structures of the world, that it applies in selecting and constructing these objective properties. In other words, action is neither "purely reactive" in Weber's phase, nor purely conscious and calculated. (Bourdieu 2000:148)

Under some conditions the natural world and the social realm appear to correspond, an experience Bourdieu (1977:164) calls *doxa*. For example, Bateson and Mead (1942; see pp. 113–14) argued that on Bali, social statuses and spatial orientations were parallel schemes. Distance from the sacred dwelling place of the deities, Mount Agung located in the center of the island, was an index of social position, and thus a higher status person should be seated on the "inland" side of a room. In traditional Bali, social order and natural order apparently correspond. Bourdieu insists that the creation of systems of knowledge is always a political act, and "the symbolic power to impose the principles of the construction of reality—in particular, social reality—is a major dimension of political power" (1977:165). In societies where systems of knowledge are stable and replicated by their members' actions, then the range of what is taken for granted is correspondingly large. Customary law "*goes without saying because it comes without saying*: the tradition is silent, not the least about itself as a tradition" (Bourdieu 1977:167). In contrast, when societies experience permanent or temporary instability, then the field of doxa correspondingly shrinks. Any social theory that views cultural behavior as the acting out of predetermined rules or codes (e.g., structuralism) overlooks this connection between systems of knowledge and political power, a point similarly addressed by Eric Wolf (see pp. 355–58).

As an example of doxa, one could cite the fading but still present cultural notion in the United States that "a woman's place is in the home." (This example was triggered by a newspaper article noting that the Texas Board of Education protested "a photo of a woman with a briefcase because it undermined family values" [Gold 2003:A14].) Behind that notion lies a set of cultural statements: housework is women's work, motherhood is sacred, and men are wanderers while women preserve the family hearth. Such statements are made to seem inevitable by reference to nature—"A woman's place is in the home because only women can give birth," or "Men are pigs—they just don't know how to clean a bathroom." Such statements are examples of doxa, in which custom hides relationships of power (a point considered by Ortner [see pp. 319–20] and Wolf [pp. 357–58]). While this particular field of doxa has shrunk since the 1970s, it remains present in certain American enclaves. The relationship between "the home" and "women" is a generative scheme—a habitus—but it has a social existence only through practice: verbal classifications ("working moms" versus "stay-at-home moms"), institutional policies (e.g., pay differences between men and women), and—most importantly—the actions of individual women and men. This element of American cultural life linking gender and work cannot be reduced to habitus, doxa, or individuals' actions; all those domains comprise a specific field of practice.

Every society creates multiple fields of practice; different societies draw on different fields of practice. One of the most common fields of practice centers on the house; this is true in America, and it is also true of rural Algeria, where Bourdieu studied the array of themes centered on the Kabyle house.

The Kabyle House: Habitus and Home

Different societies employ distinct generative structures, and in rural Algeria Bourdieu showed how the Kabyle centered an array of themes on the house (Bourdieu 1990). The Kabyle house is a rectangle, its interior divided by a partial wall into a larger well-lighted space containing the kitchen hearth, weaving loom, and grain bins, and a smaller, darker space that serves as a stable. The Kabyle house is often built on a sloping hillside, and the stable is lower than the larger living area. Tools are stored in hayloft above the stable, and women and children sleep in the loft. The long axis of the house usually runs north–south, with an entrance on the east wall and a back door on the west wall.

From this architectural form, the Kabyle peasant spins out a vast scheme of homologies and oppositions. The upper, well-lighted living area is the cultural realm; the lower, darker stable the realm of nature. The lower realm is associated with things that are dark, damp, and "natural": water, livestock manure, sexual intercourse, childbirth, and death. The upper room contains the hearth, storage jars, cooking utensils, and the large weaving loom—the women's work within the house—and also the man's rifle, which is used to protect female honor. The loom stands along the west wall, and a guest is invited to sit in front of the loom, thus facing east and toward the place where light originates. To seat a guest on the eastern wall is an offense, as this is the "wall of darkness." To invite a guest to sleep in the hayloft is an inconceivable affront, violating the propriety of the women and children and also asking the guest to stretch out in a space associated with death, since the loft is elevated on posts just as a coffin is raised on pallbearers' shoulders (Bourdieu 1990:271–283).

Through their actions, the Kabyle extrapolate cultural associations from the house to the broader social universe. The house is the women's realm, a place of weaving and cooking that is also *h'aram*, a sacred space forbidden to any man not a member of the household. The female household realm is in opposition to the male public realm—the farming fields and village assembly house. During the dry season, men and initiated boys sleep outside the house. A man leaves his house for the fields at daybreak, and a man who spends too much time at home is derided. By extension, males are associated with the full light of the sun, women with the shaded darkness of the house. The bright outside, and particularly the east side, is the source of all prosperity: the harvests of grains are produced by the union of male plough and female wet, fertile earth. East is the cardinal direction for ritual: to ensure prosperity the farmer plows from west to east, oxen are faced east to be sacrificed, and countless other ritual acts take reference from the rising sun.

The Kabyle house serves as a generative scheme, a conceptual pivot from which complex arrays of meanings are devised.

At first glance, it would seem that this is a perfect example of Lévi-Straussian structures all organized into binary oppositions. In fact, Bourdieu retrospectively observed that his article about the Kabyle house was "perhaps the last I wrote as a blissful structuralist," but the article constantly refers to the making of culture through practice (1990:9). The Kabyle experience cannot be reduced to a set of codes. The conceptual parallel between sleep and death is created as people going to sleep first lie on their right side—the position of the corpse—and then turn onto their left side, constructing meaning through practice (Bourdieu 1990:273). Various themes coalesce around the house, but men and women distinctly create them. If women are kept in the house, men are kept out of it. "Whereas for the man the house is not so much a place he goes into as a place he comes out of" (Bourdieu 1990:280), for women the house entails a different set of associations that are actively made by practice. As a bride, a woman arrives at her new house and tosses figs, wheat, water, and other items at the dwelling since they are associated with plenitude and prosperity, which her own work and fertility will bring. Carried across the threshold on a kinsman's back, she must avoid the threshold since it is a liminal space and therefore dangerous. In these and myriad ways, the Kabyle make their culture through practice, simultaneously drawing on rules, strategies, and individual actions.

"Understanding ritual practice is not a question of decoding the internal logic of a symbolism," Bourdieu writes, "but of restoring its practical necessity by relating it to the real conditions of its genesis, that is, to the conditions in which its functions, and the means it uses to attain them, are defined" (1977:114). A structural analysis that reduces a ritual practice or the complex associations of the Kabyle house to a series of binary oppositions explains less than we might imagine. Bourdieu asserts that "contrary to appearances, scarcely more understanding is derived from a structural analysis which ignores the specific functions of ritual practices and fails to inquire into the economic and social conditions of the production of the dispositions generating both these practices and the collective definition of the practical functions" such rituals serve (1977:115).

Thus Bourdieu argues that any attempt to reduce the social universe to a set of rules or operational roles distorts reality by removing the pragmatic concerns, the social actors, and the historical and economic antecedents. These historical and economic antecedents, in turn, are shaped by social orders that attempt to "naturalize" the arbitrariness of the social order (Bourdieu 1977:163–166). There is no inherent reason why Kabyle women should be associated with the house, the earth, darkness, and the tomb. Those associations are created and given a facade of inevitability by being affiliated with the natural world.

Conclusion

Pierre Bourdieu had a major influence on anthropological theory, but several issues remained undeveloped or unclear. For example, do Bourdieu's concepts of practice, habitus, and doxa render the concept of culture obsolete, or are they rather implicit critiques of the misuse of the concept of culture? Once we acknowledge that culture cannot be reduced to hidden codes, confused with individual actions, nor separated from the dynamic process of culture-making, then are Bourdieu's ideas radically new theories or important correctives to the misuse of the concept of culture (e.g., similar to Geertz's discussion; see p. 265)? Further, if anthropologists must be alert to the assumptions inherent in their own practice, then what are the implications for research methods? How precisely does one devise a research method that unites habitus, doxa, and individual social actors?

At his death from cancer in January 2002, Bourdieu had written some forty-five books and five hundred articles, works translated into a score of languages and indexed on a massive online bibliography at the HyperBourdieu website (www.iwp.uni-linz.ac.at/sektktf/bb/HyperBourdieu.html). His last major publications serve to triangulate Bourdieu's long-held interests. *Interventions politiques, 1962–2001* is a massive collection of Bourdieu's political texts, from his early writings on the conditions in Algeria to his final attacks on neoliberalism and globalization. Another book, *Science de la science et réflexivité* (2001), is a sociological analysis of science and science studies, which returns to Bourdieu's concerns with the way the practice of science shapes inquiry—a theme Bourdieu had explored in *Outline of a Theory of Practice*. In a third study Bourdieu literally returned to his home village: *Le bal de célibataires: Crise de la société paysanne en Béarn* (*The Bachelors' Ball: The Crisis of Peasant Society in Béarn*, 2008) begins with an account of a Friday-night dance in his home village. Bourdieu notices that the men standing, drinking, and watching rather than dancing are the community's unmarriageable men; from this small observation Bourdieu pursues an analysis of kinship, the devaluation of peasant life, and changes in family structure (Wacquant in McLemee 2002).

Throughout the many themes of his intellectual project, Bourdieu insisted on the empirical groundedness of his theoretical concepts. He once commented that non-French readers misunderstood his anthropological and sociological work because they "have offered a reading of it limited to its purely theoretical dimension. This has often led them to ignore its properly empirical dimension" (1993b:270). He added, "One cannot grasp the most profound logic of the social world unless one becomes immersed in the specificity of an empirical reality" (1993b:271). Bourdieu outlined a theoretical perspective on the social universe that, as Loïc Wacquant observed, is distinguished by its "relational and reflexive character. Bourdieu's theoretical approach proceeds from a thoroughgoing *relationalism* which grasps both objective and subjective reality in the form of mutually interpenetrating systems of relation," a position "designed to capture the fundamentally recursive and relational nature of social life" (Wacquant 1993:236). This research led Pierre Bourdieu from the Algerian countryside to the great institutions of Paris and then back to his home village at the foothills of the Pyrenees.

References

Bateson, Gregory, and Margaret Mead
1942 *Balinese Character: A Photographic Analysis*. New York: New York Academy of Sciences.

Bourdieu, Pierre

1963 The Attitude of the Algerian Peasant toward Time. In *Mediterranean Countrymen: Essays in the Social Anthropology of the Mediterranean*. J. Pitt-Rivers, ed. Pp. 55–72. Paris: Mouton.

1966 The Sentiment of Honour in Kabyle Society. In *Honour and Shame: The Values of Mediterranean Society*. J. G. Peristiany, ed. Pp. 191–241. Chicago: University of Chicago Press.

1977 *Outline of a Theory of Practice*. R. Nice, trans. Cambridge: Cambridge University Press.

1984 *Distinction: A Social Critique of the Judgement of Taste*. R. Nice, trans. Cambridge, Mass.: Harvard University Press.

1988 *Homo Academicus*. P. Collier, trans. Stanford, Calif.: Stanford University Press.

1990 *The Logic of Practice*. R. Nice, trans. Stanford, Calif.: Stanford University Press.

1993a *The Field of Cultural Production: Essays on Art and Literature*. R. Johnson, ed. New York: Columbia University Press.

1993b Concluding Remarks: For a Sociogenetic Understanding of Intellectual Works. In *Bourdieu: Critical Perspectives*. C. Calhoun, E. LiPuma, and M. Postone, eds. Pp. 263–275. Cambridge: Polity Press.

1996 *Photography: A Middle-Brow Art*. With Luc Boltanski et al. S. Whiteside, trans. Stanford, Calif.: Stanford University Press.

1998 *On Television*. P. P. Ferguson, trans. New York: New Press.

2000 *Pascalian Meditations*. R. Nice, trans. Stanford, Calif.: Stanford University Press.

2001 *Science de la science et réflexivité: Cours du Collège de France, 2000–2001*. Paris: Raisons d'agir.

2002a *Interventions Politiques, 1961–2001: Science Sociale et Action Politique*. F. Poupeau and T. Discepio, eds. Marseille: Agone.

2002b *Le Bal des Célibatires: Crise de la Société Paysanne en Béarn*. Paris: Seuil.

2008 *The Bachelors' Ball: The Crisis of Peasant Society in Béarn*. R. Nice, trans. Chicago: University of Chicago Press.

Bourdieu, Pierre, and Alain Darbel, with Dominique Schnapper

1991 *The Love of Art: European Art Museums and Their Public*. C. Beattie and N. Merriman, trans. Cambridge: Polity Press.

Bourdieu, Pierre, and Jean-Claude Passeron

1979 *The Inheritors: French Students and Their Relation to Culture*. Chicago: University of Chicago Press.

1990 *Reproduction in Education, Society and Culture*. London: Sage Press. [Originally published 1970.]

Bourdieu, Pierre, and Loïc Wacquant
1992 *An Invitation to Reflexive Sociology*. Chicago: University of Chicago Press.

Calhoun, Craig
2000 Pierre Bourdieu. In *The Blackwell Companion to the Major Social Theories*. G. Ritzer, ed. Pp. 696–730. Cambridge, Mass.: Blackwell.

Calhoun, Craig, and Loïc Wacquant
2002 In Memoriam: Pierre Bourdieu (1930–2002). www.theglobalsite.ac.uk/times/202calhoun.htm.

Collins, James
1993 Determination and Contradiction: An Appreciation and Critique of the Work of Pierre Bourdieu on Language and Education. In *Bourdieu: Critical Perspectives*. C. Calhoun, E. LiPuma, and M. Postone, eds. Pp. 116–138. Cambridge: Polity Press.

Gold, Scott
2003 Ayes of Texas Are Still on Hold. *Los Angeles Times*, May 14, A14.

McLemee, Scott
2002 Loïc Wacquant Discusses the Influence of Pierre Bourdieu, Who Died Wednesday, and His Latest Projects. *Chronicle of Higher Education*, January 25.

Postone, Moishe, Edward LiPuma, and Craig Calhoun
1993 Introduction: Bourdieu and Social Theory. In *Bourdieu: Critical Perspectives*. C. Calhoun, E. LiPuma, and M. Postone, eds. Pp. 1–12. Cambridge: Polity Press.

Riding, Alan
2002 Pierre Bourdieu, 71, French Thinker and Globalization Critic. *New York Times*, January 25.

Wacquant, Loïc
1992 Towards a Social Praxeology: The Structure and Logic of Bourdieu's Sociology. In *An Invitation to Reflexive Sociology*. P. Bourdieu and L. Wacquant, eds. Pp. 1–59. Chicago: University of Chicago Press.
1993 Bourdieu in America: Notes on the Transatlantic Importation of Social Theory. In *Bourdieu: Critical Perspectives*. C. Calhoun, E. LiPuma, and M. Postone, eds. Pp. 235–262. Cambridge: Polity Press.

24

Eric Wolf

Culture, History, Power

Eric Wolf (1923–1999) challenged anthropology to explore new directions, his research focusing on three sets of interrelated issues: the nature of peasant societies, the connections between power and culture, and a critique of the concept of culture as ahistorical, unitary, and stable. From his research on peasant communities in Latin America and Europe, Wolf contended that those rural communities could not be understood as cultural isolates, but were segments of larger systems operating at national and global levels. Further, such societies were never reflections of unchanging cultural configurations, but the expressions of specific histories. As he expanded the breadth of his inquiry during his career, Wolf consistently sought the connections between the local patterns and broader dimensions of economy and politics, insisting upon an anthropology concerned with history and power. Wolf built on the Marxist concern with structure and added the essential element of human agency. In a series of extremely influential articles and books written over a forty-year career, Wolf revisited these issues without ever being redundant.

Background

Wolf was born in Austria into a family of secularized Jews where the "virtues of the Enlightenment . . . were extolled: the great German poets, morality without religion, progressive liberalism, playing the violin" (Wolf 2001:1). The fever of anti-Semitism in

Central Europe increased during the 1930s, and when the Nazis occupied Austria in March 1938, Wolf and his family sought refuge first in England and then in the United States in 1940. Wolf enrolled at Queens College, New York, trying various majors before encountering anthropology. In 1942 Wolf joined the U.S. Army's 10th Mountain Division, fighting through the Alps, and winning a Silver Star for bravery (Wolf 2001:3; Prins 2000). Wolf returned to university on the GI Bill, completed his B.A. in 1946, and entered graduate studies in anthropology at Columbia University.

The theoretical mix was shifting in Columbia's anthropology program. With Boas's death in 1942, Ruth Benedict was the department's premier anthropologist and culture and personality studies were dominant. Wolf later criticized Benedict for her lack of concern with either the history or material conditions of cultures, treating them as if "cultures and personalities seemed to exist in some timeless no-man's land" (2001:4). After World War II, this paradigm was challenged by a cadre of new, left-leaning graduate students—Marvin Harris and Eleanor Leacock among them—and by Julian Steward who joined Columbia's faculty in 1946. Unlike Benedict, Steward's theoretical position explicitly considered history, environment, and economy. Steward began a multiyear research project on Puerto Rico, and Wolf was recruited to conduct doctoral research in a rural, coffee-growing region in the central part of the island (Wolf 1951).

Wolf once suggested that his career was marked by three phases of fieldwork, theoretical interests, and political action (Baumann 1998). The first phase focused on peasant communities and nation-states; it commenced with Wolf's 1948–1949 fieldwork in Puerto Rico, followed by research in Mexico and Europe. When Steward left Columbia for a position at the University of Illinois, Wolf joined him as a research associate (1952–1955). Wolf then held teaching positions at the University of Virginia (1955–1958), Yale (1958–1959), and Chicago (1959–1960), before taking a permanent position at the University of Michigan (1961–1971). The second phase in Wolf's career began in the mid-1960s with his activism against the war in Vietnam and was characterized by his increasing attention to global processes and local consequences. In 1972 Wolf moved to the

City University of New York where he taught for the next two decades. This phase produced such important studies as *Peasant Wars of the Twentieth Century* (1969), numerous articles on peasant political mobilization and revolts, and culminated in the 1982 book *Europe and the People without History.* The final phase of Wolf's career centered on issues of culture, power, and ideology (Wolf 1999, 2001). In addition, Wolf addressed other theoretical matters, writing important articles on the advantages and shortcomings of the concept of culture (1984), the nature of society (1988), ideology and power (1990), and his last major monograph, *Envisioning Power: Ideologies of Dominance and Crisis* (1999). His theoretical writings always developed from specific ethnographic problems; Wolf noted, "My articulations of general theory have emerged out of that substantive work rather than having been the starting point for it" (2001:306)—a point essentially true of Eric Wolf's entire career.

Peasants

Wolf's initial fieldwork in rural Puerto Rico led him to focus on the study of peasants. During the first half of the twentieth century, ethnographers tended to focus on tribal societies—hunters and gatherers, subsistence farmers, fishing folk—but after World War II studies of peasant communities were a major focus of anthropological inquiry well into the 1980s. In early studies anthropologists commonly approached the peasant community as a more or less isolated remnant of an earlier tradition. For example, Latin American indigenous peasant communities were viewed as vestiges of age-old cultural patterns that had been reduced or disturbed through contact with Europeans. Writing about the "folk culture" of the Yucatán, for example, the American anthropologist Robert Redfield could write of "the great violence done the culture of the [indigenous] communities ancestral to Chan Kom by the Spanish conquest," scarred by a "seam across the fabric that marks the incomplete juncture made between the Spanish conceptions and those which were aboriginal" (1941:134–135). Such a perspective saw peasant communities as graftings of different cultural traditions. Historical perspectives were "limited to providing information on diffusion, points of origin, or geographical dispersion" (Monaghan 2000:2).

Eric Wolf's research was markedly different. Peasants are rural cultivators integrated into larger economic, social, and political systems; their production is, to varying extents, diverted to dominant outsiders, usually urban elites associated with a nation-state (Wolf 1966:1–17). The "peasantry always exists within a larger system," Wolf wrote (1966:8). In his article, "Types of Latin American Peasantry" (1955), Wolf distinguished peasants from other non-urban groups based on three criteria: they are rural agriculturalists, who retain control over land, and whose goal is subsistence rather than business. These criteria marked peasants as distinct from other rural producers tied to larger markets (e.g., fur trappers or rubber tappers), from agriculturalists who do not control their land (e.g., plantation workers or sharecroppers), and from cultivators who approach farming as a business enterprise (e.g., plantation owners or farmers). Thus defined, the peasantry contains significant variation, and Wolf discussed two types in depth: the closed corporate peasant community and the open peasant community.

The closed corporate peasant community "represents a bounded social system with clear cut limits, in relations to both outsiders and insiders. It has a structural identity over time" (Wolf 1955:456). Land ownership is based on community membership. Community members produce for their household needs, selling only limited surplus to buy goods from the outside. In Latin America, Wolf notes, such communities have tended to be indigenous villages situated on marginal land farmed with traditional technologies (e.g., hand tools, ox-drawn plows). They exist, in part, because their land is too poor for appropriation by national elites. Their poor resource base, in turn, ensures their poverty. As Wolf simply notes, "The community is *poor*" (1955:457, emphasis in the original).

Within the closed corporate peasant community in Latin America, Wolf argued, power is intertwined with the religious system that defines "the boundaries of the community and acts as a rallying point and symbol of collective unity" (1955:458). A male-dominated hierarchy is linked to the politico-religious system. Men gain prestige as they ascend to various positions in the system, but as they advance they are obliged to fund expensive communal events and expenditures (feasts, religious celebrations, processions). Therefore, as men gain prestige, they lose wealth. The politico-religious system inhibits the development of class divisions and asserts the power of the community over the individual. The closed corporate peasant community tends to be conservative and mistrustful of outside innovations (Wolf 1955:457–461).

Thus, the closed corporate peasant community attempts to survive on marginal land, meeting basic subsistence needs and the requirements of the politico-religious system. These factors force the peasant to deal with the larger national economy in specific ways. Consumption of food is limited, and outside foods and other products are rejected. Hard work is extolled, avarice denounced, and the family reigns over the individual. The family may sell extra produce to gain needed cash for other products, but the exchanges are relatively small and occur in regional or circulating markets where peasants make modest sales and small purchases (Wolf 1955:459–460).

The open peasant community is different (Wolf 1955:461–466). The majority of production is directed to cash crops, usually agricultural products of the humid lowlands: sugarcane, coffee, cocoa. Land is owned privately, although often of marginal quality and worked with traditional technology. The open community obtains capital investment from the outside economy, but in modest and uncertain amounts that are insufficient to modernize production or stabilize the markets. Developed in response to the outside economy's demands for cash crops, the open peasant community is directly tied to national and global markets that establish prices, provide cash, and produce consumer goods. Individuals accumulate and display their wealth. As commodity prices rise and collapse, the fortunes of individual families wax and wane—as does their status and power in the community. Thus, Wolf writes, "We are dealing with a type of community that is continually faced with alignments, circulation, and realignments, on both the socioeconomic and the political levels" (1955:465).

Wolf presented these two types of peasant communities as opposite idealized forms, and he also briefly sketched out five other types of Latin American peasantries but pleaded ignorance of these forms and did not develop the models fully (1955:466–468). Wolf did not suggest that peasant communities were either "open" or "closed," a point missed by some commentators (Wolf 2001:194).

Wolf made several important points in this article—there are multiple forms of peasantry, there are parallels between Latin America and other regions—but his most important point is this: peasant societies, however configured, represent rural cultivators responding to larger, external forces. In Latin America closed corporate peasant societies may be "Indian" and "traditional," but they are not "traditional Indian" communities—they reflect the consequences of the Spanish conquest and its aftermath. In Java, the closed corporate peasant community developed only after the Dutch established their empire in the Indonesian archipelago. The closed corporate peasant community is not always the product of foreign conquest—it may result from internal forces and be produced by peaceful or warlike encounters—but it is always the result of "the dualization of society into a dominant entrepreneurial sector and a dominated sector of native peasants" (Wolf 1957:8). Writing of Mexico and Java, Wolf stated,

> It is my contention that the closed corporate peasant community in both areas represents a response to these several characteristics of the larger society. Relegation of the peasantry to the status of part-time laborers, providing for their own subsistence on scarce land, together with the imposition of charges levied and enforced by semiautonomous local authorities, tends to define the common life situation that confronts the peasantries of both societies. The closed corporate peasant community is an attempt to come to grips with this situation. (1957:12)

Peasant communities are not impoverished remnants of "traditional" social forms, but employ specific social, economic, and political institutions that reflect rural cultivators' varying strategies for survival. Understanding these rural communities requires connecting the local to the national and global. This demands an anthropological history attentive to the dynamic factors to which a society responds.

Wolf's analysis contained a critique of the idea of cultures as tightly integrated, temporally persistent, and "seemingly immune to the turmoils of history and unaffected by the implications of power" (2001:307). This last point is one of Wolf's central ideas. In a 1957 paper Wolf wrote that anthropologists "have erred in thinking of one culture per society, one subculture per social segment, and that this error has weakened our ability to see things dynamically" (quoted in Wolf 2001:225).

Wolf argued that power relations—expressed in political, religious, ethnic, or other schemes, but always with economic consequences—define the limits and possibilities for social maneuver. For example, the closed versus open peasant communities delineate distinct fields of social action. Yet, within these fields there is room for maneuver, including maneuvers to circumvent or change these fields. Wolf observed,

> Most "cultural" anthropologists have seen cultural forms as so limiting that they have tended to neglect entirely the element of human maneuver that flows through these forms or around them, presses against their limits or plays several sets of forms against the middle. . . . At the same time, dynamic analysis should not omit note of the different uses to which the form is put by different individuals, of the ways in which people explore the possibilities of a form, or of the ways in which they circumvent it. Cultural form not only dictates the limits of the field of social play but also limits the direction in which the play can go in order to change the rules of the game when this becomes necessary. (quoted in Wolf 2001:225)

Wolf's ideas in this 1957 paper are strikingly similar to those outlined by Pierre Bourdieu twenty years later (see chapter 23), touching on what would later be called "agency." Wolf emphasized, however, that power and economy were primary limits on local practice, in this diverging from Bourdieu's theory of practice. For example, Wolf (2001:216) was adamant that "such actions be understood within both structural limitations and unforeseen opportunities" delimited "within larger historical fields or arenas" (2001:318). This position is exemplified in Wolf's *Europe and the People without History*.

Global Processes, Local Consequences: *Europe and the People without History*

This book is a broad overview of the global connections of power and economy between AD 1400 and 1900, the period of European imperialism and the rise of international capitalism. The title is meant ironically: Wolf, obviously, recognized that the peoples of Africa, Asia, Oceania, and the Americas have histories, but these histories were seldom discussed in Eurocentric school texts and classrooms. Yet those histories are, in fact, interconnected, and historical patterns are the products of such interconnections. To some degree, this has always been true, but the pace and intensity of those interactions increased after AD 1400. Before then, Europe was a marginal extension of Eurasia, a thinly populated assortment of small kingdoms, feudal city-states, and rural villages. In 1400 Islamic kingdoms and the Ottoman Empire controlled a vast region from southern Iberia across northern Africa and from the Balkans to Baghdad, the capital of the Islamic caliphate and a city of four hundred thousand. Europe's major exports were furs, timber, and (non-African) slaves, exchanged via Venice and other port cities for silk, spices, and ivory from the East. The Italian port cities further benefited from the Crusades, transporting troops, marketing the spoils of war, and establishing colonies in the Levant and Byzantium (Wolf 1982:106). As late as 1300, however, Europe's political landscape did not suggest the emergence of future nation-states. The kingdom of England held more lands on the Continent—what would later become France—than it did in Wales or Ireland and was ruled by a French-speaking nobility. Spain, Russia, Italy, and Switzerland did not exist, while states like Bohemia, the German Empire, and the Byzantine Empire would not last into the modern era. Yet, in only two centuries, the political landscape completely changed, and European nation-states vied for global domination. What changed?

In essence, Wolf argued, the modes of production changed. Rural cultivators were tied to local lords who, although the characteristics of the arrangements varied, always achieved "the transfer of tribute from surplus producers to surplus takers," underwriting the lord's political and military powers (Wolf

1982:105). Agricultural intensification, technological innovations, and the extension of arable land increased the available surplus, thus supporting a dominant class, the costs of war, and a lord's desires for conquest. Greater political consolidation required even larger surpluses, achieved either by foreign conquests, commerce, or enlarging the royal domain—a process that ultimately led to far-flung empires, as European states sailed to and colonized distant lands and peoples. Yet, those invaded lands were not merely passive prey, but their riches—precious metals, slaves, and crops—in turn transformed Europe. In Europe, Asia, Africa, and the Americas, the modes of production were fundamentally reorganized after 1400.

Wolf adopts "mode of production" from Marx as referring to the "complex set of mutually dependent relations among nature, work, social labor, and social organization" (Wolf 1982:74). Humans simultaneously are part of nature and transform nature through culture. The environment limits or allows for specific forms of human existence—igloos aren't built in the tropics—and yet humans, as Marx said, confront "the material of nature as one of her own forces" (Wolf 1982:72). Humans encounter and reshape nature through labor, but always as members of a social group. Specific sets of coworkers—the staff of an office, for example, or the carpenters and other construction workers on a building project—are in turn linked to other sets of producers and consumers. The "links" consist of exchanges of labor, Marx argued. In capitalist societies labor exchanges are expedited through the flow of money via markets: the carpenter is paid for his week's work, remembers his car insurance payment is due, pays his insurance bill, and a fraction of that goes to the insurance office staff. But if such monetary market exchanges characterize capitalist societies, labor exchanges are differently configured in other societies. In a hunting and gathering society, for example, meat may be exchanged in customary portions to different kin members; no cash is exchanged, no market is involved. At a basic level, the carpenter and the hunter are equally "part of" nature, but they are connected to nature via distinct combinations of technology, work, labor, and social organization. Marx referred to those distinctive combinations as "modes of production."

Marx discussed various modes of production, treating the capitalist mode of production in greatest depth, and illuminating how different groups of humans are strategically linked by social labor. Since Wolf was interested in the connections between an expansionistic Europe and the peoples of Africa, Asia, and the Americas after AD 1400, he found three modes of production most relevant: a capitalist mode, a tributary mode, and a kin-ordered mode.

The most salient characteristic of *capitalist mode of production* is that the rich use money to control the means of production—the technology, the factories, the markets—and can separate the means of production from the workers who actually produce. Workers must sell their labor in the marketplace. The wealthy holders of the means of production can force workers to produce enough to cover not only the producers' cost of labor, but to also generate a surplus—a surplus that reverts to the owners of the means of production rather than to the producers. In turn, capitalists attempt to increase productivity—lowering labor costs, increasing output, investing in technology, and so on—resulting in an upward spiral of surplus production and an increasing burden on workers. Thus the three characteristics of the capitalist mode of production are (1) capitalists control the means of production; (2) laborers must therefore sell labor to capitalists; and (3) this results in a spiral of capital accumulation, labor exploitation, and reorganizations of production. Consequently, capitalism divides society into classes (Wolf 1982:78–79).

The *tributary mode of production* is different: "The primary producer, whether cultivator or herdsman, is allowed access to the means of production, while tribute is exacted from him by political or military means" (Wolf 1982:79–80). Tribute systems do not create labor markets because producers are not separated from the means of production. In a tribute system, peasants farm their own land with their own tools but are forced to pay taxes and tribute. This does not mean that the tributary mode of production is any less exploitative than capitalism; despots regularly exploit their subjects to starvation. Some tribute systems are centralized powerful states, yet others are fragmentary and relatively weak systems in which modest tribute is accumulated by local lords. This range of possible power relations encompasses Marx's "feudal mode of production" and "Asiatic mode of production," which Wolf considered variants of a tributary mode of production (Wolf 1982:80–81).

The *kin-ordered mode of production* is fundamentally distinct: kinship is used to establish rights and relationships among people, including over social labor. This mode of production is so varied that it is easier to state what it does not do: it does not organize social labor by capital or tribute. Kin-ordered societies may vary based on whether resources are widely distributed and generally available or restricted to members of specific kin groups (Wolf 1982:91). Where resources are generally available, people will respond principally to environmental constraints and social dynamics, often resulting in "band societies" characterized by mobility, social fluidity, and the absence of coercive political authorities. Where resources are "owned" by specific social units, the rights and claims to natural resources and social labor may be passed from one generation to the next. Significant differences may exist *within* such kin groups—between senior and junior sublineages, between ascendant and declining families—and enormous differences may exist *between* different social units. But, there are limits to the inequalities tolerated in kin-ordered modes of production. A wily leader can only exploit the kinship ties of a society to a certain degree before either his ambitions are checked, the society fissions, or those very ties are reorganized—often into a form of tributary mode of production (Wolf 1982:94–96). An ambitious leader will seek resources outside of his own kin-ordered society, for example, raiding neighbors or trading with outsiders. Such opportunities, Wolf observed,

> are greatly enhanced when kin-ordered groups enter into relationships with tributary or capitalist societies. Such relationships afford opportunities for the seizure and transfer of surpluses beyond those available within the kin-ordered mode. Chiefs can then employ these external resources to immobilize the workings of the kinship order. This is why chiefs have proved to be notorious collaborators of European fur traders and slave hunters on two continents. Connection with the Europeans offered chiefs access to arms and valuables, and hence to a following outside of kinship and unencumbered by it. (1982:96)

This brief comment exemplifies *Europe and the People without History*. Employing the modes of production as conceptual tools, Wolf presents an analytical synthesis of the multidirectional connections that reshaped the world between 1400 and 1900. This broad synthesis cannot be adequately summarized here, but a few examples give a sense of Wolf's scope and analysis. With its 1415 capture of a north African port, Portugal began a process of expansion paralleled by Spain, Holland, France, and England. The predatory search for distant wealth took different forms. "In South America, the search for wealth centered on gold and silver. In North America it was the beaver that was sought. . . . In Africa the main commodity came to be "black ivory"—people, to be sold primarily in the Americas" (Wolf 1982:195).

Certainly the broad outlines of this history are well known, but Wolf's special contribution is to connect the global with the local. For example, the search for beaver fur in North America resulted in a rapid European expansion, in the process deranging Native Americans' "accustomed social relations and cultural habits" and prompting "the formation of new responses" (Wolf 1982:161). Economic relations were reordered, warfare between Native American groups intensified, and as France and England and then England and the American colonies battled over North America through the eighteenth century, a complex chain reaction was triggered as native allies were recruited, armed, fought each other, and then, equipped with firearms and horses, moved into the Great Plains to hunt bison for meat and hides (Wolf 1982:160–163). The vast global networks associated with the cotton trade—planted in the American South, East Africa, Egypt, and India, woven into fabric in Lancashire and Bombay, and exported across the globe—had complex local consequences: the forced removal of native peoples in the American South as cotton plantations expanded west, the maintenance of slavery into the nineteenth century, the creation of new laboring classes within India, and—most fundamentally—the creation of capitalism. Cheaper ocean shipping resulted in greater trade in basic foodstuffs. Already suffering through the Great Depression of 1873–1894, cheap American and Russian wheat flooded into Europe and destroyed peasant agriculture, "sending a migrant stream of ruined peasants to seek new sources of livelihood in the burgeoning Americas. Ironically, many of them made the journey westward on the same ships that carried to Europe the wheat that proved their undoing" (Wolf 1982:319).

Europe and the People without History contains an insistent critique of a central notion of American cultural anthropology: the concept of "cultures"—distinctive sets of ideas, languages, and common practices that are perpetuating and "more or less coherent" to recall Benedict's phrase. Such cultures were treated as analytical units, with ethnographies of Kwakiutl culture, Trobriand culture, Nuer culture, and so on. Further, "culture" was viewed as determinative; culture "caused" specific human actions. The Dobuan in Benedict's *Patterns of Culture* is "dour, prudish, and passionate" *because* his culture demands such behaviors. Wolf wrote,

> We can no longer think of societies as isolated and self-maintaining systems. Nor can we imagine cultures as integrated totalities in which each part contributes to the maintenance of an organized, autonomous, and enduring whole. There are only cultural sets of practices and ideas, put into play by determinate human actors under determinate circumstances. In the course of action, these cultural sets are forever assembled, dismantled, and reassembled, conveying in variable accents the divergent paths of groups and classes. These paths do not find their explanation in the self-interested decisions of interacting individuals. They grow out of the deployment of social labor, mobilized to engage the world of nature. The manner of that mobilization sets the terms of history, and in these terms the peoples who have asserted a privileged relation with history and the peoples to whom history has been denied encounter a common destiny. (1982:390)

Whether informed by Boasian particularism, Benedict's configurational approach, or Radcliffe-Brown's structural-functionalism, *any* view of culture as coherent, static, and isolated is wrong, Wolf argued. Such perspectives are blind to the connections between societies and to the factors that shape such social forms. Those factors, Wolf later asserted, are

> specifiable ecological, political-economic, and ideological processes. Put another way, neither societies nor cultures

> should be seen as givens, integrated by some inner essence, organizational mainspring, or master plan. Rather, cultural sets, and sets of sets, are continuously in construction, deconstruction, and reconstruction, under the impact of multiple processes operative over wide fields of social and cultural connections. (1984:396)

Culture and Power

Wolf extended his critique of the culture concept and linked it to an analysis of power in his final original study, *Envisioning Power: Ideologies of Dominance and Crisis* (1999). Just as we realize that culture is not a unitary thing, animated by its own search for coherence, but is actually a vast array of interconnected phenomena, Wolf argued, then it is similarly evident that not all "members" of a culture share equally cultural knowledge, and neither is that information or knowledge passed uniformly from one generation to the next. Wolf asserts that "culture is not a shared stock of cultural content. Any coherence that it may possess must be the outcome of social processes through which people are organized into convergent action or into which they organize themselves" (1999:66).

Understanding these processes requires examining the relationships between culture and power. After an impressive intellectual history of the origins of key concepts of "culture," "ideology," and "power" (Wolf 1999:21–64), Wolf arrived at a nested set of questions: (1) What are the different forms of power, what are the domains and levels on which they are employed, and how are these difference linked? and (2) What are the connections between power and the various forms of social, political, and ideological means that specific sets of social actors deploy? As Wolf observed,

> There may be no inner drive at the core of a culture, but assuredly there are people who drive it on, as well as others who are driven. Wherever possible, we should try to identify the social agents who install and defend institutions and who organize coherence, for whom and against whom. (1999:67)

This implies power. Power operates differently in interpersonal settings, institutional contexts, and whole societies (Wolf 1999:5), and Wolf distinguishes four modes of power in his writings (Wolf 1990, 1999). The first mode, individual power, is akin to what we mean by "force of personality" as when, for example, observers commented on Pablo Picasso's personal and creative aura (Brassaï 1966). Individual power, "as potency or capability . . . draws attention to the endowment of persons in the play of power but tells us little about the form and direction of that play" (Wolf 1990:586). A second mode of power is characterized by the ability of one person to impose their will on another, but says little about the arena of social action where that imposition occurs (Wolf 1990:586). A third, and for Wolf more interesting, modality is *tactical* or *organizational power* "that controls the contexts in which people exhibit their capabilities and interact with others" (Wolf 1999:5), calling "attention to the instrumentalities of power" and how individuals and social groups "circumscribe the actions of others within determinate settings" (Wolf 1990:586). Wolf calls a fourth modality *structural power*: "The power manifest in [social] relationships that not only operates within settings and domains but also organizes and orchestrates the settings themselves, and that specifies the direction and distribution of energy flows" (1999:5). Structural power is the "the power to control behavior by governing access to natural and social resources" (Wolf 2001:375).

Structural power is deployed in two directions; it has empirical effects in the real world—mobilizing social labor, controlling resources—and it is engaged in the world of symbols and ideas. Allocation and connotation are intertwined. "The ability to define what things are," Wolf writes, "is also the ability to define what things are to be had by whom, how, when, and where, with whom and against whom, and for what reasons" (2001:375). For example, if I identify a building as "my house," I am doing more than just describing a building; I am referring to an array of property relationships, concepts of ownership, legal guarantees and obligations, and so on that delineate my (or better said, my bank's) control over that resource. Conversely, by calling a building "my house," I am making that array of resource controls seem natural, referring to "my house" just as I would talk about "my toes" or "my hair," as if the building were similarly an extension of my person. The phrase "my house" is neither a pure expression of material relationships nor a completely arbitrary creation; rather it expresses both resource control and symbolic construction. Structural power always has this "double nature" (Wolf 2001:375).

Structural power is seldom stable. Once-dominant forces may lose control over resources and over their ability to define. This instability means that there are constant efforts to maintain control or to challenge it, to define relationships or unhinge those definitions. As the forms of control change, then symbolic associations will change. In an address to the American Anthropological Association, Wolf argued,

> Power is implicated in meaning through its role in upholding one version of significance as true, fruitful or beautiful, against other possibilities that may threaten truth, fruitfulness or beauty. All cultures, however conceived, carve out significance and try to stabilize it against possible alternatives. In human affairs, things could be different—and they often are. . . . I would add that there is always the possibility that they may come unstuck. Hence symbolic work is never done, achieves no final solution. The cultural assertion that the world is shaped in this way and not in some other has to be repeated and enacted, lest it be questioned and denied. (1990:593)

Wolf explores these issues in three ethnographic cases: the Kwakiutl, the Aztecs, and the Nazis. These cases, Wolf felt, were remarkable for their excesses: the destruction of wealth in the Kwakiutl potlatch, the devotion to human sacrifice among the Aztecs, and the orgy of violence and genocide unleashed over a dozen years in Nazi Germany.

The potlatch observed by Boas and other late nineteenth-century observers had been reshaped by conditions of decline—first of population due to death from European disease, alcohol, and out-migration (Wolf 1999:76–77), and second by the weakening of sociopolitical relationships at several different levels: between a chief and his "house" (*numaym*; pl. *numayma*), an associated social group that combined elements of kinship, residence, and clientship among the differently ranked members of a numaym (men/women or nobles/commoner/slaves), and also between different numayma and the tribal groups in which they coalesced (Wolf 1999:82–88). The potlatch with its feasts, theatricals, and lavish gifts was primarily about "the display and affirmation of privileges and in transfers of valuables in the presence of witnessing gifts" (Wolf 1999:112). Rather than manifesting a Dionysian core value, as Benedict asserted, the potlatch was about structural power.

So was Aztec sacrifice. Beginning as a small band of mercenaries, by the mid-1400s the Aztecs had consolidated their control over much of the Valley of Mexico, and their armies expanded south toward Tehuantepec and east to the Veracruz coast. Tribute and trade further extended their reach. The affairs of state, however, were never settled. Population climbed in the Valley of Mexico, perhaps increasing to 1 million, with an estimated 160,000–200,000 living in the capital, making Tenochtitlán larger than most of the cities of Europe. Earthquake, floods, and killing frosts produced severe famines. The successes of Aztec armies were tempered by defeats by the Tarascans (1479–1480), the dogged independence of nearby Tlaxcala, and a score of other never-conquered nations. Aztec sacrifice, Wolf argued, was one element in a broader response "to defend and legitimize the social order against the challenges of crisis and change" (1999:161). Aztec cosmology "was deeply implicated in the formation, maintenance, and expansion of their state" (Wolf 1999:188–189), providing a justification of class hierarchy, asserting the sacredness of the Aztec king, and formulating a cyclic view of time with its key junctures as moments of cosmic dangers mediated by the flow of human blood. Human sacrifice rose to an "unparalleled intensity," and its explanation "must take account of their cosmological understandings about the creative and transformative capacities of violence, as well as the use made of these ideas in their imperial ideologies" (Wolf 1999:193).

The rise of Nazism in the early 1930s shared features with other millenarian or revitalization movements, which Anthony Wallace had described as "deliberate[ly] organized attempts by some members of society to construct a more satisfying culture by rapid acceptance of a pattern of multiple innovations," noting that "the persons involved in the process must perceive their culture . . . [as] unsatisfactory; and they must innovate not merely discrete items, but a new cultural system" (1979:422). Such a notion, Wolf asserted, helps us to conceptually grasp Nazism

> because it points us towards questions about the tensions and contradictions produced by antecedent social and political arrangements in the Germanies. At the same time, it was unlike most other efforts at revitalization, in that it aimed to enhance vitality by linking it to apocalyptic visions of racial corruption and sought renewed life for the Germanic few by destruction of the many who were judged to be "subhuman." This ideological vision it pursued with singular tenacity, becoming increasingly lethal, both to its followers and to its victims. It took a world war and the death of millions to halt this homicidal project. (1999:198)

This homicidal project was entwined with a set of key concepts: *Volk*, race, *Reich*, and *Fuhrer*. The notion that each people (Volk) had its own qualities or essence was an eighteenth-century concept transformed into a justification of superiority: that Germans were a primordial people, uncontaminated by other nations. This notion intersected with even older folktales, dating back to the Middle Ages, in which Germany's greatness would remerge in an empire or Reich led by a new emperor (Wolf 1999:210–212). The defeat of the Second Reich in World War I, the loss of territory, and the enormous burden of reparations meant that Germany's government had few resources, scant support, and limited authority, which evaporated during the 1929–1933 depression (Wolf 1999:220–222). The resulting chaos provided the perfect environment for Hitler and the Nazis, who exploited the fissures in German society and recruited from its fragments. In large rallies, Hitler proclaimed his worldview in messianic speech, a "rhetoric built on experiences of a world turned upside down . . . and it was amplified into visions of evil forces that needed to be controlled and turned back" (Wolf 1999:226). Principal among those evil forces, Hitler proclaimed, were the Jews. The remedy for Germany's ills was the return of racial health to the Volk. This took various forms, but its most horrific consequence was the murder of millions of Jews and other "undesirables" (Wolf 1999:235–250). Nazi ideology recalled and transformed long-established German beliefs in Volk, Reich, and Fuhrer and developed an ideology of racial health implemented in the horrors of Auschwitz, Chelmno, Buchenwald, and other death camps. Power and ideology, as always, were inseparable.

The cases Wolf analyzes in *Envisioning Power* were characterized by intensifying stresses, crises caused by environmental, demographic, economic, social, or political factors. The response was to create extreme ideologies, partly constructed from preexisting concepts and institutions but reshaped to address the issues of structural power—the allocation of resources, the mobilization and deployment of social labor, the classifications of peoples. Ideologies were not static cultural schemes; rather they were creations of specific historical moments and cultural traditions (Wolf 1999:274–279). Ideology had distinctive consequences among the Kwakiutl, the Aztecs, and in Nazi Germany because they had different imaginary worlds: a world where the flow of goods stimulated the circulation of vital powers, a universe where the gods demanded human blood to maintain the cyclical existence of the world, or a pure Volk unweakened by contaminating Jews (Wolf 1999:283).

The comparative studies demonstrate the importance of considering culture and power. Culture remains a useful, though untidy, concept partly because we lack any other good explanation of "how the human mind can produce such great socially patterned variability" (Wolf 1999:288). Further, "culture" is a useful concept because it forces us to look at connections—between the generically human and the locally specific and between domains of "material relations to the world, societal organization, and configurations of ideas" that we might otherwise treat separately (Wolf 1999:289). It is essential, Wolf argued, to bind culture to considerations of structural power. Such a consideration will lead to several lines of inquiry: how a society is divided into segments, how resources are allocated, and how cosmologies and ideologies present such arrangements as the natural order of things. "Cosmologies and ideologies," Wolf observed, "connect questions of power with the existential concerns of everyday life"

(1999:290). Writing the last lines of his book in the last years of the twentieth century, Wolf concluded, "At this millennial transition, the human capacity to envision imaginary worlds seems to be shifting into high gear. For anthropologists and others, greater concern with how ideas and power converge seems eminently warranted" (1999:291).

Conclusion

A review of Eric Wolf's life and ideas demonstrates how he revisited key concepts over forty years without being repetitious. From his first ethnographic research in rural Puerto Rico until the end of his life, Wolf was concerned with a set of central issues. Wolf's analysis proceeds from the following premises. Culture is not a discrete set of ideas, but is always connected to the material world. Individual cultures are never isolates, but are always impacted by other social groups. Individual cultures are not the static expressions of internal values; they are always the dynamic consequences of historical antecedents. Finally, culture is always implicated in matters of power because power is present in all social arrangements. Power may be expressed in four modalities—individual power, the power of one person over another, tactical power, and structural power. Wolf was most interested in structural power, particularly in its double-edged prospects: the control of resources and its construction of symbolic meaning. These relationships are not static, nor are all symbolic domains equally implicated in power. Sorting through those relationships illuminates and, hopefully, explains central domains of human existence.

In this work, Wolf influenced a number of anthropological endeavors. First, Wolf extends the Marxist concepts of modes of production by adding the elements of human agency and historical contingency. For example, the class between kin-ordered and capitalist societies was not just an impersonal collision between modes of production but was animated by individuals: chiefs who sought external sources of wealth, plantation owners demanding cheap labor, and so on. Second, Wolf contributed to studies of globalization and core-periphery studies, somewhat parallel to the "world-systems" theory outlined by Wallerstein (1974, 1979, 1984), linking local realities to national and international systems of power and economy. But for anthropological theory, Wolf's central contribution was his critique of the concept of culture.

Wolf's friend and colleague, the anthropologist Aram Yengoyan, notes the twin sources of Wolf's critique of culture. "One was his early concern about the presumed bounded quality of culture and the insistence on the homogeneity of this boundedness," a central notion of American cultural anthropology exemplified by Boas, Benedict, and others, "couched in terms of coherent entities, each expressing its own particular world view" (Yengoyan 2001:xiii). The second stemmed from Wolf's keen recognition that this romantic view of culture, that there were distinctive peoples with shared corporate spirits, was itself a historical artifact—an ideological rationale for emerging nation-states who justified themselves as the expression of a people's will, spirit, *Geist*. In that sense, Wolf would argue, the very concept of culture was born in the struggle for power.

References

Baumann, Gerd

1998 How Ideological Involvement Actually Operates. An Interview with Eric Wolf. *Easa Newletter* no. 23, October.

Brassaï

1966 *Picasso and Company*. New York: Doubleday.

Davies, Norman

1996 *Europe: A History*. Oxford: Oxford University Press.

Monaghan, John

2000 A Retrospective Look at the Ethnology Volumes of the Handbook of Middle American Indians. In *Ethnology*. J. Monaghan, ed. Pp. 1–6. Supplement to the Handbook of Middle American Indians, vol. 6. Austin: University of Texas Press.

Prins, Harold

2000 Remembering Eric Wolf. Department of Anthropology, University of Massachusetts–Amherst. Online at www.umass.edu/anthro/Remembering-Wolf.html.

Redfield, Robert

1941 *The Folk Culture of Yucatan*. Chicago: University of Chicago Press.

Wallace, Anthony

1979 Revitalization Movements. In *Reader in Comparative Religion: An Anthropological Approach*. W. Lessa and E. Vogt, eds. Pp. 421–29. 1956. Reprint, New York: Harper & Row.

Wallerstein, Immanuel

1974 *The Modern World System: Capitalist Agriculture and the Origins of the European World-Economy in the Sixteenth Century*. New York: Academic Press.

1979 *The Capitalist World-Economy*. New York: Academic Press.

1984 *The Politics of the World Economy*. New York: Cambridge University Press.

Wolf, Eric

1951 Culture Change and Culture Stability in a Puerto Rican Coffee Community. Ph.D. diss., Columbia University.

1955 Types of Latin American Peasantry: A Preliminary Discussion. *American Anthropologist* 57:452–471.

1957 Closed Corporate Peasant Communities in Mesoamerica and Central Java. *Southwestern Journal of Anthropology* 13:1–18.

1959 *Sons of the Shaking Earth*. Chicago: University of Chicago Press.

1966 *Peasants*. Englewood Cliffs, N.J.: Prentice Hall.

1969 *Peasant Wars of the Twentieth Century*. New York: Harper & Row.

1982 *Europe and the People without History*. Berkeley: University of California Press.

1984 Culture: Panacea or Problem? *American Antiquity* 49(2):393–400.

1988 Inventing Society. *American Ethnologist* 15752–61.

1990 Distinguished Lecture: Facing Power. Old Insights, New Questions. *American Anthropologist* 92:586–596.

1999 *Envisioning Power: Ideologies of Dominance and Crisis*. Berkeley: University of California Press.

2001 *Pathways of Power: Building an Anthropology of the Modern World*. Berkeley: University of California Press.

Yengoyan, Aram A.

2001 Foreword: Culture and Power in the Writings of Eric R. Wolf. In *Pathways of Power: Building an Anthropology of the Modern World*. By Eric R. Wolf. Pp. vii–xviii. Berkeley: University of California Press.

25

Marshall Sahlins

Culture Matters

The theoretical contributions by Marshall Sahlins resist neat summary. His writings and ideas explore diverse fields of anthropological inquiry, such as the political economies of traditional non-Western societies (1959, 1963, 1972), the historical ethnography of Oceania (1981, 1992, 2004), broader issues regarding historical ethnography (1993, 2004), and the often implicit connections between anthropological models and the assumptions of Western intellectual traditions (1972:xiii–xiv, 1996:395–407). Not only has Sahlins approached quite different topics, but he has done so from varying theoretical stances.

Sahlins's early research was molded by the evolutionary perspective of Leslie White (e.g., Sahlins 1959, 1960). In his influential works on economic anthropology (Sahlins 1968, 1972), Sahlins argued that economic behavior was enmeshed in the other domains of social life rather than governed by universal formalist "laws" (for a similar point, see Mauss, pp. 127–30). For example, in the essay "The Original Affluent Society," he argued that hunting and gathering societies, rather than being doomed to wander endlessly in a desperate scramble to elude starvation, in fact were "affluent" because their material needs were satisfied, not by producing much but by desiring little and "enjoying an unparalleled material plenty—with a low standard of living" (1972:1–2). Although ecological limits might exist, "culture would negate them, so that at once the system shows the impress of natural condition and the originality of a social response" (Sahlins 1972:33).

By the early 1970s Sahlins explicitly rejected utilitarian theories of culture, including the materialist theories he previously employed (e.g., 1961). Arguing that utility theories "are naturalistic or ecological," such that culture is seen as driven by the need to either preserve the human species or maintain the social order, Sahlins insisted that anthropologists should "no longer be content with the idea that custom is merely fetishized utility" (1976a:viii, x). Utilitarian theories—such as Malinowski's theory of needs (pp. 139–42) or White's theory of cultural evolution (pp. 181–87)—inevitably failed to recognize that

> The unity of the cultural order is constituted by . . . meaning. And it is this meaningful system that defines all functionality; that is, according to the particular structure and finalities of the cultural order. It follows that no functional explanation is ever sufficient by itself; for functional value is always relative to the given cultural scheme. (Sahlins 1976a:206)

The single discernible "constant" that runs through Sahlins's work is his insistence on the importance of culture for understanding human experience. For example, addressing the "intuition of culture as dependent on biological nature" (1996:401), Sahlins argues,

> If anything, it is the other way round: human nature as we know it has been determined by culture. As Geertz observes, the supposed temporal precedence of human biology relative to culture is incorrect. On the contrary, culture antedates anatomically modern man (H. sapiens) by something like two million years or more. Culture was not simply added on to an already completed human nature; it was decisively involved in the constitution of the species, as the salient selective condition. The human body is a cultural body, which also means that the mind is a cultural mind. The great selective pressure in hominid evolution has been the necessity to organize somatic dispositions by symbolic means. (1996:403)

In short, Sahlins argues, culture matters.

Background

Born in Chicago in 1930, Sahlins attended the University of Michigan, where he studied under Leslie White and received his B.A. and M.A. degrees; he received his Ph.D. from Columbia University in 1954. Sahlins's dissertation examined historical patterns of social stratification in Polynesia (Sahlins 1959). His subsequent ethnographic fieldwork focused on Fiji, where Sahlins conducted a twelve-month project in 1954–1955, followed by a half-dozen shorter field studies in New Guinea and Fiji over the next thirty years. Most of Sahlins's research has been based on extensive studies of historical sources rather than on ethnographic fieldwork. Initially he relied on other anthropologists' ethnographies as the basis for his comparative studies (Sahlins 1959), but he progressively incorporated archival materials and firsthand accounts of traditional culture in Oceania (e.g., 1992), a shift in emphasis with theoretical consequences discussed below.

After teaching as a lecturer at Columbia, Sahlins returned to the University of Michigan as an assistant professor in 1957 and advanced to the rank of full professor in 1964. Sahlins was also politically active, co-organizing the 1965 National Teach-In against the Vietnam War (Sahlins 2000:205–268). Sahlins taught at Michigan until 1973 when he joined the faculty at the University of Chicago. Sahlins has been a visiting professor at universities in the United States, France, Australia, Japan, and China. In the course of a distinguished scholarly career, Sahlins has received numerous honors and prizes, including honorary doctorates from universities in Europe, Brazil, and the United States. The recipient of grants from the National Science Foundation, the Guggenheim Foundation, and the National Endowment for the Humanities, Sahlins is a member of the American Academy of Arts and Sciences, the National Academy of Sciences, and the British Academy. In 1983 he was named to an endowed professorship at Chicago, and he retired from the University of Chicago in 1997 where he is professor emeritus. In 2002 he cofounded Prickly Paradigm Press, a Web-based publisher of short, provocative works in the social sciences, where Sahlins serves as executive publisher (see www.prickly-paradigm.com).

Politics and Economy in Traditional Societies of the Pacific

Sahlins's early writings were concerned with the political economies of traditional Pacific Islanders' societies. His 1954 dissertation, published as *Social Stratification in Polynesia* (1959), was a comparative study designed "to relate differences in an aspect of the social systems of aboriginal Polynesia—stratification—to differences in the adaptation of the cultures to their environment" (Sahlins 1959:ix). Contrasting ethnographic cases from Hawaii to Samoa, Sahlins argued that there was a positive correlation between a society's degree of stratification (a ranking based on the number of status levels, chiefly prerogatives, and control over resources) and its level of productivity (as indicated by the ability to produce food surpluses measured by the number of people participating in a network of food exchange) (1959:9–12, 107–110). Sahlins's (1959:247) conclusion that a culture's basic adaptation (environment and technology) shapes its social organization and ideological tenets could have been written by Leslie White (see pp. 182–83).

In one of his most frequently cited articles, "Poor Man, Rich Man, Big-Man, Chief: Political Types in Melanesia and Polynesia," Sahlins broadened his comparative reach and narrowed his focus. He compared the social and political contexts of two broadly practiced approaches to leadership among Pacific Islanders, those of Melanesian "big men" versus Polynesian chiefs. The Melanesian big man's political position is achieved and based on personal power, "the outcome of a series of acts which elevate a person among the common herd and attract about him a coterie of loyal, lesser men" (Sahlins 1963:289). A big man's position is "a creation of followership" acquired by demonstrating that the man "possesses the kind of skills that command respect—magical powers, gardening prowess, mastery of oratorical style, perhaps bravery in war and feud" (Sahlins 1963:290–291), which is continuously constructed through *renown-building*—sponsoring feasts and ceremonies, distributing gifts in elaborate displays—actions that construct a loyal faction of supporters. Through such actions, the big man acquires a "fund of power" (Sahlins 1963:292).

In contrast, chiefs in traditional kingdoms of Tahiti and Hawaii do not acquire power; power is inherent in the position to which an individual succeeds. "Power resided in the office; it was not made by the demonstration of personal superioity" (Sahlins 1963:295). Chiefs derived their authority from the office they inherited; "the qualities of command that had to reside in men in Melanesia, that had to be personally demonstrated in order to attract loyal followers, were in Polynesia socially assigned to office and rank" (Sahlins 1963:295).

Such different political types are rooted in other variations between Melanesia and Polynesia (Sahlins 1963:285–288). Political units in Melanesia have smaller territories and populations than in Polynesia. In Polynesia, "the political geometry is pyramidal," so that the populations of villages and hamlets are integrated as subunits of a larger political body. Thus a Polynesian chiefdom consists of "a pyramid of higher and lower chiefs holding sway over larger and smaller sections of the polity" that encompass an entire island or archipelago (Sahlins 1963:294). In contrast, Melanesian polities are "segmental" with each village or cluster of hamlets a self-governing entity equal in its political status (Sahlins 1963:287). Sahlins argues that big-men polities have an internal, self-regulating feature that inhibits their development: as big-men polities become larger, there are increased demands on followers to provide resources, discontent inevitably arises, and the big man's support evaporates. Thus, efforts to expand big-man political systems usually lead to their fragmentation and collapse. "Developing internal constraints, the Melanesian big-man political order brakes evolutionary advance at a certain level. It sets ceilings on the intensification of political authority, on the intensification of household production by political means, and on the diversion of household outputs in support of political organization" (Sahlins 1963:294). For these reasons, "Melanesian big-men and Polynesian chiefs not only reflect different varieties and levels of political evolution, they display in different degrees the capacity to generate and sustain political progress" (Sahlins 1963:300).

In *Stone Age Economics* (1972), Sahlins explores other cases in which cultural patterns shape or limit various dimensions of "progress," whether expressed in the acquisition of political power or of additional wealth. Much as big-men polities face internal limits to their capacity to gain additional power, in societies where the economy is organized by domestic groups and kinship relations—or "the domestic mode of production" (Sahlins 1972:41, 74–86)—households have an internal "anti-surplus" principle in which once the household's needs are met, there is no incentive to produce more. These households would produce much less than they could: "Labor power is underused, technological means are not fully engaged, natural resources are left untapped" (Sahlins 1972:41). In such households, Sahlins writes,

> domestic control becomes an impediment to the development of the productive means. . . . Kinship, chieftainship, even the ritual order, whatever else they may be, appear in the primitive societies as economic forces. The grand strategy of economic intensification enlists social structures beyond the family and cultural superstructures beyond the productive practice. In the event, the final material product of this hierarchy of contradictions, if still below the technological capacity, is above the domestic propensity. (1972:101–102)

If more complex political economies like Polynesian chiefdoms are to develop, then "everything depends on the political negation of the centrifugal tendency to which the [domestic mode of production] is naturally inclined" (Sahlins 1972:131).

Stone Age Economics received a generally positive critical response and was lauded as "outstanding and enjoyable" (Stirling 1975:327), "a major contribution to economic anthropology" (Neale 1973:372), and "the most valuable single contribution to the theory of economic anthropology in the last ten years" (Dalton 1972:312). Critics scolded Sahlins for being overly or insufficiently Marxist in his approach (Neale 1973:373; O'Laughlin 1974:1326–1364)—what Scott Cook referred to as "a flirtation with materialism a la Marx in areas where a marriage seems more appropriate" (1974:358). Scott Cook's (1974) review essay is a substantial critique of *Stone Age Economics*, which argues that Sahlins did not present theoretical propositions rooted in materialism. As Cook points out, the important structures in Sahlins's analysis are not located in the "material conditions of existence" (see p. 204), whether he is discussing the limited desires of hunter-gatherers, the internal limits of big-man polities, or the centrifugal tendency of the domestic mode of production. All these structures are outside the realm of infrastructure, and thus Sahlins's position "stands in direct opposition to the Marxist view" (Cook 1974:370). Cook raises a final criticism: "What are Sahlins' 'social relations,' 'institutions,' 'social structures,' 'lineage orders' or 'socio-cultural systems' apart from concrete human behavior in empirically specifiable situations? At no point in *Stone Age Economics* has he defined the exact nature of these implicit forms" (1974:377).

Rephrasing this criticism, what are "structures" in a culture? Institutions like "matrilateral cross-cousin marriage" or "reciprocal meat exchange" or "the potlatch" do not just float about in the atmosphere; they only exist in individual humans' actions in a given historical moment. Further, what is the role of the individual, the social actor who maneuvers among such social structures, manipulates or avoids them, accepts or changes them? How did big men *ever* become chiefs?

At this point, we encounter the complex issues of structure, history, and agency, which become central to Sahlins's writings, as well as the ideas of Wolf, Ortner, Bourdieu, and others (see pp. 292–94). Sahlins's evolving theoretical position correlates with his more intensive historical ethnography. As his research involved deeper readings of historical sources (native documents, the accounts or mariners and missionaries, and the archives of the Kingdom of Hawaii), Sahlins became more interested in understanding the theoretical implications of specific historical moments, attempting, as later noted, "to 'ground truth' as it were, big issues of the relations between cultural order and temporal change: relations between structure and event, between agency and society, and, most generally, between the anthropological and historical disciplines" (Sahlins 2000:271).

For example, in *Anahulu: The Anthropology of History in the Kingdom of Hawaii*, Sahlins discusses the ways in which an anthropology of history illuminates how, "In distinctively Hawaiian ways, the organization of the kingdom and then of the valley transmitted the historical forces emanating from the larger world," such as the expansion of European and North American empires and economies (1992:2). Yet, those outside forces were not reflected in Hawaii in a "simple or direct way" because "the historical forces and influences are played out through the particular persons"—foreign and Hawaiian—"authorized to represent them." The changes in politics and economies that Sahlins describes "unfold in the specific forms of an Hawaiian cultural order" (1992:2).

History and Structure

Sahlins's essential theoretical position is that historical processes and individual actions intersect in a world of symbolic systems that anthropologists call culture. It is impossible to segregate the flow of human existence from the cultural realm. Human actions cannot be reduced to utilitarian principles because the utility of any human actions is calculated in terms of cultural systems. Sahlins asserts that

> the distinctive quality of man [is] not that he must live in a material world, circumstance he shares with all organisms, but that he does so according to a meaningful scheme of his own devising, in which capacity mankind is unique. It therefore takes as the decisive quality of culture . . . not that this culture must conform to material constraints but that it does so according to a definite symbolic scheme which is never the only one possible. Hence it is culture which constitutes utility. (1976a:viii)

Thus, in his criticism of E. O. Wilson's *Sociobiology: The New Synthesis* (1975), Sahlins rejects the idea that human behaviors—such as aggression or mating patterns—are the evolved consequences of natural selection that impart adaptive advantage. In an extended discussion of kin selection, Sahlins argues that while "systems of kinship and concepts of heredity in human societies, though they never conform to biological coefficients of relationship, are true models of and for social action" (1976b:25), in human societies, "kinship is a unique characteristic of human societies, distinguishable precisely by its freedom from natural relationships (1976b:58). Culture, Sahlins insists, "is the indispensible condition of this system of human organization and reproduction. . . . Human society is cultural, unique in virtue of its construction by symbolic means" (1976b:61).

This does not imply that those symbolic structures are unchanging or that the individual actor simply implements prefabricated, culturally defined behaviors like a computer executing a program. Rather, Sahlins argues,

> History is culturally ordered, differently so in different societies, according to meaningful schemes of things. The converse is also true: cultural schemes are historically ordered, since to a greater or lesser extent the meanings are revalued as they are practically enacted. The synthesis of these contraries unfolds in the creative action of the historic subjects, the people concerned. For on the one hand, people organize their projects and give significance to their objects from the existing understandings of the cultural order. . . . On the other hand, then, as the contingent circumstances of action need not conform to the significance some group might assign them, people are known to creatively reconsider their conventional schemes. And to that extent, culture is historically altered in action. (1985:vii)

A recent example from American social history illustrates Sahlins's point. On August 18, 2002, the *New York Times* altered its policy and allowed gay unions to be publicized on what had been called the "Wedding" pages. This decision followed the state of Vermont's recognition of civil unions, a *New York Times* editorial in favor of recognizing same-sex unions, and discussions between the *Times'* top management and representatives of the Gay and Lesbian Alliance against Defamation (GLAAD) and National Lesbian and Gay Journalists Association. The decision required some editorial changes: the section was retitled "Weddings/Celebrations," and in same-sex unions the individuals had to be identified in the accompanying photo captions ("Mr. Brown (left) is a securities broker, while Mr. Jones (right) is a producer of off-Broadway plays"), but these changes were minor. Interestingly, this new example of American culture simultaneously reflected historical processes (changes in American attitudes about homosexuality), the change and continuity of structural forms (the new unions were recognized according to a symbolic code based on analogous heterosexual weddings), and those historical processes and structural forms were enacted by human actors—the newspaper management, the representatives of gays and lesbians, and the couples who sent in their announcements.

Sahlins argues that "although in theory structure is supposed to be a concept antithetical to history and agency, in practice it is what gives historical substance to a people's culture and independent grounds to their action. Without cultural order there is neither history nor agency" (1999:412). Of course, this does not mean that culture is static:

> The relationships generated in practical action, although motivated by the traditional self-conceptions of the actors, may in fact functionally revalue those conceptions. Nothing guarantees that the situations encountered in practice will stereotypically follow from the cultural categories by which the circumstances are interpreted and acted upon. Practice, rather, has its own dynamics—a "structure of the conjuncture"—which meaningfully defines the persons and the objects that are parties to it. And these contextual values, if unlike the definitions culturally presupposed, have the capacity then of working back on the conventional values. Entailing unprecedented relations between the acting subjects, mutually and by relation to objects, practice entails unprecedented objectification of categories. (Sahlins 1981:35)

Sahlins's theoretical concerns are firmly rooted in the historical ethnography of Oceania. For example when Native Hawaiians initially interacted with Europeans, they did so in reference to traditional customary relationships that in precontact settings would serve to reproduce cultural patterns. Thus, when Hawaiians first gave gifts of small pigs and banana plants to Captain Cook, those objects were presented as offerings to deities (Sahlins 1981:37–38). In time, however, such offerings were reconsidered as transactions between native chiefs and ship officers and quickly developed into a form of trade. Echoing Marcel Mauss—and his own writings in *Stone Age Economics*—Sahlins writes, "Trade does not imply the same solidarities or obligations" as offerings to divinities; rather, "trade differentiates the parties to it, defines them in terms of separate and opposed, if also complementary, interests" (1981:38). In the process, the relationships between people and the objects they exchange are reassessed and recalculated, resulting in "novel relations to each other" produced in the interplay of structure and practice (Sahlins 1981:52):

> The engagement of different categories of Hawaiian society—women, men and chiefs—to the foreigners . . . was traditionally motivated: the interests they severally displayed in the European shipping followed from their customary relationships to each other and to the world as Hawaiians conceived it. In this sense, Hawaiian culture would reproduce itself as history. Its tendency was to encompass the advent of Europeans within the system as constituted, thus to integrate circumstance as structure and make of the event a version of itself. For again the pragmatics had its own dynamics: relationships that defeated both intention and convention. The complex of exchanges that developed between Hawaiians and Europeans, the structure of the conjuncture, brought the former into uncharacteristic conditions of internal conflict and contradiction. Their [i.e., Hawaiian men, women, and chiefs] differential connections with Europeans thereby endowed their own relationships to each other with novel functional content. This is structural transformation. The values acquired in practice return to structure as new relationships between its categories. (Sahlins 1981:50)

These theoretical concerns run through Sahlins's writings of the past thirty years—distinct from his earliest writings but recurrent in his work since at least the early 1970s. And Sahlins's position is exemplified in his writings on the death of Captain Cook.

Killing Captain Cook

On January 17, 1779, Captain James Cook sailed into Kealakekua Bay on the west coast of the Big Island of Hawaii. His ships, the *Resolution* and the *Discovery*, anchored among hundreds of canoes filled with thousands of singing and rejoicing Hawaiians.

Cook was rowed to shore, where he was met by native priests who wrapped him in fine red tapa cloth and led him to a temple, passing among kneeling throngs of Hawaiians who called out that Cook was the returning god Lono. Feted and honored as a deity, Cook remained in Hawaii for a month as his expedition received gifts of fresh foods and the sexual attentions of local women. After hoisting anchor, Cook set sail, but the foremast on the *Resolution* broke and forced him to return to Kealakekua Bay for repairs on February 11. Cook's return was completely different from the initial arrival: the bay was empty, the locals stole and pilfered from the British vessels, and relations between natives and navigators deteriorated. When the *Discovery*'s cutter was stolen during the night of February 13, Cook resolved to capture the king and hold him hostage until the boat was returned. Accompanied by a small force of marines, Cook took the king, Kalaniopu'u, hostage and returned to the shore amid an increasingly threatening mob. After firing at a chief brandishing an iron dagger (which, ironically, was an earlier gift from the British), Cook was stabbed to death, his body trampled and broken by the mob. The surviving British seamen thrashed through the waves to their boats and gained the safety of their ships. Two days later parts of Cook's body were returned to the *Resolution* by two priests who asked the remaining mariners when Lono would return (for sources, see Beaglehole 1967, 1974; Sahlins 1981, 1985, 1995; cf. Obeyesekere 1997).

Sahlins analyzed the fate of Captain Cook as an example of how a culture's structures—in this specific case, the Hawaiian notion of the return of Lono—set cultural limits on individuals' actions. The apotheosis and death of Cook exemplifies how "culture may set conditions to the historical process, but it is dissolved and reformulated in material practice, so that history becomes the realization, in the form of society, of the actual resources people put into play" (Sahlins 1981:7).

> During the passage inland to find the king [Kalaniopu'u], thence seaward with his royal hostage, Cook is metamorphosed from a being of veneration to an object of hostility. When he came ashore, the common people as usual dispersed before him and prostrated, face to the earth; but in the end he was himself precipitated face down in the water by a chief's

> weapon, an iron trade dagger, to be rushed upon by a mob exulting over him. . . . In the final ritual inversion, . . . Cook's body would be offered in sacrifice to the Hawaiian king. (Sahlins 1985:106)

Cook's death was not just the unfortunate killing of a British navigator; it was

> Death of Cook: death of Lono. The event was absolutely unique, and it was repeated every year. For the event (any event) unfolds simultaneously on two levels: as individual action and as collective representation; or, better, as the *relation* between certain life histories and a history that is, over and above these, the existence of societies. . . . Hence on the one hand, historical contingency and the particularities of individual action; and on the other hand, those recurrent dimensions of the event in which we recognize some cultural order. (Sahlins 1985:108)

To oversimplify, given the Hawaiian myth of the return of Lono and the confrontation between Lono (Cook) and the king (Kalaniopu'u) in which the king is triumphant, the divine appearance and inevitable death of Captain Cook make sense as a historically contingent event (what if Cook had *not* returned?) that is only comprehensible in terms of another culture's sets of meanings, "a situational set of relations, crystallized from the operative cultural categories and actors' interests" (Sahlins 1985:125).

But is Sahlins's interpretation correct? In 1992 the anthropologist Gananath Obeyesekere (1992, 1997) published a critical response, *The Apotheosis of Captain Cook: European Mythmaking in the Pacific*. Obeyesekere's criticism touched off one of the more spirited debates in recent anthropology (for an overview of the controversy, see Borofsky 1997). Obeyesekere's central point is that the Hawaiians never considered Cook to be divine; rather, the British navigators who recorded the 1779 events imposed their own Western European structures onto the encounter with native peoples:

> I question this "fact" which I show was created in the European imagination of the eighteenth century and after and was based

> on antecedent "myth models" pertaining to the redoubtable explorer *cum* civilizer who is a god to the "natives." To put it bluntly, I doubt that the natives created their European god; the Europeans created him for them. (Obeyesekere 1997:3)

The debate between Sahlins, Obeyesekere, and their respective proponents flared across the pages of reviews and journals. Sahlins's *How "Natives" Think: About Captain Cook, For Example* (1995), is a book-length salvo that is by turns detailed and scholarly, witty and wicked. Obeyesekere responded with a countervolley in the second edition of *The Apotheosis of Captain Cook*, which included a new essay, "On De-Sahlinization." At times the controversy descended to parody and personal attack, but a nested set of central issues emerged from the acrimonious swirl. First, did the Hawaiians think Cook was Lono or rather a high-status chief? Second, is the idea that foreign "discoverers" were gods a Hawaiian structure or a European myth-model? Third, how can an anthropologist presume to speak for the individuals of another culture; how can the cultural categories of another society be defined by any outsider?

The first issue is simultaneously empirical and theoretical. Sahlins musters a commanding array of primary sources, principally but not exclusively European narratives, and deploys multiple accounts to arrive at a series of inferences. By his own admission, Obeyesekere is not a specialist in Polynesian history and ethnography (1997:xvii). Yet, Obeyesekere claims, simply amassing more and more "evidence" does not prove Sahlins's interpretation, because the underlying motives of the accounts are never exposed, analyzed, and deconstructed. It makes no difference how many British navigators said Cook was considered divine because those accounts contain hidden agendas.

The not-so-hidden agenda in this case, according to Obeyesekere, was a justification of Western imperialism. Cook was the fatal beneficiary of the myth-model that European conquerors were viewed as divine beings by the peoples they subjugated, natives who acquiesced to the natural superiority of their conquerors. The flaw in Sahlins's argument, according to Obeyesekere, is that Sahlins uncritically accepted the British accounts: *"There is not a single instance of his questioning the agendas, motiva-*

tions, or social contexts underlying the writing of these texts" (Obeyesekere 1997:201, emphasis in the original). Obeyesekere claims that "Sahlins simply ignores the complicated nature of text writing by missionaries and navigators . . . as he holds imperturbably to the position that these texts accurately describe Hawaiian culture and voices" (1997:200).

Obeyesekere is incorrect. For example, Sahlins writes,

> Many of the main authorities are also significant actors in the events they relate, in one way or another authorized to represent the structures in play. . . . But at least as important as the supposed "biases" introduced by the particular interests of the journalists [i.e., authors of the sources] is the fact that their interests and biases are constitutive of what they are talking about. As much as the texts are "distortions" of "reality," they represent the organization of it. (1992:4)

This is a significant, subtle point. Obeyesekere argues that the historical accounts are necessarily biased by Western myth-models, biases that his non-Western upbringing in Sri Lanka equipped him to discern (e.g., 1997:8–9, 21–22, 223–224). Obeyesekere insists that the European sources tell us little about the native point of view, and—to add another layer to the controversy—that Sahlins's use of those sources embodies his own biases—personal, intellectual, and cultural—which result from being a member of a dominating Western society (Obeyesekere 1997:220–225, 248–249).

In contrast, Sahlins argues that the "biases" of the accounts are really reflections of the "values" of the encounter, mirroring the worldviews and prejudices of the participants. If the account of Cook being viewed as a god were merely the projection of Western myth-models, then why did it only occur in Hawaii and not in Tahiti or British Columbia or any other place where the expedition interacted with native peoples? As to the biased sources, Sahlins's position is that

> the discussion of sources is not meant to be a testimony to the persistent faith that by describing the class status or some evident reason for the "bias" we will be able to make the appropriate compensations and thus arrive at "the facts." On the

> other hand, neither is our criticism offered in the postmodernist hope of attaining an ineffable lightness of historiographic being, a liberating sensation of the impossibility of knowing anything coherent and the futility of worrying about it. For an ethnographic history, the so-called distortions of first-hand observers and participants are more usefully taken as *values* than as *errors*. They represent the cultural forces in play. Insofar as the principal authorities are also significant actors, the ways they constructed Hawaii were precisely the ways by which Hawaii was constructed. (1992:14)

In such dynamic encounters, cultural structures and historical processes and contingencies are engaged through human actions. The death of Captain Cook exemplified this process, but so too, ironically, does the debate between Sahlins and Obeyesekere. Writing of the fatal visit of Cook and its aftermath, Sahlins concludes that

> there is something more to this tempest in a South Pacific teapot than a possible theory of history. There is a criticism of basic Western distinctions by which culture is usually thought, such as the supposed opposition between history and structure or stability or change. . . . Yet this brief Hawaiian example suggests there is no phenomenal ground—let alone any heuristic advantage—for considering history and structure as exclusive alternatives. Hawaiian history is throughout grounded in structure, the systematic ordering of contingent circumstances, even as the Hawaiian structure proved itself historical. (1985:143–144)

As to Obeyesekere's other claim that Sahlins's ethnographic history is necessarily biased, inevitably a product of unequal power relationships of (mostly) Western ethnographers who presume to "speak for" their (mostly) non-Western subjects, Sahlins's response is two-pronged. First, this criticism rests on the notion that "the unequal power relationships between anthropologists and their interlocutors" makes cross-cultural understanding impossible, which is itself a presumption of power:

> To say that such a history cannot be done, that a priori we can only succeed in constructing others in our own image, would,

> however, be an ultimate assumption of power. It would take divine omniscience thus to know in advance the limits of what we can understand about humanity. (Sahlins 1997:276)

Second, this criticism ignores the possibility of exchange, of intersubjective discourse: "Anthropology is an attempt to transcend the customary parochial limits of such discourse" (Sahlins 1997:276), and "anthropology struggles to go beyond its membership in a particular society by virtue of its relationship to others" (Sahlins 1997:273).

> All this is an argument for what postmodern anthropology has made us allergic to: ethnographic authority, the so-called construction of the other. A better phrasing would be *construing* the other. And whether ethnographic authority in this sense turns into Orientalism or some such imperialist conceit depends on how it is achieved rather than whether it is attempted. There is no choice here. The attempt is a necessity: Either anthropology or the Tower of Babel. (Sahlins 1997:273)

Conclusion

Sahlins's most recent works extend and develop his ideas on history, structure, and agency. Sahlins's book *Apologies to Thucydides: Understanding History and Culture and Vice Versa* (2004) contains three topically separate studies: (1) an extended and fascinating comparison of the Peloponnesian War (431–404 BC) between Sparta and Athens and the bloody conflicts between two Fijian kingdoms, Rewa and Bau, between 1843 and 1855; (2) issues of culture and agency in history as reflected in the 1951 pennant victory of the New York Giants over the Brooklyn Dodgers and the 1999–2000 controversy over the young Cuban boy, Elián González, who survived a deadly voyage to Florida only to become embroiled in a religio-political conflict between the Cuban exile community in Florida and Cuban government; and (3) the events and consequences of an 1845 assassination among rival half brothers of a chiefly lineage in Fiji, a political murder that embodies all the issues of cultural structures and historical contingencies ("the indeterminacy involved in who would wind up killing whom—while also endowing it with determinate historical effects") that integrate the collective and the personal (Sahlins 2004:220). The book is a bravura example of Sahlins's work: deeply detailed, witty throughout, moving deftly from the specific case to broader theoretical issues that inform his theoretical perspective:

> Cultural totalities are also historical particularities: so many distinctive schemes of values and relationships that variously empower certain subjects, individual or collective, as history-makers and give their acts special motivation and effect. Who or what is a historical actor, what is a historical act and what will be its historical consequences: these are determinations of a cultural order, and differently determined in different orders. No history, then, without culture. And vice versa, insofar as in the event, the culture is neither what it was before nor what it could have been. (2004:292)

References

Aya, Rod

2006 Review of *Apologies to Thucydides: Understanding History as Culture and Vice Versa,* by M. Sahlins. *American Anthropologist* 108(2):433–434.

Beaglehole, J. C.

1967 *The Journals of Captain James Cook on His Voyages of Discovery, Volume III, The Voyage of the Resolution and Discovery, 1776–1770.* London: The Hakluyt Society.

1974 *The Life of Captain James Cook.* Stanford, Calif: Stanford University Press.

Borofsky, Robert

1997 Cook, Lono, Obeyesekere, and Sahlins. *Current Anthropology* 38(2):255–265, 276–282.

Cook, Scott

1974 "Structural Substantivism": A Critical Review of Marshall Sahlins' *Stone Age Economics. Comparative Studies in Society and History* 16:355–379.

Dalton, George

1972 Review of *Stone Age Economics* by Marshall Sahlins. *Annals of the American Academy of Political and Social Science* 404:311–312.

Goody, Jack

2006 Review of *Apologies to Thucydides: Understanding History as Culture and Vice Versa* by Marshall Sahlins. *Transforming Anthropology* 14(2):198–199.

Kirch, Patrick V.

1992 *Anahulu: The Anthropology of History in the Kingdom of Hawaii*. Vol. 2: *The Archaeology of History*. Chicago: University of Chicago Press.

Neale, Walter

1973 Review of *Stone Age Economics* by Marshall Sahlins. *Science* 179:372–373.

Obeyesekere, Gananath

1992 *The Apotheosis of Captain Cook: European Mythmaking in the Pacific*. Princeton, N.J.: Princeton University Press.

1997 *The Apotheosis of Captain Cook: European Mythmaking in the Pacific*. 2nd ed. Princeton, N.J.: Princeton University Press.

O'Laughlin, Bridget

1974 Review of *Stone Age Economics* by Marshall Sahlins. *American Journal of Sociology* 79:1361–1364.

Sahlins, Marshall

1959 *Social Stratification in Polynesia*. Monograph of the American Ethnological Society. Seattle: University of Washington Press.

1960 Evolution: Specific and General. In *Evolution and Culture*. M. Sahlins and E. Service, eds. Pp. 12–44. Ann Arbor: University of Michigan Press.

1961 The Segmentary Lineage: An Organization of Predatory Expansion. *American Anthropologist* 63:322–345.

1963 Poor Man, Rich Man, Big-Man, Chief: Political Types in Melanesia and Polynesia. *Comparative Studies in Society and History* 5:285–303.

1968 *Tribesmen*. Englewood Cliffs, N.J.: Prentice Hall.

1972 *Stone Age Economics*. Chicago: Aldine.

1976a *Culture and Practical Reason*. Chicago: University of Chicago Press.

1976b *The Use and Abuse of Biology*. Ann Arbor: University of Michigan Press.

1981 *Historical Metaphors and Mythical Realities: Structure in the Early History of the Sandwich Islands Kingdom*. Association for Social Anthropology in Oceania, Special Publications no. 1. Ann Arbor: University of Michigan Press.

1983 Other Times, Other Customs: The Anthropology of History. *American Anthropologist* 85:517–544.

1985 *Islands of History*. Chicago: University of Chicago Press.
1992 *Anahulu: The Anthropology of History in the Kingdom of Hawaii*. Vol. 1: *Historical Ethnography*. Chicago: University of Chicago Press.
1993 Goodbye to Tristes Tropes: Ethnography in the Context of Modern World History. *Journal of Modern History* 65:1–25.
1995 *How "Natives" Think: About Captain Cook, For Example*. Chicago: University of Chicago Press.
1996 The Sadness of Sweetness: The Native Anthropology of Western Cosmology. *Current Anthropology* 37(3):395–415.
1997 Reply to Borofsky. *Current Anthropology* 38(2):272–276.
1999 Two or Three Things I Know about Culture. *Journal of the Royal Anthropological Institute* 5(3):399–421.
2000 *Culture in Practice: Selected Essays*. New York: Zone Books.
2004 *Apologies to Thucydides: Understanding History as Culture and Vice Versa*. Chicago: University of Chicago Press.

Stirling, Paul
1975 Review of *Stone Age Economics* by Marshall Sahlins. *Man* 10(2):326–327.

Postscript
Current Controversies

In 2002 Clifford Geertz observed that the world was characterized by "the simultaneous increase in cosmopolitanism and parochialism" in which, in the aftermath of the polarities of the Cold War, the broad reaches of a globe interconnected by the Internet, the flow of capital, and multinational companies contrasted with "intensely parochial provincialisms"—such as Afghan tribes, the struggles of Chechen or Kurdish or Basque separatists, or turf battles between African American, Latino, and Salvadoran gangs in south central Los Angeles (Geertz 2002:13–14). While it may seem paradoxical that humanity is simultaneously becoming more fragmented and more interconnected, Geertz suggested that this is actually "a single, deeply interconnected phenomenon" (2002:13). In turn, this tendency requires anthropologists to rethink basic ideas about concepts such as nation, society, and culture—ideas that imply units that may no longer exist.

Not surprisingly, the discipline of anthropology is experiencing a similar sense of fission. Geertz writes,

> Things are thus not, or at least in my view they are not, coming progressively together as the discipline moves raggedly on. And this, too, reflects the direction, if it can be called a direction, in which the wider world is moving: toward fragmentation, dispersion, pluralism, disassembly, multi-, multi-, multi-. Anthropologists are going to have to work under conditions even less orderly, shapely, and predictable, and even

> less susceptible of moral and ideological reduction and political quick fixes, than those I have worked under. (2002:14)

The American Anthropological Association (AAA) is the largest professional organization of anthropologists with more than ten thousand members. The American Anthropological Association's mission statement defines anthropology as "the science that studies humankind in all its aspects, through archaeological, biological, ethnological and linguistic research"—a definition that probably seemed more solid in 1903 when it was first published than it does today.

Some of the changes within anthropology are indicated by the topics of symposia and paper sessions at the annual AAA meetings. For example, in November 1988, among the more than 370 sessions, there were symposia on "Paleolithic Europe," "Gender Representation in Mexico and the Andes," "Current Research in Orang Al (Malay Aboriginal) Studies," "Reconceptualizing Carnival," "Hunter-Gatherers and Early Villages," "Guatemalan Indian Identity in Transition," "Primate Biology and Behavior," "Cultural Dimensions in North American Society," "Post-Transitional Iberia," "Visions in the Sky: Studies in North American Ethnoastronomy," "Reconsidering African Kinship," and "Cognition and Ideology in European Culture." The majority of these sessions combine an analytical theme—such as kinship, gender, or identity, among others—with a region: North America, Africa, Iberia, and so on. The implication is that these individual themes are illuminated by cases drawn from a specified region, not a "culture area" per se but a geographic unit within which comparisons are relevant.

Nearly twenty years later the situation has changed. At the 2007 meetings there were 534 sessions, an increase of 44 percent over the 1988 conference. The session titles indicate other changes, with symposia about "Pathways to Justice: Exploring the Global Justice Movement, Archaeology and Anthropology," "The Application of Biological Anthropology: Addressing Social and Health Inequalities in an Increasingly Complex World," "Rethinking America: The Imperial Homeland in the 21st Century," "Anthropology, Environmentalism and Justice: Exploring Interconnections," "Children's Human Rights in the 21st Century: Challenges and Progress Worldwide," "Pop Mediation in Hip Hop and Reggeton: The Role of Everyday Practitioners, the State and Corporate Media," and "Queer Belonging, Sexual Citizenship." Many of these symposia reflect the theme of the 2007 meeting, "Difference, (In)equality, and Justice"; the 1988 AAA meeting had no explicit theme. By the 2007 AAA meetings, there were few symposia topics that fit the popular conception of what anthropologists do. Even more interesting was the way that the 2007 symposia generally avoided the geographical descriptors that anchored a topic to a specific region or culture area. Rather, the 2007 topics emphasized the global interconnections or focused on "memberships" that supersede national or regional boundaries.

Yet, at the same time there is evidence of global interconnections, there are indications that the profession of American anthropology became more fragmented between 1988 and 2007. The American Anthropological Association is composed of a number of constituent units—variously referred as divisions, sections, or societies (societies are once-separate organizations that have joined the AAA). In 1998 there were twenty divisions, sections, and societies within the AAA; in 2008 there were thirty-six. The proliferation of units reflects two dimensions of distinction: new units defined by the topics or themes of study and new units based on the self-identities of the anthropologists. The majority of the new constituencies were thematic, such as the Anthropology and Environment Section, the Association for Feminist Anthropology, the Society for East Asian Anthropology, the Evolutionary Anthropology Section, the Middle East Section, or the Society for the Anthropology of Consciousness, among others. Yet a few of the new constituencies were based on the identities of the anthropologists themselves; by 2007 the National Association of Student Anthropologists and the Association for Black Anthropologists (present at the 1988 meetings) were joined by the Association for Latina and Latino Anthropologists, the Association of Senior Anthropologists, and Society of Lesbian and Gay Anthropologists.

Not all anthropologists are members of or participate in the American Anthropological Association, but it is broadly representative of the trends Geertz identified: interconnection and fragmentation. First, there are many more anthropologists, working in diverse applied and academic settings; that their interests have diversified is not surprising. Second, it may be that anthropology was never a unified field, but its internal fractures were camouflaged by the discipline's own self-myths. American anthropology has enshrined its diversity in the "Four Fields Approach," comprised of sociocultural anthropology, biological anthropology, archaeology, and linguistics. Various scholars contend that this is more an ideological construct than an accurate description of intellectual practice. For example, Robert Borofsky (2002) conducted a thematic analysis of 3,264 articles published in *American Anthropologist* between 1899 and 1998, and he found that a mere 9.5 percent actually drew on more than a single subfield. Borofsky concluded that the collaborations between fields have never been significant and that the "Four Fields Approach" is a disciplinary "myth," a symbolic scheme that resolves but does not eliminate anthropology's central contradiction as a scholarly field: "The contradiction anthropology lives with is its tendency toward specialization, all the while aspiring to be an intellectually holistic discipline" (Borofsky 2002:472).

Anthropology is changing in the same way the world is. If the world is simultaneously becoming more "cosmopolitan and parochial," then perhaps we should not be surprised that anthropology will reflect those trends, with specific sets of research becoming intertwined in surprising ways at the same time the discipline of anthropology is less unitary.

"One of the advantages of anthropology as a scholarly enterprise," Clifford Geertz once noted, "is that no one, including its practitioners, quite knows what it is" (2000:89). Inevitably, we fail at the attempt to define anthropology as the study of some *thing*—as geology is the study of Earth's formation processes or entomology is the study of insects. Rather, anthropology is "a loose collection of intellectual careers," Geertz suggested, an "indisciplined discipline" that "is a far from stable enterprise" (1995:98). Geertz referred to the field as

> a kind of gathering-of-fugitives consortium whose rationale has always been as obscure as its rightness has been affirmed.

> The "Four Fields" ideology, proclaimed in addresses and enshrined in departments, has held together an uncentered discipline of disparate visions, ill-connected researches, and improbable allies: a triumph, and a genuine one, of life over logic. (2000:90)

Lacking a crystal ball, we cannot know the future of these debates, but alternative and integrative positions may be emergent. For example, the anthropologists discussed in part VI—Fernandez, Bourdieu, Ortner, Wolf, Sahlins—are all variously concerned with the factors that "structure" cultural life—whether tropes, habitus, key scenarios, modalities of power, or the structure of conjuncture—*and* the individual social agent. None of these anthropologists, who otherwise vary in their theoretical positions, argue that cultural life is neither the acting out of preordained patterns nor the unfettered creations of individuals. In a similar vein, the anthropologist Roy Rappaport wrote,

> Two traditions have proceeded in anthropology since its inception. One, objective in its aspirations and inspired by the biological sciences, seeks explanation and is concerned to discover causes, or even, in the view of the ambitious, laws. The other, influenced by philosophy, linguistics, and the humanities and open to more subjectively derived knowledge, attempts interpretation and seeks to elucidate meanings. . . .
>
> Our two traditions have not always lived very easily together even when, or perhaps especially when, they have cohabited in the same minds. But any radical separation of the two is misguided, and not only because meanings are often causal and causes are often meaningful but because, more fundamentally, the relationship between them, in all its difficulty, tension, and ambiguity, expresses the condition of a species that lives, and can only live, in terms of meanings it itself must construct in a world devoid of intrinsic meaning but subject to natural law. Any adequate anthropology must attempt to comprehend the fullness of its subject matter's condition. (Rappaport 1994:154)

Anthropology, thus, is complex and diverse because humans are complex and diverse. Our theories, inquiries, and data will reflect that challenging, but fascinating, complexity. An exit from the dichotomous science/humanism debate may be represented by a different kind of anthropology. As Laura Nader writes, "An anthropology between science and humanism, nature and culture, the past and the present, Us and Them, and anthropology and the wider world, forces fuller consideration, a different kind of breadth, and a different kind of science" (2002: 441).

While we anthropologists follow and attend such debates, we should remember the importance of anthropological fieldwork in shaping our theoretical perspectives. In each of the twenty-five profiles in this book, there is an example of an anthropologist revising her/his theoretical position in light of anthropological data. Notably, Clifford Geertz, despite being a major figure in anthropological theory, wrote, "It has not been anthropological theory, such as it is, that has made our field seem to be a massive judgment against absolutism in thought, morals and esthetic judgment; it has been anthropological data: customs, crania, living floors, and lexicons" (1984:264).

There is a vital intellectual synergy between theory and data in anthropology. As we acquire insights into specific moments of the human experience, we gain basic insights into human nature. A partial list includes

- Race does not account for variations in human behavior.
- Other cultures are not "fossilized" representatives of earlier stages in human evolution.
- There is a complex dialectic between individual and culture in every society. Individuals are shaped by and shape the culture they experience.
- Culture is not a thing of "shreds and patches," but neither is it a smoothly integrated machine. Different elements of culture meet the adaptive requisites of human existence, express the creativity of human actors in their use of symbols; and reflect the transmitted experiences of humanity.
- Our knowledge of other peoples is shaped by our own cultural experience.
- There is nothing simple about understanding another culture.

The anthropologist Eric Wolf called anthropology "the most scientific of the humanities, the most humanist of the sciences" (1964:988). This is a catalyst of our controversy, but also the basis of our intellectual contributions. As Gregory Reck has written,

> Anthropology's uniqueness and contributions [have] resided, as always, in its simultaneously comfortable and uneasy location between things, between the sciences and the humanities, between history and literature, between ourselves and the other, between objectivity and subjectivity, between the concrete and the abstract, between the specific and the general.
>
> Living in the cracks between these worlds comes with the territory. It is our nature and strength. For as long as we are anthropologists . . . we will retain the primary goal of understanding the human species, realizing that multiple routes lead to that understanding. (1996:7)

The pursuit of that understanding is reflected in anthropology's multifaceted, multidimensional visions of culture.

References

American Anthropological Association

1988 Program of the 87th Annual Meeting. Phoenix, Arizona, November 16–20. Washington, D.C.: American Anthropological Association.

2007 Program of the 106th Annual Meeting: "Difference, (In)equality, and Justice." Washington, D.C., November 28–December 2. Washington, D.C.: American Anthropological Association.

Borofsky, Robert

2002 The Four Subfields: Anthropologists as Mythmakers. *American Anthropologist* 104:463–480.

Geertz, Clifford

1984 Anti Anti-Relativism. *American Anthropologist* 86:263–278.

1995 *After the Fact: Two Countries, Four Decades, One Anthropologist.* Cambridge, Mass.: Harvard University Press.

2000 *Available Light: Anthropological Reflections on Philosophical Topics.* Princeton, N.J.: Princeton University Press.

2002 An Inconstant Profession: The Anthropological Life in Interesting Times. *Annual Review of Anthropology* 31:1–19.

Nader, Laura
2002 Missing Links: A Commentary on Ward H. Goodenough's Moving Article "Anthropology in the 20th Century and Beyond." *American Anthropologist* 104:441–449.

Rappaport, Roy
1994 Humanity's Evolution and Anthropology's Future. In *Assessing Cultural Anthropology*. R. Borofsky, ed. Pp. 153–166. New York: McGraw-Hill.

Reck, Gregory
1996 What We Can Learn from the Past. *Anthropology Newsletter* 36(4):7.

Trencher, Susan
2002 The American Anthropological Association and the Values of Science, 1935–1970. *American Anthropologist* 104:450–462.

Wolf, Eric
1964 *Anthropology*. Englewood Cliffs, N.J.: Prentice Hall.

Index

About the Author

Jerry D. Moore is professor of anthropology at California State University, Dominguez Hills, where he was selected "Outstanding Professor" in 2003. He received his Ph.D. in anthropology from the University of California, Santa Barbara. He has directed archaeological research in Peru, Mexico, and the United States and has conducted ethnoarchaeological and ethnohistoric research in Peru and Mexico. Moore has been a Fellow in Pre-Columbian Studies at Dumbarton Oaks Research Library and Collection; a Visiting Research Fellow at the Sainsbury Centre for Visual Arts, University of East Anglia; and a Getty Scholar at the Getty Research Institute, Los Angeles. He is the author of *Architecture and Power in the Ancient Andes: The Archaeology of Public Buildings* (1996), *Cultural Landscapes in the Ancient Andes: Archaeologies of Place* (2005), and numerous articles and professional reviews in anthropological journals.